CHINA'S FUTURES

CHINA'S FUTURES

PRC ELITES DEBATE ECONOMICS, POLITICS, AND FOREIGN POLICY

Daniel C. Lynch

STANFORD UNIVERSITY PRESS

Stanford, California

Stanford University Press
Stanford, California

Special discounts for bulk quantities of Stanford Business Books
are available to corporations, professional associations, and other
organizations. For details and discount information, contact the
special sales department of Stanford University Press.
Tel: (650) 736-1782, Fax: (650) 736-1784

Printed in the United States of America on acid-free,
archival-quality paper

Library of Congress Cataloging-in-Publication Data

Lynch, Daniel C. (Daniel Christopher), author.
China's futures : PRC Elites Debate Economics, Politics,
and Foreign Policy / Daniel C. Lynch.
pages cm
Includes bibliographical references and index.
ISBN 978-0-8047-9257-8 (cloth : alk. paper)
ISBN 978-0-8047-9419-0 (pbk. : alk. paper)
1. China—Politics and government—2002—Public opinion.
2. China—Foreign relations—21st century—Public opinion.
3. China—Economic conditions—2000—Public opinion.
4. China—Social conditions—2000—Public opinion. 5. Elite (Social
sciences)—China—Attitudes. 6. Public opinion—China.
7. China—Forecasting. I. Title.
DS779.4.L96 2015
951.06—dc23
2014033657

ISBN 978-0-8047-9437-4 (electronic)

Typeset by Thompson Type in 10/15 Sabon

Contents

Preface: Competing Chinese Conceptions
of the PRC's Possible Futures

A MARCH 24, 2014, GOOGLE SEARCH uncovered nearly 13 million Internet pages addressing some aspect of "the rise of China." In the twenty years since William H. Overholt first published his prophetic book with that title,[1] the world has become enthralled with the idea of an increasingly powerful People's Republic growing economically at 9 percent a year, endlessly into the future. What would the implications of such a world-historical development be for the structure of international relations? Would Anglo-American civilization conclusively lose its (already fading) global preeminence? How might a power transition be managed peacefully, given the awesomely destructive weapons that both China and the United States possess?[2] Would the transition be less problematic if economic reform and opening lead China onto a path of democratization? As recently as the 1990s, many observers considered that it would be impossible for the PRC to rise successfully and yet remain authoritarian. Even today, quite a few political scientists continue to insist that democratization is, if not inevitable, at least strongly likely, given China's transformative economic changes and the associated social pluralization.[3] If democratization is inevitable or at least highly likely, why should anyone be concerned that a successful Chinese rise might lead to the power transition becoming acrimonious or even violent? Or, from an entirely different angle, is it not possible that democratization would be more likely to occur in the event China's massively complex mix of economic, environmental, and demographic challenges—unprecedented for any country in modern history—were to cause the rise to stall?

All of these questions (and more) are at the forefront of contemporary debate among political and other social scientists, international relations scholars, policy analysts and government officials, journalists, business people, NGO professionals, and everyday concerned citizens. China's stunning economic successes invite intense and widespread rumination about how the PRC and the world will together change if the PRC's rise succeeds—or, in other words, if China realizes "the China Dream" concept that Xi Jinping co-opted from left-leaning nationalist groups (but then reformulated) on his ascent to power in November 2012. Xi uses "the China Dream" to describe—albeit vaguely—the thoroughly desirable end state to which China's development is inevitably leading, with success expected about 2050.[4] Xi is far from alone in issuing confident predictions concerning China's future, although his motivations are distinctive. Any casual survey of the global media and blogosphere creates the impression that nearly everyone is taking a stab at it, and certainly a large plurality of the world's leading social scientists and public intellectuals are doing so. Some observers express their predictions with more conviction than others; often, the most confident "predictioneers," to use Bruce Bueno de Mesquita's term, are social scientists.[5] Although strongly self-confident predictions can be useful for helping to focus thought, stimulate debate, and shape research agendas, they should always be treated with caution and skepticism. The starting point of this book is the simple observation—elaborated in Chapter 1—that no matter how scientific a predictioneer's model may appear to be, the future can never be known, because (1) there are too many factors in play that will affect it, and (2) even if the factors could be mapped and measured, human agency ("free will"—critical though circumscribed), along with chance events, will always intervene to make predicting with reliable accuracy impossible.

On the other hand, it would be foolish and irresponsible to abandon all efforts at thinking systematically about what the future may bring— or, in our case, which of several plausible, but competing, developmental trajectories China might take in the specific subarenas of the economy, politics, public culture, and foreign policy. As elaborated in Chapter 1, thinking through different possible trajectories and their varying implications can be useful for formulating policy (for government, business, or any other affected entity) in the present—not only in the negative sense of preparing for the worst but also to spot those developments that seem to provide opportunities for encouraging positive change. Analyzing current trends for insight into which of the competing trajectories seems the most probable is, obviously, not the same as analyzing the future itself, which, by definition, is impossible—because nothing in the future has happened yet.

To date, very few of the observers struggling to get a handle on China's developmental course have devoted their energies to analyzing systematically the varying *images* of the future circulating within China itself; that is, the discussions and debates concerning China's possible trajectories that the PRC's huge cadre of smart, well-informed, hard-working, and public-minded policy analysts (whether in academia, think tanks, government, or business) engage in every day. In any country, images of the future—or competing conceptualizations of the national trajectory as manifest in economics, politics, culture, foreign policy, and other issue-areas—help to shape real-world policy making (and private sector decision making) in the present and consequently the trajectory itself. Especially in a still superauthoritarian country like China, images articulated by elites (broadly conceived) are likely to be highly valuable—even though so far underexploited—windows on what the future might hold. Researchers can study these images in an effort to understand different possible trajectories even if the analysts who circulate them are acting within the boundaries of broad Party guidelines. This is because of the near-certainty that the authoritarian power center will exert the dominant influence over which of several different paths China ends up taking. So whether intellectual (or other) elites affect the leaders' thinking, or, in contrast, the leaders shape the elites' research and assessment agendas, either way, the images elites circulate can serve as a mirror on the policy choices the power center is most likely to face.

Elite images are obviously not the only important factor shaping a country's developmental trajectory. Material factors related to geography, demography, the economy, and the environment are also critically important, along with exogenous factors originating in foreign countries or global society. But this book assumes that what high-profile figures within the Chinese establishment think and say about their country's developmental trajectory, along with their recommendations for how the trajectory should be altered to achieve a more desirable future, can be used as potent indicators providing insight into what the future may become. It should make a significant difference that, as explained in Chapter 2, the overwhelming majority of China's economists vigorously criticize current economic arrangements and demand liberal alternatives; while, as elaborated in Chapters 5 and 6, the country's foreign policy specialists are mostly tough-minded realists convinced of the absolute rightness of China's international claims and the inevitability of the national rise succeeding. It would equally make a difference (in the opposite direction) if a majority of Chinese political scientists were calling for—*and saying they expected*—democratization, while the majority of international relations specialists were cautioning that because China's territorial and other contested claims are "constructed" rather than absolute, China must compromise with neighboring countries and Taiwan for the sake of global stability. To repeat, this is not to argue that elite images invariably shape policy, or that Chinese intellectuals determine the CCP's policy agendas. Under certain circumstances this surely does happen—Party-state leaders constantly solicit the views of policy-oriented intellectuals—but ultimately the CCP sets the boundaries and shapes the agendas of discourse.[6] The critical point is that even when Chinese analysts are simply *reflecting the demands of the Party Center* in the images of the future they create and circulate, studying these images—how they reflect what is expected and what (possibly in contrast) would be normatively desirable—can be highly useful in trying to assess what the trajectory is likely to become, precisely because the elites are operating inside parameters imposed by the (still) awesomely powerful Party-state.

Each of Chapters 2 through 6 addresses Chinese thinking about a particular issue-area and how current trends either are or are not, in the minds of Chinese elites, leading to a desirable future. Chapter 2 examines the economy and demography. Chapter 3 focuses on the structure and dynamics of the political system. Chapter 4 turns to communication and culture construction, or the new "network society" made possible by rapid media and telecommunications development. Chapters 5 and 6 focus on different dimensions of China's trajectory in international relations. The concluding Chapter 7 outlines various possible scenarios for China's future (the next decade or so), approaching the task by tying together the core findings of each of Chapters 2 through 6 and briefly addressing more recent developments such as the pledges made concerning economic reform at the CCP's "Third Plenum" in November 2013 and the near-simultaneous declaration of an "Air Defense Identification Zone" over most of the East China Sea. For this is the central tension in the Chinese images uncovered in this research: Some elites, especially economists, view China's rise as perched precariously on the edge of a devastating crisis, which would center on a sharp slowdown in economic growth even *if* complex, risky, and divisive reforms are implemented; whereas others, especially international relations specialists (though not all of them), express a heedless hubris that nothing could stop China's rise; therefore, the time has come to assert China's CCP-defined national interests much more boldly and vigorously than at any point since at least the mid-1990s. These two groups do not even seem to talk to each other, though the economists are far more aware of (and worried about) the brashness of the IR specialists than the other way around. Through systematic reading and interviews, one arrives at the inescapable conclusion that most IR scholars do not even bother to concern themselves with what the economists are writing, even though the economists' warnings of inevitable trouble strike at the core of the nationalist IR specialists' boundless optimism, which fuels or reinforces risky policy choices. This central tension and its implications will become evident in the chapters to follow.

SOURCES AND METHODS

The book is based primarily on analysis of Chinese-language *neibu* (internal-circulation only) and open-source journal articles, most with a strong policy focus; books and book chapters published by establishment PRC presses; some Party newspaper articles; and, to reinforce points of fact, occasional reports from foreign (especially Western) news outlets. *Neibu* journals can be particularly valuable to researchers because the restrictions on their circulation combined with their policy focus work together to ensure that contributing authors (usually academics—from both universities and think tanks—but also Party and government officials and the occasional businessperson) speak more candidly (sometimes surprisingly so) than analysts publishing in open journals or books. *Neibu* journals vary in the number—and type—of PRC Party-state officials technically permitted to read them, although circulation figures and the specific restrictions are never detailed in the journal issues themselves. None of the *neibu* journals to which a foreign scholar can, through various avenues, secure access is likely to be of the "top secret" variety. The subjects that available journals cover are indeed sensitive but not usually the *most* sensitive issues facing China; for example, only rarely does one find articles frankly addressing the resistance movements in Xinjiang and Tibet, or offering forthright assessments of corruption among higher-ranked (and *never* the highest-ranked) leaders. But contributors to *neibu* journals often do inadvertently reveal fascinating details about the problems facing China. From a meta-analytical perspective, they also make obvious that Chinese policy is always being vigorously, sometimes even fiercely, debated. The image of a monolithic China in which everyone thinks alike—the image that all Chinese are unreasonable nationalists, for example, or that all support without qualification breakneck, investment-led, economic growth—is manifestly false. China today is a kaleidoscopically plural society—although still, to be sure, always subject to the Leninist state's discipline should the leaders decide, for whatever reason, to crack down, either on a whole category of activity/discourse or on a particular person who has irritated a local tyrant.[7]

The *neibu* journals serve as venues for the most cogent analyses of China's problems and the most contentious debates, but even mainstream academic journals and books are far livelier and more forthright today than even a decade ago, with a few notable exceptions (for example, probably no open journal in the PRC's history was more lively and forthright than the iconoclastic and unpredictable *Strategy and Management*, banned by Hu Jintao in August 2004). Consequently, I also make extensive use in this book of mainstream Chinese academic journals and books, with most of the materials I use published between 2006 and 2013. Although it would have been impossible (and even undesirable, as explained in the following discussion) to survey such sources strictly at random—partly because foreign scholars inevitably have only limited access to PRC books and journals, especially *neibu* journals—I constantly kept in mind the possibility that my sample could become systematically biased. To avoid this pitfall, whenever I came to a point in my reading where I felt that all or most of the voices were trending in one direction, I would self-consciously go back to the journals to confirm that I had not overlooked dissenting voices. It was important to make certain that the "trending" I was detecting accurately reflected the broader universe of publications concerning the issue-area. My core criterion for including an article, book, or book chapter in the sample was simply that the author of the text had to be systematically addressing some aspect of China's trajectory, with an eye on the policy implications for shaping what the author considered to be a more desirable future.

A second criterion was that the citations had to be distinctive and original in the context of all the citations that might have been included in the sample. Within the universe of published policy- and future-oriented Chinese publications to which a foreign scholar might have access, only a small percentage will be novel, distinctive, original, or insightful, whereas countless others simply echo the findings of other scholars or, more often, the propaganda line of the Party Center as expressed in slogans and code-terminology. For this book, I wanted to analyze and discuss only writings that appeared genuinely to *contribute* to debates, not by "piling on" through copying-and-pasting verbiage from other people's publications— or the Party-state's—but instead by offering fresh perspectives, whether critical of the state or supportive, in a spirit in which "CCP talk"—so full of vacuous slogans and arcane code-terminology—is largely ignored except in a polite few opening lines.

To locate the high-value-added citations required first wading through giant stacks of other publications, most of which ended up being rejected because they were either obviously derivative or else purely propagandistic. So, for example, I decided to exclude from the sample all articles and chapters devoted simply to echoing the pet political slogans of the Party General Secretary, without offering any substantive analysis of the slogans or their implications. I certainly had no objection to including citations in which, for example, the author would seriously analyze and ultimately embrace Hu Jintao's twin concepts of "harmonious society" and "harmonious world." But to make it into the sample, the author had to probe the concepts, explain their origins, elaborate on their significance, forthrightly address their weaknesses, and/or candidly assess prospects for their successful implementation—somehow, in other words, add value, advance understanding, or offer an alternative interpretation. To be included, writers did not necessarily have to oppose the Party leadership or reject the leaders' slogans; they simply had to demonstrate an analytical, critical cast of mind in receiving and reflecting on the Party line. The goal of the research was to map the *range of debates* on the trajectory, not to insist on uncovering a mythical, unified "Chinese state of consciousness," whether supportive or subversive. In the end, I did find dominant tendencies in the discourse for each of the separate issue areas. But with the notable exception of the economics discourse, in which a high degree of (liberal) unity prevails, the differing points of view on display in each chapter are in some respects even more revealing than the underlying commonalities and shared assumptions.

A second kind of often-seen but low-value-added article or book chapter may not be purely derivative or propagandistic but will be "light" or even "cute" in tone, not taking the country's challenges seriously. The authors of such essays will invariably raise a few problematic issues but then spend most of their time cheerily insisting (without confronting any discomforting evidence) that "everything will work out in the end thanks to the Communist Party's wise leadership." This special genre of bland, "happy ending" pieces does, in a sense, showcase writers predicting the future, but not in a way that inspires confidence the writers have given the matter serious thought. The thoughtlessly happy pieces are not the sort of articles one would want in a sample of Chinese writing on the future—and therein lies a key reason that sampling at random would be problematic for more than just reasons of access. Because articles and books of this lighthearted and "fluffy" genre are overwhelmingly voluminous, joining the pure propaganda and endless copying-and-pasting of others' works in clogging the bookshelves and diluting the contents of otherwise high-quality journals, any random sample would have captured far too many such analytically useless pieces, whose authors seem to be motivated more by a determination *not* to inquire into China's trajectory with intellectual rigor, but instead to signal ingratiatingly to the Party that "I am with the program and not a troublemaker; no matter what those doom-and-gloom naysayers may conjure up next, I will always serve you loyally." Under Mao, this kind of fear-driven and/or opportunistic obsequious behavior was termed *biaotai*, or "expressing one's attitude"—and the attitude always had to be positive and enthusiastic, no matter what the person behind the pen might actually think. As subsequent chapters make clear, the works of numerous optimists and regime supporters did meet the sample criteria and were consequently included. What distinguished the writings of these supportive and optimistic analysts from those who wrote in the platitudinous happy-talk genre was that in the course of arriving at their optimistic conclusions, the serious analysts who were adding value to the debates forthrightly engaged at least some of the points being made by the skeptics and the pessimists.

Also requiring active exclusion from the sample was the omnipresent Party propaganda issued by the leaders themselves or by their official mouthpieces—*in a manner suggesting that even they had other things on their mind when they were delivering the speech or composing the article in question*. A carefully crafted, meticulously detailed policy statement could certainly be included but not something like the paint-by-Party-numbers speech Hu Jintao delivered to a CCP conclave in July 2007. This speech begins with Hu announcing: "The Communist Party of China (CPC) takes Marxism-Leninism, Mao Zedong Thought, Deng Xiaoping Theory and the important thought of Three Represents as its guide to action and theoretical basis [for policy] . . ."[8] To be sure, speeches like this should not be dismissed as politically meaningless; clearly, they must serve some important political purpose, probably of a ritualistic nature. But such speech and articles do not serve the purpose of this book, which is to map the range, in multiple issue-areas, of *genuinely believed-in* Chinese images of the future. Essays serving this purpose—meeting the needs of the sample—take the iron-hard reality of Party domination as a fact and then proceed to explore what this and other dimensions of reality as the authors perceive it imply for desired or likely futures. In contrast, the *biaotai* genre and the constantly echoing ritualistic Party propaganda must actively be excluded from the sample so that we can focus our inevitably limited analytical attention on the exciting, incisive, creative, and weighty debates that are flourishing in the Chinese policy-making community.

The methodological necessity, in other words, was to *separate*—painstakingly and with constant attention to the possibility of inadvertently introducing systematic bias—signal from noise. Sampling purely at random would have been much easier and taken far less time but in this case would have been irresponsible and lazy, an abandonment of sound methodological principles—because it would have resulted in a book devoted primarily to the analysis of noise: pointless from start to finish.

An additional problem regarding construction of the sample was the question of what to do about people "everyone knows" are influential in China, and consequently famous; or, conversely, are famous, and therefore obviously influential. I made a decision to reject any effort to predetermine—inevitably by "dead reckoning" (that is, "guessing")—who the famous or influential analysts and commentators are, then solely concentrate on their books and articles. Trying to construct a sample in that way would have been "too clever by half" insofar as it would almost certainly have introduced all manner of hidden distortions into the sample because how a person becomes famous in China—and how I then come to discover who the famous people are—are both opaque and mysterious processes very likely to be tainted by hidden biases.

At the same time, I decided that it would equally be mistaken to *exclude* well-known writers automatically, under the (surely false) assumption that they are all vacuous products of hype. Rejecting famous commentators simply because they are famous would have introduced an entirely different set of equally distortive biases. Well-known writers were included just so long as they met the core criteria of publishing substantive, debate-advancing articles, books, or book chapters on the subject of the trajectory in the types of outlets sampled within the time period specified.

Finally, I chose not to examine blogs, microblogs, or other popular publications. I do not deny the potential importance of such materials in shaping China's trajectory or in reflecting how the CCP intends for the trajectory to be shaped. The potential importance of Internet discourse is one reason I devote all of Chapter 4 to examining Chinese debates over what the ongoing communications revolutions mean for a polity that is still Leninist in structure. I posit the *problématique* as being China's transformation into a "network society," the powerful concept developed by sociologist Manuel Castells in the 1990s. Gustavo Cardoso, the coeditor with Castells of a 2005 volume on the subject, defines the revolutionary—but still too-early-to-fathom—implications of the network society's global advent in terms that suggest profound changes may be on the horizon for the PRC's Leninist political structure:

Perhaps what we are witnessing [worldwide, including in China] is not the disintegration and fractioning of society, but the reconstruction of social institutions and, indeed, of the structure of society itself, proceeding from autonomous projects carried out by society's [individual and group] members . . . In this perspective, the autonomization of individuals and groups is followed by their attempt to reconstruct meaning in a new social structure on the basis their self-defined projects. By supplying the technological resources for the socialization of the projects of each individual in a network of similar subjects, the Internet, together with the mass media, becomes a powerful social reconstruction tool.[9]

The advent and deepening of the network society imply that within a decade or so it may well become imperative to study images of the future circulating exclusively through the Internet, in addition to images published in outlets the CCP ultimately controls. But, for now, it seems reasonable to focus on Party and Party-supervised publications, given that the CCP continues to maintain its monopoly on legitimate political power while vigorously policing media and Internet content, trying to steer the content in nonpolitical, or even frivolous, directions—except insofar as the network is useful as an administrative tool.[10] Were the CCP to lose substantially more control over the network and broader information flows—or decide to abandon its efforts to control—then clearly, Internet content initiated by private citizens would become far more important to monitor and analyze.

In addition to studying written works, I conducted thirty-five formal interviews at universities and think tanks in Beijing and Shanghai in 2010,

2011, and 2012. (All interview subjects were promised anonymity, but one person preferred that I cite him by name.) Overrelying on interviews would be problematic methodologically, partly because only scholars predisposed to being friendly with foreigners will sit for them. But interviews can be exceptionally helpful for clarifying points made in books and articles and exploring potential new lines of thinking.

There are many people I would like to thank for helping to make this book possible. Let me start with the ever-effervescent and witty Professor Stanley Rosen, to whom this book is dedicated. Although I've had the pleasure during my years at USC of working with numerous colleagues who are highly accomplished and erudite, yet also friendly and down-to-earth, Stan occupies a category all his own, as a truly good guy: friendly to everyone, invariably supportive of younger faculty and students, and often hysterically funny (the life, inevitably, of any USC party), while yet maintaining his status as a keen and deeply insightful observer of China and the profession of studying China. I can't imagine how substantially less rewarding my sixteen years at USC would have been if Stan had not already been firmly ensconced here as the senior Chinese politics specialist by the time I arrived. It helps that Stan is from Brooklyn, as many of my family members are, and that he is a big fan of sports and jazz music. I could not even begin to quantify the many valuable things I have learned from Stan over the years, to say nothing of the voluminous entertaining trivia he has poured into my mind. Stan is not responsible for the content of this book, of course, and he may well disagree with some of its conclusions. But he has played a central role in creating and maintaining the supportive climate in which a book like this—which requires years of patient work—can come to fruition.

Clay Dube is another special person I want to thank because of the critical role he has played in helping to turn USC into an exceptionally exciting place for studying China. Deploying his formidable administrative skills, his talent from bringing diverse people together, his own extensive knowledge of China, and his disarming friendliness and gift for garrulous gab, Clay has done a masterful job in building the USC U.S.–China Institute since assuming the leading role in that challenging task in 2006. One highly enriching result among many is that Clay has arranged for a continuous parade of outstanding outside speakers to come and visit USC, year after year: journalists, scholars, government officials, businesspeople, and many others, from countries throughout the world, including, of course, China itself. Without a doubt, my being able to participate in the numerous high-quality events Clay has organized has indirectly helped enriched this book. Institution building is a rare talent; we have been fortunate at USC to have Clay in place doing that selflessly every day.

Let me also thank the audiences before which I have presented various parts of this work in progress over the past few years, including at the annual meetings of the Association for Asian Studies and the International Studies Association; the City University of Hong Kong in July 2010; Taiwan's Institute for National Policy Research in December 2010; Renmin University of China in May 2011; Georgia State University's Confucius Institute in April 2012; the Thai Royal Naval Academy in August 2013; Southern Methodist University's conference on "Asia's Contested Waters" in September 2013; and, in between, presentations not only at USC's U.S.–China Institute, but also its Center for International Studies and Korean Studies Institute. I also owe a huge debt of gratitude to the Chinese University of Hong Kong's Universities Service Centre, four leading PRC universities in Beijing and Shanghai that I have decided not to name, and two PRC think tanks that I have also decided not to name—as well as the kind individuals who helped arrange my visits to those leading institutions of contemporary China studies.

USC's Dornsife College, the USC U.S.–China Institute, the School of International Relations (my home department), and the School's Center for International Studies all provided generous and timely grants to help fund my research trips to China, including Hong Kong.

Two anonymous manuscript reviewers both went far beyond the call of duty in offering constructively critical and penetratingly thoughtful suggestions for how I could improve the manuscript. All authors say their reviewers worked especially hard; I can assure you that mine truly did. Consequently, I approached revisions feeling a strong sense of obligation to these generous and insightful scholars. With all the effort they put in, I certainly did not intend to let them down. The same holds true for Michelle Lipinski, the Stanford University Press Acquisitions Editor who, from the very first day I submitted the manuscript, has been exceptionally enthusiastic and supportive. When people like Michelle go out of their way to express confidence and high aspirations for a book, I not only feel gratitude but also an enhanced motivation to make the book as strong as possible. I would not want to disappoint either Michelle or the anonymous reviewers, nor give them any grounds for thinking their confidence was misplaced.

And the same also holds for Margaret Pinette, whose meticulous and careful copy editing—striking just the right balance—was far more important in enhancing the book's overall impression of coherence than most readers will be aware. I think of Margaret, Michelle, and the two anonymous reviewers—along with the many other professionals in the Stanford University Press network, most of whom I don't even know, but who worked, and continue to work, on various aspects of the book behind the scenes—as all part of a team, a team of which I am very proud to be a member.

CHINA'S FUTURES

CHAPTER I

The Pitfalls of Rationalist Predictioneering

SPECULATION CONCERNING THE IMPLICATIONS OF China's rise—both for China itself and the world as a whole—should be understood in the context not only of post–World War II social science debates but also of the deeper historical transformations in European (and eventually global) thought that followed in the wake of the eighteenth-century Enlightenment. Perhaps the most profound of these transformations, in the estimation of intellectual historian Franklin Baumer, is that human society (or societies) came to be imagined as not merely "being"—in a state of constancy—but instead as "becoming": potentially, though not inevitably, something better.[1] Out of this change, by the mid-twentieth century, a multidisciplinary new social science emerged under the heading of "futures studies," devoted to the systematic analysis of national and global trajectories. Although it would be difficult to pronounce this discipline a success—given the practical impossibility of studying events that have yet to happen—contributors to futures studies debates have, in the process of directly confronting the vexing problems associated with trying to conceptualize national or global trajectories, developed ideas that social scientists, journalists, government officials, and others ruminating about China's future could benefit from considering. By reflecting on the central *problématiques* debated in futures studies, we in the mainstream social sciences and larger community of people concerned about China's trajectory could enrich our thinking about how best to conceive of China's future.

As with the other social sciences, futures studies grew ultimately out of the mix of Enlightenment philosophy with the real-world—often painful—practical experiences of people living in societies undergoing the wrenching changes associated with industrialization and what was once called "modernization." Psychologist and philosopher Thomas Lombardo, who founded a Center for Future Consciousness in Arizona, reminds us that "not only did the Age of Enlightenment bring with it a positive hope for the future of humanity, it also embraced the principles of science, including scientific determinism, and hence . . . the great expositor of the Enlightenment, Condorcet, offers a variety of extrapolative predictions on the future of humanity."[2] Yale University sociologist Wendell Bell concurs on the importance of this revolution in worldview but stresses the structural changes that came to industrializing societies as a result of economic growth and the rise of the modern state:

As the complexity of society increases, or decreases as it sometimes does, so does the potential for an increase in the scope of *planning* flow and ebb. Collecting taxes, managing estates, irrigating the land, and waging wars require planning . . . Yet it was not until the twentieth century that economic and social planning grew into the comprehensive activities that reach into the everyday lives of nearly every individual. It was not until the creation of the modern state that everyday life became so fully under conscious regulation, encouragement, or direct control.[3]

Once the modern state was firmly in place, bureaucrats, politicians, industrialists, intellectuals, and members of the general public could all begin to imagine national leaders using state power to direct their country or even the world as a whole to a perpetually brighter future, realizing both rational Enlightenment objectives as well as some of the more Romantic visions associated with futuristic utopian science fiction, which itself emerged in the nineteenth century.[4] As a result, even in the depths of the Great Depression—and on the eve of a world war—Americans and others could celebrate a quasi-utopian future at the 1939 New York World's Fair:

The theme of the fair was "The World of Tomorrow"; the opening ceremonies were held in a vast enclosure called "The Court of Peace" . . . Here, all about one, was the embodiment of the American dream, 1939 model. Bold modern architecture, sometimes severe, sometimes garish, but always devoid of the traditional classical or Gothic decoration, and glowing with color . . . Miracles of invention and of industrial efficiency to goggle at . . . In this fantastic paradise there were visible no social classes, no civil feuds, no international hates, no hints of grimy days in dreary slums, no depression worries. Here was a dream of wealth, luxury, and lively beauty, with Coca-Cola at every corner and the horns of the busses jauntily playing "The Sidewalks of New York."[5]

Yet World War I; the Depression; the rise of Fascism, Nazism, and Stalinism; and then World War II all together made clear that the powerful forces unleashed by industrialization, scientific development, and the rise of the modern state could also be put to profoundly destructive uses. This seemed to create the tension in which futures studies came together as a distinctive field in the 1950s. The inevitability of a fabulous, bountiful, and just future promised by some strands of Enlightenment or Romantic thinking now seemed hopelessly naïve, particularly with the advent of nuclear weapons. If there were to be a brighter future—for any single nation or for humanity as a whole—it would have to be built by human beings, and the human track record of recent years did not inspire automatic confidence:

The Western optimistic belief in progress declined [in the years following World War II] and pessimistic and nihilistic philosophies became more popular . . . The belief that the future was determined and could scientifically be predicted was rejected by many writers and thinkers . . . There were many possible futures rather than one inevitable future. These different futures could be evaluated for desirability ("preferable future"), and which future was actually realized would depend on the choices and actions of humans.[6]

Prior to the 1970s, futures studies in the United States was dominated by Cold War imperatives and often directly financed by the Pentagon and other Washington agencies. The field began to broaden and internationalize starting in the 1960s, in tandem with the general sociocultural ferment throughout the world at that time. A landmark event was the convening in 1967 of the First International Future Research Conference in Oslo, Norway; this was followed by the founding in 1973 of the World Futures Studies Federation in Paris. Yet "the imbalance in futures research . . . continued through the 1980s, especially in the case of large-scale, highly organized well-financed research projects where the clients' goals determined the definition of the problem and the focus of research, especially where those goals involved war, counterinsurgency, and Cold War tactics and strategies."[7] Even today, much futures research is conducted in secret or "in-house," financed by governments or corporations. But the overall intellectual endeavor is substantially broader today than ever, and its activities (conferences, publications) span the globe.

In his influential overview of the field, Yale's Wendell Bell identifies "nine major tasks" for futures studies useful to keep in mind when considering Chinese assessments of the People's Republic of China's (PRC's) trajectory: (1) the study of possible futures, (2) the study of probable futures, (3) the study of images of the future, (4) the study of the knowledge foundations of futures studies, (5) the study of the ethical foundations of futures studies, (6) interpreting the past and orientating the present, (7) integrating knowledge and values for designing social action, (8) increasing democratic participation in imaging and designing the future, and (9) communicating and advocating a particular image of the future.[8] This book focuses on Tasks 1, 2, and 3; or more precisely, it pursues Task 3 as a means to answering the questions posed by Tasks 1 and 2: studying images of China's future as articulated by Chinese elites—or, what amounts to the same, these elites' conceptualizations of China's trajectory (what they perceive the actual trajectory to be, in addition to their preferred trajectory) as indicators of what the future may become, or at the very least correctives to some of the unjustifiably overconfident predictions that can be found in certain corners of social science.

Bell makes the critical point that research of this nature requires a willingness to challenge conventional wisdom, where necessary, in ways that will not always be popular: "The exploration of possible futures includes trying to look at the present in new and different ways, often deliberately breaking out of the strait-jacket of conventional, orthodox, or traditional thinking and taking unusual, even unpopular, perspectives."[9] There are many ways in which conventional, orthodox, or traditional thinking potentially straitjackets analysis of China's future, but two stand out:

1. The belief that China's rise will inevitably continue without serious interruption, leading the PRC to become in short order the most powerful country on Earth—either (a) for everyone's benefit, as end-

lessly increasing prosperity deepens social pluralization and eventually causes democratization; or (b) to the world's detriment, as China remains uncompromisingly authoritarian while—emboldened by increasing wealth and strength—it embarks on a course of predatory expansionism.

2. The sharply contrasting belief that China will inevitably fail, either collapsing into chaos or grinding into a permanent morass of low or zero growth. Chaos would produce all manner of nontraditional security challenges for China's neighbors and global society at large; grinding into a morass (or what Chinese economists call a "middle income trap") might or might not lead China to adopt a more cautious foreign policy; it also might or might not increase the chances of democratization.

This study takes as its starting point the assumption that China's future is ultimately unknowable. But it also acknowledges that some developments are more likely than others and contends that systematic study of elite Chinese depictions of the future (what is likely versus what would be desirable) can help us to sort the more from the less likely trajectories. Elite images can also be deployed as potent tools useful for correcting certain overly confident predictions of China's path offered by Western (and other) social scientists and professional commentators—the countless "predictioneers" who claim in books, blogs, journals, and newspapers to possess a special insight into the future.

APPROACHES TO THE FUTURE I:
RATIONALIST PREDICTIONEERING

Not all social scientists and commentators are convinced that elite (or any other) images must be studied systematically to predict or even control the future. One of the most intellectually stimulating (if extreme) books to take this position in recent years is influential political scientist Bruce Bueno de Mesquita's *The Predictioneer's Game: Using the Logic of Brazen Self-Interest to See and Shape the Future*, published in 2009. BDM, as he is often known, states straightforwardly in his Introduction that "the principal claim of this book" is that "it is possible for us to anticipate actions, to predict the future, and by looking for ways to change incentives, to engineer the future across a stunning range of considerations that involve human decision making."[10] BDM goes on to claim that "it so happens I have been predicting future events for three decades, often in print before the fact, and mostly getting them right . . . According to a declassified CIA assessment, the predictions for which I've been responsible have a 90 percent accuracy rate."[11] BDM assumes that humans and the institutions they create, including states, are rational agents locked into interdependent relationships with other rational agents. By knowing the preferences of these agents and the payoff schedules associated with their various possible moves, action—and therefore the future itself—can be predicted and even manipulated: "In my world, science, not mumbo-jumbo, is the way to anticipate people's choices and their consequences for altering the future. I use game theory."[12]

The Achilles heel in BDM's position—certainly for anyone trying to wrestle with a problem as complex as China's future—is the question of preferences. BDM writes that politics and other complex social phenomena are all predictable: "All that is needed is a tool—like my model—that takes basic information, evaluates it by assuming everyone does what they think is best for them, and produces reliable assessments of what they will do and why they will do it."[13] But clearly this entails first finding out what everyone thinks is best—factors related to the identity of actors. As Alexander Wendt frames this problem: "Identities refer to who or what actors *are*. They designate social kinds or states of being. Interests refer to what actors *want*. They designate motivations that help explain behavior . . . *Interests presuppose identities* because an actor cannot know what it wants until it knows who it is, and since identities have varying degrees of cultural content, so will interests."[14] In BDM's model, preferences are critical, but identities are either held constant, as everyone is assumed to seek maximization of material utility, or else are imputed in a cursory process. BDM trained in graduate school as a South Asianist, and on that basis asserts that he respects and values area and culture expertise: "But I don't think it's the way government or business should organize itself for problem-solving purposes . . . Country expertise is no substitute for understanding the principles that govern human decision making, and it should be subordinate to them, working in tandem to provide nuance as we actively seek to engineer a better future."[15]

Such a perspective implies that any halfway decent social scientist should be able rather easily to trace the trajectory of China's rise, by simply (1) imputing the identity of rational utility maximizers to Chinese elites; (2) determining their preference schedules; and (3) mapping out how the elites would then pursue their resulting interests, subject only to the restrictions imposed by the moves of other actors, China's material limitations, and chance events. Other than for purposes of embellishment, it would be a waste of time to research how Chinese elites conceptualize their country's trajectory, because Chinese conceptualizations would be very similar to the conceptualizations of elites in other rising countries facing similar structural conditions. "The principles that govern human decision making" are, according to BDM, universally valid; questions of identity can provide nuance and color to a prediction but are not fundamentally important. "We surely would think it ridiculous if chemists believed that oxygen and hydrogen combine differently in China than they do in the United States," BDM writes, "but for some reason we think it entirely sensible to believe that people make choices based on different principles in Timbuktu than in Tipperary (we might be different from mere particles, but we're not all that different from one another)."[16]

Presumptions such as these are probably what led some Western observers of the past to make dubious or even flat-out wrong (at least as of this writing) predictions concerning China's future, such as that the PRC would inevitably democratize or that it would become a contended global actor working happily together with its East Asian neighbors and the United States to solve world problems peacefully and in accordance with international norms.[17] Of course the beauty of such predictions is that they can never be falsified because predictioneers tend not to specify the time period in which the positive developments must inevitably unfold.[18] Here, though, Bueno de Mesquita is, to his credit, considerably bolder and more intellectually honest. He is willing to go out on a limb with his predictions, and, in so doing, he helpfully (but unintentionally) illustrates the weaknesses inherent in forecasts that ignore, or incautiously impute, actor identity.

Even BDM has to put actor preferences in his models, one way or another. But instead of studying preferences or identity systematically—for example, by researching conceptualizations of national trajectories as articulated by elites strongly constrained by an authoritarian state's guidance—he reserves his own intellectual energies (and they are formidable) for the game-theoretic analysis. He takes a more relaxed approach to assigning preferences. For example, he had undergraduate students read online newspapers to help develop a set of predictions regarding Pakistan and Iran–Iraq relations in the last chapter of *The Predictioneer's Game*. The students "had almost no prior experience with any of the material or models. They had limited access to experts, so they relied on the Internet and major news outlets to put their data together. I mention this to be clear that any hard-working, motivated person can replicate what they did [that is, no special area expertise is required]. All this being said, my students used my model, and I certainly reviewed their work—so any misses are the model's and mine."[19]

Unfortunately, one of the predictions proved to be a very big miss indeed. After the students had gathered the data, BDM ran his model and predicted in the spring of 2008 that Washington's commitment to using military force inside Pakistan to go after Islamist militants "will collapse shortly after the American presidential election. The new president is not likely to do much of anything about the rise of terrorist influence within Pakistan at least through 2009," when the forecast period would end.[20] But as we now know, all throughout that period the (new) Obama administration continued to gather intelligence and stage operations in Pakistan and Afghanistan, culminating in the dramatic killing of Osama bin Laden in April 2011. If BDM had consulted a specialist on American politics and foreign policy—that is, a U.S. area specialist—perhaps he would have come to realize that regardless of what his model predicted, President Barack Obama was very likely to continue pursuing Al Qaeda militants, partly because he was a Democratic president who had come into office on an antiwar platform and therefore had to prove his tough foreign policy credentials, as all Democratic presidents have felt pressured to do since the advent of the Cold War. By ignoring such subtle factors as these, rooted in an inevitably nuanced and complex American area-studies history, BDM's mechanistic model blunders into a big miss. More careful attention to national identity and leadership preferences could easily have allowed him to avoid this failure.

For his final prediction—a grand prediction, indeed—BDM addresses the threat to the human community posed by global warming. To assess the far-off future, BDM must make key (but unacknowledged) assumptions concerning not only preference schedules in the present and how they affect actor decisions but also the continuity of such preferences over time; that is, *culture*. BDM predicts that once global warming reaches a certain critical threshold, automatic mechanisms will kick into gear restoring the world to equilibrium, as rising temperatures "create enough additional sunshine in cold places, enough additional rain in dry places, enough additional wind in still places, and, most important, enough additional incentives for humankind that windmills, solar panels, hydroelectricity, and as yet undiscovered technologies will be the good, cheap, evenly distributed, and clean mechanisms to replace the fossil fuels we use today," thereby ending the trend of warming.[21] BDM is not worried about market failure, politics, inequality, or limitations in human ingenuity ultimately obstructing the automatic adjustment mechanism.[22] But what is particularly interesting about his prediction in the context of this book is the assumptions he makes regarding continuity of preferences over time—in fact, over many decades. BDM predicts that "Americans who worry about global warming, like their European Union brethren, [will] remain committed through about 2030 or 2040 to tougher standards than were announced at Kyoto. But after that, they join forces with those who put economic growth ahead of regulating carbon dioxide and other emissions . . . The voice that dominates debate after 2040 or so is the voice of Americans who today are not convinced global warming is for real."[23] Here, BDM assumes that the actors in place today will be the same actors in place after 2040, essentially unchanged and clinging to their preferences of 2010. Indeed, in Figure 11.3 ("What Will the Biggest Polluters Do about Greenhouse Gas Emissions") he runs his analysis all the way to 2130.[24] On this basis, he confidently predicts that global warming will produce its own solutions. He also arrives at what could be a dubious policy recommendation for the present: "Frankly, we will see that agreements like the Kyoto Protocol and the efforts at Bali [in 2007] or Copenhagen [2009] to reduce greenhouse gasses, especially carbon dioxide emissions, are not likely to matter. They may even be impediments to real solutions."[25]

To generate inputs to the model that produces this conclusion, BDM imputes preferences and other characteristics to multiple actors (countries and nongovernmental organizations, or NGOs) in the present and assumes that these preferences and characteristics will continue throughout the course of the simulation, until 2130.[26] This of course assumes a transmission mechanism by which the characteristics can be handed down to subsequent generations: *culture*, in effect, even though BDM has already declared that cultural characteristics are ultimately superfluous, at best providing nuance or color to analyses, because at the core humans worldwide are all rational and the same. By introducing a cultural variable in an ad hoc, unexamined, fashion, BDM weakens what would otherwise be a reasonably defensible prediction. He assumes that cultures (and the preference schedules embedded in them) are essential and unchanging over time. Yet the actors he studies in his model include the likes of Japan, Russia, the European Union (EU), and China: all places that have changed radically over the past 100 years. Why should we expect that they will not change equally radically over the next 100 years? Perhaps there is a reason—another ad hoc hypothesis that BDM leaves unexamined. The point is not to suggest that his prediction is destined to be wrong or is entirely without merit. The point is simply that he needs to suspend his certainty that a rationalist model, casually imputing preferences instead of uncovering them painstakingly, can easily predict outcomes from complex human interactions even decades or a century in advance.[27]

APPROACHES TO THE FUTURE II:
INSIGHTS FROM THE DISCIPLINE OF HISTORY

A very different approach to analyzing future trajectories is proposed by historian David J. Staley. In *History and Future: Using Historical Thinking to Imagine the Future*, Staley declares flatly that "the future cannot be predicted"; yet this should not prevent researchers "from creating useful representations about the future . . . History is an excellent method for creating such useful representations."[28] In arriving at this recommendation, Staley first distinguishes between what he calls history1 and history2, analogous to future1 and future2. History1 refers to the actual past, whereas history2 refers to *representations* about the past, by which Staley means all writing about history. By extension, "Future2 will refer to anything we can imagine about future1 [what will become the actual future], that is, any representation of or narrative about future1. Future1, like history1, is not present and is as 'absent' as the past. Therefore, in order to achieve understanding or insight about future1, we require a substitute: a future2."[29]

Instead of aspiring to make "scientific" predictions, Staley proposes varying *scenarios* as the most reasonable end product of research into the future: "Both the designer and user of a prediction assume that the prediction is a certainty . . . A scenario, by contrast, is a statement that assumes uncertainty. It describes not a certain world but only a possible world."[30] This does not mean that researchers who design scenarios are tolerant of sloppiness or that they aim to be vague. On the contrary, they aspire to a more sophisticated and nuanced rigor in methodological approach because their goal is to arrive at conclusions more strongly in accord with reality. Researchers who design scenarios can achieve these goals partly because they are not afraid to reject demonstrably false social science orthodoxies such as the insistence that variation in culture or worldview must always be causally irrelevant given that people everywhere are essentially identical in their rationality. Scenario-designing researchers attempt—as would any genuinely thoughtful and reflective social analyst—to use their *whole brains* in designing and carrying out their projects, not just one overdeveloped *part* of the brain. The result is more nuanced and accurate research conclusions: "Understanding that any such future2 is probably not going to correspond exactly to future1, the scenarist instead seeks the next best thing: a narrative about the future that is plausible, that corresponds as closely to future1 as possible."[31]

As with history, so a future2 scenario can either reinforce prevailing interpretations inside a dominant paradigm or else propose something new. Although "most works of history add to or elaborate upon a mental map of the past, . . . on occasion a historian composes a history2 that alters the mental map, the historiographic boundaries of a debate."[32] Scenarios, too, can either reinforce or alter existing images of the future. In this book's concluding chapter, I discuss some possible scenarios for China's future over the next ten to twenty years, but the book's primary objective is to present the most prominent scenarios being written or articulated by China's own elites. Sometimes the Chinese images have the (direct or indirect) effect of challenging dominant paradigms from Western social science, or from the Western commentariat. It is significant, for example, that so many analysts working in democratic countries expect China to become democratic after the country reaches a certain level of per capita gross domestic product (GDP), but what do China's own elites—operating inside the system—think about such predictions? What are *their* expectations for China's future? Considering that Chinese elites are likely to have far more influence over the PRC's trajectory than social scientists and commentators in democratic (and other foreign) countries, the question is a critically important one to ask. The key is to realize that Chinese elites are fully aware of most Western social science predictions concerning China, and the Chinese Communist Party (CCP) exercises its awesome agency to try to prevent the predictions it dislikes from coming to pass. Separately, Chinese elites have their own categories for thinking about the future, which mean a great deal to them even if Western social scientists are largely, or entirely, unaware of them. One example would be "achieving China's recentering in world history."[33] I have little doubt there are many other Chinese categories that I myself have never encountered and probably never will. But it is important to try, because the Chinese conviction in the power of the PRC's own agency and its capacity to shape rather than be shaped is no illusion. China is a very powerful country.

Nevertheless, although predicting with absolute certainty is impossible—and Chinese (especially CCP) agency is formidable—certain trends and developments in the present seem likely to produce unavoidable, inescapable consequences in the future. This is why the first issue-area I discuss in this book (in Chapter 2) is China's economy. As we will see, there are certain demographic trends now underway—most notably, an aging population, a shrinking of the working-age cohort, and a sex imbalance—that cannot possibly be reversed in short order. Even if the CCP were to abandon its one-child policy (the original source of these problems), the population structure could not possibly be put back onto an economically more supportive track before at least two decades, even assuming all goes well and Chinese couples start producing babies again with giddy enthusiasm. The altered demographic structure will remain an objective material reality certain to act as drag on China's economic development for at least two decades into the future—and that is in addition to the various other "drags" to be discussed. No matter what Chinese elites (such as the superoptimistic international relations [IR] analysts discussed in Chapters 5 and 6) imagine their country's economic future to be, not even the CCP's agency can solve the demographic problem—although the Party-state could take measures to begin ameliorating the problem. Probably analogous structures exist in politics (constellations of interests), society (mutual role expectations), and culture (norms and values).

APPROACHES TO THE FUTURE III:
FACTORING IN COMPLEXITY AND CHAOS

There is another important respect in which hard scientific predictions of the future can be dangerously misleading. The world is far too complex for prediction on most sociopolitical issues to succeed in any but the most general terms. The logic here derives from chaos and complexity theory. As explained by political scientists Euel Elliott and L. Douglas Kiel:

Chaos theory is the result of natural scientists' discoveries [beginning in the 1950s] in the field of nonlinear dynamics . . . Nonlinear systems reveal dynamical behavior such that the relationships between variables are unstable. Furthermore, changes in these relationships are subject to positive feedback in which changes are amplified, breaking up existing structures and behavior and creating unexpected outcomes in the generation of new structure and behavior. These changes may result in new forms of equilibrium; novel forms of increasing complexity; or even temporal behavior that appears random and devoid of order: the state of "chaos" in which uncertainty dominates and predictability breaks down.[34]

Concepts from chaos and complexity theory can be useful in thinking critically about predictions concerning China's future, primarily for two reasons:

1. Some of the prognostications offered by Western (and other) social scientists and commentators have an overly linear "feel" to them, insisting that China is on a recognizable trajectory similar to the trajectories of other economically developing or rising powers of the past. (Consequently, it will "certainly" democratize, it will "almost inevitably" challenge the United States in a power-transition struggle, and so on). Such predictions ignore the possibility—even the likelihood—suggested by chaos and complexity theory that things will almost certainly *not* turn out as expected, although they will also probably not turn out exactly the *opposite* of what is expected (that would still be linearity, but in a different direction).[35]

2. Some of the images articulated by Chinese elites themselves posit linearity—especially the strongly confident expectations in the Chinese IR world concerning the inevitability of China's continued rise in status and influence. At the root of this confidence is the (usually, it appears, unexamined) assumption that nothing can stop China from continuing to amass comprehensive national power at a much faster rate than its competitors: The trajectory that began in the 1980s is assumed to be firmly in place and unalterable. Because the rise is imagined as unstoppable, there is no question in the minds of many Chinese IR analysts that China will achieve its deeply controversial international objectives: unifying Taiwan; beating back Vietnam, the Philippines, and Malaysia to secure rightful control over most of the South China Sea; raising the cost to Japan and the United States of continuing to administer the Senkaku/Diaoyu Islands to the point that eventually they give up; forcing India to back down on the two countries' McMahon Line boundary dispute; compelling South Korea to accept China's dominant position in North Korea; and so on—*all, it is expected by Chinese predictioneers, at relatively low cost*, because of the almost mystical guarantee that China's material and eventually soft power will continue to soar inevitably. Currently, Japan and

the other wrong and obstinate countries are arrogantly blocking the realization of a grand, world-historical master trend: China's return to global centrality and all-surpassing greatness, the realization of one critical dimension of the China Dream. But the obstinate countries will eventually abandon their arrogance in the face of endlessly increasing Chinese comprehensive national power.

The problem common to both the Western and Chinese linear predictions is that every significant assumption the prognosticators make about the present and each phase of the future must be accurate for the trajectory to remain on its expected track. If even one significant assumption proves false, the actual future could end up profoundly different from the predicted future. This is the problem known in chaos and complexity theory as "sensitivity to initial conditions." Anyone who predicted in 1950 that China would hew tightly in its developmental course to the path taken by the Soviet Union failed to consider sensitivity to initial conditions—the slight or not-so-slight differences between the two countries that ensured that China would veer onto a substantially altered (though not entirely different) course just a few years after the PRC's establishment. Accumulating differences in each new phase of the post-1950s future, as it became the present, led the two countries onto even more radically different trajectories by the time China's leaders decided to launch "reform and opening" policies in the late 1970s.

Or, to take a more recent example: Some scholars and pundits were predicting confidently in the 1990s that China would democratize in the same way as Taiwan or South Korea, or even Thailand and the Philippines. These predictioneers were overlooking the profound differences among these countries at their "starting points." As historian Staley phrases the problem: "Many physical [and social] systems can produce wildly different results with only a *slight* alteration in one of the variables . . . The best we can do, argue scientists who study non-linear systems, is to posit the most probable future states (plural) to which the system might eventually settle."[36] Therefore, Staley proposes that researchers apply their efforts at offering plausible (and perhaps competing) contingent scenarios instead of brashly self-confident predictions.

Yet, at the same time, the reality of uncertainty and complexity should not be taken to mean that the world operates entirely on the basis of random events, which would render systematic thinking about the future (or even the present) pointless and absurd. Staley and others influenced by chaos and complexity theory agree that order will emerge in the course of a country's political, economic, and cultural change. But given the multiplicity of variables at play, the sensitivity to initial conditions, the intervention of a not-always-rational human agency, and other factors, including chance events—predictive models of linear development cannot easily succeed in capturing the kaleidoscopically complex processes and sequencing of change, nor even the ultimate outcomes—except, perhaps, for certain subcomponents of the change process more likely to be governed by the laws of natural science (in the environment, epidemiology, or demography, for example).

Concretely, Staley outlines a rather simple and straightforward approach to research into the future, which pivots on the chaos and complexity theory concept of "attractors." A developmental economist, Samir Rihani—who also uses this concept in his practical work giving advice to governments—defines attractors as powerful if often difficult-to-specify supervariables that can potently explain ranges of complex-but-patterned behavioral tendencies in any system, including human societies:

[An attractor] in its simplest form could be a *point* attractor, as seen in a pendulum swinging under gravity that invariably comes to rest pointing vertically downwards. Its different *states* while it is in motion ultimately converge on that attractor; they are said to drain into that basin of attraction. The next level is the *limit-cycle* attractor . . . The attractor in this case is an envelope of space or time that includes every single state assumed by the system within the cycle . . . Point and limit-cycle attractors occur in linear systems that are at or near equilibrium. Life becomes more complicated as we move away from these simple instances.[37]

A good example of how attractors differ in linear and nonlinear systems might be an engine originally controlled by a governor that maintains the speed of the engine within a certain range, relying on positive and negative feedback. Plotting the speed over a long period of time yields a torus, or doughnut shape. That is when the system is still linear; "However, if the governor were to fail suddenly [taking us completely outside the realm of linearity], the engine would then race along driven by a multiplicity of internal and external factors. We have now moved into the domain of nonlinear phenomena, including complex systems, where basins of attraction are often referred to as *strange* attractors."[38] As a development economist, Rihani is interested in analogizing complex mechanical or biological systems to societies and using the attractor concept to model "strange" or otherwise massively complex social, political, and economic dynamics. He observes that even "minor events [which serve as attractors] can, and often do, shift the economy [or society] in new and unexpected directions. And the same can be said of polities."[39]

Obviously in this view, a society's development trajectory cannot be mapped or predicted as easily as Bueno de Mesquita and certain others would contend, even holding constant the knotty problems of contingency and human agency. To Staley, the solution is to uncover those sociopolitical attractors that seem *most likely* to pull the system potently in one direction or another over the course of the time period of interest—always allowing for the possibility that some unrecognized endogenous or exogenous factor could at any point throw the system into an *apparently* chaotic (but still not random) pattern of nonlinear development, or indeed, that it has already entered a period of nonlinear development. In thinking about trajectories, then, the goal of scenario writing cannot be "to predict the one path the future will follow, but [instead] to discern the possible states toward which the future might be 'attracted.'"[40] The clear implication for research into China's future is that analysts should find and focus on those factors that seem most likely to shunt the system first onto one path and then possibly onto another, as events unfold, along with other factors that could pull the system onto entirely different courses. The pushing and pulling itself would then describe the trajectory: The order in China's development would be emergent.

Keeping such considerations in mind, I posit in this book that, to the extent elite Chinese images of the future are systematically articulated, coherent, and focused, they should be regarded as one highly potent attractor (or set of attractors, with variations in content depending on the specific issue-areas) contributing to the shape of China's emerging trajectory—even if (perhaps especially if) the elite images are not generated autonomously, but instead reflect, to some degree, the demands of the Communist Party power center. That is to say, even though the Chinese system is, from one point of view, developing along material lines governed by powerful—often linear-like—logics (economically, as discussed in Chapter 2, and as a network society, discussed in Chapter 4), the subjective assessments Chinese elites offer in trying to interpret and shape these developments—their collective (though dispute-driven) discourse—*itself* acts as a powerful attractor. This idea is captured succinctly by sociologist Wendell Bell: "Futurists see images of the future as being among the *causes* of present behavior, as people either try to adapt to what they see coming or try to act in ways to create the future they want."[41]

The material attractors are undeniably potent—and are recognized as such by Chinese elites.[42] Economic development and the Internet ushering in the network society have combined with globalization to generate substantial new sources of wealth in Chinese society. They have also helped to remake China into a profoundly more pluralistic society. This ongoing, multilayered process seems, on balance, to act as an attractor pulling China's political system in the direction of liberalization or even democratization. At the same time, the CCP fights vigorously and sometimes viciously against this pull. Beginning in the 1990s, following China's spring 1989 nationwide democracy uprising and the subsequent collapse of the Soviet Union, the CCP embarked on a relegitimization strategy centered on cultivating a conviction among Chinese citizens that their great nation is viewed with contempt by foreigners and is consequently forever at risk of being cheated, bullied, exploited, and maligned by Westerners and Japanese who remain, despite the friendlier pose they strike, essentially evil: just as were their ancestors of 75 to 150 years ago. Only the CCP can save China from foreign depredations, past, present, and future. Therefore, all patriotic Chinese must support the CCP. The centerpiece of the original relegitimization effort was the comprehensive Patriotic Education Campaign, a massive, open-ended effort launched in stages between 1991 and 1994 for the purpose of replacing discredited Communist ideology with a semireligious apotheosis of the PRC nation-state.[43] But, even to this day, the campaign—which succeeded in cultivating an angry and sometimes venomous nationalism in certain segments of the population—continues to be implemented vigorously, partly, it appears, to counterbalance the increased social pluralization produced by economic restructuring and the advent of a network society. This CCP determination to keep itself in power even at the risk of heightening tensions with foreign countries (because much of the nationalism is strongly antiforeign) would itself, obviously, act as a powerful attractor pulling China *away* from liberalization and democratization—precisely the CCP's intent.[44] The behind-the-scenes maneuvering of economic elites who benefit from the status quo—especially the managers and employees of state-owned enterprises—has the same effect. The People's Liberation Army (PLA) benefits from nationalism and the Party's capacity to control the population but also requires relatively rapid economic growth to arm itself to a level necessary to achieve its ambitions; for this reason, some in the PLA might view with irritation state-owned enterprise (SOE) elites who block the economic liberalization that would be necessary (if not sufficient) to ensure China returns to a high rate of economic growth. It is not impossible to imagine Army leaders quietly lining up in favor of economic reform while remaining staunchly opposed to political liberalization. But first the PLA leaders—along with most of the other influential opinion makers in the Chinese IR world—must recognize the reality of the country's sharply deteriorating economic condition, a problem the PRC's economists have been warning about for years but that, until very recently, most people in China (including elites) and in other countries have ignored or even flatly denied.

CHAPTER 2

Economic Growth: Marching into
a Middle-Income Trap?

OUTSIDE ASSESSMENTS OF CHINA'S ECONOMIC PROSPECTS in the years ahead range from the highly optimistic to the extremely pessimistic—with pessimism steadily displacing optimism since about 2011. One influential optimist would be Edward Steinfeld, a political economist at the Massachusetts Institute of Technology (MIT). Steinfeld argued in a highly acclaimed 2010 monograph, *Playing Our Game*, that there is strong reason to be hopeful about China's economic *and* political futures, because for many years now—and accelerating in the 2000s—the CCP has been borrowing the institutions and emulating the practices of the industrialized democracies. The term Steinfeld uses to describe this process is *institutional outsourcing*. Provocatively, he defines this process as "ceding to a third party the power to define key societal rules that govern and shape social interaction . . . China has outsourced the power to define its domestic institutions—and thus shape its developmental trajectory—to [global] commercial entities and other outsiders."[1] Steinfeld is aware that the PRC has still not "arrived" yet as an industrialized democracy. But, by the late 1990s, he argues, CCP leaders had come to the realization that they "had little choice but to push convergence [in Chinese institutions and practices] toward global norms."[2] Beijing's intent was probably to push convergence only to the extent necessary to keep the Party in power. But eventually, Steinfeld argues, the institutional outsourcing "developed a dynamic that is leading to—and indeed, has already created—a different order entirely."[3]

Steinfeld's book appeared at just the right time for it to make a major impact: mid-2010, the high point of foreign optimism about China's economic prospects. During the two-year period from mid-2009 until mid-2011, innumerable foreign observers insisted that the CCP's decisively bold response to the global financial crisis (GFC) allowed China to emerge stronger and healthier economically than ever before, certainly in comparison to the woefully beaten-down Western countries, Japan, and South Korea. As detailed in the following discussion, almost *no* Chinese economist was, at the time, expressing comparable optimism—although quite a few Chinese international relations (IR) specialists were doing so (as discussed in Chapters 5 and 6). But rare indeed was the Western or other foreign observer who did not jump onto the "China as number one" bandwagon—or at least keep silent if he or she harbored any doubts.[4] This may be difficult to imagine today, given that voicing skepticism about China's economic performance has, in the years since 2011, become widespread to the point of being de rigueur on certain occasions. The sharp and sudden change in sentiment was documented in a newsletter issued by BCA Research in early 2012. BCA analysts pored over a sample of leading English-language newspapers dating from January 2002 to December 2011, to count all of the articles discussing the possibility of China suffering an economic "hard landing" or a comparable crisis. Throughout the mid-2000s, approximately 100 such articles appeared each month. Astonishingly, this number fell to *almost zero* by mid-2009, evidently because the outside world was dazzled by the CCP's proudly trumpeted "successful" response to the GFC and subsequent "Great Recession."[5] Even as late as the first quarter of 2011, there were still only about 200 bearish assessments published each month in the newspapers sampled. By the end of 2011, however, the number had increased dramatically, averaging about 500 articles per month: at one point in the late fall it spiked to 1,100.[6]

Well before 2011—and even well before 2008—Edward Steinfeld's MIT colleague, political economist Yasheng Huang, established himself as one of the leading critics of the CCP's development strategy, with the criticism rooted in meticulous, highly regarded research. Although Steinfeld—also a formidably accomplished researcher—contends that the 1990s marked a decisive turning point in a liberal direction for China, as the country transitioned successfully from state-led to market-driven economic growth, Huang, in his widely acclaimed 2008 book, *Capitalism with Chinese Characteristics*, argued precisely the opposite: that the early 1990s marked a transition *away* from the market-oriented reforms of the 1980s—during which private firms began to flourish, particularly in the smaller towns and villages—back to a model in which the state smothers or at least sharply constricts the freedom of the private sector. Huang summarizes as follows: "My argument is that the best way to characterize the Chinese economic system today is that it is a commanding-heights economy. This system has many failed antecedents among the statist developing economies of the 1970s."[7] Huang's contention was strikingly iconoclastic in the context of the late 2000s, because at the time many—perhaps most—political economists were depicting China's trajectory as similar to the trajectories of South Korea, Taiwan, and other East Asian success stories. But Huang flatly rejected this analogy as tendentious and uninformed, because "the East Asian economies, notwithstanding their high levels of industrial policy interventions, were far more privately owned than China is today" and consequently far more dynamic.[8] In thinking about the future, then, Huang worried that "China faces substantial challenges in its transition to a genuinely efficient form of capitalism."[9]

As we turn now to analyses offered by China's own academic (and occasionally, business) elites, it becomes evident that in key respects *both* Steinfeld and Huang are right in their assessments. Steinfeld is right to the extent that Chinese policy analysts—or at least those writing in available *neibu* journals and recently published, trajectory-analyzing books—articulate a trenchant critique of China's economy rooted in what a Peking University professor acknowledges is the "standard economics" model developed—and still dominant—in the West.[10] There seems to be no coherent and compelling alternative model in Chinese economics capable of competing with the standard (Western) model to shape the thinking of CCP leaders. There is a New Leftist school of nationalist-leaning commentators whose adherents praise China's economic performance even under Mao. In books, these critics warn against deepening liberalization, but one searches in vain to find any articles by members of this school in the *neibu* policy journals. The New Leftists' chief concern—rising inequality—is a concern that mainstream economists now fully share.[11] Simply put, the New Leftist school did not appear to have much influence during the Hu Jintao years and does not as of this writing seem to have much influence under Xi Jinping. As discussed in Chapter 7, the "economic reform" document issued at the close of the CCP's Third Plenum (November 2013) vacillates between reformism and conservatism but does not champion nationalistic leftism.[12] Even the toppled Bo Xilai's "Chongqing model"—elements of which are discussed in Chapter 3—was an amalgam of standard and New Leftist economics. It was not at all the "neo-Maoist" model it was often depicted as being.[13]

Standard (Western) economic analysis may well be dominant to the point of hegemonic in Chinese universities, think tanks, and private businesses these days, but my survey of books and journal articles on China's economic trajectory makes clear that most Chinese economists are strongly dissatisfied with the degree to which the prescriptions of standard economics are being taken seriously by CCP policy makers. The critical discourse these analysts articulate should be treated as a significant "attractor" certain to exert some degree of influence over China's developmental trajectory in the years ahead, especially given that the power of this discourse seems likely to be reinforced by the actual deterioration in economic conditions it describes.[14] Precisely how much influence the discourse will exert—how powerful as an attractor it will prove to be—is impossible to specify, but assuming that Chinese officials responsible for economic policy have been reading and hearing the economists' criticisms day in and day out, over many years, the logic of the criticisms almost certainly will have already begun to affect their thinking. Indeed, the rhetoric, if not yet the policy reality, emerging from the November 2013 Third Plenum suggests that even the highest-ranking leaders are now intent on at least paying lip service to the critics' views. Whether they have the power and determination to overcome the opposition of vested interests in order to implement the liberalizing reforms the economists are demanding remains to be seen.[15]

Just who, exactly, opposes the reforms? In a biting *neibu* assessment published in November 2009, Zhou Ruijin of the Chinese Academy of Social Sciences (CASS) Graduate School uses tough language to castigate four categories of "special interest groups backed by public power," whose members constantly scheme to undermine or block significant economic change:[16]

1. *Monopolistic SOEs.* Every year, "some SOE monopolies" (Zhou does not name any) make superprofits and neither return (much of) the money to the state nor distribute it to society. Instead, they either reinvest the money in real estate or expanded productive capacity or else distribute it among themselves for personal enjoyment.[17]

2. *The real estate industry.* Zhou argues that this is an industry steeped in corruption at every phase in the process of property development, from local governments seizing land from the farming (or other) families that have leased it, to rezoning the land for nonagricultural use, auctioning off land-utilization rights, and then subsequently "supervising" the projects that follow. This entire process, Zhou contends, is "choking with the exchange of power for money."[18]

3. *SOEs benefiting from* guojinmintui *("advance of the state, retreat of the private").* Certain SOEs have been able to take advantage of the backing they receive from local political authorities to squeeze the market space of specially targeted private enterprises, putting them out of business or taking them over maliciously. While the SOEs are working through the marketplace to implement these schemes, the local government is hitting the private enterprises behind the scenes with special new taxes, fees, and regulations.[19]

Zhou summarizes by offering a hard-hitting definition of special interest groups: "Where powerful capitalist elites and powerful governing elites conspire and exchange together—manipulating the government's public policy, carving up and consuming national assets, and seizing and squandering public resources that ultimately belong to the whole people—here we have typical 'special interest groups.'"[20] Some of these groups even succeed in "purchasing [intellectual] specialists to advocate for and explain away their monopolistic behavior, to manufacture discourse power for them."[21] It is not exactly clear what sort of intellectual specialists Zhou has in mind; evidently, he means a combination of journalists, academics, and lawyers. He writes that "the most serious problem is when 'special interest groups' penetrate and subvert the legal system," not so difficult because judges have wide scope for interpreting laws that are often vague or incomplete in their coverage.[22]

Material special interest groups in Zhou's sense are surely pulling China on a very different path from the one that most economic analysts recommend in policy-oriented books and *neibu* journals. Precisely what the outcome of this contest will be is of course unclear. The important point to stress is that if China's own economic analysts are right in their critiques, the country's current economic trajectory is unsustainable. Yet this does not necessarily imply the Party Center will change tack. The leaders may no longer be capable of shifting China's economic course because by now they may lack sufficient power relative to the special interest groups—or, indeed, they or their family members may be integral members of the groups. To the extent that either of these hypotheses proves correct, China's economic problems will certainly mount—no matter how nicely packaged and presented was the outcome of the November 2013 Third Plenum.

THE SUMMARY ASSESSMENTS OF CHINESE ECONOMISTS

Some Chinese analysts work at the macro level and try to explain the general problems facing multiple sectors of the PRC's economy. In May 2009, an entity called the China's Future Direction Editorial Group published a book entitled *China's Future Direction: Uniting High-Level Policymaking and National Strategic Arrangements*.[23] Nowhere in the book are the members of the editorial group identified, but the publisher, Renmin Chubanshe, "is an official publishing house of the Chinese Communist Party and Chinese government for books on politics and ideology."[24] For this reason, the book can probably be taken as an authoritative guide as to how senior Party figures were assessing these problems (or allowing them to be assessed) on the eve of the GFC.[25] This is important because the assessment of economic conditions would have been written *before* China's initially "successful" (but ultimately damaging) response to the crisis. Consequently, the authors could not have been influenced by either the praise resulting from the initially positive results of the 2008–2009 stimulus package (which did stop China from sliding into a deep recession) or by the criticism that followed in the wake of the shocking realization, beginning in the summer of 2009, that the stimulus had led to the government losing significant control over money and credit expansion.

From 2005 through 2008, the real (inflation-adjusted) M2 money supply increased at an average annual rate of 5 percent. But then in 2009 the growth rate suddenly skyrocketed to 17 percent, and it would remain elevated until well into 2010. At the same time, real growth in lending by establishment banks and the shadow banking sector[26]—which was also increasing at an annual average rate of about 5 percent between 2005 and 2008—soared to 21 percent (establishment banks) and 17 percent (shadow banking) in 2009. Just as with the M2 money supply, the growth rate in bank loans would remain elevated until several months into 2010. After mid-2010, both M2 and establishment bank loan growth rates returned to roughly their pre-2009 averages, albeit with occasional fluctuations. However, these growth rates were now in relation to the substantially higher absolute levels of money and credit issued in 2009 and 2010.[27]

Growth rates in nominal terms were always higher still and subject to wider fluctuations. Thus, nominal bank credit and bank loans increased at rates of about 10 percent a year from 2004 to 2006, rising to 15 to 17 percent from late 2006 until the end of 2008. Then, in 2009, nominal bank lending exploded: increasing by an astonishing 32 percent, whereas total credit in nominal terms increased by 36 percent. After the state finally responded in early 2010 by imposing tighter restrictions on establishment bank lending, that sector's nominal rate of annual growth gradually fell back to 15 percent by the beginning of 2011. It remained at that level until mid-2012, when the rate rose briefly to 17 percent after the government decided to loosen policy as it confronted the prospect of declining GDP growth on the eve of the Eighteenth Party Congress (November 2012).[28]

However, just as the government began succeeding in its struggle to reassert control over money and credit growth through tighter regulation of establishment banks, an already introduced, irresponsible new "actor" (actually, a congeries of multiple actors) suddenly appeared on the scene to challenge the government's restrictions: the various and sundry players in the shadow banking sector. Actually, this sector had always been around during the reform-and-opening period, serving the useful purpose of channeling finance to the private sector. But only in 2010 and afterward did its activities start to pose a significant problem for China's macroeconomic managers.

As explained in a comprehensive report by the U.S. Federal Reserve Bank of San Francisco:

China's shadow banking system includes direct credit extension by nonbank financial institutions (especially trust companies and brokerage firms) and informal securitization through the pooling of proceeds from wealth management products [WMPs] provided by banks . . . China's shadow banking activities typically involve direct lending to the real estate sectors . . . Shadow banks are also closely tied to commercial banks. Trust companies, for example, rely heavily on banks to obtain funding since they cannot accept retail deposits. Banks are also allowed to hold controlling shares in trust companies. Another example is direct company-to-company lending, where large, state-owned enterprises obtain bank loans at low interest rates then lend the funds to small and medium-sized private enterprises (SMEs) that are in need of credit.[29]

Prior to 2008, data on total credit issued in China normally corresponded quite closely to data on bank lending. This situation began to change in 2008, when the government deflated a minor (by today's standards) real estate bubble as well as a major stock market bubble by tightening restrictions on bank lending. For the first time, entities in the shadow banking system stepped in to fill the void—meeting some of the demand for credit—so that a data gap appeared between total credit issued and total bank lending: Total credit issued exceeded total bank lending by three to four percentage points. This probably proved fortuitous because it would have helped some businesses survive the late-2008 GFC, which the CCP could not have easily foreseen. From late 2008 until mid-2009, total credit issued then fell back into close alignment with total bank lending. The data gap evaporated—but only temporarily.

A substantially new situation began to develop in 2010, when the government was forced once again to try to contain an asset bubble—this time, a far more serious real estate bubble—by tightening monetary and credit policy. The government's efforts succeeded with the establishment banks—at least in their *roles* as establishment banks (because they also contribute to the shadow banking sector)—but was much less successful with the shadow banking entities. Consequently, in the years since 2009, total credit issued has always exceeded total bank loans, reflecting the lending activities of the shadow banking sector. Until mid-2012, however, the gap held steady at about the same 3 to 4 percent margin as in 2008, which meant that the shadow banking activities were still rising and falling in tandem with establishment bank loans. State policy thus did have *some* effect on the shadow banking sector, even though regulators could not directly control it.

Then came the dramatic and alarming change. From mid-2012 until at least mid-2013, the shadow banking system's so-called social financing—which represents the gap between total loans and bank loans—began to grow at a much higher rate, doubling the apparently acceptable 3 to 4 percent spread between bank loans and total credit to a far more worrisome 7 percent.[30] Given the opacity of many shadow banking system transactions, which makes them difficult to regulate—in the context of the rapid growth in volume and magnitude of shadow banking activities—China's regulators and establishment financial institutions became concerned for a second time (as in 2009) that money and credit expansion were escaping their control. Reflecting the anxious official mind-set, the Bank of China's board chairman, Xiao Gang, warned in an October 2012 *China Daily* analysis that shadow banking was, in speed and nature, developing to the point that it could eventually pose a systemic risk to China's macroeconomy:

It is difficult to measure the precise amount and value of wealth management products [WMPs, the most prominent investment vehicles sold within the shadow banking system]. Fitch Ratings says that WMPs account for roughly 16 percent of all commercial bank deposits, while KPMG reports that trust companies [which supply the WMPs] will soon overtake insurance to become the second-largest sector in the Chinese financial industry. According to a report by CN Benefit, a Chinese wealth-management consultancy, sales of WMPs soared 43 percent in the first half of 2012 to 12.14 trillion yuan ($1.9 trillion).

There are more than 20,000 WMPs in circulation, a dramatic increase from only a few hundred just five years ago . . .

China's shadow banking is contributing to a growing liquidity risk in the financial markets. Most WMPs carry tenures of less than a year, with many being as short as weeks or even days. Thus in some cases short-term financing has been invested in long-term projects, and in such situations there is a possibility of a liquidity crisis being triggered if the markets were to be abruptly squeezed.

In fact, when faced with a liquidity problem, a simple way to avoid the problem could be through using new issuance of WMPs to repay maturing products. To some extent, this is fundamentally a Ponzi scheme.[31]

The authors of the *China's Future Direction* volume are highly critical of numerous features of the Chinese economy, but even they failed to anticipate the deeply damaging loss of control over money and credit expansion in 2009–2010, to say nothing of the even greater loss of control threatened by the out-of-the-blue rapid expansion of the shadow banking system after 2010. What is interesting, however, is that the six bottlenecks the book's authors do identify as most likely to menace China's economic development efforts in years to come will *all* be much more difficult to resolve if the state's control over money and credit expansion continues to unravel.

The six bottlenecks that most concern the authors of *China's Future Direction* are as follows: (1) insufficient domestic demand from consumption (a concern of almost all Chinese economic analysts), (2) worsening shortages of natural resources, (3) historically unprecedented environmental pollution and ecosystem destruction, (4) increasing socioeconomic inequality, (5) numerous structural imperfections in the economic system, and (6) the looming sharp reduction in the supply of low-wage labor, which they expected to begin in 2015.[32] The authors focus most of their attention on bottlenecks 1, 4, and 5:

1. *Insufficient domestic demand from consumption.* Sounding very much like Yasheng Huang, the authors note that demand from domestic consumption drove economic growth in the 1980s but then started to slide in the 1990s and continued sliding throughout the 2000s. The authors calculate that consumption as a percentage of GDP fell from 61 percent in 2000 to 54.1 percent in 2004.[33] To avoid wasting

productive capacity and/or stockpiling inventories excessively, "There was no choice but to rely on expanding investment and increasing exports in order to maintain economic growth." Inevitably, however, this led to more production overcapacity and increased international trade tensions, even before the GFC.[34] The authors worried that consumption would continue to be insufficient indefinitely into the future because households fear that, if they fail to save, they will be unable to afford catastrophic health care costs, their children's educational expenses, unexpected unemployment, or retirement.[35] Even expanding and perfecting the social safety net would not be sufficient to change consumer psychology overnight, and psychology, as we will see, is far from being the only factor explaining underconsumption. Although the authors of *China's Future Direction* offer the hopeful observation that the low consumption rate means "our capacity for increasing consumption is enormous,"[36] their summary conclusion is that underconsumption is going to bedevil China's economy for many years into the future, "acting as a constraint on China's high speed growth."[37]

2. *Shortages of natural resources.* The authors do not discuss this problem in detail, other than to warn that shortages will drive prices up, creating long-term inflationary pressures.[38] Taking energy resources alone, the U.S. Energy Information Administration (EIA) reports that China surpassed the United States to become the world's largest consumer of energy in 2010. The EIA predicts that China will consume 50 percent more energy than the United States by 2020 and 100 percent more by 2030.[39]

3. *Serious environmental pollution.*[40] Chinese-style extensive economic growth and weak environmental protection rules have, the authors acknowledge, led to staggering environmental damage in the country—equivalent, they calculate, to the destruction of 10 percent of GDP every year from the late 1980s through 2007.[41]

4. *Inequality.* The authors calculate that real income inequality between cities and the countryside increased from a ratio of 1.8:1 at the beginning of reform and opening (c. 1980) to 3.22:1 in 2005. Proper accounting for social guarantees, education, and other public goods would

yield a ratio closer to 5:1 or 6:1 in 2005. Income inequality not only causes problems of social instability and in that way challenges CCP governance; it also threatens economic development directly because it reflects a reduced capacity of most households to consume.[42] In some ways, the authors argue, *regional* inequality can even be thought of as "causing" the overcapacity problem because a primary reason the bountiful productive capacity of eastern China is underutilized is that consumption demand in the central and western parts of the country is comparatively weak. Solving the consumption demand problem would lead, the authors contend, to the overcapacity problem being solved automatically.[43]

5. *Imperfections in the economic structure.* The only partial use of the market mechanism to allocate goods, services, and financial capital leads to inefficiency and high transaction costs. The most important manifestation of this problem is the cozy relationship between establishment banks and state-owned enterprises. The authors assert straightforwardly that "because Chinese state-owned commercial banks for quite a long time have been directed by the government and serve state-owned enterprises, they very rarely consider borrowers' ability to repay and credit risks." As a result, the system is predisposed to issuing too much credit, resulting inevitably in the accumulation of nonperforming loans (NPLs), which eventually lead to a reduction in both aggregate demand and banks' willingness and ability to lend.[44] Meanwhile, the SOEs that receive the lion's share of the establishment bank loans are highly inefficient. In the mid-1990s, they employed 59 percent of the urban labor force; by 2005, this figure had fallen to 20 percent: "But SOEs still consume the vast majority of societal resources. Chaotic management and lack of competitiveness are fairly common phenomena for SOEs."[45] Quite the opposite is the case for private enterprises, the authors find—but private enterprises are for the most part kept out of the stock and bond markets and cannot easily obtain loans from the state-owned banks.[46] Consequently, private enterprises are starved for finance and often must turn to the shadow banking system for credit.[47] From a macrolevel perspective, resources are thus constantly being directed away from efficient producers to

the wasteful SOEs, "weakening the capacity of China's economy to achieve sustained growth."[48]

6. *Reduction in the supply of low-wage labor.* The authors discuss this problem only briefly, noting that labor shortages began to appear as early as 2004. They predict that wage increases will eventually prompt capital (foreign and domestic) to leave China in favor of less expensive locales.[49]

In a *neibu* article published in October 2009, two macroeconomists with the State Council's National Development Commission—Chang Xinghua and Li Wei—suggest that the potentially catastrophic decline in consumption as a percentage of GDP probably stems from the post-1998 reduction in households' share of national income.[50] With regard to the initial distribution of income (before government intervention), households' share fell from 53.12 percent in 1998 (the high point after 1992) to only 39.74 percent in 2007 (low point in the series). The share going to enterprises rose from 33.57 percent in 1998 (low point) to 45.45 percent in 2007 (high point). Even the share going to government increased from a low of 12.71 percent in 1996 to a high of 14.81 percent in 2007.[51] Chang and Li suggest that this makes China's economic structure very different from those of most other countries—and heading in the wrong direction on the eve of the GFC. The government's share in China was higher in 2007 than that of any other country or region in a sample of fifteen states plus the Eurozone.[52] Enterprises' share in China was higher than in any other country except Mexico, the Czech Republic, Italy, and Poland.[53] Even after *re*distribution following government intervention, Chinese households received a comparatively low share of national income. Households received 69.29 percent after redistribution in 1996 (high point) but only 59.57 percent in 2007. This was not, however, the low point in the series. The low point (57.83 percent) came in 2004. The social welfare policies of Hu Jintao and Wen Jiabao were beginning by 2005–2006 to make a positive difference, however meager.[54] Enterprises, meanwhile, increased their share of income after redistribution from 13.33 percent in 1992 (low point) to 20.84 percent in 2007. (The high point for enterprises was 21.79 percent in 2004). All of this contrasted sharply with the situation in the United States—the only other country analyzed in the section on redistribution. From 1992 through 2007, American households received a fairly steady 72 to 77 percent of national income after redistribution. This, Chang and Li believe, was the main reason American consumers were able during that period to drive GDP growth in the United States and the world at large.[55]

Chang and Li do not foresee China's anomalous situation changing at any point in the near future.[56] The dynamics of inequality in income distribution measured in this way are such that the inequality tends to feed on itself. Enterprise profits are more likely than wage income to be invested in assets that will generate additional income; asset income, in turn, is much more likely to be reinvested than distributed as wages that might be spent on consumption. Partly for this reason, Chang and Li expect that China's economic development model will continue to be based on investment-driven (and, to a much lesser extent, export-led) growth. Efforts to achieve restructuring toward domestic consumption-driven growth *cannot* succeed in the immediate future, they contend, because of this built-in, positive-feedback reinforcement mechanism. Households will continue to receive a low—perhaps declining—share of national income relative to enterprises and the government. In a context of productive overcapacity at home and the post-GFC reduced ability and willingness of trading partners to absorb Chinese exports, such income distribution patterns and trends are "planting the seeds of hidden calamity for our country's efforts to achieve sustainable economic development."[57]

An analyst at the State Information Center's Forecasting Department agrees that "it is hard to be optimistic about [household] consumption."[58] In wrestling with the question of how to sustain growth in the aftermath of the GFC, Zhang Monan notes that household income growth slowed substantially in early 2009—and not only because of the GFC. The problem was deeper and longer term—ultimately, it was structural. The widely trumpeted increases in automobile and home appliance purchases in 2009 resulted, Zhang argues, simply from a combination of special government efforts to encourage such consumption and the wealth effect produced by the (temporary) stock market recovery and soon the epic housing bubble (see the following discussion). Unfortunately, all of this was unsustainable:

"There is insufficient basis for consumption to continue increasing rapidly; in fact, we cannot rule out the possibility it will decline."[59]

At the same time, Zhang is among the many who worry that China will never again be able to increase net exports at the growth-driving rates achieved in the mid-2000s.[60] The post-GFC Great Recession was, she argues, quite unlike any other since World War II, because (1) it followed in the wake of a financial crisis, and financial crises always leave businesses (assuming they face a hard-budget constraint) and households too saddled with debt either to invest or consume at growth-driving rates; and (2) the recession hit most or even all of the world's most powerful economies at precisely the same time: It was a truly *worldwide* contraction. Point 1 implies that many of the entities that could have generated the demand necessary to drive growth out of the recession have been forced instead to divert their resources into paying off debt.[61] Point 2 highlights the fact that there is no large and undamaged economy "out there" capable of pulling the rest of the world out of its pit and igniting a new era of high growth. Both of these negative factors "will continue to exert a profound impact on our own country's exports" for years into the future: China faces "an endless era of stagnant external demand."[62]

Notably, not all Chinese analysts think China should worry about declining export growth because they never accepted the idea that encouraging export-led growth—for example, by keeping the renminbi artificially undervalued—was ever a good idea in the first place. Liu Jiejun of the National Bureau of Statistics makes a strong case to this effect in a keenly analytical article for a *neibu* publication. Liu's chief contention is that maintaining an undervalued renminbi limits development of the service industries, whose vigor many authors consider to be critical for increasing employment, reducing inequality, spurring urbanization, and facilitating the desired change to domestic consumption-led growth. Liu portrays the effort to ensure the renminbi remains undervalued as "a protectionist measure for manufacturing industries and a discriminatory measure for service industries" because services—especially at China's level of development—are far less likely than manufactures to be exportable.[63] Keeping the renminbi undervalued therefore encourages investment to flow into manufacturing for the wrong reasons. Much more of it should instead be encouraged—or simply allowed—to flow into the service industries. Liu complains that even foreign capital is, as a result of currency policy, flowing into Chinese manufacturing when instead it should go to the service sector. In consequence, keeping the renminbi undervalued in a misguided quest to increase exports is yet another unwise policy leading China down a suboptimal economic path.[64]

Liu stresses that although currency revaluation would certainly result in some firms failing, it would more broadly encourage technical transformation and industrial upgrading. He finds that during the last period of sustained revaluation (2005–2008), 59.9 percent of small- and medium-sized Chinese enterprises "proved willing to take the initiative and use affirmative, fundamental methods to increase their long-term competitiveness."[65] The enterprises most likely to fail under currency appreciation would be *undesirable enterprises*: those producing cheap and easily breakable products that potentially damage the health of Chinese and foreign consumers and harm China's national reputation. Such firms would not be missed after they disappeared; indeed, they should be shown the door. If the resources they used were redeployed to the service sector, multiple economic, social, and foreign policy objectives could be achieved simultaneously.[66]

Many other economists contend that, from a long-term perspective, artificially stimulating demand for Chinese products by whatever means is no longer a sensible policy (if, indeed, it was ever sensible), because years of overinvestment and policy-fuelled export growth have resulted in China being saddled with far too much productive capacity and underutilized infrastructure. Just how serious is this problem? In 2012, the International Monetary Fund reported that China's average industrial capacity utilization rate fell from an already-low (in comparative terms) 80 percent in 2007 to an astonishingly-low 60 percent in 2011. The reason for this eye-popping decline was precisely the huge investment spike in unnecessary capacity financed by the monetary and credit expansion of 2009–2010.[67] Economist Zhang Monan focuses her attention on the all-important Chinese steel industry, a source of national pride ever since Mao decided to import the Stalinist model in the 1950s. Zhang presents data showing that the steel industry operated at only 73.1 percent of capacity during the first seven months of 2009, even though the CCP insisted that China's year-over-year GDP growth rate never fell below 6 percent during the period.[68] Steel slowly recovered, however, with the capacity utilization rate rising back to 82 percent (still low by international standards) in 2012. However, the paradoxical reason for this recovery was the CCP's decision in 2009 to throw open the floodgates of money and credit expansion in order to fuel investment—including in steel production itself. Most of the new investment during the 2009–2010 high-tide period was in infrastructure, particularly railroads—which require huge amounts of steel to construct.[69] Although some of the new infrastructure put into place starting in 2009 will probably prove genuinely beneficial over the long term by increasing economic productivity, other projects—such as the high-speed rail network or the dozens upon dozens of new airports being built in even the tiniest of towns—will surely prove wasteful.[70] With relatively few people able or willing to pay the high prices necessary to use the fancier new infrastructure, the local governments (and other investing entities) that borrowed heavily to build the showcase projects will increasingly find themselves saddled with debilitating debt—at least until the central government bails them out, at the expense of China's household savers.

For all of these reasons (and more), the Director of the China Society for Economic Reform, Gao Shangquan, denounces the entire Chinese model—past, present, and (implicitly) future—in his contribution to a volume on Chinese megatrends leading up to the year 2040. Gao begins by noting that, even though China's GDP did increase fourteenfold from 1949 through 2009, the country's consumption of mineral resources increased fortyfold.[71] This alone is reason enough to pronounce the Chinese development model a failure, Gao contends, because the model's need for enormous (and growing) quantities of natural resources makes it patently unsustainable. It *has* to be abandoned; there is no choice. But in the meantime, Gao laments, the CCP responded to the GFC by going mindlessly into default mode and encouraging local governments to run wild with investment for investment's sake: anything to keep the GDP growth rate at or above the sacred 8 percent level. It was, to Gao, a foregone conclusion that such a "strategy" would lead to colossal waste as the governments (and SOEs) invested in unnecessary projects—which eventually would leave them mired in debt. Gao contends that the fundamental problem is an ingrained shortsightedness on the part of China's macroeconomic managers: They impulsively try to put out fires using whatever tools happen to be at hand but in the process create even bigger problems for themselves (or their successors) down the road. After many years of taking such an approach, the CCP has rendered China's economy "dysfunctional" for at least three reasons:

1. The market mechanism does not function comprehensively to allocate resources, most notably for land, energy, and financial capital. Prices for these resources do not signal in the way they should according to the tenets of standard economics. Most land is controlled by local governments and serves as an important source of fiscal income and as a tool for attracting business investment. Gao notes that local government officeholders will be in power for only a few years but will auction off land to be used over many decades. The incumbent government will want to see results from land auctions now, even if this means the land will be abused or polluted and therefore lose future value. The same is true for minerals, whose artificially low prices encourage overexploitation. At the same time, the shortsighted governments refuse to make investments in education, public health, or sustainable agriculture because the payoffs from such projects can come only many years into the future, by which time today's officeholders will have moved onto other jobs, in other locales.[72]

2. More than some people might realize, the Chinese government constantly interferes in the functioning of the economy by continuing to play the role of director in decision making, especially with regard to enterprise investments. Gao believes this is particularly problematic for a country like China, because (a) there is no nationwide standardization in the decision-making procedures used by the local governments that direct most of the investment, and (b) there is a divorce between the act of decision making and the assumption of responsibility for the decision's consequences (partly because failures may become apparent only after the officeholder moves on): a classic moral hazard

problem. This all too often leads decision makers to throw caution to the wind when deciding on investment projects. The macrolevel consequence is that "our country has an extremely high investment rate but a distorted investment structure," in which there is far too much investment in productive capacity and showcase infrastructure projects, but far too little in education, pollution abatement, and the provision of other public goods.[73]

3. The current fiscal and tax system discourages reform of the problematic model. Local governments have felt under fiscal pressure ever since the tax reforms of 1994 (after which a much greater share of revenue was allocated to the central government) and abolition of the agricultural tax in 2004 (a centrally imposed requirement designed to reduce the financial burden on peasants).[74] To keep the tax revenues flowing in, and to increase local employment (which increases tax revenues indirectly), "Local governments will tolerate or even encourage investment in certain highly polluting projects," even in those sectors where China already suffers from overcapacity.[75] Gao cites as an example the iron and steel industry. Governments know perfectly well that from a China-wide perspective, there is far too much capacity in this sector. But they will not consider closing down their own local plants (indeed, they might build new ones) because they want or need to keep the revenue generated from investment and production (and the original land auction) flowing in to service debt, fund social services, and maintain local employment—while also raking off some of the benefits for themselves.[76]

Citing concerns similar to Gao's, the CASS Department of Economics Economic Tracking Analysis Study Group calls in *Leadership Reference*, a *neibu* journal, for the Chinese government to shift out of its post-GFC, state-directed economic recovery mode—because it detected as early as 2010 that the recovery mode was in the process of becoming a problematic "new normal."[77] Massive investment was the main factor allowing China to recover quickly from the GFC-induced crisis as well as to avoid the worst; the key players in allocating this investment were governments at all levels of the hierarchy. The CASS study group acknowledges that the government-directed investment approach had the advantage of speed and certainty: With their power and authority, the local governments could organize the channeling of investment to deliver a positive shock to China's economy quickly. The problem is that both the initial successes and the soon-to-follow negative consequences (including waste and debt) tempted the authorities to "double down," that is, to assume even more control, borrow even more money, and direct even more investment. If such practices were allowed to become institutionalized as a new normal, China would fall into a serious trap, characterized by two dilemmas:

1. If the economy were to become addicted to super-high levels of investment to sustain growth, inevitably growth will have to stall or go into reverse at some point because super-high levels of investment are by definition unsustainable (they lead to debt, overcapacity, and waste).

2. Even before reaching an absolute limit, superhigh levels of investment become increasingly inefficient as the more viable projects are quickly exhausted.[78] This helps to explain why the effectiveness of issuing new credit and increasing the money supply to spur GDP growth has declined precipitously in the years since the GFC. The *Financial Times* calculated in November 2011 that "overall, the credit intensity of gross domestic product in China—the amount of credit generated to produce one unit of GDP—has more than tripled, from 1:1.3 a few years ago to 1:4.3 in the first quarter of 2011."[79] A year later, the *FT* quoted Michael Werner of Bernstein Research as observing that "2012 marked one of the weakest years in terms of translating credit growth into GDP growth. During the year, RMB 15.6 trillion of credit was formed while nominal GDP growth was just RMB 4.6 trillion. This means that for every RMB of credit generated in 2012, just RMB 0.30 of economic growth was generated. This marks the lowest level on record save for the 2009-H1 '10 period that was highlighted by the aggressive fiscal and monetary stimulus."[80] The ongoing expansion of the shadow banking system's activities suggested that this decidedly negative trend was almost certain to continue.

The CASS study group's proposed solution was for the CCP to insist on a gradual reduction in government-directed investment, to be replaced by societal investment—with projects determined by private businesses and households.[81] But "this would require smashing monopolies, encouraging fair competition, loosening control over enterprises (especially in the service sector), and increasing the level of credit support for non-SOEs"; therefore, it was a long-term objective rather than an immediate aim.[82] It would also be an exceedingly difficult transition to manage without triggering a sustained contraction in growth.

DEMOGRAPHY

Of all the factors affecting China's trajectory, demographic restructuring is almost certainly the one most impervious to change. Many Chinese analysts are concerned that the rapid aging of China's population will have a profoundly negative impact on its economic development prospects—starting very soon. The 2010 census results announced in April 2011 revealed an annual population growth rate of only 0.57 percent in the 2000s, down from 1.07 percent in the 1990s and much lower than anticipated. The number of workers aged twenty to twenty-four had already begun shrinking, and the overall workforce was projected to start contracting in 2016. "After adding six million workers every year to its labor force in the two decades up to 2010, China will soon see a decline at an average rate of 6.7 million workers per year"; that is to say, *every* year, for at least the next two decades.[83] The country's entire population is now projected to peak in 2026 and then decline—after which India would surpass China to become the world's most populous nation. Moreover, almost half of China's population—49.68 percent—now live in cities, where couples limit births not only because of the one-child policy but for the same reasons couples in other crowded East Asian cities limit births (see the following discussion). Consequently, short of encouraging immigration, Beijing cannot possibly prevent China's workforce from shrinking until at least the mid-2030s.[84] The number of Chinese women of childbearing age is projected by demographers to decline by 34 percent between 2012 and 2032, from 344.7 million to 228 million. As a result, "even if birth *rates* increased, it will be hard to alter the big picture of a declining total *number* of births."[85]

Even before the worse-than-expected 2010 census results were announced, Chinese demographers and economists were expressing concern that the unavoidable population trends would have a decidedly negative impact on the economy. In a 2010 edited volume commemorating sixty years of the People's Republic and musing on the Chinese development model, Zhang Yi of the CASS Research Center for Labor and Social Security warned that "this problem is serious."[86] Cadres in the big cities responsible for implementing birth control policy now tend to encourage newlyweds to go ahead and have a child—to get their quota of one out of the way, in the hope that the new parents might then decide they want a second child. Nevertheless, the obstinate couples continue to delay. Zhang explains the newlyweds' rationale as follows: (1) The cost of living is high and climbing, especially for housing;[87] (2) it takes not only money but also time and effort to educate a child, and education is crucial in a Chinese context—not only for cultural/historical reasons, but also because the society is ultracompetitive; and (3) having a child is thought likely to disrupt the mother's career.[88] Consequently, "the vast majority of scholars believe that China's current total fertility rate is in the 1.6 to 1.7 percent range [well below the rate of population replacement] . . . Officials claim 1.8, but scholars do not agree."[89] In the short run, this trend is irreversible, even if the CCP were to abandon the one-child policy, which Hu Jintao declared in April 2011 was not in the cards.[90] Nevertheless, demographer Zhang calls—almost begs—for at least a reconsideration of the policy. He argues there is little reason to worry these days that China's population is suddenly going to balloon: Attitudes have changed, and the higher a country's GDP, the lower its birthrate. "If only the cadres responsible for birth planning could grasp this [social] law, they would realize the desirability of taking less action. If they do too much, they will ruin the situation."[91] Zhang wants a single, unified policy (not one with loopholes and exceptions like the present one) in which every couple nationwide is limited to *two* births. He warns that unless such a change is implemented, the pressures of taking care of retired people could become economically overwhelming, and "our country will have walked into a demographic trap."[92]

On page 81 of his essay, Zhang presents an alarming diagram showing Japan's birth rate, death rate, and population increase rate from 1870 projected to 2050. The diagram shows the decline in Japan's population, which began in the mid-2000s, and suggests the country will lose another 10 million people as a result of fewer births between 2010 and 2050. Such a diagram is particularly interesting as an image of China's possible future. Zhang is suggesting that the China of tomorrow may well be the Japan of today, except that it would be substantially less wealthy and developed—sociopolitically as well as economically. Zhang is obviously worried that, unless radical remedial measures are adopted soon, the changes in China's population structure will put an end to the country's economic dynamism. Growth would slow to a crawl, or even stop, after which all talk of "the rise of China" would sound absurd.

With a similar set of concerns in mind, Fudan University demographer Wang Guixin recommends that the government adopt five "strategic policy changes" to slow if not stop the demographic restructuring:[93]

1. *Relax the national birth control policy.* No matter what the CCP does at this point, the population is going to age, and the labor force will shrink—but Wang thinks that an official relaxation of restrictions on births could still make a positive, if not decisive, impact. He recognizes that in the large and wealthy cities of the East, the natural birth rate is already lower than the rate mandated by the one-child policy, but still he thinks that some families would respond to a well-publicized relaxation of the policy by deciding to have another child. In turn, that would result in the birth rate nationwide moving back in the *direction*, at least, of the population replacement rate: two children per household. If such a shift could be achieved quickly, China might yet be able to maintain the "demographic dividend" (which results from the working-age population being larger than the dependent population)—or at least avoid a worsening of the demographic deficit—for another twenty to thirty years. Such a highly desirable outcome would help "ensure that sufficient human resources are available to develop the economy, create wealth, and raise the society's supporting capacity" for the very young and the very old.[94]

2. *Spur the economy to grow at a faster rate.* Wang perceives a race between the aging of China's population and the development of its economy; to put it another way, he worries that aging too rapidly will cause the economy to start growing at a much slower rate, relegating China to middle-income status indefinitely. Aging is inevitable, but Wang thinks that by investing in "old age industries" (specializing in the goods and services older people want and need), China can maintain a growth rate that is reasonably high. He does not say how high, nor does he offer detailed advice on what policies the government should adopt to encourage investment in the old age industries. But he does offer two policy slogans to summarize for decision makers the essence of his recommendations: "Get old and rich at the same time" (*bian lao bian fu*), and "Use wealth to support the old" (*yi fu yang lao*).[95] The Party-state may not be able to change demographic reality in short order, but it could take steps to manage the transition to an older society more smoothly and less disruptively by putting into place policies that could reduce the negative economic impact.

3. *Reform the hukou (household registration) system while improving social welfare support.* Wang agrees with most other analysts that reforming the *hukou* system so that cities and the countryside can ultimately fuse together (*cheng xiang tongyi*) would encourage more migrants to settle in the cities securely.[96] He does not offer a detailed explanation of how a quickened pace of urbanization could help to ease the demographic transition, but by implication he seems to be suggesting that if migrants could more easily settle permanently in the cities, they would receive higher levels of social welfare support; that, in turn, would put them in a better financial position to raise additional children—who would then enjoy all the rights and privileges of multigenerational urban *hukou* holders. Moreover, the migrants' parents could more easily move to the cities to live with their children and grandchildren. The (grand)parents would no longer have to suffer the emotional void associated with the "empty nest syndrome"; they would also be in a position to contribute their labor and wisdom to the running of the multigenerational new urban household. At the same

time, the elderly migrants would find themselves in a better position to receive, and pay for, social welfare services, including health care provision.[97]

4. *Develop a multifaceted model for supporting the elderly.* China should not expect to rely entirely on families to take care of elderly people, nor should it rely entirely on publicly funded caregiving facilities. To be sure, the families must continue to play the primary role in shouldering the responsibility, both because of Chinese tradition and because funding a fully developed support system for the elderly is beyond the means of the PRC government. Yet families cannot do everything by themselves, and some functions are best provided to groups of elderly people together, taking advantage of economies of scale. Wang calls on Chinese society to fuse the efforts of government, community, and market to generate an appropriately complex (given the complexity of the problem) and creative response to the challenges an aging population poses. The scope and scale of the challenges China faces are unprecedented in history; the only choice is for Chinese people from all sectors to respond with sociocultural innovation.[98]

5. *Cultivate a deep awareness of the problem and a new social consciousness.* Wang believes that Chinese people must develop an entirely new mind-set to meet the challenges posed by demographic restructuring because currently they are psychologically unprepared. The CCP should take the lead in nurturing the new mind-set, but all socially responsible entities must play a role. The Party-state, NGOs, businesses, and other organizations should begin laying the groundwork for the new social consciousness *now*—because the effects of population restructuring will manifest far sooner than most people realize. The new social consciousness would, Wang hopes, lead Chinese people to esteem and even valorize respecting, assisting, and taking care of the elderly—not only their own parents and grandparents, but elderly people in general. Wang depicts efforts to encourage the new mind-set as a necessary component of a multifaceted new national strategy whose ultimate aim would be to "construct an enthusiastic, healthy, happy, harmonious, and sustainably developing aging society."[99]

Some observers are not convinced that the aging population will prove quite as problematic as demographers and economists are warning. For example, four analysts with Essence (Anxin) Securities suggest in a *neibu* article that "the market" will ultimately solve these problems automatically. Sounding a bit like Bruce Bueno de Mesquita on the global warming question (see Chapter 1), financial analysts Fan Yan, Cheng Dinghua, Zhang Zhi, and Du Haibin readily acknowledge that the demographic trends are real. They even go so far as to suggest that the shortage of "low-end" (*diduan*) workers may start to cause economic difficulties sooner than even most demographers expect. The reason, they say, is that workers in this category are very likely to retire as soon as financially possible. These workers have been forced to spend their entire lives toiling for long hours at arduous and often unsafe jobs. Many will be physically incapable of working to the legal retirement age in China of fifty for women and fifty-five for men.[100] Consequently, the end of the demographic dividend is approaching much faster than most people realize. By no later than 2017, "China's aggregate low-end labor supply is likely to start falling precipitously."[101] The middle- and higher-end labor segment "is still a long way from reaching its high point," but even the people in these categories will not be as numerous in absolute terms as would be economically optimal because each successive generation since 1980 has produced fewer and fewer children per couple, leading to what has now become the first phase of an inexorable downward spiral.[102]

Fan and his coauthors emphasize four challenging but not devastating implications of these developments for China's economic trajectory:

1. *Wages will rise.* For low- and middle-end workers, wages have already been rising for many years but will now begin to rise faster, holding other factors constant. "Especially in the central and western parts of the country, from 2003 through 2009, wages increased at a compound annual rate of 16 percent, and during the same period, the wages of urban residents increased at a compound annual rate of 12 percent."[103] The problems posed by rising wages for businesses are obvious, but Fan and his coauthors argue that the adaptability of Chinese businesses should not be underestimated. They also point out that rising wages

are positive for Chinese households and could play a critical role in effecting the universally desired macroeconomic shift to a model of domestic consumption-led growth.

2. *The maximum potential GDP growth rate will fall.* In the early stages of reform and opening, villagers started flooding into the cities to become workers. This automatically led to improvements in micro- and macroeconomic productivity—resulting in real economic growth— because manufacturing and mining are inherently more productive than the types of agriculture then dominant in China. Given the enormous size of China's rural population, migration also translated into comparative cost advantages for Chinese manufacturers relative to those of other countries. This helped to fuel the growth in net exports, especially after World Trade Organization (WTO) entry in 2001. But now, Fan and his colleagues write, as the low-end labor supply reaches its maximum, and labor costs continue steadily to rise, productivity almost certainly will begin to fall. This is because most of the villagers suitable for urban work have already made the transition. The pool of those still available to make the transition would be precisely those who, for whatever reason, decided (or had it decided for them) that they are less suitable for urban work and residence. Consequently, Fan and his coauthors calculate that the total supply of low- and middle-end labor will begin to decline at precisely the same time as productivity gains almost certainly will diminish— assuming that no massive government retraining campaign is put into place for people still living in the villages. Any decline in productivity gains can only mean that the maximum potential GDP growth rate must fall, unless there is some revolutionary change in technology (currently not anticipated) that throws the entire development model onto a completely new track.[104]

3. *Inflationary pressures originating within China will therefore increase.* The reason is simply that wages will probably rise faster than productivity. Households will demand more goods and service, but manufacturers, retailers, and service providers (in addition to the remaining farmers) will not be able to counterbalance by lowering their costs to a comparable degree on the basis of improvements in the productivity

of their operations. Moreover, in the absence of profound changes in governance and the financial system, this interplay is likely to unfold in a context in which the rate of money supply growth and credit expansion continues to exceed by a substantial margin the rate of GDP growth—even *nominal* GDP growth. The larger the gap, the stronger the inflationary pressures.[105]

4. *Profit rates for enterprises will steadily fall.* The reason is both that the economic growth rate will slow and rising salaries and wages will consume a larger share of enterprise budgets—including both state and private enterprises.[106] This, however, is the point at which Fan and his colleagues suddenly morph into optimists. All of the points they make in the first part of the article would lead readers to expect that China is certain to face economic challenges so vexing that they might prove insoluble. However, this is not that argument that these authors wish to make. Instead, they contend that the falling profits will goad enterprises into exiting the low-end manufacturing sector and moving into more capital- and technology-intensive industries, some using cutting-edge technologies. "The majority of traditional industries will gradually decline," but this would be a positive development, the authors contend, because the (often government-supported) traditional industries are hidebound and inefficient. Meanwhile, China's smart and energetic entrepreneurs are fully capable of shifting into new lines of production and service provision, in sectors that could lead the country to a greener, more prosperous future than would be possible under the current model. Although there would undoubtedly be some initial pain associated with the transition, the Chinese governing elite's wisest policy choice would be to jettison the current model by removing its pillars of support and allowing the market to work its magic through the processes of creative destruction. Moreover, Fan and his colleagues express confidence that the CCP will eventually commit to the wiser course. Population dynamics make it unavoidable: "Based on these demographic structural changes, we forecast that mass-consumption products and technology-intensive industries will become the new economic direction that China takes in the decades to come."[107]

URBANIZATION AND THE PROPERTY BUBBLE

In the aftermath of the GFC, as worries about China's economic future began slowly to diffuse more widely throughout Chinese (and eventually global) society, economist Zhou Tianyong, Vice Director of the Central Party School Research Institute, published an influential monograph with the People's Daily Press making a detailed case for *intensified urbanization* as the key to China sustaining its economic growth.[108] Zhou argues that in comparative terms, China remains—despite the full array of its stunning economic achievements—surprisingly underurbanized. He calculates that with a per capita GDP of US$3,200 in 2008, China's urbanization rate "should" have been fifteen to twenty percentage points higher than it actually was. This means that there will still be some 200 million people living in the villages who should have already migrated to the cities, and 100 million living in the cities only temporarily ("because the costs of staying on are too high") who should have settled down in an urban area to stay.[109] Keeping in mind that the urbanization rate actually *fell* significantly in the 1990s and 2000s,[110] Zhou warns of four significantly negative consequences—unless the tide can be turned:

1. Underurbanization will prevent the service industries from developing to their fullest potential, which in turn would unnecessarily limit employment opportunities. This is because recent migrants to the cities have a strong propensity to work in the service industries as well as to increase their consumption of services.[111]

2. Whenever industrialization occurs at a faster rate than urbanization, the kind of industry that becomes dominant tends to be heavy industry and more wasteful and polluting industry. At the same time, keeping people scattered throughout the countryside ensures that their use of resources will be inefficient because they will not be in a position to take advantage of urban economies of scale. Scattered populations also present the Party-state with greater challenges in generating an effective response to environmental destruction and the provision of public goods. Increasing the rate of urbanization could therefore help China to simultaneously solve both the industrial imbalance and environmental problems.[112]

3. Regions of the world with lower rates of urbanization tend to suffer not only from higher levels of income inequality between cities and the countryside, but also from more pronounced urban–rural socio-cultural differences. Failure to address the income inequality problem can cause the sociocultural differences to widen over time into a gulf. Eventually these differences may crystallize into political cleavages that can fuel intense conflict. Fostering increased migration to the cities should, therefore, prove helpful to China not only economically but also politically, assisting in the process of building a more harmonious society of the future.[113]

4. Continued underurbanization will make it more difficult for China to effect the necessary transition to domestic consumption-led growth. When villagers move to the cities, advertisers find it easier to reach them, and the entire experience of living in a city can seduce the migrant worker into embracing a lifestyle centered on conspicuous consumption. It also becomes relatively easier for migrants to satisfy their consumption desires because their incomes rise after they take city jobs, and they live and work physically closer to retail outlets. Put simply, urbanization facilitates consumption, and this important observation leads Zhou to conclude that "only when urbanization and industrialization advance at the same rate will a country's aggregate supply and aggregate demand be in equilibrium."[114]

Zhou's logic suggests that, with only half the population living in cities as of 2010, China should still have the potential to grow economically at a relatively rapid rate for many years. But what factors caused China to be underurbanized in the first place? What must change so that urbanization can work its putative magic for economic development? Perhaps somewhat surprisingly, Zhou rejects the notion that the *hukou* system is a critical obstacle; he finds that, despite this system, "numerous migrant workers have been able to go live legally in the cities. There are no longer any serious [legal] obstacles to staying on."[115] Others would presumably dispute this point, but Zhou's objective is to shed light on another factor that receives far less attention: Chinese villagers hesitate before moving permanently to a city because what they would lose from making such a move is far too valuable in comparison with what they would be most likely to gain. The problem, Zhou explains, is China's land system. Chinese villagers do not own the land they farm. Ownership is collective, which means in practice that the land is controlled by the village (or township) government. As long as villagers continue to farm, the land whose use rights they contract from the collective serves as a critically important asset from which they can extract utility. But once the villagers return the land to the collective—or, indeed, once the collective seizes the villagers' land under various dubious pretexts—they no longer have the ability to benefit from controlling and exploiting this asset. This means that villagers who either give up the land they farm or have it confiscated by village elites are unlikely to have the resources necessary to set up residency in a city (even holding the *hukou* factor constant)—particularly, as explained in the following discussion, in the post-2008 era of astronomically high (and rising) housing prices.

Zhou underscores that this situation makes China strikingly different from South Korea and Taiwan when they were both growing rapidly in the 1960s and 1970s. Thanks to the government-imposed land reforms of the 1950s, Korean and Taiwanese farmers found it much more affordable to move to the cities, where many of them were able to secure employment in the manufacturing and service industries.[116] The Chinese land reform of the 1950s was followed by coerced collectivization. There has been no new land reform initiative since institution of the household responsibility system c. 1980.

In combination with the post-GFC explosive growth in money and credit, the land system also contributed to the staggering real estate bubble of recent years. Yin Zhongli of the CASS Institute of Finance puts this problem into historical perspective in an article in the *neibu* journal *Leadership Reference*.[117] Yin begins by explaining that reform of the residential system—requiring urban residents to buy or rent their homes in the marketplace rather than (as in the past) receiving them as compensation from work units—began in 1998 and was "basically completed" by 2000.[118] Yet the market did not function as effectively as anticipated because the land system ensured that local governments enjoyed monopolistic control over new land to be rezoned as suitable for development. The

Land Management Law (*tudi guanli fa*) specifies that collectively owned land (and all rural land is collectively owned) may not be sold directly by farm households to developers planning to use the land for nonagricultural purposes. This is true even for land that has already been approved for nonagricultural use. Local governments, "representing" the collective, must first obtain the land from farm households through purchasing back land-use rights or confiscating. The governments and only the governments have the legal right to lease the purchased or confiscated land to developers. This means that governments are the only players on the sellers' side in the primary land market, which leads Yin to conclude that "the land market is supermonopolized" and that "land prices are easy to manipulate."[119] Governments can set different prices for different proposed forms of land use; for example, they can set higher prices for upscale residential real estate projects and lower prices for new factories that would increase local employment. Many developers naturally want the higher returns that come from lucrative upscale commercial and residential real estate projects and so have little choice but to pay the higher prices. They will then charge more for the structures they build, trying to pass the higher costs on to consumers. This leads not only to upward pressure on house, condominium, and apartment prices and rents but also to upward pressure on the prices of consumer goods sold in retail outlets—because (newer) retail outlets must occupy the commercial buildings that developers construct.

The 1994 tax reforms and 2004 abolition of the agricultural tax ensured that local governments would face a strong incentive to take advantage of their monopolistic positions.[120] The central government's share of all revenues rose from 22 percent in 1993 to just over 50 percent in the mid-2000s. Absolute levels of local government revenue continued to increase, but so did the governments' responsibilities—especially after the Hu-Wen administration mandated establishment of a better social safety net in the mid-2000s.[121] Local governments were permitted in the 1994 tax reform to retain two critical sources of revenue: (1) certain taxes associated with the real estate industry and (2) the income derived from selling land use rights. Initially the governments focused on increasing revenues by selling land use rights to enterprises at low prices. The expectation was that the enterprises would invest in productive capacity that would create jobs for local residents, thereby indirectly causing tax receipts to rise. But following the 1998 housing reform, local governments soon came to realize that selling land use rights to real estate developers at rapidly rising prices would be a substantially more effective way to generate revenue. In 1999, government revenue from leasing out land use rights amounted to only 6.8 billion yuan China-wide. By 2009, the figure had risen to 1.5 trillion yuan: "Revenue from leasing out land-use rights was almost doubling every year."[122] Yin minces no words in characterizing this system: Farmers are being "exploited," he says, as "through the intermediation of land, more and more wealth is transferred from households to the government and to enterprises."[123]

Not only villages and small towns rely heavily on land sales for revenue. An analyst with the CASS Economic Research Institute, Wang Lina, reports that in 2009, some 40 percent of the Beijing and Shanghai municipal governments' general revenues came from property auctions.[124] Wang observes that absent central (or provincial) government directives, local governments will always want to sell land use rights to the highest bidder, and the highest bidder is likely to be a developer with plans to construct expensive residential or commercial real estate projects—as opposed, for example, to affordable housing for the urban poor, construction of which the CCP has been encouraging since 2010.[125] Consequently—as another scholar, Wang Xiaochang (of the Chinese Academy of Governance), notes—between 2005 and 2009, the richest 10 percent of China's population bought 50 percent of the houses, and the richest 40 percent bought 85 percent of the homes.[126]

The persistence of the housing bubble has defied all expectations, paradoxically increasing alarm among some ("the higher the prices, the greater the damage when the bubble finally bursts") and calm optimism among others ("prices are rising for sound economic reasons; it is only natural for a country whose GDP is growing at such a high rate to see its asset values rise"). House prices entered bubble territory (on a much smaller scale) in 2006 and 2007, but then declined in tandem with stock prices from late 2007 to late 2008 as Beijing recognized the bubble and intervened decisively to bring about a smooth landing. Still, housing prices remained higher in 2008 and 2009 than they were at the time when most of the people who then owned houses first purchased the properties. This put the relatively wealthy class of homeowners (in addition to the many enterprises that owned housing or other real estate projects) in the best position to profit once prices began soaring in mid-2009: As owners of assets rapidly appreciating in value, they were in the best position to buy more and/or better.[127] The initial pattern of social inequality thus worsened as a result of the bubble, with negative consequences not only for perceptions of social justice but also for China's ability to make the shift to domestic consumption-led growth. The larger the proportion of a household's income that must be spent on housing, the less the households will have to spend on other goods and services, suggesting that the housing bubble will indirectly exacerbate the problems of overcapacity and excessive reliance on investment to spur growth.[128]

Wang Xiaochang—the scholar with the Chinese Academy of Governance—argues that the reason property prices began rising rapidly in 2009 is straightforward and noncontroversial: The government encouraged far too much more money and credit to be released into the economy than was necessary to escape or prevent the (likely) ravages of the GFC and Great Recession. In the beginning sections of this chapter, I provided some basic data on China's money supply and credit expansion since the mid-2000s, along with an explanation of how the rise of the shadow banking system made controlling money and credit even more difficult after 2010. But Wang's characterization and contextualization of post-GFC money and credit expansion help additionally illuminate the causes of the housing bubble. Wang summarizes by observing that Chinese financial institutions of all types issued 9.5 trillion yuan in new credit in 2009, "equivalent to the total amount of credit issued in the previous four years combined."[129] He then calculates that fully 4 trillion yuan (42 percent) of the 9.5 trillion yuan in new credit either directly or indirectly entered the property market, fueling the surge in prices. Only about 2 trillion yuan of the new credit "became GDP."[130] That the government would allow—or even encourage—far more money and credit to be issued than was necessary for increasing GDP was, in the judgment of Wang, "highly irresponsible—it was only because monetary policy became problematic in this way that we ended up with house prices rising."[131]

To the extent the huge infusion of money and credit was simply a panicky response to the GFC, its long-term damage could probably be contained. But to the extent the excessive expansion reflected deep-rooted dysfunctional tendencies in China's political-economic system—related not only to the rise of shadow banking, then in its early stages, but also to production overcapacity and the irresistible impulse on the part of SOEs and local governments to invest—the 2009 money and credit expansion might be taken as a worrying sign for the future.

Cao Jianhai is one analyst among many who argues that the credit expansion spree reflected deep-rooted dysfunctional tendencies. In 2009, the year of the splurge, China's official GDP growth rate reached 8.7 percent. Cao, a researcher with the CASS Industry and Economy Research Institute, argues that this result would not have been possible had the government not "saved the real estate industry" by unleashing the banks.[132] Cao notes that M2 money supply increased 27.7 percent in 2009 while the selling price for newly constructed commercial real estate projects rose 24.2 percent. This was in stark contrast to the prices for consumer goods; the Chinese consumer price index actually fell slightly in 2009— it finished the calendar year down 0.68 percent.[133] Cao is suggesting that GDP was being calculated on the basis of the false assumption that *real* property prices were rising over 20 percent; that there was no bubble, in other words, but instead genuine increases in social wealth of an enormous magnitude. Cao also questions official data that suggest *profit* in the real estate industry in the year 2009 amounted to fully 8.12 percent of GDP.[134] Was the increase in wealth implied by the term *profit* real or merely notional? The questions Cao raises are critical because to the extent GDP and GDP growth are now reliant on artificially high and rising property prices that are *not acknowledged* as being artificial—in addition to being reliant on unsustainable investment in productive capacity and infrastructure—GDP will eventually have to fall. In effect, actual GDP— the production of genuinely useful goods and services priced according to rational principles—would already be much lower than reported, because a substantial proportion of the reported figures would reflect the mere notional wealth stored in the form of artificially overpriced real estate not acknowledged by the state as being artificial: inflation, in effect. The crisis would result from the eventual need to reequilibrate notional GDP (or wealth) to actual GDP (or wealth).[135]

Cao additionally expresses concern that SOEs and private firms alike decided to begin investing heavily in real property in 2009 at the expense of their main lines of production. This had the effect of further feeding the bubble and expanding the circle of people and firms caught up in the frenzy of speculation, thereby exposing the firms to risk should the bubble collapse. Company balance sheets would appear artificially healthy as long as prices continued to rise, but the ever-present threat of a bubble collapse—the simple fact that it *was* a bubble and thus "false" (a mere monetary or credit phenomenon)—implied that the most heavily exposed companies were not at all healthy. Even those that were in decent shape before and then entered the property game simply as a way to make some easy additional money could find themselves increasingly vulnerable to the possibility of devastating loss the more reliant they became on the sugar-high-like nature of artificially rising prices.

The issue of firms becoming dependent on rising property prices is a concern shared by many analysts. Elaborating on the firms' motivation for starting down this slippery slope, Wang Lina of the CASS Economic Research Institute explains that enterprises listed on the stock exchange could buy property in 2009 and then, at the end of the year, truthfully report a rise in the value of their assets accomplished by just sitting back and watching prices rise. The rise in the value of their assets would in turn help the firms' stock prices to rise, which further improved the firms' position, giving added incentive to speculate in real estate. Yet another source of the motivation was that once the firms reported an increase in the value of their assets, they could borrow additional money from banks, given that "land is the best collateral."[136] Some might even find a way to increase their borrowing for the ultimate (though probably disguised) purpose of buying even more property, betting on an endless upward movement in prices. Little wonder, then, that enterprises with initially no connection to the real estate industry would join in the property speculation game and, from a political perspective, would side with the powerful groups at the center of the real estate industry in opposing government measures to slow or stop the price rises—despite the havoc and suffering a collapse of the bubble would be certain to cause.

This expansion in the network of interest groups and individuals who would benefit from property prices continuing to rise illustrates the vexing dilemma Beijing faces in trying to achieve sustainable economic development. On the one hand, firms making property plays are contributing to investment, and investment has in recent years been the weightiest contributor to Chinese GDP growth—by a wide margin. On the other hand, the Party-state has repeatedly committed itself to trying to effect a shift to domestic consumption-led growth. Reliance on real estate investment that is purely speculative rather than based on sound analysis of market needs and trends would be among the worst kinds of investment for an economy to become dependent on—because the wealth increases such investment appears to generate are to a large extent illusory.[137] Yet the wider the circle of enterprises, organizations, and individuals chasing the (ultimately) illusory gains associated with an asset bubble, the more politically and economically challenging the task faced by government officials trying to contain and deflate the bubble without precipitating a crisis.

As early as April 2010, an analyst writing under the name of Zai Fu—who did not reveal his or her institutional affiliation—complained bitterly in a *neibu* policy article that special interest groups with large property holdings were already scheming to subvert a CCP initiative to cool the property market through imposition of a nationwide tax on real estate transactions.[138] Zai Fu identified three such groups trying to block the tax:

1. *Interest clusters of policy makers (officials)* who themselves or whose family members own substantial tracts of residential or commercial real estate. These groups opposed the tax first because implementing it would require that everyone clearly register their property ownership, "which would expose the actual situation of these officials and their families, presenting considerable political risk."[139] They would also have to *pay* the tax every year, a substantial sum of money. What the groups were frantically seeking at the time was simply a delay in

implementation of the new measures so that they could buy time to unload some of their properties or reregister them under different names.

2. *Real estate developers.* Members of this group had paid large sums of money to the monopolistic local governments in exchange for the rights to develop plots of land, and now they faced the prospect of seeing their net revenues fall. Moreover, once word leaked out that a tax was definitely going to be implemented, people holding real estate as speculative investments (rather than for more serious purposes) might impulsively decide to sell their properties, flooding the market all at once and consequently depressing prices. Real estate developers did not like the tax but had to exercise caution in expressing their opposition. Zai Fu writes that developers had no choice but to content themselves with using various back channels (not excluding the payment of bribes) to persuade policy makers to stop the tax from going forward.[140]

3. *A certain segment of local government officials.* "It is undeniable," Zai Fu writes, "that at the present time, there are still some local government officials who have united together in common interest; the rise in real estate prices is precisely in accord with these officials' interest."[141] Either they personally owned real estate, their administrations depended on real estate price appreciation for revenue, or both. Even more so than the real estate developers who opposed the tax, local officials anxious to block it were not in a position to express their opposition openly. Instead, they insisted publicly that they supported the tax because it certainly would be a good idea in the long run. At the present, however, although it might make sense to implement the tax in a small number of first-tier cities, it would be a very bad idea to impose it on smaller cities and towns such as their own. The officials insisted not only that the tax would have a negative economic impact but also that it was far too technically complex a tax for smaller cities and towns to collect.

Yet not all of the local governments that objected to the tax did so for purely cynical reasons related to personal corruption. Ding Yuanzhu, a researcher with the Chinese Academy of Governance, writes sympathetically that most localities in China truly do need rising revenues to meet the complex and expanding demands imposed on them by higher-level governments. Ding arrived at this conclusion after conducting fieldwork in an unnamed province, where he discovered that the provincial government had increased its expenditures on social services substantially in the preceding three years and earnestly hoped to continue doing so. The main source of revenue the government used to pay for the projects was money earned from auctioning off land to developers. On the one hand, then, high and rising real estate prices directly hurt the poor and middle classes; at the same time, rising prices also provide significant revenues that local and provincial governments *could* use for the purpose of increasing assistance to the relatively less well off. Should property prices collapse, governments would have no choice but to drastically slash the provision of social services.[142]

Then, too, the local governments by 2010 desperately needed property prices to continue rising so that they could pay off the debts they incurred in the process of implementing the Center's 2009 stimulus program. These debts will surely act as a drag on Chinese economic growth for many years to come; the only uncertainty is to what extent, and who, ultimately, will pay the price.[143] Chen Zhi, whose institutional affiliation is not given, explains the problem in a *neibu* article entitled "An Insider's Account of the Risks Involved with Local Financial Platforms."[144] Because local governments are not allowed to borrow money directly from banks, they established financial platforms that serve as surrogates for borrowing the needed or desired funds. The platforms date back to abolition of the agricultural tax in 2004, but they mushroomed in number and became bolder in their borrowing in the aftermath of the GFC. In early 2010, Chen counted more than 3,800 financial platforms active throughout China.[145] He visited one in an unnamed southwestern city to profile the platform manager. This particular platform invested 80 percent of the funds it raised in local government infrastructure projects—which may or may not have been viable or necessary—and the other 20 percent in a local SOE (whose line of business Chen does not identify). Because the government relied on leasing out land use rights for most of its revenue, if property prices failed to rise, or if they fell, the financial platform would not be able to pay back its loans. It was therefore highly risky for the state-owned banks to lend money to the financial platform, but they did so anyway.[146] Chen invites the reader to imagine this happening in 3,800 locations throughout the country. To the extent the projects in which these platforms invest prove unviable, failing to generate revenues sufficient to repay the loans, the entire Chinese economy would be at some risk should the property bubble collapse. Beijing has sufficient financial resources to prevent a total economic collapse, perhaps, but bailing out the local governments would prevent the Center from using these resources for socially optimal purposes. Ultimately, the resources must come from Chinese households, via the banking system and the SOEs' hoarding of profits at the expense of wages. This means that local government debts will unavoidably contribute to consumption growth remaining repressed for many years to come.[147]

The broader issue concerns the role of *leverage* in fueling China's property bubble. Particularly in 2009 through 2011, some foreign commentators denied that Chinese property was in a bubble because, they said, Chinese purchasers tend not to go heavily into debt when buying houses (in particular); rather, they pay much higher down payments than their counterparts in, for example, the United States.[148] Yet Chen Lixin of the Chinese Academy of Land and Resource Economics declares flatly in a 2009 *neibu* article that "since 1998 [when housing reform began], household mortgages for family residences have become an important driving force promoting development of the real estate industry."[149] Chen explains that the role of leverage in Chinese real estate is not simply to help families buy houses. She writes that, to a perhaps dangerous degree, the entire real estate industry relies on bank loans for the majority of its working capital. Generally, she states, real estate developers hold bank loans equaling about 70 percent of their assets, with some reaching as high as 85 percent.[150] When real estate prices rise, the real estate companies' assets rise in value, which means they can obtain even bigger loans from the banks to use as working capital.

The banks, meanwhile, also own real property, so that their balance sheets also strengthen when property prices rise. For both of these reasons, banks become willing to lend more money to developers when prices rise, and developers then have more money to purchase land-use rights from the monopolistic local governments—which are all too eager to sell at the highest possible prices. Add into this mix the fact that "in order to promote the expansion of domestic demand, the government at the macro level has [since 1998] implemented an expansionary monetary policy," and it is easy to understand why property developers would come to rely on bank loans: They are easy to get, and they carry a low (sometimes even a negative) real interest rate. As long as property prices are rising, the developers, the banks, the local governments, and the SOEs that get into the game can all prosper. The problem, of course, is that a *fall* in real estate prices—a collapse or even correction of the bubble, which would bring prices back into line with actual values—"could lead to a sharp contraction in banks' asset values," precipitating a cascading crisis potentially severe and widespread enough to pose a "systemic risk."[151] Indeed, a correction seemed finally to be underway by the beginning of 2014. An analyst for the CCP's *China Daily* warned in March 2014: "Signs have emerged that the curtain is falling on the decade-long golden period for China's real estate . . . Along with slowing price rises is the drastic drop in home sales . . . There is no doubt that a chilly autumn is coming for China's housing market."[152] The analyst warned that CCP authorities should be poised to move quickly to prevent the bubble's deflation (should it continue) from "causing systematic economic collapse."[153]

INEQUALITY

Inequality is a root issue in China touched on at many points in this chapter. It is also a topic that numerous Chinese observers treat directly, noting both the moral/ethical and political consequences of fostering inequality as well as inequality's negative impact on economic growth. "Our country's Gini coefficient has already surpassed 0.5," revealed Wang Zhanyang of the Central Socialism Institute in a 2010 interview. "China has now joined the ranks of those with the highest Gini coefficients in the world. This is obviously a very serious problem. It is a trend that in the present reality not only isn't being stopped but is continuing to worsen."[154]

A professor at Renmin University's School of Labor and Human Resources, Zheng Gongcheng, counts four ways in which the social distribution system is failing in China.[155] First, workers' incomes are not growing as rapidly as enterprise profits.[156] This is related to the inequality in income distribution among households, enterprises, and government discussed earlier. Zheng calculates that in developed countries, wages and salaries normally amount to about 50 percent of enterprises' operating costs, but in China they amount to a stunningly low 10 percent. In developed countries, workers' income amounts to some 55 percent of gross national income, but in China the figure has fallen in recent years from just above 50 percent to only 42 percent.[157] Thus, a province like Guangdong now rivals Taiwan and South Korea in per capita wealth, and yet the incomes of farmers and workers are increasing at such a low rate that they can barely keep pace with inflation.[158]

Second, income is often deducted from workers' wages under a variety of dubious pretexts. Sometimes firms will simply not pay their employees or will delay their pay for a very long time. Bureaucrats will impose mysterious taxes and fees while their own incomes suspiciously rise. Lack of a democratic political system and limits to what the media are permitted to report sharply restrict the workers' options. The legal system does not always (or even usually) work to their advantage, particularly if the person filing a complaint lacks the urban *hukou* status.[159]

Third, social welfare and social services are underprovided. This has distributional consequences, not only because the poor are more likely to have need for social services but also because such services are more likely to be provided in wealthier parts of the country, which leads to those areas becoming even wealthier still. The gap between rich and poor widens. Zheng invites his readers to consider the effects of inequality in education and public health provision. Inadequate access to such goods and services (or access to only low-quality education and public health) reduces the life chances of poor people's sons and daughters—especially the sons and daughters of farmers and migrant workers.[160]

Finally, the existing tax system is regressive rather than redistributional in impact.[161] Zheng takes some solace from the fact that in 2009, for the first time ever, the percentage increase in central government spending for social guarantees surpassed the percentage increase in central government revenues. (Social expenditures increased 16.6 percent while revenues increased 11.7 percent.) This, to Zheng, indicates that progress is possible. The future has the potential to turn brighter than it now appears, but the change to a new course is nowhere near consolidated and secure.[162]

What if, despite these preliminary positive indicators, inequality continues to worsen? "From ancient times to the present, the cycle of order and chaos has always unfolded in production and distribution."[163] Zheng argues that production and distribution are integrally related: No country can have sustained increases in production if wealth and income are unequally distributed to a high degree. This is not only because inequality makes it difficult to achieve domestic consumption-led growth. It is also because inequality fuels anger, which erupts in actions that cause socioeconomic disruptions. Zheng finds a causal relationship between the increase in mass incidents of recent years and the widening wealth and income gaps.[164] In 2007, he administered a survey to 4,000 people, over 80 percent of whom said they did not think China was at the present time achieving social justice. Not only poor people said this; many well-off people working for SOEs and private enterprises made the same observation.[165] Even nonaltruistic privileged people worried that increasing inequality leads to the crime rate rising.

Zheng concludes with the shocking observation that, in China today, some sick people who are poor will rob or steal so they can go to prison to receive free medical care, while some old people without pensions commit crimes so they can "retire" in a prison securely. This is how bad the inequality situation has become; this is what happens in a society when the government refuses to take seriously the need for a comprehensive social security program.[166]

Some analysts argue that increasing inequality is intrinsic to the core economic growth model. Jettison the growth model, and the government could increase social spending at a lower rate while paradoxically having a bigger impact. The chief problem, once again, is the extraordinarily high investment rate. According to economist Liu Shangxi, of the Ministry of Finance Research Institute, "the so-called 'rich get richer, poor get poorer' phenomenon is in the end realized through investment."[167] A policy environment (including suppressed real interest rates) and a social reality (*guanxi* and socioeconomic status giving some groups and individuals special access to financing) encourage the privileged classes—including SOEs as a category—to invest instead of giving workers and staff higher wages and salaries. Reinvested returns to asset investments further fuel inequality in a continuing downward spiral. To be sure, some of the investment does create some jobs, "but there is a limit" because of the low employment elasticity of Chinese GDP growth (see the following discussion).[168] The government recognizes this problem but finds itself in a dilemma. If it pressures firms to reduce investment and start providing employees with higher wages and salaries, GDP growth will at least initially fall because household consumption behavior is too deeply ingrained to change overnight: It would take some time for demand from rising consumption to replace the demand lost from declining investment. There is even some possibility that GDP could contract during the adjustment period and that the contraction could become self-sustaining, as households—alarmed by the very real prospect of job losses—decide (ironically) to *restrict* their consumption, leading to private sector firms failing in a vicious cycle. Readjustment in the face of entrenched inequality is therefore rife with risks: "In the end, we could fall into the 'Latin America trap' [middle-income trap] and not be able to climb back out."[169]

Some Chinese analysts calculate that not only is the rate of wage growth too low, but employment growth itself is far too anemic to support a reduction in inequality. It might be expected that this problem should take care of itself as demographic trends lead to the workforce shrinking. But there is no guarantee that any wage increases resulting from a reduction in labor supply would be sufficient to reduce inequality to the degree necessary to shift China in the direction of domestic consumption-driven growth. For that to happen, China must—according to the assessment of Song Xiaowu, President of the China Society for Economic Reform—first urgently raise the elasticity of employment increases associated with GDP growth.[170] Song calculates that, in the 1980s, a one-percentage-point increase in GDP resulted in slightly more than 2 million additional people being employed. In the 1990s, this figure fell to one million. During the

2000s, the number continued to hover around one million, "but in some years amounted to only 800,000 or so. At present, our country's employment elasticity is approximately 0.1."[171] Song cites International Labor Organization (ILO) and Asian Development Bank (ADB) data to compare China's elasticity with the elasticities of other countries. The ADB reports that the figure for all Asian developing countries together during the 1990s was 0.3 to 0.4. Meanwhile, the ILO reports that among the BRIC countries (Brazil, Russia, India, and China), China had the lowest employment elasticity from 1992 though 2004. While China's employment elasticity languished at 0.1, Brazil's was an impressive 0.9, India's was 0.3, and Russia's was 0.2. The ILO additionally reports that the elasticity of European Union countries collectively was 0.78 in 2007, while that of all the Organisation for Economic Co-operation and Development (OECD) countries was 0.48. Song concludes sardonically that it is "worth researching" how the country with the world's largest population could end up choosing an economic development model with one of the world's lowest employment elasticities.[172]

Song's primary contention is that the "seriously twisted income distribution structure" *itself* causes the low employment elasticity, which in turn causes the income distribution structure to become even more unequal. He explains by demonstrating that if the salaries-and-wages share of GDP had in 2007 remained at the same level as in 1990, 46 million more people would have been employed by the later date.[173] Song's reasoning is that, if incomes were more evenly distributed, households currently unable to afford certain goods and services that require the employment of comparatively more people to produce or provide would be able to afford them, increasing demand for the goods and services and employing the now-unemployed people in a virtuous cycle.[174]

Song argues that the reason income is not more evenly distributed is the prevalence of government-mandated monopolies. Such monopolies have less reason to increase efficiency because they can sit back and rely on exclusive access to key resources; special rights to produce certain kinds of goods that other firms are not permitted to produce; and the provision of government-directed investment, credit, and tax support. The monopolistic firms can charge high prices for what they produce and not have to worry about competitors charging less; at the same time, they receive myriad subsidies in various guises that allow them to keep production costs relatively low. The result is that monopolistic firms find themselves with substantial net revenues that they can either reinvest or share among the firms' more favored employees. Resources are in this way denied to those who would put them to more efficient use and bestowed on the privileged groups that work for government-backed monopolies. These managers and employees will receive higher incomes than would result from market competition, but, precisely for this reason, fewer people society-wide can be employed. If, instead—in any given locale—consumers could pay lower prices for the goods and services now being sold by monopolies, they would have more money left over to buy other goods and services. This would increase effective demand for these other items, allowing the firms that produce or provide them to hire more workers. Song estimates that, in 2007, about one-third of the difference in income and social welfare benefits between the best- and worst-treated employment sectors in China resulted directly from the existence of monopolies. If the monopolies were eliminated, an additional 7 million people could be put to work immediately—which then would have a further positive effect on reducing inequality.[175]

As noted, at the most general level, changing demographics should eventually help to reduce unemployment pressures, which were particularly severe in the immediate aftermath of the GFC, underscoring China's still-heavy reliance at that time on exports to support production.[176] But for one category in particular, unemployment could remain a serious (and even worsening) problem for many years to come. This is the category of new college graduates, whose numbers are increasing rapidly. The reason for this is straightforward: In January 1999, the Chinese government announced a plan to expand educational opportunities at the high school and college levels. As an immediate result, the number of newly admitted college students increased by an astonishing 400 percent between 1999 and 2006;[177] by 2009, some 29,790,000 young Chinese were enrolled in some form of higher education.[178] Hong Chengwen, a professor in the Department of Education Management at Beijing Normal University, addresses the employment issues raised by this dramatic new development in *World*

Megatrends and Challenges China Will Face in the Coming Decade.[179] Hong reports that in 2008, nearly one million college graduates were unable to find jobs.[180] Presumably he was referring to *new* college graduates, because Song Xiaowu finds the problem to have been substantially more serious. Song calculates that, in 2009, 6.11 million students would graduate and then compete with 3.5 million more who had graduated in previous years but had still not found jobs.[181]

The primary reason, according to Hong, is that "the economic structure at this point in the development process still needs low-skilled laborers but not as many people with college degrees."[182] As early as 2004, steadily rising wages signaled the beginning of shortages for skilled manual laborers; these shortages now seem to be intensifying as the population structure steadily ages. But college graduates are evidently unwilling to perform manual labor.[183] They expect instead to be able very quickly to walk into a high-paying white-collar job, as indeed almost all college graduates could do in previous years, when graduates were scarce. One might imagine that, given China's widely remarked need for economic structural change, new college graduates should be well placed to bring such change about. They would have the vigor, the knowledge, and the creativity to effect the transformations needed. The problem is that China's economy continues to be dominated, in key respects, by SOEs. Entrepreneurs can find it difficult to secure financial support for starting new businesses. The situation is even more difficult for young entrepreneurs because securing financial support requires the sort of *guanxi* and real-world experience that only older people are likely to have. Chinese society remains authoritarian to the degree that college graduates are very likely to have to attach themselves to some organization or Party-linked patron to climb the social ladder. But only when China achieves the sort of industrial upgrading that results in strong demand for college graduates—and only when college graduates adjust their expectations downward—will the ranks of the unemployed in this sector decline. Hong calls for more government action to find jobs for new graduates, but this seems unlikely to solve the problem as long as graduates' services are not yet needed and they disdain working at lower-end jobs.[184] The worry, meanwhile, is that unemployed college graduates could eventually pose threats to political stability.

SUMMARY

Chinese economics commentators may disagree on specifics, but almost all of them—or at least those publishing in the available outlets—accept as universally valid a liberal model of how economies should function and what must be done to realize efficient, sustainable economic growth. The economists are also in near-unanimous agreement that Chinese practice is substantially at variance from the requirements of the liberal model and that this is already causing China serious harm. To the extent China fails to implement "standard economics," most writers worry the future will be compromised. Many openly discuss the possibility of the PRC getting stuck in a "middle-income trap" of permanent mediocrity, while other countries pass it by or widen their lead. The only solution is for the Chinese state boldly to begin implementing liberalizing reforms: to stand back and allow the natural talents and energies of the Chinese people to start guiding the economy onto a sustainably developing path. But this will not be easy, because China's economic problems are depicted as resulting causally from deep-rooted structural factors: logics embedded in the political-economic system. Few of the economics writers call explicitly for political reform. But most suggest implicitly that some sort of fundamental political change will be necessary for a more liberal economic order to take root and to flourish. And this, in turn, will be essential if China is to have any hope of achieving sustainable economic growth and continuing its national rise.

CHAPTER 3

The Leninist Political System Confronts
a Pluralistic, Wealthy Society

FROM THE MID-1980S UNTIL THE MID-2000S, social science debates on the future of China's political system were lively and constructively contentious. In recent years, the debates have faded in visibility and vigor, possibly because there seems to be no sign of substantive political liberalization or democratization on the horizon or possibly because the political changes that have come to China (for example, the livelier and less subservient National People's Congress, or the politicized microblogs discussed in Chapter 4) do not yet seem to have gelled into a coherent new model whose component parts articulate in a logically compelling pattern. The country seems always to be on the cusp of political change, yet still locked within the confines of a Leninist iron cage. Many scholars, journalists, and NGO professionals do continue to research the possibility of China developing a freer and more politically influential civil society and (Internet-based) public sphere: important precursors to democratization in other times and places. But the contributors to this valuable body of work seem (appropriately) to be much more tentative today than many of their predecessors were twenty years ago.

As the democratization debate faded toward the end of the 2000s, the debate over what kind of international actor China would become after (presumably) consolidating its rise became more prominent. This debate was, in any case, always interlinked with the debate on the potential for the PRC to democratize: Both centered on questions concerning the "personality" of the Chinese state, its identity as a domestic and international actor. Was the CCP's intrinsic predisposition to govern humanely and justly at home, while cooperating with foreign countries and working for the common global good—even on territorial issues? Or was the Chinese state so self-absorbed and committed to authoritarianism or even militarism that its leaders would never accept yielding control over the levers of policy making to the Chinese people at large, and would never accept that other countries' perspectives on issues such as territorial disputes could possibly have any validity? To the extent the PRC did have a truculent personality, could it be socialized into becoming a less-problematic entity through participation in international regimes and acceptance of global norms?

From the early 1990s until approximately 2005, the Tiananmen uprising (so large in scope and scale that it seemed likely that a latent demand for democratization would persist even after the brutal crackdown), the collapse of the Soviet Union, and all the myriad internal changes in China of a positive nature combined to convince some analysts that democratization was inevitable or at least highly likely, with the only questions being how long the process would take and how exactly it would unfold.[1] Other scholars, however—most prominently Andrew Nathan—came to the very different conclusion that precisely the same economic successes that had convinced some analysts of democratization's inevitability were combining with China's increasing international prestige to strengthen the CCP's authoritarian control over society, both by deepening the material resource pool available for the Party to use in co-opting strategic segments of the population and by allowing it to claim credit for restoring China to international greatness.[2] Nathan never declared that "authoritarian resilience" would last forever, but neither did he specify when or how it might end—until perhaps 2009, when he began to suggest that the regime's legitimacy deficit combined with increasing activism on the part of Chinese civil society could produce a crisis of some sort; if that crisis became coupled with a split in the Party leadership, a turbulent transition might occur, although not necessarily a transition to a smoothly functioning democracy.[3] Generally, though, most observers in the mid- to late 2000s depicted the Chinese political system as robust and creatively adaptive, even though it faced numerous challenges.[4] The sudden disappearance of the great debate on China's potential for democratization led Kevin O'Brien to wonder openly in 2011 whether most specialists on Chinese politics now considered the matter to be closed and accepted that authoritarianism—though surely continuing to change in important ways—is fundamentally here to stay.[5]

At least one group, however, persisted in articulating optimism—although this group was focused more directly on China's international behavior than on its potential for domestic political change. A cluster of scholars and other observers who had been arguing all along that China's rise would be peaceful and ultimately beneficial for the region and the world rose to unprecedented prominence in the mid- to late 2000s. Prior to about 1996, even avowed optimists had to admit that, at the time, China did not show signs of becoming a responsible international actor predisposed to internalizing global norms. But they also insisted that either (1) domestic political liberalization would eventually change the Chinese state's core identity, which in turn would make the PRC more cooperative internationally, and/or (2) intensified participation in globalization would eventually force China into behaving more cooperatively and accepting socialization to global norms—after which the socialization process would, over time, remake China's national identity through the mechanisms of "deep learning."[6] In a virtuous cycle, socialization to international norms could eventually then facilitate democratization itself, because, following the Cold War, it appeared that a powerful new global "constitutive" norm was taking shape: an expectation that all "normal" countries (especially the great powers) must either already be, or else be in the process of becoming, democratically governed.[7] If, in contrast, a country is not democratic and does not appear to be embarked on a process of becoming democratic, then—according to the powerful, emerging norm—it cannot be regarded (or "constituted") as normal. It would instead be abnormal, according to this norm, and therefore potentially a problem in international relations.

Even though few people were arguing in the mid- and late 2000s that China was destined to become democratic, many were suggesting that the PRC was a "status quo" power not likely to menace its neighbors or unsettle global order; in other words, they were suggesting that it might not matter much (for outsiders) whether the PRC became democratic. A consensus seemed to be emerging that China's rise was an inherently positive development in world politics and that the PRC, regardless of its internal political arrangements, would benevolently bring wealth, order, and peace to Asia and the world—just so long as neighboring countries and the United States managed to restrain themselves. This academic near-consensus aligned neatly with the CCP's proclamation in 2003 that China's rise would be peaceful and its subsequent declaration in 2005 that the point and purpose of China's rise were to create a brand-new harmonious world. Although not all analysts of China accepted this imagery, those who rejected it faced the prospect of becoming marginalized within the field.

New developments following the Beijing Olympics (2008) and the GFC helped to reopen both the question of China's potential for democratization and the parallel question of what kind of international actor the PRC would become if its rise succeeded. The international question is discussed in Chapters 5 and 6. The remainder of this chapter is devoted to the PRC's prospects for democratization or at least political liberalization, as seen in particular from the vantage point of China's own academic and political elites.

At no time in its history did the authoritarian PRC appear more powerful, wealthy, and confident than in 2009–2010. Most outsiders accepted the CCP's claims of stunning economic success likely to continue indefinitely into the future. And yet not only, as we have seen (in Chapter 2), was the economy in fact being mauled and maimed at the time by severely destructive policies whose consequences would only become visible later. Politically, dissatisfaction with corruption, pollution, and many other integral components of the Chinese model continued steadily to increase, frequently exploding in "mass incidents." At this point, the January 2011 (and afterward) "Arab Spring" served helpfully to remind observers of Chinese politics that democratization movements or political instability in general can emerge suddenly and without warning in any part of the world—even in regions already written off by some as unsuitable for democracy.

But China had never been written off; rather, specialists simply stopped talking about the PRC's potential for democratization. Most observers agreed that, by 2010, China—or at least urban China—had achieved all of the major socioeconomic preconditions generally considered necessary for democratization, particularly a moderately high GDP per capita—which some political scientists go so far as to contend *causes* democratization, in the strong sense of the term.[8] At the same time, the global constitutive norm pressuring China to democratize continued to hover "out there," reminding Chinese elites day in and day out that influential observers in the other great powers looked on the PRC as abnormal and out of sync with global trends ("on the wrong side of history"). The external pressure could eventually interact with domestic developments to convince the CCP to begin experimenting with political liberalization.

This lingering possibility; the general world turmoil that followed in the wake of the GFC; and China's apparent (though, as we have seen, ultimately illusory) economic dynamism, helped to revive the debate over China's political future after 2010. Once again—just as in the 1990s—some foreign scholars began arguing the position that liberalization leading eventually to democratization would be inevitable for the PRC, even if it remained unclear when, and exactly how, the process would begin. The revival of this debate, in turn, interacted with rapid Internet development (discussed in Chapter 4) to rekindle the debate inside China itself.

On the outside, Larry Diamond, one of the world's leading specialists on democratization, cogently developed the argument that China would, one day, inevitably democratize in an article appearing in the January 2012 *Journal of Democracy*:

Increasingly, the CCP faces the classic contradiction that troubles all modernizing authoritarian regimes. The Party cannot rule without continuing to deliver rapid economic development and rising living standards—to fail at this would invite not gradual loss of power but a sudden and probably lethal crisis. To the extent that the CCP succeeds, however, it generates the very forces—an educated, demanding middle class and a stubbornly independent civil society—that will one day decisively mobilize to raise up a democracy and end CCP rule for good.[9]

Diamond contends that a CCP collapse could come "quite possibly within the next ten years," although the first post-Communist regime would probably be "a much more dangerous form of authoritarian rule, perhaps led by a nationalistic military looking for trouble abroad in order to unify the nation at home." But this would only be a temporary phase, because "the military is incapable of governing a rapidly modernizing, deeply networked, middle-class country facing complex economic and social challenges." Eventual democratization would be inevitable, though precisely how China would arrive at the positive end point remained an open question; Diamond chose not to address the issue of potential pathways in his 2012 article, a short article whose primary purpose was to introduce one of the *Journal*'s occasional special issues on China.[10]

Despite Diamond's cautious optimism ("cautious," because the care he exercised in choosing what terminology to use suggested an awareness of—and determination to avoid—the pitfalls of predictioneering), the fundamental question remains unanswered: How certain can we be that democracy is the only type of political system ultimately possible for China? Or how certain can we be that, if attempted, democracy would take root in China and become consolidated, particularly given the economic problems discussed in Chapter 2? Should we not consider the possibility that the experiences of other countries in other times and places—the sources of social science models generalized by some as valid for all states—may not serve as reliable guides to the trajectory of China's political system? After all, China not only differs from other recently democratized Asian states (Taiwan and South Korea, for example) in the structure of its political system, performance of its economy, and functioning of its communication system. China also differs from Taiwan and South Korea in its relationship with the current global hegemon, the United States, as well as on deeper questions of national identity.

Indeed, part of the CCP's motivation for *rejecting* democratization seems to be a determination to resist incorporation into what champions of globalization insist is an increasingly borderless, "posthistorical" world order not dominated by any single nation-state; that is, not having a center and therefore far more fair and just than world orders of the past. Most Chinese analysts (and leaders) adamantly reject such imagery, countering that the global order that has slowly taken shape during the past quarter century unquestionably *does* have a center—the United States, which self-servingly promotes the posthistorical, "cosmopolitan" concept as a ruse designed to divert attention from its own dominance and trick countries such as China into accepting it. The profound problem for some Chinese patriots and almost all nationalists is that yielding to the strong and enticing pull of the United States and its insistence on the universal validity of liberal-democratic values (which do seem to be widely shared, including in Asia—all the more unsettling for many Chinese elites) would, for some, imply the highly traumatic disappearance of China as a distinctive political entity with a world mission of its own to fulfill. This homegrown mission—part of what Xi Jinping evidently intends to signal by the "China Dream" (see Chapters 5 and 6)—is to turn China into one of the world's strongest and most impressive or even feared countries in order to erase the "shame" of the past 150 years, during which China was decentered in history and international relations by the West and (for a few decades) Japan. The only way to "prove" that the period of history in which China could not claim to be the center was an aberration—abnormal or even unnatural—is to recenter the country and insist that recentering was, all along, inevitable: restoring the world to its proper state through the relegation of the West, Japan, and other Asian states to secondary, or even subservient, positions. The many Chinese elites who articulate such a vision tend to dismiss pressures from the West, Japan, and other Asian countries to democratize as political ploys designed to weaken China even to the point of causing it to disintegrate or dissolve, after which the PRC's components parts would disappear into the cosmopolitan global mix deceptively directed by the United States.[11]

But the mere fact that many (though far from all) Chinese political and academic figures articulate such a grandiose vision does not, of course, imply that Chinese recentering is inevitable, any more than Chinese democratization is inevitable. We have already seen how complex and knotty economic and demographic problems seem likely to slow the pace of China's rise in the years ahead, possibly even to the point that the country becomes mired in a middle-income trap. But even if China is able to muddle through economically, the question of how Chinese political institutions will change—and in what direction—is entirely open. Neither inevitable democratization nor inevitable perfection of the authoritarian system seems a defensible position to take at this point—although *possible* democratization or *possible* perfection of the authoritarian state certainly would be a reasonable position to take.

As explained in the Preface, the fundamental presupposition of this book is that what a country's own elites are thinking and articulating about their nation's trajectory in a given issue-area will correlate significantly with what the trajectory eventually becomes. The correlation will not be perfect; many other factors will enter the equation. But it will make a material difference if the authors to be reviewed in this chapter state clearly and consistently that they expect China to democratize successfully and soon. (Consider the alternative of elites proclaiming the likelihood or desirability of Chinese authoritarianism continuing indefinitely.) Holding all other factors constant, when elites in a country share widely in a belief (which they also articulate publicly) that something is deeply wrong with their country, necessitating fundamental political change, that country's political trajectory is more likely to depart from its initial starting state than if the elites mostly agree there is little need for fundamental change.

This chapter focuses on internal Chinese debates from recent years on the future of the PRC's political system: the core institutions and processes. Almost all of the contributors to these debates agree that thirty years of reform and opening have brought tremendous changes to Chinese society—mostly (but not entirely) positive changes—to which the political system, however, has yet to adapt. A few liberals do say (albeit mostly in not-for-attribution interviews) that the highly visible tensions in state–society relations of recent years are bound to lead eventually to democracy; a few conservatives contend that China already *is* a democracy and is performing well in most major respects.[12] In this chapter, I will examine not these outlier arguments but instead five more carefully developed and apparently influential approaches to conceptualizing the political trajectory which seem to resonate among broader communities of analysts:

1. The standard CCP orthodoxy, as explained in the 2009 volume on *China's Future Direction* (published by Renmin Chubanshe), along with various other publications;

2. Shanghai scholar Xiao Gongqin's revised neoauthoritarianism, which as of 2012 placed substantially more emphasis than his earlier publications on preparing for eventual democratization;

3. Neoleftist nationalist Pan Wei's exposition of the so-called China model, which recognizes no major flaws in China's current trajectory and opposes political liberalization;[13]

4. The evidently CCP-sanctioned liberal model of Yu Keping;[14]

5. The disgraced (albeit not yet formally rejected) Chongqing Model, which is important to discuss at least briefly as an illustration of one model that Party leaders seemed to rule out in 2012, and yet whose combination of pseudo-neo-Maoism; populism; an uncompromisingly harsh (and thus generally popular) stand against (some) crime and corruption; and, somewhat paradoxically, a proclivity to co-opt many of the economic liberals' policy proposals suggest that the model, or some variant of it, could yet return to center stage at some point in the future.

STATE–SOCIETY TENSIONS

A widely held view among Chinese political analysts is that tensions are mounting between state and society and that the tensions both demand and herald political change. The only question is, what kind of political change? "China is increasingly pluralistic," notes a liberal academic, "and will continue to become even more so as long as the economy continues to grow on the basis of being market oriented. The market brings with it a proliferation of new social roles, in ways that aren't always foreseeable."[15] This new pluralism—intertwined with inequality—creates the state–society tensions. There have been a fair number of examples of these tensions exploding to the surface in recent years, "but for the most part, they're now latent. I would expect these tensions to become increasingly obvious in the next ten to twenty years and for people to start talking about them more."[16] Today, talking about the tensions is difficult because drawing attention to them can be portrayed as violating the Party Center's demand to stress harmony—and the Center has shown no hesitation in crushing those who stray too far from the mandated line. "The conflict is already a social fact; as people gradually start talking about it more, that also itself becomes a social fact"—one that this academic observer considers likely to put even more pressure on the state to liberalize.[17]

But when might this liberalization occur? A self-proclaimed liberal optimist states that China's democratization, although inevitable, "might not come for many decades—two to three generations from now."[18] This academic believes that "we are now in the middle of a very long process that dates back to the nineteenth century." Moves being made by the leadership in the area of economic reform continue to pave the way for eventual political change, but change can come only slowly: "The leaders can solve only one *big* problem per generation in China—our problems are too complex and too numerous."[19]

Another scholar acknowledges the state–society tensions and the challenges facing CCP leaders but believes the Party elites are too timid to pursue political reform: "The leaders don't want to do *anything*; they are far too risk averse."[20] Some at the top champion the paradoxical and ultimately untenable objectives of "controllable democracy" or "inner-Party democracy," either of which would result in a degree of liberalization but with the CCP still firmly in charge. Yet even these tightly limited types of reform are not likely to be pursued in the near future, because "the system itself ensures that no bold person can rise to the top."[21] What is more, economic growth—although it does promote social pluralization—on balance undermines the prospects for political liberalization because it convinces China's leaders that they are succeeding with their current approach and so should avoid risking political reform. This academic does not rule out the possibility that Xi Jinping could take it upon himself to pursue some sort of political liberalization before his scheduled two terms end in 2022. But, by the time he acts, it could be too late: Contemporary China increasingly resembles the Qing Dynasty after 1900, the academic finds, "stubbornly postponing reforms until they are unavoidable, by which time it's too late; meanwhile, all kinds of disruptive forces are grabbing selfishly for power."[22] Readers will fully be aware that the outcome of the Qing collapse was decades of militarism and civil war; consequently, this scholar is hinting at possible disaster should the CCP continue to reject political and economic reforms.

AN ORTHODOX CCP TAKE ON CHINA'S
FUTURE POLITICAL DIRECTION

In May 2009, Renmin Chubanshe, an "official publishing house for political and ideological books of the Chinese Communist Party and the
Chinese government,"[23] published a volume by the China Future Directions Editorial Group (whose individual members are not identified)
entitled *China's Future Direction: Uniting High-Level Policy-Making
and National Strategic Arrangements.*[24] In Chapter 2, I discussed this
group's views on China's economic trajectory. Here I discuss the forty-
one pages the group devotes to the evolution and future possibilities for
Chinese politics.

The group begins by acknowledging all of the changes in Chinese
society (including the new tensions stressed by interview subjects) that
have appeared in the wake of economic development. The group concedes
that the expanded realms of freedom in social interaction and personal
expression accompanying media and telecommunications development
(see Chapter 4) have given rise to a strengthened democratic consciousness in Chinese society—a consciousness that, in the context of the new
economy, can serve as "the scaffolding for democracy" after the matura-
tion of political and social institutions makes it safer to put democracy in
place. "National conditions" have thus changed substantially in recent
years, and yet the group still contends that it would be unwise to tinker
with the political system too soon. China remains a developing country
in which moving at too quick a pace could produce chaos or violence. The
group cites the turmoil that followed the Kenyan elections of December
27, 2007, as an example of what would probably happen in China should
the CCP relax control over politics, even though Kenya has *not* developed
economically and culturally in ways similar to China in the decades since
reform and opening.[25]

In what ways, then, must China continue to develop to establish the
preconditions for safe experimentation with democracy? Here the group
is looking for signs of "other kinds of social development" beyond economic advance. In particular, Chinese society "must—one step at a time—
establish institutions that will facilitate democratic compromise [among

competing interest groups] and rational behavior," whereas "the people in society must gradually develop the willingness, habit, and ability to uphold social rules, respect differences [among individuals and groups], and form and express their opinions rationally."[26] If democracy is attempted in a setting in which the quality of the people has not yet improved in these ways, voters will make mindless choices and engage in other sorts of irrational political behavior that will leave them susceptible to manipulation by demagogues and "political opportunists." The people thus have a responsibility to cultivate themselves through education and nurturing the habits of self-discipline before the society can safely experiment with democracy—even if the economy is already highly advanced.[27]

This fear of the Chinese people's alleged irrationality or stupidity—which, as explained in Chapter 4, also partly undergirds the CCP's restrictive Internet policies—is not the only reason given for approaching democratization cautiously (if at all). Another explanation is that democracy must inherently be viewed with suspicion because it is associated with the West. Although this is a common theme in the CCP's rejection of democracy going back decades, in recent years the theme has come increasingly to be expressed in the sophisticated terminology of Western social science. What exercises CCP writers today is the concern that democracy's acceptance in countries throughout the world reflects not some inherent, scientifically demonstrated suitability of democracy for developing societies, but instead the West's global "discourse hegemony," which flows automatically (or so it is claimed) from Western economic and military power.[28] From the early 1980s, after the Soviet Union lost its appeal as an alternative model, until the turn of the century, the group argues, many people in Third World countries thoughtlessly championed "Western democracy" on the basis not of rational calculation but instead their infatuation with the dazzling material accomplishments of Western civilization. There is no denying these accomplishments; the problem is that for developing countries to achieve such material successes they must *reject* democracy. If they accept democracy, they will never develop because their states will be too weak to discipline society and implement the wrenching changes necessary for development to take place. Developing countries require states that can "mobilize" people; they need "a democratic political system in which the level of institutionalization is higher" and in which the degree of state power regulating democratic processes is greater.[29]

This is why the authors of *China's Future Direction* are delighted with what they contend is the "failure" since approximately 2000 of the third wave of global democratization.[30] Importantly, this failure—exemplified by Vladimir Putin's rise to strongman status in Russia (a development the authors praise)[31]—is presented as causally associated with a *weakening* of Western discourse hegemony, which itself resulted partly from the successes of China's rise in material power terms. China's rise, the weakening of Western discourse hegemony, and consequent failure of the third wave "do not, however, imply that democracy itself is dead." Instead, the developments herald "the flourishing of new opportunities for different countries to experiment with different kinds of democracy."[32] The problem in the recent past has been that Western discourse hegemony resulted in the West monopolizing the definition of democracy. The West abused its hegemony to reject as undemocratic the political systems of China and other developing countries. But now, "China's historically unprecedented great development proves the success of China's democratic political construction" while at the same time legitimizing the political endeavors of other states (for example, Russia) ostracized by the West as authoritarian.[33] "Proceeding from Chinese reality and tradition, we should enthusiastically explore and gradually construct a kind of new-style [CCP-led] democratic system that, on the one hand, provides guarantees for talented and righteous people to excel and, on the other hand, results in their rights being comprehensively supervised."[34] In the process, "we should reflect on the values that democracy would serve. These values should be excellent national governance and a good quality of life for the people. We should proceed from these values . . . and not pursue democracy merely for the sake of democracy"—as recommended by sometimes ill-intentioned people in Western and Asian democratic countries.[35]

The authors find that as long as Chinese comprehensive national power continues to increase, the world should remain safe for the CCP to continue pursuing its unique brand of "excellent national governance" and "democratic political construction." Comprehensive national power is critical because it allows Beijing on the one hand to assert that it accepts as universally valid "the concepts of 'liberty, democracy, and human rights'—which, though they originated in the West, are all good things just so long as they are not abused." On the other hand, national power allows China to *resist* the imposition of "narrow" definitions of these Enlightenment values and to defend its national right actively to *interpret* these values for the purpose of deciding which aspects are suitable for CCP objectives and which aspects are not. Without increasing national power, China would be unable to exercise this "right to interpret": "The right to interpret these values must belong to each nation, and not just to a minority of countries; otherwise, all sorts of absurdities will possibly appear."[36] The authors are optimistic that trends will continue to work in China's favor: "The world is advancing. China is rising. The era in which the countries with material power also own discourse power is gone and never to return."[37]

The last statement is in tension with the claim that CCP-style Chinese democracy can be safe only if China's rise in relative material power terms continues. At points such as this one, the authors present China as a still-developing country making progress in the soft-power contest with the West on the basis of the persuasiveness of CCP argumentation and the dignity with which it resists the West's gratuitous insults. At other points—most points, in fact—the CCP wins and can only win on the basis of Chinese material power increasing, which implies that the era in which countries with material power also automatically possess discourse power is still very much with us, only now China is joining the ranks of the materially powerful. But this is the argument to which the authors keep returning: "A world under the control of a hegemon not only cannot have [genuine] democracy, but it would also find it difficult to maintain a long period of peace. In contrast, if globalization brings in its wake pluralization and multipolarization [the rise of new power centers, especially China], the forms of democracy would become more numerous" and legitimate (because grounded in national realities), and globalization itself would continue to develop sustainably on the foundation of diversity and harmony among essentially unlike units.[38]

What would be impossible, the authors argue, is for "American-style democracy" to become universally entrenched and accepted as legitimate. This is because the universal entrenchment and legitimization of American-style democracy could only succeed by imposition through the realization of American hegemony and unipolarity—and yet hegemony and unipolarity are intrinsically and objectively both impossible and illegitimate.[39] Thus, the only way—paradoxically—for democracy to take root and to flourish is for the United States to stop insisting that all countries must accept democracy and stop rejecting and ridiculing the political institutions of countries like China. In turn, the only way the United States will do this is if countries like China—or China in particular—continue to increase their relative material power: "A more democratic world cannot possibly be a chaotic world without [multiple] poles [of power]. At the same time as poles restrict the formation of hegemony, they also gradually give shape to a new ethical basis [for international relations] and new 'rules of the game.'"[40] A world without multiple poles—a unipolar world of American hegemony—would be (1) chaotic and thus dangerous and not developing, (2) susceptible to constant warfare and strife, and (3) bereft of morality and ethics. This is why China's rise on the basis of rejecting "Western democracy" and Western discourse hegemony is so important for the world's future, not just China's. It is also why the CCP's determination to find a different road for China's political trajectory is presented as being of world-historical—almost cosmic—significance.

What does it all add up to on the question of China's political trajectory—and in particular the question of whether China will become democratic? The group declaims that this question has already "fundamentally been answered." China will continue to develop the democracy it already has, "organically uniting the principle of insisting on the Communist Party's leadership, the people being their own masters, and the country being governed according to rule by law."[41] Taking this road is both "an historical necessity" as well as "the choice of the people"—which solves both the problem of ensuring that the decision is a wise one (it could hardly be unwise to accept what is historically necessary) as well as legitimate according to the principles of the Enlightenment (because the people have chosen it). Because the decision is wise, "in taking this road, China will gradually become rich and powerful, democratic, civilized, and harmonious."[42] But the process will take a long time, and to stay on track, China must, the group warns, pay greater attention to, and seize tightly, the following three preconditions: (1) The democracy China pursues must be socialist democracy with Chinese characteristics; that is, it must be a democracy administered by the CCP and that excludes any elements the CCP determines to be negative;[43] (2) the democracy must continuously change on the basis of practical experience and in view of the primary tasks of increasing national strength and developing the economy; the only constants, the groups expects, will be elections of some sort, compromise among different interest groups, and supervision by the CCP;[44] and (3) the democracy will uphold the successes already achieved even while ceaselessly carrying out new experiments, or, in the words of the group, "under the precondition of the Four Cardinal Principles [fundamental dominance of the Communist Party and of CCP ideology], we will advance the construction of democratic politics by means of enthusiastically carrying out reform of the political system."[45] Some change is thus possible, and even desirable, but not to an extent that would end the authoritarian system with the CCP on top.

XIAO GONGQIN: REVERSE SULTANIZATION, PREPARE FOR GENUINE DEMOCRATIZATION

Something like the collapse of the Qing repeating is a scenario that worries Xiao Gongqin, one of the few Chinese thinkers who devotes systematic analytical attention to focused research on China's political trajectory: contrasting the course of the country's likely evolution with what Xiao considers to be its desirable evolution.

In an influential 2009 collection of essays, Xiao—whose primary appointment is in the history department of Shanghai Normal University—warns that China is rapidly becoming mired in a "soft political crisis."[46] By this he means a smoldering stalemate in which, "under conditions of low political participation . . . , social contradictions continue to increase"—most notably inequality and injustice at the local level, usually related to corruption—as leaders of the central state vacillate and ultimately decide not to use their still-formidable powers to resolve the contradictions. "Conditions of low political participation" become important because civil society institutions, which might otherwise fill the power-balancing gap left by central government reticence, remain underdeveloped in a posttotalitarian order. At the local level, this allows a bureaucratic class working with business elites to lock in a new power structure that cannot be challenged effectively by organized societal opposition.[47] The country as a whole appears on the surface to be stable politically, but unsolved problems and pressures building toward a larger crisis continue inexorably to mount.[48]

Xiao borrows the term *sultanistic regime* from Western political science to describe this sort of political system: "the worst kind of authoritarian political formation," a "retrogressive type of extreme formation unconstrained from top to bottom or bottom to top," "personalistic," "arbitrary."[49] Although the situation may appear calm and stable, as the economy forges ahead on the basis of high levels of state-directed investment, "the whole society actually operates in a semi-anarchic condition: orders are not implemented, laws exist but are not obeyed, and local emperors take charge," leading to a "comprehensive corruption syndrome" in which the central state gradually loses its capacity to achieve large-scale social objectives such as reorienting the economy to domestic consumption-driven growth, reducing pollution and resource waste, and protecting intellectual property rights.[50] "Muddling through" is not an option: Either the central Party-state will reassert itself vigorously to take control of the situation, establishing a neoauthoritarian order, or China will plunge into a dark and dispiriting political-economic pit.

Whereas in the past, Xiao placed intellectual emphasis on the need for a new vigor and assertiveness on the part of the central Party-state—hence his identity as a well-known neoauthoritarian—in a May 2012 interview he said that his most recent thinking focuses on how China can ultimately achieve democracy.[51] Xiao first emphasizes that he remains a neoauthoritarian insofar as he opposes liberal demands for the immediate installation of electoral democracy. If elections were held today, the result, he says, would be populism, "and Chinese-style populism could be the world's worst: Just look at what happened here during the Cultural

Revolution."[52] Populism would eventually destroy the democracy out of which it emerged, Xiao contends.

But, in contrast, reinvigorated centrally led authoritarianism could help advance a *long-term* democratization process that Xiao believes began in the 1970s. He identifies five stages in this process, each of which only becomes possible after the immediately preceding stage is consolidated:

1. *Stage 1* began with reform and opening and continued until suppression of the nationwide democracy uprising in June 1989. The political activists of this period struggled to prevent the comeback of ultra-leftwing authoritarian and paternalistic rule. But conditions were not ripe for China's democratization, and Xiao criticizes the 1970s and 1980s activists for having tried uncritically to transplant Western models of political organization to China—models that could not have flourished even if CCP leaders had been willing to accept them. Xiao calls the 1970s and 1980s activists "romantic, moralistic, and unreasonably unwilling to compromise" yet argues at the same time that they did lay important groundwork for China's eventual democratization by putting the fundamental transition permanently on the agenda.[53]

2. *Stage 2 (1992–2002)* began with Deng Xiaoping's reform-reviving tour of the south in January and February 1992 and featured stunning economic development under "enlightened authoritarian" rule.[54] Xiao recognizes that many people in the West consider the entire post-1989 period to be a "democratic winter," but he thinks that four developments established important preconditions for future democratization: (a) formation of a market economy and the rise of NGOs, which created a "second culture" through pluralization of societal interests and perspectives; (b) the rise of a middle class; (c) progress in establishing a legal culture and the rule of law (now receding in those parts of the country most affected by sultanization); and (d) increased legitimacy of CCP rule, necessary but not sufficient to ensuring an orderly political transition when the time eventually comes.[55]

3. *Stage 3*, the current stage, began when Hu Jintao and Wen Jiabao took power in 2002–2003, but its tasks remain unfinished. Xiao identifies the most important task for this stage as being "the project of

establishing the people's livelihood" (*minsheng gongcheng*), by which he means not only continuing GDP growth at a reasonably high rate (he specifies 5 to 7 percent), but also redistributing wealth and improving social justice. Unless a meaningful degree of redistribution and justice is achieved, any democratization attempted would collapse into populism and fail. The Hu-Wen government made laudable progress in pursuing these goals in the early years of its rule, but, after the mid-2000s, this government proved itself to be pathetically weak-willed in the face of sultanization, which worsened inequality and social injustice. For this reason, Xiao makes it a point to praise the Chongqing model's redistributive economic policies, even though he says that he disliked Bo Xilai the person for his dictatorial tendencies. Xiao rejects the so-called Guangdong model of liberalization because it does not take seriously the need to redistribute wealth, instead promoting the idea of letting the market decide social and economic outcomes even though market functioning in China is profoundly distorted by special interest group manipulation.[56]

4. The centerpiece of *Stage 4*—which can only begin in earnest after "the project of establishing the people's livelihood" succeeds in Stage 3— will be building a genuinely effective, robust, and healthy civil society. This is what Xiao has spent most of his time thinking about in recent years, even though he acknowledges that even in a best-case scenario China is unlikely to complete Stage 3 before the early 2020s.[57] The kind of well-functioning civil society that China will have to put into place during Stage 4 for democracy to succeed must, Xiao believes, feature four characteristics: (a) institutionalization of the rule of law, with no exceptions based on individual or institutional status (for example, neither princelings nor the Party itself would be exempt); (b) state tolerance for the expression of dissenting views in a significantly freer and more open public sphere; (c) guarantee of such civil rights as the right to petition, the right to demonstrate, to right to hold assemblies, and the right to organize politically; and (d) gradual acceptance of genuine political competition, perhaps starting experimentally in the wealthier parts of the country but with the understanding that eventually the experiments would expand.[58]

Xiao elaborates on the political importance of establishing a well-functioning civil society in a May 2012 article in *Exploration and Free Views*, a publication of the Shanghai Social Sciences Association, which bills itself as a nongovernmental organization. In "Rebuilding Civil Society," Xiao first emphasizes that civil society has a prominent place in Chinese history, appearing in embryonic form as far back as the Song Dynasty (960–1279) and then taking off in the modern era during the late Qing. It only disappeared after decades of warlordism, Japanese occupation, and civil war, followed by CCP repression in the 1950s.[59] Xiao's primary point, however, concerns the present and future. China has achieved a level of economic development in which social differentiation and the pluralization of socioeconomic interests are facts of life to which the political system must unavoidably adapt. At present, because civil society institutions are underdeveloped and often treated with contempt by the Party-state, naturally differing socioeconomic interests have few institutionalized, well-functioning processes for working out their conflicts peacefully. This is why China now suffers from so many seemingly aimless confrontations between social agglomerations and the local state: "atomized individuals clashing directly with the government."[60] Such clashes may or may not resolve immediate grievances, but, for long-term healthy social functioning, China needs intermediate civil society institutions to aggregate and articulate socioeconomic interests, communicating and compromising with elements of the government and competing interest groups. It is important to note that Xiao considers that, in China, the organization of civil society is likely to be state led and state sanctioned, with the result that he attaches the label "corporatist" to the type of civil society he expects to emerge over the course of the 2020s during Stage 4.[61]

Arguing that even imagining the defining features of Stage 5, when China would become democratic, is next to impossible until Stage 4 is well underway, and reminding that even Stage 3 is unlikely to be consolidated before another five to ten years, Xiao expresses reluctance to discuss in detail what the Chinese democracy that could emerge in the 2030s might look like. He does, however, make one critical point: Because he expects the civil society that develops in Stage 4 to be of the state-led corporatist variety, he considers it likely that Chinese democracy will come to resemble the democracies in other countries with state-led corporatist civil societies: most notably, Japan, South Korea, Taiwan, and Singapore. He mentioned these four political systems by name.[62] He is not, however, basing his argument on culture, claiming a Confucian or East Asian model of democratization. He is saying that if the reinvigorated authoritarian state necessary to suppress sultanization and achieve the "people's livelihood project" of Stage 3 succeeds, it will come to resemble the developmentalist authoritarian states that eventually accepted democratization in South Korea and Taiwan, along with bureaucrat-dominant (at least until the 2000s) democracy in Japan and quasi-democracy in Singapore.[63]

Few other scholars develop as systematic a vision of China's current political predicament and prospects for escape as Xiao. One who seems clearly to have been influenced by Xiao is Wang Yukai of the Chinese Academy of Governance (the official English translation for the *Guojia Xingzheng Xueyuan*). What makes Wang's thinking worth briefly outlining is the fact that, in teaching at such an institution as the Academy, he would come into contact with numerous current and aspiring Chinese officials—precisely the people who would be on the front lines of implementing the fight against sultanization and trying the strengthen the neoauthoritarian order.

Similar to Xiao, Wang—whose ultimate hope is, like Xiao's, democratization—finds the greatest obstacle to political reform in "the fusion between political power and capital" that began in 1992 and that becomes tighter by the day: "In the event that reform touches on the interests of fused political power and capital, it basically cannot advance an inch."[64] Consequently, what China must do at the present is (1) consolidate state autonomy vis-à-vis material social interests, (2) increase state legitimacy in the eyes of the public by dealing effectively with Party-state corruption, and (3) begin to implement inner-Party democracy and from it find a path to broader political reform. "I believe that political reform in China should not start from the bottom and go to the top but should start from the top and go to the bottom"—that is, it should be led by an enlightened and socially autonomous authoritarian state, not by ill-informed politically mobilized groups in society.[65] There are, Wang believes, three critical considerations for China's more enlightened authoritarian leaders to keep in mind if they eventually decide to start pursuing top-down political liberalization:

1. They must proceed slowly and make certain at every stage that the specific reform policies they are considering will be consistent with the material needs of economic growth.
2. Society and economy will continue rapidly to evolve; to stay on top of this ever-changing situation, the Party must learn to become more flexible, nimble, open minded, and creative. It must study how to adapt intelligently to constantly emerging new situations—or else it could lose control and/or become irrelevant to the fundamental forces driving Chinese change.
3. More concretely, the leaders should begin expanding inner-Party democracy at the county level of government by increasing the number of locales in which base-level cadres directly elect the leading cadres; afterward, the local party secretary or county chief would have to answer to both the base-level cadres and the county-level People's Congresses. After this reform is implemented successfully at the county level, Wang says the Party should try implementing it at successively higher levels of the governing hierarchy.[66]

Wang does not offer an assessment of how likely the Party-state is to act on his recommendations. But, like Xiao, he implies that if it fails to do so—by first addressing sultanism effectively (though Wang does not use that term) and then by pursuing gradual political reform—the Party-state will be swamped by the ongoing socioeconomic changes, both positive and negative. Judging from the tone of his writing, he may be even more worried than Xiao that the Party-state must move *quickly* to rectify this increasingly parlous political situation or else risk losing control.

PAN WEI'S VISION OF "THE CHINA MODEL"

In December 2008, Peking University Professor of International Studies Pan Wei convened a conference on the subject of "the China model" as it appeared on the eve of the PRC's sixtieth anniversary. More than forty scholars participated in the conference, giving papers or remarking on other scholars' papers. In February 2010, Beijing's Sanlian Bookstore published a volume capturing the conference proceedings. Pan Wei himself wrote the introductory chapter. Elaborating on themes he has developed over many years, Pan—a well-known and influential neoleftist scholar—argues that everything is generally going well for China and that not only is substantial reform unnecessary, but it would also be dangerous because it could throw China off track.[67] Pan is therefore severely at odds not only with the mainstream economists discussed in Chapter 2 but also with Xiao Gongqin and others concerned about sultanization, promoters of democracy, and even promoters of the Chongqing model. As explained in the paragraphs to follow, Pan believes that, because the China model has emerged naturally out of a series of crucibles in Chinese history, it is inherently right for China. He argues that there is a single, unique road for China to take—a road that may not always be clear but that with effort can be discovered through mining the past. This road, if taken, will guarantee that China can continue to cruise smoothly into the future. "Only if we lack self-respect and self-confidence"—and decide to follow models proposed by foreigners—would China fail.[68]

Pan flatly rejects the idea that there is anything substantially wrong with the functioning of the Chinese economy. Indeed, he considers that the GFC proved that, at least for China, the China model is far superior to economic liberalism and that committing to the China model economically would ensure there is a very good chance China will surpass the United States in GDP within twenty-five years—even doubling the United States in GDP by 2050.[69] Pan is not worried about demography, pollution, resource constraints, or inequality resulting in China getting trapped in middle-income-country status. He evidently reads the economists' critiques but refutes them with elaborate counterpropositions.

Pan finds "four great pillars" upholding the Chinese economic model (organically linked, as explained in the following discussion, to the political model), all of which many of the economists discussed in Chapter 2 regard as problem zones: (1) the state controlling land as a key factor of production; (2) the state owning core financial institutions, large-scale resource-extraction enterprises, industrial enterprises, and public goods–providing enterprises; (3) the labor market being largely "free"; and (4) the existence of parallel free markets in certain commercial products and financial services. Pan finds a harmony and balance between the state and private/market dimensions of the Chinese economy and considers these to be keys to the country's successes.[70] So how, exactly, do each of the pillars provide the functions required of them to make the whole model work?

1. *The state controlling land as a key factor of production.* Pan believes that state control over land distribution allows China to maintain the stability of village society. It ensures relative fairness in people's access to land (so critical to all forms of production). Because governments derive the bulk of their revenues from land sales, the system also allows tax rates for the industrial economy to remain low. Finally, state control over land ensures that basic infrastructure for industry can be supplied at a lower cost than would otherwise be possible.[71] Although some of these points are factual, it is noteworthy that Pan declines to discuss all of the problems resulting from state control over land, as identified by mainstream economists, political analysts such as Xiao Gongqin, and proponents of the Chongqing model. Nowhere does Pan make mention of local governments effectively confiscating land from villagers and then selling it corruptly for real estate development. He only sees goodness in the China model and contends that because there is essentially only goodness there, tinkering with the system would be extremely risky.

2. *The state controlling the pillars of the economy.* State control over finance, Pan contends, ensures that the financial system will remain stable and will serve industrial production rather than becoming (as in the West) its own "gold-seeking empire." Because the financial system is in this way kept disciplined, the state can more easily influence the functioning of the macroeconomy. Meanwhile, state control over large enterprises ensures that investment will flow to those expensive basic infrastructure (and national defense) projects that private enterprises would find it difficult to undertake; moreover, the infrastructure can be supplied at a low and stable price, which increases China's competitiveness relative to foreign countries.[72] Finally, state control over public goods–providing enterprises ensures, as might be expected, the

speedy development and flourishing of entities providing education, scientific research, public health and sanitation, sports, and culture.[73] Once again, however, Pan passes up the opportunity to discuss the pathologies of state ownership and in particular the well-known problem of financial repression (the interest rate on household savings being kept low so that loans to state-owned enterprises will be cheap), which contributes to overinvestment in often wasteful, unviable projects. As explained by many of the economists discussed in Chapter 2, not only does this lead to the massive misallocation of scarce resources—which no society can afford indefinitely—but it also contributes to underconsumption (itself threatening to economic growth), because most households deposit their wealth in savings accounts that typically earn interest below the rate of inflation.[74] The Pan article can be frustrating for readers not because the points it makes are ipso facto wrong or unreasonable but instead because he simply declines to engage the arguments of other analysts who would disagree. He seems to *know* the counterarguments well enough to reject them, but he never explains fully why he thinks the arguments are flawed.

3. *The labor market being largely free.* This ensures, Pan argues, that (a) the vast majority of workers will enjoy relatively fair employment opportunities, and (b) labor will be low-cost, which will have salutary effects on China's international competitiveness.[75] There might seem to be a contradiction between (a) and (b), but Pan does not explore it. In particular, if the CCP were to allow collective bargaining and labor unions, employment opportunities (and conditions of employment) might improve substantially for Chinese workers, albeit at the cost of reducing China's international competitiveness and its attraction as a destination for foreign direct investment. A nationalist-leftist like Pan might argue that international competitiveness is more important than the treatment accorded to individual workers.

4. *Parallel free markets in commercial products and financial services.* As with labor, Pan here finds the logic of economic liberalism compelling. He argues that the parallel "free" markets for certain commercial products and in finance (a) ensure competition and therefore

efficiency in China's economy; (b) guarantee ultimate social equality insofar as competition leads to continuation of a claimed Chinese tradition that "wealth cannot last beyond three generations" (Pan thinks that China's is an inherently fair society in which crystallized social classes have never been important or sustained historically); and (c) lead to the "flexibility of supply," which simply means that producers and suppliers will move to meet needs as expressed in marketplace demand.[76] Although it is not clear why the logic of free market functioning should be seen as desirable in this and the labor case but not in those areas in which the state directs the economy, Pan insists on the point: The harmonious interaction of the state- and market-driven sectors is the key to China's economic success.

Moreover, it has always been this way—ever since the founding of the People's Republic. Pan rejects the notion that China's economic successes only began with the advent of reform and opening in 1979: "The global financial crisis that started in 2008 smashed the myth of the 'invisible hand,' while also smashing the myth of 'advance of the state, retreat of the private' (*guojinmintui*). Looking back at our Republic's economic development, the success has been a success of sixty years," not just a success of the period in which relatively liberal policies were pursued. (Pan says nothing about the Great Leap Forward or the endemic problems of the Maoist economy.) Both are critical organically to the Chinese economic model, which may not be perfect—nor transferrable to other settings (every country must discover its own essentially distinctive path)—but does work for China. Losing self-respect and confidence in the model and slavishly importing Western institutions and practices uncritically would lead to catastrophe: the end of China's rise:[77]

The foundation of the Western model is invasion-oriented military, political, and economic mechanisms. China has never embraced such a foundation and never should. The reason for the Chinese renaissance is that it has carved out a unique road . . . Today, China's urgent responsibility is to reject infatuation with Western teachings and prevent foreign doctrines from leading our country into a trap.[78]

It is important to note that Pan finds precisely same logic applies in politics. He contends that the cornerstone of the Chinese political model—going back 3,000 years—is a "people-based" (*minben*) orientation. In turn, there are four pillars to the people-based model, comparable to the four pillars of the economic model: (1) democratic concepts appropriate for contemporary people-based politics; (2) selective mechanisms for choosing officials and "the people's representatives" through competitive examinations and exam-like procedures; (3) advanced, uncorrupt, and united governing groups; and (4) effective government mechanisms for dividing up responsibilities, balancing power, and rectifying mistakes.[79] The critical point is that Pan thinks all of these desiderata have always been present in all of Chinese history—or at least during those periods when Chinese practice has been faithful to the Chinese model. In other words, the Chinese model of politics is essential and elemental to the point that it transcends dynasties and revolutions and therefore has profound implications for the future. In a sense, the model *is* the trajectory for politics, and for Pan the only question is the extent to which China will remain true to this intrinsically correct trajectory. There is no possibility for any root change. Efforts to change at a fundamental level—such as through "Western-style" democratization—may be attempted but would only lead to trouble. To Pan, the Chinese model of politics is ultimately inescapable for China because it is, after all, the Chinese model. But much damage could be done by otherwise well-meaning people who would attempt policies at variance with the model's demands; therefore, the model must be specified and propagated so that political actors will understand and embrace it:

1. *Democratic concepts appropriate for contemporary people-based politics.* The 3,000-year-old *minben* tradition specifies that the only reason government exists is to exercise the responsibility of taking care of the whole people's welfare. If the government fails to provide this function, rebellion is justified, and the people should overthrow the government. Throughout Chinese history, Pan finds, dynasties or even the superficial *form* of the state would often change—but not the political system (the China model) itself. Even the apparently profound

political developments that shook China starting in the late nineteenth century were changes *within* the Chinese model—although Pan does allow that these changes were influenced by Western thought. Thus, "under the Republic, people-based government was called 'the people's livelihood.'" Under the People's Republic, it was called "serving the people." Ultimately, they were all the same; there has never been a radical break throughout 3,000 years of history.[80] Moreover—and of critical importance—people-based government is fundamentally different from "'Western democratic doctrine,' which recognizes the 'rights' of powerful social organizations." In China, interest group politics and political party contention have no necessary legitimacy. Instead, the whole people will—through the government—exercise the responsibility of taking care of the whole people's welfare. It has always been this way; the only thing that has changed or been "modernized" is use of the term *the people's representatives* to describe the government.[81]

2. *Selective mechanisms for choosing officials and the people's representatives*. Pan notes an "obvious contrast" between China's "meritocratic" system (he supplies the English translation) and the competitive party processes of the West. Imperial China used the examination system; since 1949, the Communist Party has carefully vetted officials to ensure a high quality of personnel to fill important positions. Such a system "ensures that the government is both sensitive to popular opinion and able to shoulder responsibilities; it is in particular able to shoulder the responsibilities of weighing short-term versus long-term interests, particular versus integrated interests, and development versus order interests."[82] Pan is thus strikingly at odds with the political economists discussed in Chapter 2 who worry that the Chinese government is actually shortsighted, corrupt, and incapable of preserving either a just order or—in the end—perhaps any order at all. He would also be at odds with those inside as well as outside China who note profound differences between the Maoist approach to bureaucratic recruitment and the approaches that prevailed before 1949 and after 1979. Pan may be right that the governing elite in China has always selected officials carefully and not trusted the process to voters or the

unmediated interplay of interest groups. But he does not explain why the specific criteria in use can change so radically. The implication is that the criteria may appear different on the surface but are ultimately always consistent with people-based politics.

3. *Advanced, uncorrupt, and united governing groups.* This refers to the Chinese tradition in which carefully vetted officials "are the first to worry about the problems of the realm and the last to enjoy its pleasures."[83] Pan is not going so far here as to claim that contemporary Chinese governing groups are incapable of being corrupt. Rather, he is saying that, to the extent they are corrupt, it is because their practices are departing from the Chinese model. There is nothing inherently flawed about the model itself—nothing intrinsic to it causing the corruption. Indeed, he finds that the Leninist system works well for China, because: (a) The officials are all indoctrinated in a guiding set of thoughts, which increases the likelihood they will implement the Party line in a disciplined fashion; (b) the Party itself is structured by rules and norms designed to maximize discipline in carrying out centrally-determined objectives—this helps to ensure that nepotism, factionalism, and other problems can never become serious; (c) the armed forces remain under the control of political leaders; (d) ethnic separatism can more easily be countered and the national territory preserved intact; (e) all ethnic minorities in China and even ethnically Chinese citizens of foreign countries can be united and directed toward achieving common objectives; and (f) the government will remain this-worldly and can thus more easily prevent the "social turmoil" caused in so many other countries by religious groups.[84]

4. *Effective government mechanisms for dividing labor, balancing power, and rectifying mistakes.* Pan aims to distinguish the Chinese mechanisms from faulty Western separation-of-power models. He lists ten kinds of mechanism (but does not discuss the mechanisms in detail): (a) *minben* (government is people based) doctrine acting as a soft check on those at the top who wield administrative power; (b) the division of labor between Party and government; (c) mutual, flexible restraints stemming from the jostling for power between vertical bureaucratic hierarchies (*tiaotiao*) and the provincial (or lower) state (*kuaikuai*);

(d) the hard constraint facing top leaders which results from term limits and a (sometimes relaxed) mandatory retirement age; (e) democratic centralism (both aspects of it); (f) the Party's disciplinary apparatus and the judiciary both constraining the behavior of government officials; (g) the regular shifting of officials from their current positions to new posts and the regular shifting of officials from their current regions to new locations; (h) the "supervision" effected by the National People's Congress and National People's Political Consultative Conference; (i) pressures from public opinion—strengthened by advanced communication technologies—and all manner of internal reference materials shaping government policy decisions while fostering increased transparency; and (j) the differing perspectives of all the interacting bureaucracies leading to shifting balances of power within the government, pressuring officials to take particular care in formulating policies.[85]

Pan has been concerned about such issues for many years, since long before "the China model" became a commonly used term. In 2003, he published a *neibu* article vigorously and colorfully mocking "democracy infatuation" and denouncing the idea that China was destined to be swept by global democratization's "third wave."[86] This was a time when evidently many more people thought democratization was possible for China; thus, Pan's use of language may have reflected genuine alarm at where China was heading. He insisted that "the great democratization wave of recent years has not brought developing countries prosperity and progress"; on the contrary, "the majority of 'new democratic countries' are wracked by corruption, economic malaise, and civil war," as "the smell of blood floats through the air."[87] Pan listed ten reasons the American political scientist Robert Dahl gave for why democracy is normatively desirable, but then concluded:

Reading this list one cannot help feeling embarrassed for this formerly very serious scholar. With one stroke, he obliterates all the accomplishments of the Soviet Union and China, forgetting how "the third wave" tramples on humanity's dignity, forgetting the wars of American westward expansion.[88]

In what was clearly an adumbration of his later thinking on the China model, Pan announced that he would devote his research to mining the Chinese historical record to rediscover essentially Chinese practices and patterns that could prove useful in solving such contemporary problems as crime and corruption. He decided that the key to achieving these objectives was "to establish independent judicial organs that are *not* responsible to voters and electoral institutions";[89] if they were responsible to voters and electoral organs, they could easily become corrupt. "The 'people's democratic dictatorship' under the Communist Party's 'authoritarian leadership' reflects China's demands of the times. If this were not so, then how could this great and powerful nation accept us?"[90]

For another illustration of the functionalist, conservative logic implicit in China model formulations, we turn to a short piece contributed to the Pan Wei–coedited volume by He Xuefeng, Director of the China Rural Management Research Center at Central China Science and Technology University in Wuhan. Although most of the economists discussed in Chapter 2 (as well as proponents of the Chongqing model) denounce the so-called two-pillared system, which prevents rural residents from settling securely in the cities, He praises the system as integral to the China model's genius. The reason is that, under the two-pillared system, recent migrants to the cities can always return to the villages in the event of an economic crisis.[91] If, instead, villagers were granted ownership rights to village land and decided to sell it off before migrating, they would find themselves trapped in the cities in the event of a crisis. They would then be unemployed and in a position to cause unrest.[92]

He acknowledges that the little land to which villagers have access will never be enough for them to raise their social status. But it will be sufficient to provide them with basic sustenance—at least for 95 percent of the rural population. Rural residents also have in the villages a sense of belonging and of roots: an identity, which is difficult to put a price on but is widely recognized as all-important. On balance, "the quality of life for Chinese villagers is far higher than the quality of life facing poor people living in the cities of other developing countries."[93] All the talk about ending the two-pillared system to facilitate a shift to domestic consumption-led growth is misguided, He contends, because ending the system would result in the CCP having substantially less room for making economic policy mistakes. The two-pillared system ensures that the country can continue on its stable march to sustained development—because villagers are far less likely under the system to become troublesome elements causing urban disorder.[94] He pronounces Bo Xilai's goal of increasing Chongqing's urbanization rate from 47 percent in 2010 to 70 percent in 2020 "unthinkable." Perhaps by 2040 the two-pillared system could be dismantled, but definitely not now: "I would prefer that the speed of reform be a little slower."[95]

REMNANT LIBERALISM

In absolute terms, many people in China are calling these days for a more liberal political order: academics, journalists, NGO activists, business people, and even some Party-state officials. The problem is that few editors will dare to publish the writings of liberalization/democratization advocates in *neibu* journals—and publishing in *neibu* journals is one important (albeit not decisive) indicator that an author has some influence within the system as it currently functions and/or is trusted to convey, in general terms, a correct interpretation of reality as defined by the Party Center. As detailed in Chapter 2, countless writers call for economic liberalization and the deepening of economic reform. This seems to be far less sensitive than calling for political reform—even though as senior a figure as former Premier Wen Jiabao himself occasionally called for political reform. For example, at a press conference convened to close the March 2012 National People's Congress, Wen proclaimed that he was worried Chinese economic reforms will fail unless the country also starts pursuing political reforms.[96]

One liberal-leaning scholar who does enjoy the right to publish in *neibu* journals is Yu Keping, whose titles include Director of the Comparative Politics and Economics Research Center at the CCP's Central Translation and Compilation Bureau (a policy-oriented Party think tank); Director of Peking University's Center for Research on Chinese Government Innovation; and professor at multiple universities. Yu is perhaps best known for his 2006 essay, "Democracy Is a Good Thing," which was reproduced in a number of official outlets, including the *People's*

Daily.[97] At approximately 1,800 characters, this short essay is not itself especially remarkable. It makes a number of conventional points such as that democracy may not be flawless but is still the best political system humankind has yet to invent. What is noteworthy about this essay is that it was widely reproduced, and Yu—while holding important positions—has been free to publish other essays on similar subjects without apparent hindrance in the years since "Democracy Is a Good Thing." Apparently, the CCP's latitude of acceptance for arguments such as Yu's is wider than its latitude of acceptance for concrete, on-the-ground political experimentation. Nevertheless, the CCP's tolerance suggests that room for on-the-ground experimentation could itself expand in the future—just so long as the Party retains ultimate control.

Yu develops his "democracy is a good thing" theme in a subtle yet powerful critique of the "China model" discourse that he published in the open journal *Social Observation* in December 2010.[98] Yu goes to great lengths in this essay to praise proponents of the China model for reminding China's attentive public that whatever political experimentation the country engages in will have to be grounded firmly in real-world Chinese experience. There is no "off-the-shelf" model available from foreign countries for China to import. But Yu carefully turns the essentialism of (at least) Pan Wei's version of the China model on its head, by arguing that China's road is still open; that, in effect, the model is still in the process of being discovered:[99] "Although some typical, unique features of [the model] have already started to become apparent, our endeavors at modernization are not yet complete; we are still in the process of exploring for the 'China model' and it could be that the road of exploration will be quite long."[100] Yu's insistence that the road is open is subversive because it challenges the determinism implicit in Pan's formulation, as well as the determinism intrinsic to CCP orthodoxy. For Pan, Chinese political actors can rather easily discover the essential Chinese road by studying a carefully constructed version of history. What agency they do have can be used only to throw China off an otherwise destined—and glorious—course. But to Yu, agency is all-important and Chinese actors must exercise it diligently and courageously. Although Yu concedes that the PRC's political trajectory will unavoidably be grounded in China's concrete historical experiences, he stresses the process of open-ended discovery: the pragmatic exploration that will lead the country to a more desirable political future.

And yet, in his contribution to the *World Megatrends and Challenges China Will Face in the Coming Decade* volume, Yu makes a strikingly different case.[101] He contends in the *Megatrends* essay that democracy of some sort will eventually be inevitable for China: "We must deeply recognize that advancing democracy is an unstoppable world historical trend, the inherent logic of human development, and a core demand intrinsic to socialism."[102] Whereas Yu rejects the China model proponents' insistence that history has already predetermined China's political trajectory, he implies in the *Megatrends* essay that the trajectory *is* effectively predetermined—only by global trends, not by a (carefully constructed) Chinese history. A great Chinese civilizational renaissance may well be historically inevitable, but Yu suggests that only by following the global trend of democratization can it be achieved. What is more, the Communist Party's primary mission *must* be to help realize the renaissance: "If we fail to pursue democracy, then we are not true members of the Chinese Communist Party. Developing democracy is a road that must be taken in the great renaissance of the Chinese nation and is an historical responsibility that the Chinese Communist Party must bear."[103]

In all of his essays,[104] Yu consistently promotes liberal-democratic solutions to China's problems, and for many years his arguments have received a high degree of official tolerance. Almost certainly part of the reason is that Yu has been effective at illustrating how liberal-democratic solutions could help Party leaders to achieve their already-announced goals. For example, in 2005, Yu published a *neibu* article explaining how increasing the level of citizen involvement in governance, promoting the rule of law, affirming the Party-state's responsibility to the people, and raising the level of transparency in public policy decision making could all—in tandem with other measures—help the CCP to achieve its goal of building a harmonious society. Sounding at points like Xiao Gongqin, Yu argues that Chinese society has changed substantially with the successes of reform and opening. The new situation requires corresponding changes in politics for the country to become harmonious.[105]

Another liberal author challenging the China model (and, to a lesser extent, CCP orthodoxy) is Han Yunchuan, a professor at the Central Party School's Social Development Research Center. Writing in the *neibu* journal *Internal Reference Materials on Reform*, Han identifies five "errors in recognition" on the part of CCP cadres that block political reform:[106]

1. *The doctrine of the Chinese system's superiority.* This is the most pernicious of the recognition errors—and pointing it out seems in some ways to be an indirect rejoinder by Han to promoters of the China model, as well as the hubristic international relations analysts discussed in Chapters 5 and 6. Han notes that champions of the Chinese political system's inherent superiority claim the system is uniquely dynamic and effective. They fail to acknowledge the system's limitations and faults; they refuse to recognize that the systems of other countries might well surpass China's in performance. Promoters of the PRC-as-superior doctrine naturally reject the notion that China should pursue political reforms. Han counters that *all* Leninist systems suffer from serious institutional dysfunctions (which he does not, however, detail). This means that even if at points the Chinese variant of Leninism may seem to be functioning well, it will always revert toward a problematic equilibrium in the absence of fundamental change.[107]

2. *The doctrine that China's developmental stage requires autocracy.* This is an argument often used by those (including the authors of *China's Future Direction*, discussed earlier) seeking to justify Chinese authoritarianism. The core of the argument is that China is "not yet ready" for democracy. Before any tinkering with the political system, the Party-state must transform the economy and culture to make China more materially prosperous and culturally advanced. In contrast, Han portrays the political realm as intertwined with the economic and cultural realms, so that political reform would be *helpful* for achieving deeper economic and cultural development. In turn, deeper economic and cultural development would then assist in the effort to promote political reform. Han states flatly that "the conditions for carrying out comprehensive reform of the political system are already present."[108]

There is no reason to wait. China has exited the developmental stage at which autocracy might be justifiable.

3. *The doctrine that Chinese culture is intrinsically authoritarian.* Han acknowledges that China's authoritarian traditions pose an obstacle to successful implementation of political reform. But he finds that there have been far too many public-minded heroes in modern Chinese history willing to sacrifice their lives for democracy for anyone to argue seriously that authoritarian cultural obstacles are insurmountable. Democracy, he argues, resonates positively in Chinese culture. Where Chinese traditions are inconsistent with democracy, the country should renounce the traditions and replace them with new practices and institutions imported from democratic countries.[109]

4. *The doctrine that implementing democracy will inevitably lead to chaos* (luan). Han counters the familiar "democracy equals *luan*" argument by observing that "only with a complete and fully functioning democratic political system can a society truly be stable."[110] He raises the example of Romania in the 1980s and suggests that it was Ceausescu's refusal to reform that eventually led to the opposition becoming extremist.[111] This is a rather striking argument to make insofar as it implies that Chinese leaders who reject reform are playing with fire and might one day find themselves facing a firing squad.

5. *The doctrine that democratization could cause China to fall apart.* Some nationalists argue that, if China were to democratize, immediately it would lose Tibet and Xinjiang and that in general democracy is not a workable system for a country with "fifty-six nationalities." But Han contends that "this viewpoint underestimates the centripetal pull of the Chinese nation."[112] Having a democracy would make it easier for the Chinese nation's centripetal pull to work its magic—and would, for example, be *necessary* to achieve unification with Taiwan. Han is implicitly suggesting that Chinese elites should not delude themselves into thinking their nation has much centripetal pull now—which is why several of the fifty-six nationalities have to be coerced into remaining inside the PRC. Liberalize the political system, and coercion would no longer be necessary.

Even some figures from the business world are demanding democratization. For example, the Chairman of the China Merchants Group, Qin Xiao—who calls frequently for economic liberalization[113]—also promotes political liberalization in a *neibu* article published on the eve of the Seventeenth Party Congress (2007).[114] Qin's concerns in this article are broad ones. He phrases the core question cogently: Is there a single path of development—eventuating in democratization—that all countries, including China, must follow? Or should China hew closely to the essentially distinctive authoritarian path identified by proponents of the China model?[115] Qin notes that the dominant thinking elsewhere in the world is the former. But in China, increasingly the latter view holds sway.[116]

Qin himself emphatically rejects the China model and insists on the validity of the universal path: "China cannot possibly realize a modern transformation under a totalitarian political system," which is how he characterizes the current order.[117] Modernization requires a political transformation simply because the core values of modernism are liberty and rationality; in turn, realizing these values requires a widespread social movement motivated by the Enlightenment thinking which Qin considers to be the antithesis of authoritarian politics. As the situation currently stands, China's modernization has been stunted. It has only reached a stage that values national independence, enriching the people while strengthening the state and improving economic efficiency. The battle is therefore only partly won; now, China must pursue the broader Enlightenment agenda.[118]

Qin positions himself squarely on the side of the liberals in China's important universal values debate:[119] "The modern model created by the West—or the system of modern civilization—is a contribution to human civilization. It belongs to all of humankind."[120] Qin reassures his readers that affirming the superiority of a regime type that originated in the West should not be taken to imply that only Western democracies are consistent with modernity. After all, many countries outside the West now fully embrace democracy. For China, Qin promotes "modernity of a different kind" (*linglei xiandaixing*), "pluralistic modernity" (*duoyuan xiandaixing*), and "localization of modernity" (*xiandaixing bentuhua*).[121] But, regardless of particularistic variations, Qin insists that, in any modern society, different groups and strata must be allowed freely to express their different interests and ambitions, even granting that this will often lead to contention and conflict. Under such unavoidable conditions, "the role of the government should be to harmonize differing societal interests in accordance with the law and democratic procedures and to achieve a balance between the public's short-term interests and long-term interests."[122] Possibly, Qin allows, China at the present time—given its wrenching development process—needs to err on the side of having a strong government, though definitely not a "totalitarian" government. But ultimately, China cannot achieve economic or any other form of modernization until the CCP accepts the need to democratize. To be sure, the change can be gradual: Qin recommends "crossing the river while feeling for stones." He suggests first experimenting with liberalization in the larger cities of the East.[123]

Other proponents of political reform argue that China should begin by perfecting so-called inner-Party democracy. In December 2009, Xu Yaotong of the Chinese Academy of Governance published a notably detailed and thoughtful assessment of this problem in the *neibu* journal *Internal Reference Materials on Reform*. Xu begins by noting that at several points during the Hu Jintao years, important Party documents identified the pursuit of inner-Party democracy as a strategic objective critical to the Party's future. Inner-Party democracy is therefore already on the books as a goal the Party ostensibly values. What exactly does the concept mean?

Xu begins by enumerating the "Eighteen Rights" of rank-and-file Party members as identified over the years in a series of Party documents (which he does not specifically cite): the right to know, the right to consult, the right to manage, the right to train, the right to make suggestions, the right to criticize, the right to supervise, the right to express views in decision making, the right to elect, the right to be elected, the right to accuse, the right to file suit, the right to defend (against charges), the right to give witness, the right to petition, the right to hold one's counsel, the right to inform the authorities of an unlawful act, and the right to recall (an official) from office.[124] "Of course," Xu notes wryly, "it is one thing for Party documents to specify the democratic rights of Party members but quite another to guarantee those rights in actual practice."[125]

Concretely, he identifies four pernicious phenomena that prevent the exercise of these rights and the development of inner-Party democracy generally—despite its being (on paper) an official Party goal:

1. *The "democratic quality" of Party members is low.* Among the CCP's nearly 80 million members, both the recognition of democratic rights and the demand for them are low. Xu suggests the solution to this problem might be a propaganda-and-education campaign, in which his article would be one small but significant salvo.[126]

2. *Those trying to exercise the Eighteen Rights sometimes face attacks and retribution.* Typically, Xu explains, the exercise of democratic rights amounts to local CCP members criticizing local CCP elites. The local elites then sometimes hit back and try to get even. Xu gives the example of an unnamed Party official in Shijiazhuang who, in the late 1980s, began pointing out the corruption of local leaders; eventually, the official went so far as to implicate a provincial Party committee member. Subsequently, over the next sixteen years, the whistleblower was subjected to uncompromising retribution, including at one point being made to serve a three-year term of reeducation through labor and then afterward being pursued by people trying to kill him. Finally, in February 2003, the whistleblower obtained his victory through the intervention of unnamed higher-level officials. "This," Xu notes, "is the kind of torment that most Party members would not be able to withstand."[127] It seems significant that the whistleblower's victory came in February 2003, because that was shortly after Hu Jintao became CCP general secretary. Xu seems to be suggesting that the Hu regime did not live up to its initial promises or to the promises it made regarding inner-Party democracy in the documents it issued in later years. However, the only solution Xu offers is the suggestion that "we must establish a powerful [intra-Party] supervision mechanism" to ensure that local tyrants cannot get away with bullying Party members trying to exercise their Eighteen Rights.[128]

3. *Institutions and formal procedures for exercising inner-Party democratic rights are underdeveloped.* In fact, Xu suggests that as institutions, they are almost nonexistent. Those that do exist "are macrolevel in perspective, abstract, and tending toward existing only in principle. They lack the necessary procedures and details that would allow Party members to put them to practical use."[129]

4. *Talk may be designed as a diversionary substitute for action.* Although Xu does not say so directly, he implies in this section that there is strong demand from below for inner-Party democracy and that the Center feels pressured to respond to the demand. It does so, however, by "saying a lot about inner-Party democracy but doing very little—or even doing nothing at all."[130] Xu argues that such a strategy is not cost free for the Party Center because it invites longer-term negative consequences. Continuing to issue documents proclaiming commitment to inner-Party democracy but then not following through "will, in the end, damage the Party's prestige . . . and undermine the effectiveness of the Party's rules . . . Eventually, no one will believe Party documents or the rules specified in them, and this could lead to a legitimacy crisis and a corrosion of the Party's capacity to administer society."[131]

By definition, inner-Party democracy implies a careful walling off of liberalization from forces in society that might prove untrustworthy. It should therefore be more appealing to conservatives such as Pan Wei, who find in the China model an essential tendency for all Chinese governments, past and present, to carefully vet aspirants for government service or participation in higher-level politics. Because Party members are vetted, Pan and others suspicious of democracy *might* be expected to view inner-Party democracy as more acceptable than full-scale democratization of the kind that Yu Keping, Han Yunchuan, Qin Xiao, and silenced or imprisoned liberals evidently want. The problem is that if the liberals are right—and if Western social scientists such as Larry Diamond are right—inner-Party democracy will not be sufficient to solve the contradiction between China's increasingly pluralistic society and culture, on the one hand, and the authoritarian political structure, on the other.[132]

THE CHONGQING MODEL

The Party Center's apparent (though still not conclusively explicit) rejection of the Chongqing model—which enthralled numerous intellectuals and others in Chinese society from 2008 until Party Secretary Bo Xilai's ouster in 2012—suggests the need to spend some time examining this model for clues as to China's possible future.[133] The model may be ruled out for now, but its widespread resonance "back in the day" as well as its concrete policy successes suggest that the model could yet stage a comeback, particularly if the economy slows, the environment worsens, and/or sultanization becomes even more intolerable. The surprise return of discredited models and individuals has been a recurring theme in PRC history.

In January 2011, when Bo was still riding high, three scholars (two based in Beijing at the time, one in Chongqing) published the clearest summation yet of Bo-ist thinking and practice, a laudatory account titled simply *The Chongqing Model*. The book's authors—Su Wei (then of the National Development and Reform Commission, later of the Chongqing Party School), Yang Fan (China University of Political Science and Law), and Liu Shiwei (Chongqing Party School)—proclaim in the opening pages that Bo's Chongqing should be regarded as (1) a local development model, (2) a model for solving widely recognized problems, and (3) a model for all of China's transformation. The purpose of the book, the authors explain, is to promote the next phase of the PRC's development, by detailing Chongqing's experimentation for a nationwide audience.[134] As elaborated in the following discussion, the Chongqing model was often cast as "leftist," and its adoption in other parts of the country would certainly have led to the revival of certain hallmark Maoist practices. But it would not have flashed the country back to the 1960s, because Bo's borrowing from Maoism was selective.

Bo first arrived in Chongqing in November 2007. By early 2009, he had launched a series of activities requiring that all cadres, at every level, go down to the countryside for a short period each year to investigate social conditions and nurture relationships with poor people. The requirements of this program were quite specific: Cadres must spend at least seven days a year in poor villages, "eating, living, and laboring with the peasant masses." Newly hired and newly promoted cadres must spend at least thirty days each year doing the same. While living in the villages, cadres must spend no more than 25 yuan (about US$4) per day on all their needs, including food and lodging. (It was expected that the cadres would often live in villagers' homes.) By June 2010, 130,000 Chongqing government employees and nearly 100,000 staff members at educational, health, and other public goods–providing enterprises had taken part in the program, living or interacting with poor people in nearly 360,000 households.[135]

The authors of *The Chongqing Model* praise this experimentation: "From these activities we can better understand social conditions and popular opinions, enriching our knowledge and advancing the structure of our thought," while "strengthening the Party's connections to the people."[136] Su, Yang, and Liu claim that the experiment was smashingly successful because the cadres came deeply to understand the plight of the poor villagers, whereas the villagers developed a level of affection for the cadres heretofore reserved only for kinfolk. So thoroughly did the cadres enjoy these activities that Su, Yang, and Liu insist they will now go willingly each year to see their new "relatives." No longer will it be necessary to force them to go.[137]

The mainstream economists discussed in Chapter 2 fully share with proponents of the Chongqing model the concern that corruption and inequality are warping China's trajectory and threatening to derail the country's rise in national power terms, as well as upset prospects for continuing to improve the people's livelihood. Among socially aware Chinese, these are now almost universally shared objectives—and certainly the Party Center has embraced such objectives at least rhetorically. What made the Chongqing experimentation unique was that its promoters offered a distinctive diagnosis of the causes of corruption and inequality along with a somewhat distinctive set of solutions. Although proponents of the model accepted many of the solutions suggested by liberal economists (some examples are given in the following discussion), they also moved beyond a purely economic analysis to charge that Party members and other social elites have become corrupt in *spirit* as they slowly succumb to the enticements of money and worldly pleasures—things that poorer people are completely unable to enjoy. The solution, then, would be not only to implement many of the technical policy innovations suggested by economists but also to force Party elites to experience some of what the poor constantly suffer in their daily lives. The issue to celebrants of the Chongqing model is thus not only one of technically recasting incentive structures so that appropriate behavior can be elicited from bureaucrats and cadres or altering economic policy so that inequality can be reduced to facilitate a shift to domestic demand-driven growth. Such objectives are important, but what is of deeper importance is to reverse the rot in the governing class by revitalizing what Chongqing proponents consider to have been the best practices of the Mao era.[138]

The model is, however, a far cry from anything that might be called "orthodox Maoism." Most fundamentally, Bo while in Chongqing demanded social unity—"harmony"—rather than class conflict. The crackdown on organized crime was violent, but Bo did nothing to encourage the masses to bombard the headquarters, drag out the power holders, or beat, smash, and loot. Bo-ist "Maoism" was far more ritualistic and controlled than the real thing. Su, Yang, and Liu ask rhetorically whether the CCP should unite chiefly with the rich or the poor. A purely Maoist answer would have been "the poor," but the book's authors insist that "Chongqing demands uniting with both. We unite with the rich because we want to attract investment; we want to help and guide the nonstate economy to develop." Only by uniting with both the rich and the poor and thereby achieving social harmony "can we guarantee the Communist Party's advanced nature and strengthen its ruling position."[139] Nothing like this would ever have been suggested by Mao—at least, not after he consolidated CCP power in the early 1950s.

Bo's objective in Chongqing, then, was not to attack or bring down the Party because of its corruption, capitalism, or revisionism but instead to save it by means of a vigorous, multipronged restorationism—an objective not so different in key respects from that of neoauthoritarian political scientist Xiao Gongqin, *except* that the ultimate goal of the Chongqing leadership was never democratization. Bo sought to consolidate Party rule indefinitely, preventing both sultanization and democratization. Chongqing celebrated Communist Party rule. On June 28, 2010, Bo personally heaped lavish praise on the CCP in a speech on promoting the people's livelihood. Perhaps partly reflecting his self-identification as a princeling (son or daughter of a PRC-founding Communist revolutionary), Bo even went so far as to declare that "our Party is much greater than the Great Yu," legendary tamer of the Yellow River and godlike founder of the Xia Dynasty.[140] The chief reason Bo cited for insisting on the CCP's greatness was that the Party's efforts at improving the people's livelihood had been stunningly effective, starting as far back as the water conservancy policies launched in the 1950s by Mao Zedong. The Party and its traditions were to Bo therefore very much worth saving, and this was the point and purpose of the Chongqing model. Consolidating party rule and improving the people's livelihood were depicted as inseparable: Neither could continue without the other. Chongqing experimentation, it was hoped, "will help to strengthen consciousness of the Party's core mission and guarantee that *the more developed we become, the more consolidated and secure the Party's ruling position.*"[141] In other words, development should lead neither to the automatic democratization that some Western political scientists think follows in the wake of economic development nor to sultanistic breakdown. By following the Chongqing model, its proponents promised, China's leaders could ensure that development would lead to the consolidation or restoration of the Party's dominant, guiding role in society, after which there would be no need to fear a general reversal.

But what exactly was meant by improving the people's livelihood? First, there was the summary slogan ever-present in Chinese political initiatives: If, during the first thirty years of reform and opening (from 1979 through 2009), China stressed "money and efficiency as the chief direction," then when the Chongqing model took root nationwide, the new slogan would be "people's livelihood as the chief direction." To be sure, the new approach would build on the old one, so that trying to make money and improve efficiency would still be esteemed as noble, patriotic pursuits. Almost all provincial and local governments now focus on improving the people's livelihood—a national priority in name, at least, since the advent of the Hu-Wen administration in 2002–2003. But "the special characteristic of Chongqing is that it regards the people's livelihood problem as even more important. It takes solving the people's livelihood problem as the nucleus of its work and the direction of its development. The energy it expends on this work is greater, the measures it takes are more effective, the area of its coverage is broader, its impact is more apparent, and it receives far more attention from all social sectors."[142]

Conceptually, this meant, first, integrating the development of rural and urban areas by "smashing the two-pillared structure" (discussed in Chapter 2) through "unifying urban and rural planning, unifying basic infrastructure, unifying economic development, unifying the labor market, unifying the provision of basic services, and unifying management of the residency permit system." Hu Jintao himself "ordered" Chongqing to pursue this objective when Wang Yang was still party secretary of the municipality in the spring of 2007. Not long after Bo took over in November 2007, the Center designated Chongqing a "new special zone" and an "experimental site" for rolling out creative new policies designed to smash the two-pillared structure. At the time, only one-third of Chongqing's 32 million residents held an urban household registration certificate, and 11 percent of the population was classified as "absolutely poor," meaning that "keeping warm and eating are problems." Twenty of the municipality's forty counties were classified as "poor counties." The degree of urban–rural inequality in Chongqing was said to be even greater than that in neighboring Sichuan province.[143]

To tackle this inequality, Bo and Mayor Huang Qifan soon unveiled innovative concrete policies. First, they promoted *hukou* reform, announcing a plan to change the *hukou* status of half of Chongqing's 20 million villagers from rural to urban by 2020. In phase 1 (the time period was not specified), 3.38 million migrant workers and students—people who were already living in the urban area—would have their *hukou* status changed. Up to 7 million more rural residents would receive the urban *hukou* by 2020. Importantly, during a three-year transitional phase, candidates for the urban *hukou* would maintain their benefits in the countryside (including the right to lease a plot of land) and then at the end of the period would decide which kind of household registration status they preferred. This would alleviate the problem of villagers taking a leap into the unknown and possibly failing to secure suitable employment in the cities but then having no way to return.

The authors of *The Chongqing Model* enthusiastically celebrate this plan. Although they acknowledge that it would have left the two-pillared system intact, they insist that giving migrants to the cities the urban *hukou* could have a profoundly positive effect on labor–capital relations with important implications for all of China's future. Laborers would feel more secure in the cities and would enjoy the numerous concrete benefits that would come from urban living. Feeling more secure, the migrants' self-confidence and sense of personal worth would increase, meaning that employers would find it more difficult to exploit the migrants disdainfully or even flat-out refuse to pay their wages. The workers would, in short, enjoy more solid, reliable rights in the cities and would consequently feel more confident and "politically efficacious."[144]

Related to the *hukou* problem, Mayor Huang revealed in August 2010 that in 2008 Party Secretary Bo had approved the establishment of something most of the economists discussed in Chapter 2 would have approved: a "land coupon exchange market" (*dipiao jiaoyisuo*) designed to reduce the insecurity of villagers contemplating a move to the city. The plan would work like this: In any given Chongqing village, a rural family might use 250 square meters of land leased from the government for the family house (the structure itself). At present, if the entire family moves to the city, its members must not only return the land they farmed to the village government but must also return the house and the land beneath it. Because the villagers do not own the houses or the land, they cannot sell them as assets; therefore, they prefer to hold onto them. But, to do that, at least some family members (typically the very old and the very young) must remain in the village and use the housing while continuing to work the land.[145]

The innovation that Bo approved in 2008 would give the villagers a coupon for the land used for the house itself, which the families could then auction off in an exchange market to entities hoping to use the land for other purposes. Of critical importance, the villagers would be permitted to keep 80 percent of the selling price: a tangible asset genuinely useful to potential migrants trying to think of ways to settle securely in the city. By late 2010, approximately one billion yuan a year was flowing from urban Chongqing to the countryside in exchange for land coupons.

This, to the authors of *The Chongqing Model*, was a concrete illustration of how Chongqing policy experimentation was reducing the gap between the countryside and the city.[146]

Yet another example of Chongqing's reformism (as opposed to radicalism) was the effort to build public housing. On December 20, 2009, Bo emphasized at a municipal economic work meeting that "we want all urban and rural families to have houses in which to live." Subsequently, Mayor Huang proclaimed in his early 2010 annual work report that, within three years' time, the city would build 20 million square meters of new public housing. Huang gave his report just before the Chinese New Year. A few weeks later, the municipal government announced that the city would build 40 million square meters of public housing by 2020, half of which would be in the urban area and half in the countryside. Huang then projected in March 2010 that by 2020, some 30 to 40 percent of Chongqing's population would be living in public housing. The authors of *The Chongqing Model* claimed that Chongqing's plans in this area were far more ambitious than those of other provinces. Only Shanghai came close, but Shanghai—much later than Chongqing—set a goal of only 20 million square meters of public housing by 2020, which was still only half the area Chongqing would provide if it achieved its goals.[147]

Nevertheless, the Chongqing authorities still expected the private sector to play an important role in supplying housing: "Either completely letting the government guarantee housing or completely allowing marketization of it would be a single-track systemic arrangement that would have great flaws."[148] The thinking was that, if both private actors and the government extensively built new houses and apartments, prices would fall for all potential buyers, and the general welfare would increase. To ensure that demand remained strong—and to fulfill social objectives—Chongqing would put no *hukou* restrictions on the purchasers of public housing. It would not even restrict people from other parts of China from purchasing Chongqing public housing and coming to reside in the city. This last point was critical, because it would have given Chongqing a comparative advantage in economic development relative to other provinces and municipalities and deepen its opening to the outside world—possibly, the authors speculated, to the point that the city could come to rival Beijing or Shanghai for openness and attractiveness to foreign investors.[149] In response, other parts of China might then be forced to adopt similar liberalization policies.

Su, Yang, and Liu insist that the sanguinary crackdown on organized crime for which Chongqing became infamous would ultimately be helpful for economic development. The crackdown began on June 20, 2009 with the arrest, during a 24-hour period, of over 1,000 alleged underworld crime figures. The "high tide" of the campaign continued for four months, with the peak coming with the arrest of Wen Qiang, Director of the Chongqing Municipal Justice Bureau, on August 7, 2009.[150] Wen would be executed the following July.[151] Su, Yang, and Liu assert proudly that the crackdown caught the attention of all of China and the world. They acknowledge (albeit rather mockingly) that many people criticized the campaign-like nature of the crackdown—including the extrajudicial procedures—but they are unapologetic. They insist that corruption had become so bad in Chongqing that it amounted to a kind of attack waged on the Party by socially backward "black groups" from the business world, groups "using sugar-coated bullets." The attack "belonged in the category of political struggle; therefore, it required simultaneously using legal and political methods—'seizing with both hands'—to respond, uniting the power of the law, the masses, and public opinion together."[152] It required, in other words, a political campaign, necessitated by the nature of the struggle: Because the judicial apparatus was under attack and already corrupted, it could not be trusted to function properly. This was why Wen Qiang's arrest was celebrated and used to legitimate the crackdown.

Su, Yang, and Liu find that the campaign was overwhelmingly popular. They illustrate by providing quotations from news stories and Internet discussion posts.[153] They conclude by contending that the crackdown would have at least six long-term positive consequences for China's political future. It would: (1) help consolidate the Party's leading administrative position, insofar as it would destroy those who had corrupted the Party; (2) advance economic development, because businesses (public and private) would no longer have to devote as many resources to paying bribes or buying off extortionists; (3) create a quality environment in which upstanding citizens and their families could live pleasant and fulfilling lives;

(4) serve as a model for other parts of the country (they report that Hubei, Guangdong, Hainan, and Hunan all launched crackdowns in imitation of the Chongqing initiative); (5) nurture a new corps of outstanding Communist Party and government cadres; and (6) through exploration, lead to the discovery of a new method for organically integrating the three principles of the primacy of Party leadership, the people acting as their own masters, and the rule of law.[154]

On balance, Chongqing under Bo Xilai was boldly experimental but not in ways radically different from what the mainstream economists discussed in Chapter 2 were proposing, nor from what the Party Center continues to demand. Indeed, some of the individual Chongqing efforts are also more quietly being explored in other parts of the country. But Chongqing nevertheless stood as a model of energy, inventiveness, pragmatism, and ruthlessness in addressing some of China's most vexing problems. It did not stand as a model of liberalism or human rights protection, which is why so many observers were appalled at the model's celebration. Because Chongqing was not nearly as far out of the Party's mainstream in policy innovation as it was sometimes portrayed to be, the model—had it succeeded and been adopted elsewhere—would ironically have been a victory for the CCP and might have helped further to entrench Party power even in the midst of profound change. Ultimately, Chongqing experimentation represented a vigorous but bloody *restorationism* on the way to China's future—a pointed rejection of political liberalization but not, in all but surface respects, a return to Maoism.

CONCLUSION

China is a complex country with multiple trends crisscrossing and mutually affecting each other (sometimes positively, sometimes negatively) in what can appear to be a confusingly kaleidoscopic mosaic. Moreover, the country is continuously changing at a rate faster than most others, both on the material level and in the mentalities of contributors to public policy debates. What meaningful and reliable concluding statement, then, can we make concerning China's political-economic trajectory and how it is likely to evolve over the next ten to fifteen years? Unavoidably, social science predictions of inevitable democratization must be rejected because they fail to consider complexity and subjectivity: There are several possible roads that China could take. Still, the parameters framing and delimiting the range of likely options that emerge from the foregoing discussion do suggest a clear dynamic, if not a single road or a conclusive end point. The dynamic is that a trenchantly critical, "liberal-trending" (if the economists discussed in Chapter 2 are included) discourse seems to be combining with the vexing problems facing China's economic model—problems that have been accumulating for years and are now increasingly visible—to exert strong pressure on Party General Secretary Xi Jinping and Premier Li Keqiang to experiment with some form(s) of political and economic liberalization.[155]

At the same time, however, adamantly conservative forces rail against domestic liberalization (especially of culture, as discussed in Chapter 4) while hubristic international relations specialists demand an increasingly assertive, aggressive, or even bellicose foreign policy (see Chapters 5 and 6). These nationalistic forces appear to have the strong support of the powerful and privileged People's Liberation Army, which answers to no one in Chinese society except the highest-ranking CCP elites. Xi Jinping and Li Keqiang have, so far, oscillated in their public rhetoric and policy pronouncements, sometimes sounding relatively liberal but mostly striking a tough, nationalistic pose externally while cracking down in questionable ways (for example, by flouting legal/constitutional rules) on "corruption" (or at least some people accused of corruption) and freedom of speech. Something like a "two-line struggle" seems to be taking shape. The technocrats (especially the economists discussed in Chapter 2) and the liberals demand change; in its absence, they assert, neither the harmonious society that requires social justice nor the national rise in international power terms can possibly succeed. The technocrats and the liberals are thus implicitly pessimistic about current trends. In striking contrast, the hubristic IR specialists and political/economic conservatives think not only that there is nothing seriously wrong with China—except for the corruption and environmental degradation (which, in any case, they believe can best be addressed by strengthening rather than limiting Party-state power). They even think—some almost mystically—that the tide of history is turning in China's favor, relative to the West and Japan, so that the last thing any sane Chinese leadership would want to do is start tinkering with the current order. Instead, the order should be preserved and consolidated, and China should throw caution to the wind and start asserting itself internationally with a risk-welcoming boldness hardly imaginable even as recently as a decade ago. The "liberal"–"conservative" (any labels would fail to capture the complexity) clash in the area of Internet politics is examined in Chapter 4. The IR scholars' hubris—which completely ignores the warnings of China's economists concerning future growth prospects—is detailed in Chapters 5 and 6. The puzzle is how these two camps (which also have their internal divisions) could perceive the same "reality" in such profoundly different ways—leading to significantly different policy recommendations designed to bring about a more desirable future. The two-line split thus becomes increasingly visible, but which side (if either) will win the struggle is impossible to say. Perhaps the November 2013 "Third Plenum" document represents an effort to satisfy both sides, at least in the area of domestic policy. The confident nationalists seem currently to have a near-lock on foreign and security policy, only backing down tactically when the United States, Japan, and other actors respond to Chinese moves with a united firmness. Each line represents a different imagined national trajectory. But only one or neither can become the actual trajectory.

The New Frontier: Changing Communication Patterns and China's Transformation into a "Network Society"

FROM OCTOBER TO DECEMBER 2010, the Chinese Young Pioneers Business Development Centre—a cause-oriented enterprise (*shiye danwei*) founded in 1949 as the Zhongguo Shaonian Ertong Dui—led a group of youth- and media-oriented organizations in conducting an intensive study of Internet use among Chinese school children ages ten to eighteen. The study consisted of a large survey plus documentary analysis, panel groups, and focused interviews. The survey portion, which involved 9,884 children and 4,319 pairs of parents, was carried out in 106 different middle schools in ten provinces or province-level cities.[1] The study found that fully 77.2 percent of Chinese in this age group ("teens") use the Internet, with 77.5 percent of users going online at home and 39.5 percent of them doing so from the convenience of their own mobile phones. Half of all the kids had their first Internet experience before the age of ten. A plurality (45.1 percent) go online "about once a week," but 15.3 percent access the Internet every day. The typical Internet session for a Chinese teen lasts about two hours and consists mostly of listening to music, chatting, playing games, watching videos, and looking up materials to do homework. Still, some 15 percent of Chinese teens claim to go online regularly to read the news.[2]

This huge social development holds imponderable implications for China's political-economic trajectory and the structural evolution of Chinese society. The worldviews of today's Chinese young people when they reach maturity will be vastly different from those of their parents and grandparents. Information-enriched, young Chinese will be substantially more "knowledgeable" about the world (especially the outside world) than their parents or grandparents, even though their "knowledge" will inevitably be distorted in various ways and incomplete. The young people will also have a significantly wider circle of contacts than earlier generations. Some 23 percent of teen respondents told the China Young

Pioneers researchers that they have 50 to 100 "good friends" they chat with regularly online; 24.5 percent said they have more than 100 "good friends." These "friends" may be living anywhere in China or even outside the country.[3] Through online exchanges, the youngsters influence each other in ways not technically feasible over long distances before the Internet's wide dissemination. Most Chinese parents now believe that the Internet in general has more influence over their children than teachers do but still less than the parents themselves or the children's schoolmates.[4]

The teenagers are of course not alone: In June 2011, the China Internet Information Center reported that the number of Chinese Internet users of all ages had reached 485 million, or 36.2 percent of the population.[5] In a separate study, the State Council's News Office found that, in 2010, more than 80 percent of Chinese netizens went online for news and information (not merely to play games or to chat). The Office reported that on average, more than 3 million "items" were being accessed every day in 2010 from news sites, public-affairs discussion sites, and blogs.[6] By the end of 2010, Chinese households, businesses, and other entities in total owned about 1 billion fixed and mobile phones, with more than 70 percent of urban households also owning a home computer.[7]

For many years, scholars throughout the world have vigorously debated the implications of permanent media and telecommunications revolutions for China's developmental trajectory. Some stress how the state has lost significant control over the flow of information and images through society, with the beneficiaries including political activists locked in contention with the forces of Party-state repression.[8] Others find, in contrast, a resurgence in state strength during the 1990s and 2000s, albeit in a transformed socioeconomic setting: a furious comeback suggesting that it could be quite a long time before the Chinese public sphere becomes anything approaching genuinely liberal, with civil society groups able to use the mass media and telecommunications systems to play open, legitimated political roles.[9] Most of the West-based writers view China through the lens of long-term Western concerns regarding freedom of the press as the "fourth estate" and use of the media and telecommunications as tools for engaging in contentious politics. Building on these perspectives, the current Chinese communication scene can also be analyzed from another important theoretical perspective, that of "the network society." Sociologist Manuel Castells is the chief architect of the network society concept. He summarized its core features in 2005:

The network society . . . is a social structure based on networks operated by information and communication technologies based in microelectronics and digital computer networks that generate, process, and distribute information on the basis of the knowledge accumulated in the nodes of the networks . . . A central feature of the network society is the transformation of the realm of communication, including the media. Communication constitutes the public space, i.e., the cognitive space where people's minds receive information and form their views by processing signals from society at large . . . Societies have moved from a mass media system to a customized and fragmented multimedia system, where audiences are increasingly segmented . . . As the network society diffuses, and new communication technologies expand their networks, there is an explosion of horizontal networks of communication, quite independent from media businesses and governments, that allows the emergence of what I call *self-directed mass communication*. It is mass communication because it is diffused through the Internet . . . It is self-directed because it is often initiated by individuals or groups themselves.[10]

Crucially for understanding China, Castells finds that transformation into a network society requires profound changes in a country's economy, politics, and culture:[11]

A network-based social structure is a highly dynamic, open system, susceptible to innovating without threatening its balance. Networks are appropriate instruments for a capitalist economy based on innovation, globalization, and decentralized concentration; for work, workers, and firms based on flexibility, and adaptability; for a culture of endless deconstruction and reconstruction; for a polity geared towards the instant processing of new values and public moods; and for a social organization aiming at the suppression of space and the annihilation of time.[12]

In the 1990s, Castells portrayed the West, industrialized East Asia, Eastern Europe, and the former Soviet Union as all becoming network societies—indeed, fusing together in a single, transnational network society—in a grand historical process that began in the 1970s and would continue for decades. Castells attributed the Soviet Union's collapse to this transformation, which radically reconfigures the economy, culture, and politics—privileging certain individuals and groups as efficiencies improve but disenfranchising others as inequality worsens.

In China, where the Communist Party continues to monopolize political power and state-owned enterprises (SOEs) still dominate key sectors of the economy, the comparable transformation began much later and is at this point still in its early stages (with the endpoint uncertain). Many Chinese observers identify the severe acute respiratory syndrome (SARS) crisis of spring 2003 as a key turning point.[13] SARS led to a mushrooming in demand for information, particularly after the central and certain provincial-level governments were exposed as lying about the number of cases. In the aftermath of SARS, Chinese netizens increasingly became accustomed to seeking information proactively and circulating it to others online. At the same time, the number of people with Internet access continued to rise rapidly. This led to a second key date in the network society's development: June 2008, when CCP General Secretary Hu Jintao made a highly publicized visit to the *People's Daily* and went online to interact with netizens discussing public affairs on the paper's "Strong Country Forum" website.[14] Hu's act signaled that the CCP approved using the Internet to discuss public affairs. The Party had long promoted using the Internet for commercial purposes, recognizing the utility of decentralized, networked communication for economic growth. Following Hu's highly publicized exchanges on the Strong Country Forum, the popularity of microblogs suddenly exploded—with growth particularly rapid in 2010, which subsequently became known in China as "the year of the microblog."[15]

The comparative newness of the network society's arrival to China, along with the obvious challenges it poses to the traditional propaganda system and other tools of sociocultural control, seem to explain the liveliness of debate on the network society in Chinese *neibu* policy and professional communication studies journals. These debates provide keen insight from inside the system into the transformations China is currently undergoing as a result of the new network logic and the pressures for change it creates. The debates are the focus of this chapter. The theoretical presupposition is that even though metamorphosing into a network society constitutes an objective *material* change—comparable in important respects to becoming a more market-oriented economy— how Chinese analysts and practitioners *interpret* the metamorphosis and propose to respond to it acts as a semi-independent factor itself influencing the country's developmental trajectory. Whether the CCP ultimately chooses to accept the network society as an unavoidable new reality that might even bring substantial benefits to the country, or instead fight it or try to direct and "guide" it as an obnoxious import from the West, will make a difference for the path China takes. And, indeed, this is the major point of contention in the Chinese debates: Some analysts proclaim the network society to be positive and in any case unavoidable; others castigate it as deeply corrosive and requiring substantially tighter control and regulation. The problem is that, if Castells is right, the CCP will in the end have no choice but to relent if it hopes for China to remain globally competitive and continue to increase its comprehensive national power. Yet that would lead to the PRC's denaturing—although not necessarily its transformation into a liberal democracy. The CCP has played the primary role in nurturing China's network society into being, through both construction of the physical network and removal of the barriers to Chinese people deploying their energies and creativity to use the network effectively. Now the Party must decide whether to ride the wave with minimal resistance or try to harness it. No one can say for certain what future state(s) the wave is leading to or exactly what influence policy can have. This uncertainty combines with the enormity of the stakes involved to fuel the lively and important debate.

THE NETWORK PORTRAYED AS A
POSITIVE SOCIOPOLITICAL FORCE

In a February 2012 analysis for the *neibu* journal *Theoretical Trends*, the chairman of the board of the Jinyindao Network Technology Corporation ("JYD Online"), Liu Baohua, writes enthusiastically that Chinese society is fast becoming one in which interpersonal, face-to-face communication is inextricably linked with mediated communication, not only via the traditional mass media (radio, television, film, and print) but, more important, via the telecommunications network, which in any case is now fusing with the mass media in content and function.[16] This enormous development has the effect of changing China into a society held together and organized on a "decentered" basis—radically different from the "traditional industrial society" in which "the center propagated information to the periphery."[17] It also, however, becomes a society in which the position, role, function, and importance of the modern individual as a "subject" is increasingly problematic because individuals are in some danger of becoming mere points on a network. Liu concretely identifies "four breakthroughs" resulting from the network society's arrival to China (which he dates to the mid-2000s):

1. Society is fast entering a condition of not having a center and/or of every point becoming a center or potential center. In such a society, "information circulation is open, free, and dispersed"; the contrast with what Liu terms "the atomic age" (in which the most consequential information "radiated" from a single center) is profound. In the network society, "information recipients also become information providers; audiences demand the right to broadcast and . . . to participate directly in the processes of producing and circulating information."[18]

2. Information is now dispersed and consumed over an extremely wide geographical area; it knows no boundaries and can be copied and reproduced without limit—except, of course, for whatever information is still guarded tightly by public or private actors and prevented from even entering "network space." Once information does go online it can no longer be controlled: A defining characteristic of network space is that "it cannot be monopolized or occupied by a single force."[19] Information on the network circulates from one point to many points, from one to one, from many to one, and from many to many—in sharp contrast to the one-to-many model that characterized China in the past. This changes the psychology of Chinese citizens because no longer are they mere passive recipients of information; they can also initiate information flow. Doing this leads to a strong "sense of participating" that makes individuals feel they have "a right to express

themselves."[20] They can also autonomously create their own online virtual communities. They are no longer restricted to membership in Party-organized or Party-sanctioned communities. The old *danwei* (unit) system is gone forever. The structure and functioning of Chinese society have changed radically.[21]

3. When people in China interact online, their identities and social statuses become fluid, flexible, and unfixed. In particular—and this relates to Liu's first point—no longer are some public communicators the subjects and others the orders-receiving (and/or talked about) objects. Everyone is now a subject, and everyone is vulnerable to being turned into a talked-about object.[22] Liu stresses the former possibility—the positive, equality-enhancing aspect of network participation.[23] But as we will see in the following discussion of the views of those who want to control the network more tightly, citizens' vulnerability is also crucial: Not everyone wants to become a talked-about object, and those who do find themselves in that status often become demoralized and angry, fueling downward spirals in the civility of network discourse in a way likely to hold negative implications for politics and culture.

4. The network changes the meaning of space and time. According to Liu, there is in effect a kind of "super-high sense of mobility" among people who take part in network exchanges because they can "go" to almost any place, from any place. Moreover, there are no time restrictions as there were in the mass media era, when people would have to sit down at regularly scheduled intervals to receive news or entertainment broadcasts and/or listen to the village loudspeaker. Now, anyone in China with a "smart" mobile phone or computer can send and receive information—including "high value-added" information akin to mass media content—from almost any place in the country, at any time of the day or night.[24]

Liu concludes by stating his belief that the advent of the network society is a highly positive development for China. He thinks that it can help the country to attain "the pinnacles of political modernization," featuring: (1) what he terms the "democratization" of information exchange, (2) increased political cohesion resulting "naturally" rather than from state coercion, (3) authority that has the consent of the governed, (4) increased openness and transparency in public policy making, (5) the institutionalization of a healthy marketplace of ideas, and (6) increased public spiritedness among citizens.[25] Thus, unlike many commentators on Chinese politics, Liu does not imagine (or does not *say* that he imagines) Party-state elites trying to block these developments in the interest of maintaining power or for other purposes. Unlike Manuel Castells, Liu also does not worry about the network becoming a tool for criminals, terrorists, and others committed to value systems incongruous with liberal sociopolitical progress to sow havoc. For Liu, the network is both positive and unavoidable, with the only valid question (at least from the point of view of public opinion guidance) being "how the elites who control and regulate the central Party newspapers and other mass media will adjust the content of their own discourse to adapt to this developmental trend."[26]

Two humanities professors at the Beijing University of Posts and Telecommunications, Cheng Yuhong and Zeng Jingping, similarly stress the positive sociopolitical implications of what they call the "virtual network society" to distinguish this society from the physical network infrastructure on which it is based. Predicting that "the influence of the network on Chinese politics will only become greater . . . as participation in the network nears the point of universality," Cheng and Zeng identify three avenues by which they think the network will increasingly influence politics:

1. The network facilitates creation of "potential groups" in real-world society. People come into contact with each other on the network and exchange ideas and information. The next step for many will be to meet their virtual associates in a "geographic space" and establish on-the-ground groups.[27] Cheng and Zeng imply that these groups would almost inevitably be imbued with some degree of anti-Party ethos because the primary motivation of citizens who demand or initiate information concerning public affairs online is disbelief in what the establishment mass media are saying and rejection of the images and characterizations these media propagate.[28]
2. The network also facilitates the creation of "virtual communities." Communities are larger and less focused than groups: "The goals,

behaviors, norms, and collective consciousness of network communities are comparatively unfixed or vague while members can freely and casually float from community to community."[29] The reason they should nevertheless be considered potentially significant politically relates to the third point.

3. Reflecting political cleavages in real-world material society, virtual communities can, under certain circumstances, form virtual social groups as an expression of institutional development. This means that the members—who at first only know each other through online contact—may come, after repeated exchanges, to share common objectives and develop the capacity to act as a group, even to the point of fomenting mass disturbances. The "targets of their objectives" are often "social conflicts of interest and contradictions in real society." Or, to put it another way, "society's interest conflicts and contradictions can be reflected through the virtual network."[30] The mere existence of some social groups emerging online from virtual communities and taking an oppositional stance toward other real-world groups "can put tremendous pressure on the targeted groups," which then feel compelled to go online to defend themselves. There is a constant interplay between often acrimonious online "debates" and actions in the real world, with developments in each feeding and fueling the other.[31]

But all of this, according to Cheng and Zeng, is ultimately desirable. They argue that network phenomena promote China's "democratic political development," which they also imply is eventually inevitable.[32] Unfortunately, however, Cheng and Zeng never get around to discussing the role of the Party-state in these processes, either as a facilitator or an obstacle.[33] As with Liu Baohua, Cheng and Zeng celebrate the arrival of the network society uncritically and imply that it will lead China almost inexorably to a better political future. They certainly do not suggest, as other writers do, that the Party-state should try to regulate the network more tightly.

Another celebrant of the Internet is—perhaps surprisingly—a member of the Hebei provincial Party committee and a vice governor of the province. Nie Chenxi, writing in the *neibu* journal *Theoretical Trends*, reiterates some of the points made by Liu, Cheng, and Zeng but places emphasis on four new developments challenging the Party's efforts to guide public opinion—developments that Nie seems to regard with enthusiasm, even though they do make the CCP's governing tasks more challenging:[34]

1. As a direct consequence of the expansion of information sources, the way Chinese people think has become more complex and multidimensional. Nie finds that, in the emerging network society, Chinese people analyze and reflect on public problems from a variety of substantively diverse perspectives. In the past, he argues, Chinese people could all-too-easily be manipulated or hoodwinked by political slogans and mantras—particularly when backed by the threat of CCP violence. Today, however, China's increasingly wealthy, information-rich, and skeptical citizens insist on being *convinced* by the Party-state, through persuasion, that official claims are accurate, and that official attempts to mobilize society for political or social action are sincere rather than cynical games. Niu argues that this development will probably prove highly positive for the future of Chinese politics and society because it reflects a deepening sense of empowerment and political efficacy on the part of Chinese citizens: necessary for any future democratic experimentation to succeed.[35]

2. The network not only expands people's social relations, which itself is important. It also leads to "social concepts"—the prevailing views of society—becoming "network dependent." This, in turn, results in "people's consciousness becoming breakable, unstable, and subject to sudden change, with huge implications for the leading position of core socialist values."[36] The core socialist values are simply the values the CCP hopes to inculcate.[37] But inculcation is rendered even more difficult than it inherently is under any circumstances by the fact that Chinese people are today so distracted by all the competing messages they encounter on the network and in addition are substantially more critical than in the past. The distractions change the mentalities of Chinese people and their criticism spawns even more criticism, with the result that collective consciousness itself starts to change—to the

point that it may now already be impossible for Chinese people to become socialized to *any* set of core values. Nie states this matter-of-factly rather than in the alarmed tone adopted by some other writers (see the following paragraphs).

3. The roles of the public opinion guiders and the guided—the media workers and the audiences—are no longer separable because audiences can now themselves initiate and circulate content.[38] This is similar to the point made by Liu Baohua in the preceding discussion, but Nie emphasizes not the emancipatory implications but instead the particular difficulties the development poses for the Party's self-appointed mission to guide public opinion—difficulties that, paradoxically, could ultimately *strengthen* the Party's guiding role if the CCP can address them effectively.

4. Social objectives and social responsibilities become less clear and less certain as continuous changes appear in the relationships between long-term and short-term interests, material and spiritual interests, and individual and collective interests. This is related to the fragmentation of consciousness produced by psychological dependence on network participation. Even understanding what individual and collective interests are in any given situation becomes fraught because of the widespread perception (and perhaps reality) of growing complexity.[39]

On the horizon, Nie foresees (1) mass participation in public discussions continuing to expand, "accelerating the tendency for public opinion to become fragmented and sometimes fuel conflict"; (2) yet simultaneously, particular issues suddenly—and typically without warning—becoming the focus of nearly everyone's attention, leading to "rising temperatures" and (again) social conflict; and (3) reality and virtual reality becoming mixed together—the boundaries between them blurred—with a crucial corollary being that decentralized network communication not under any single actor's control will come to have great capacity for mobilizing social groups for public action even as the traditional mass media lose this capacity.[40]

Despite these knotty challenges, Nie is confident that the Party-state can adapt to the network society by improving the content of its traditional mass media, training media workers more effectively, and making more proactive use of the new technology. At the same time, he contends that official cultivation of the network society—partly through more energetic development of China's culture industries—would increase the PRC's comprehensive national power.[41] The connection to national power and the dynamism the network confers to society and culture appear to be the underlying reasons that Nie is enthusiastic about the network society's advent.[42]

One particular point stressed by most of those who celebrate the network society is that the new communications technologies can also be used by the government to improve its effectiveness. This would seem to be obvious, yet many officials nevertheless resist the changes or fail to seize the opportunities they present. The clearest example of a useful-for-governing network technology would be microblogs. First, a definition: In a Chinese context, Twitter-like microblogs convey messages "typically limited to no more than 140 Chinese characters"; this can include short politics-related (or other) comments, links to longer blogs, links to photographs, links to websites, links to discussion boards, and so on. China's first microblog service was Fanfou, which debuted in May 2007.[43] Take-off began a year or so later, after Hu Jintao made his June 2008 visit to the *People's Daily*: "From that point on, Party committees, governments, and leaders at all levels encouraged netizens to discuss politics and give their advice. Some leaders even invited select netizens—especially 'Internet opinion leaders'—to come and meet face-to-face."[44] At the beginning of 2010, Chinese microbloggers had registered 63 million accounts. By June 2011, the figure had soared to 195 million. This is the main reason that 2010 became known as "the year of the microblog." But the growth continued, with preliminary projections suggesting that 300 million microblog accounts would be registered by the end of 2011.[45]

One way in which Party-state entities encouraged citizen microblog participation was by establishing their own blogs. In November 2009, following an incident in which a thousand or more demonstrators took to the streets of Kunming to protest the demolition of an architecturally distinctive building, the Yunnan provincial government established the "Yunnan Microblog" to facilitate "reporting developments on a timely basis and guiding public opinion." The move attracted extensive attention, and the blog soon became immortalized online as "China's first government microblog."[46] By the spring of 2011, the blog had attracted some 120,000 followers—the most at that point for any government microblog in China.[47]

Throughout 2010, municipal-level public security bureaus took the lead in establishing microblogs nationwide, "to report information, provide services, collect clues [in criminal cases], conduct investigations, report developments in open cases, and increase efficiency in investigations."[48] By early 2011, 1,228 public security microblogs were active. Officials used them primarily in cases involving corruption, municipal construction problems, and missing or runaway children. Then on the eve of the "two meetings" in March 2011, National People's Congress representatives and Chinese People's Political Consultative Conference members opened microblogs and encouraged citizens to offer their opinions on issues concerning public policy.[49] Even the Party Secretary of Xinjiang, Zhang Chunxian, set up a microblog in March 2011, becoming the first provincial Party secretary to do so.[50] Zhang soon had 3.2 million followers and found himself dubbed by the Chinese media "the highest-ranking official in the history of blogs."[51]

Also in March 2011, the concrete usefulness of microblogs in governance became evident in the aftermath of the cataclysmic Japanese earthquake, tsunami, and nuclear power disaster. Rumors swirled throughout China—especially along the eastern seaboard—that the country's salt supply would soon become contaminated by radiation. This led to panic buying, shortages, and price increases. Announcers on traditional mass media news broadcasts solemnly denied the rumors, but this had little effect. Finally, on March 20, the government decided to use official microblogs to mock and ridicule the rumors—working inside the network. Evidently because information received through the network is viewed in many circles as more credible than information received through the traditional mass media (and possibly also because of the sheer power of ridicule), the rumors faded, and the Party-state learned a valuable lesson about how to use the new communications technologies to achieve governance goals.[52]

There is a problem, however, with this kind of successful Party-state adaptation: It may delay recognition on the part of China's leaders that the network society is something qualitatively different from what China had in the past. In other words, a short-term adaptation might actually impede successful long-term adaptation. This is suggested by the views of a Nanjing municipal propaganda official who analyzed government microblogs for an article in *Modern Communication*. Cao Jingsong—identified as a vice-minister (*fu buzhang*) of the Nanjing Municipal Party Committee Propaganda Department—was visiting Fudan University's School of Journalism as a postdoctoral fellow when he published what began as another enthusiastic celebration of microblogs recommending new thinking by the authorities but then quickly dissolved into something more conservative and familiar. Cao calls for flexibility on the part of officials, for active recognition of the distinctiveness of microblogs as new media, and for enlivening information content in official pronouncements. But his ultimate recommendation is not for the Party-state to submit to engaging in online dialogue with netizens. It is instead for the authorities to find creative new ways to guide netizens more effectively. Perhaps overlearning the lesson from the squelching of the contaminated salt rumors, Cao lists as the primary potential function of government microblogs their usefulness in setting the record straight when rumors fly during crises. He does say that blogs can be used to meet popular demands for more accurate and higher-quality information, but his ultimate objective is to manipulate netizens' thoughts and perceptions more effectively. Cao even finds that microblogs are useful for social intelligence gathering because they

. . . allow the government to penetrate the base more deeply and better understand complex social psychology and social contradictions. They let average people feel that they are respected ["feel" rather than actually "be" respected] and improve the people's understanding of the government's work . . . [while] promoting harmonious relations [between officials and the people].[53]

In a somewhat contradictory article published later, Cao criticizes the view that propaganda can be effective in cultivating whatever kind of government image the Party-state might desire.[54] Cao charges that some public policy analysts still assume the mass media can flood the airwaves and print with positive stories about the government and that this will automatically result in the government's image improving in lockstep. Such a view may or may not have been valid in decades past, but Cao argues that it cannot be taken seriously today. Chinese citizens now have access to many alternative sources of information, and they assess this information critically and comparatively, sharing their observations with others both through the network and interpersonally. In this context, the propaganda that the Party-state circulates cannot be too far removed from what citizens already believe. It must be close to preexisting perspectives and reasonably candid; otherwise, Chinese people will reject the state's claims out of hand and come to regard later propaganda initiatives with heightened suspicion. The only solution, Cao contends, is for the Party-state to improve government performance so that it becomes more consistent with the image of the government that the leaders hope to cultivate: "When popular opinion is unable to accept government decision-making, the government should quickly adjust, choosing instead policies whose content the public will broadly accept . . . This is the way to craft and uphold an image of the government as working for the people."[55] The communication dynamics of the network society in this way *compel* the government either to become more responsive and effective in meeting people's real-world needs or else pay the costs associated with ineffective communication appeals and steadily declining legitimacy.

Many other writers agree with the claim that the network society is in effect altering the balance of power between state and society. One such writer is Wang Yukai, a professor at the State Council's Chinese Academy of Governance. Wang—who, based on his job, is presumably in a good position to observe bureaucratic behavior—finds that microblogs, in particular, are at least moving China in a democratic *direction*; they have this effect by altering the practice of governance through three different avenues:[56]

1. By facilitating information exchange and the mobilization of public opinion, microblogs allow groups and individuals in Chinese society to exercise more effective "supervision" over government officials, who, in turn, now imagine themselves to be—or potentially to be—working

constantly under the watchful eye of Chinese netizens: something like "panopticonism" in reverse (although Wang does not use this term).[57]

2. Realizing the fact of network supervision—for example, the possibility of having one's photograph taken while out sporting a superexpensive watch, after which the citizen-photographer then circulates the photograph through the Internet—officials slowly come to realize they must change their entire attitude toward relations with the public; they must redefine the role of a PRC bureaucrat to adapt to the network society. Such profound attitudinal changes cannot come overnight, but Wang finds officials increasingly realize they must fundamentally reform their approach toward dealing with the public as well as managing the technical side of designing and implementing policy. Taking steps to avoid even the appearance of corruption is only the starting point. Officials are also becoming more conscious of the need to make certain that policies are genuinely responsive to people's needs—the only reliable path in the age of decentralized information exchange to convincing citizens that the government "truly puts the people's interests first." Reality must increasingly match the slogans.

3. Consequently, network opinion mobilization has the effect of pressuring government officials to render their policy making "more scientific, democratic, and law-abiding," while also motivating them to vet potential policies more carefully for errors and loopholes—gaps which, if exploited, could ignite social fury.

Despite his professed optimism concerning these political and administrative trends, Wang concludes on a note of worry and conservatism that "for this positive force of public opinion to have structure and be of high quality, it must be guided carefully and managed" by Party-state propaganda officials.[58] In particular, online behavior "that centers on taking advantage of citizen participation to spread rumors or commit crimes must be sanctioned rigorously in accordance with the law."[59] Of course this presents a conundrum because the same class of officials under pressure from public opinion would then sit in judgment of that opinion and wield the power to decide whether it "has structure," is "of high quality," and is "in accordance with the law." Because Wang tacks this section onto the end of an article that otherwise expresses an enthusiastic optimism about the network society, one possibility is that he is making the statement to appease relatively conservative elements in the leadership who might read a *neibu* article. If that were the case, Wang's felt need to appease would suggest the limitations of the Party-state's willingness or ability to adapt flexibly to the new communications ecology. On the other hand, if he sincerely believes the Internet must be "guided and managed" more tightly by the Party-state, Wang himself could be said to exemplify the CCP's resistance or perhaps its sheer inability to recognize the fundamentally novel and therefore difficult-to-model operational code of a network society.

Microblogs are particularly praised or criticized for creating "public opinion storms": generating discussion about "hot topic issues" that can sometimes lead to mass incidents. A study conducted by the Shanghai Jiaotong University Public Opinion Research Office found that, in 2010, microblogs played a critical role in conveying information and mobilizing discussion on fifty-eight of seventy-two (81 percent) "comparatively influential public-opinion hot-topic issues," and directly catalyzed eight of the seventy-two (11 percent).[60] Another study—by the People's Daily Internet Center Office of Public Opinion Supervision—concluded that the news topics most likely to become "hot" to the point of producing a storm include a long list: officials, the police, municipal management officers (*chengguan*), small businesses, migrant workers, housing prices, and consumer price inflation.[61] Among these, the top two issues most likely to cause "explosions" are (1) conflicts between government officials and the people, and (2) conflicts between labor and management. The underlying reason, the authors of the study suggest, is rising social injustice, which was particularly visible in 2010 because of soaring house prices.[62] The authors state frankly (albeit in a *neibu* publication) their belief that citizens would be much less likely to use the network to foment dissatisfaction and unrest if the government enjoyed a higher level of legitimacy. They visualize the network in a larger political and socioeconomic context and recommend regulating it with a lighter touch. They think the network could be useful as a tool for helping the Center to manage misbehaving lower-level cadres by putting pressure on them. They even go so far as to suggest that, if left alone, opinions expressed in network discourse would reach a kind of balance or equilibrium—perhaps analogous in some ways to what earlier generations of Western scholars imagined results in liberal-rational marketplaces of ideas.[63]

THE CASE FOR TIGHTER CONTROL

Yet in sharp contrast to the image of a marketplace of ideas that could be leading China toward democratic politics, many Chinese observers portray the Internet and broader network as a Hobbesian zone of chaos and verbal violence destroying norms of civility and demoralizing the citizenry. They present the network, in fact, as a space eerily reminiscent of China during the Cultural Revolution—although few ever make the analogy explicit, at least not in print. These observers consequently reject celebration of the network society (they regard celebration as naïve romanticization) and call for tough regulation and control.

In an August 2011 article for *Modern Communication*, Professor Gu Liping—the Party Secretary of Nanjing Normal University's School of Journalism and Communication—offers three illustrations of how online communities are "rebellious" and viciously destructive:[64]

1. *Kidnapping.* By heaping unwarranted shame on certain public figures—such as business leaders who, some netizens think, have not donated sufficient money to support worthy causes—virtual communities sometimes compel people to do what they would otherwise prefer not to do and have no obligation to do. The communities in this way create a kind of mob mentality that leads to innocent people being judged guilty of "crimes" in the absence of dispassionate procedures and forces them to pay restitution for the crimes before securing "release."

2. *Character assassination.* Because of the often anonymous nature of virtual communities, individuals who in real life might be polite and unassuming sometimes "go wild" online and let fly with rants—heaping exaggerated and unjustified criticism on guiltless public figures. A related pattern of behavior in this category is circulating true information about targets under attack but information that the targets would

much prefer to remain private, such as their personal health status, financial situation, sexual proclivities, address or telephone number, and so on. Any citizen can be targeted for the release of such private information. All that is needed is someone holding a grudge and having access to the tools necessary to abuse the network.

3. *Negative emotionality.* Gu finds that people falling into negative or irritable moods often vent those moods openly and without restraint online—and they frequently take some hapless innocent person as a target. Gu calls this "network violence." He argues that it leads to even more people developing negative attitudes and expressing them publicly, to the point that a downward spiral soon develops and online discourse becomes poisonous. Gu worries that such discourse will warp the minds of (in particular) young Chinese who grow up on a diet of Internet vitriol.[65] He makes the case that if the Party-state were to adopt a fully laissez-faire attitude toward network management—as proponents of the communications revolution as an unalloyed positive force recommend—China would sink into a pit.

Gu articulates three reasons for virtual communities' claimed destructiveness:

1. Given the anonymous nature of much online participation, social restraints fail to work as effectively as in real life. Inside the network is "a legal and moral vacuum" in which "extreme liberalism" prevails: freedom in the absence of effective regulating norms.[66]

2. A "herd mentality" (*cong zhong xinli*) develops online, probably because of the combination of anonymity and the sense of having safety in numbers. The result is that people who collect in angry virtual communities often develop an exaggerated sense of power rooted in a self-righteousness mentality. This leads them to become heedless of the dangers associated with confrontation. On the network, "it is easy for individuals to lose their egos and self-control, and even easier for them to display their irrational, animal-like side."[67] A liberal public sphere requires citizens to be rational if it is to function effectively in support of a democracy. If citizens are instead fundamentally irrational and "animal-like," then clearly, according to Gu's logic, they must

continue to be disciplined and guided by the only reliable source of modern rationality in China: the Party-state.

3. Internet opinion leaders sometimes intentionally promote nasty behavior while followers gladly take it up. Dehumanizing again, Gu quotes without citation an anonymous "French scholar" as having once proclaimed that "any time any kind of animal forms a group, it will willingly subjugate itself to the control of a leader."[68] Gu contends that when the centralized mass media dominated China, social opinion leaders emerged logically from among people with credentials and justified social status and who often made media appearances. But in today's network society, opinion leaders tend to be "nonprofessionals, or from the grassroots."[69] These individuals are gifted only at oversimplifying complex problems by reducing them to easily understood and distorted claims—useful primarily for agitation. Network opinion leaders do not resemble the responsible editors of the mass media era: professionals who supervised journalists and directed them to cover genuinely important stories solely in the pursuit of truth and clarity. Network opinion leaders simplify and inflame for the purpose of satisfying their own selfish and often perverse needs and desires.[70]

Some of the writers who characterize the network as an irrational zone of Hobbesian contestation point to *rumors* as a central manifestation of the problem—including the rumor concerning the salt supply becoming irradiated in March 2011. Jiang Shenghong, a researcher at the Tianjin Academy of Social Sciences Institute of Public Opinion Research, analyzed the circulation of rumors in an April 2012 article for the *neibu* policy journal *Leadership Reference*.[71] Jiang found that, in the one-month period from mid-March to mid-April 2012, "relevant departments" were forced to deny and contain the damage caused by 210,000 "rumor-laden information messages" (not necessarily 210,000 different rumors).[72] The ubiquitous rumors flourishing inside the network are problematic because they "damage citizens' interests; disturb social order; instigate mass panic; influence the public's trust in government, society, and political institutions; undermine China's international image; and easily become a factor causing social turmoil and threatening public peace." Jiang gives as an example a rumor of March 2012 that gunshots were heard one night in Beijing as troops entered the city to resolve the factional political struggle involving Chongqing Municipal Party Secretary Bo Xilai.[73] Jiang recognizes that rumors similar to this one also flourished in China prior to the advent of the network society, but he stresses that the network increases the number of such rumors and the speed with which they can diffuse to huge audiences, thus magnifying their consequences exponentially.[74]

Jiang identifies nine causes of network rumors, which collectively might be read as an indictment of China's transformation into a network society:

1. In a time of social transition, uncertainty and a sense of insecurity among some people are only natural—especially when there is no denying that bad things do happen in China. Such a setting provides a hotbed for rumor circulation.[75]

2. The Chinese people suffer from a deficiency of scientific knowledge. This renders them ill equipped intellectually for rejecting preposterous assertions. Yet people do nevertheless *believe* in "science"—almost religiously—so that if rumormongers clothe their stories in pseudoscientific garb, the rumors will seem more credible.[76] Although Jiang may be factually correct in his assertion (though he supports it by providing only anecdotes, not evidence), the undercurrent in his suggestion is that Chinese people are almost childlike (although not animal-like, as Gu Liping suggested in the preceding paragraphs)—and, consequently, incapable of functioning as rational adults in a liberal pubic sphere. The people require the modern, rational Party-state to tutor and guide them.

3. The government's approach to information sharing is insufficiently timely and transparent. Here, Jiang—who encourages government officials to make more active use of microblogs—departs from the harsher critics of network phenomena by acknowledging that the Party-state's practice in the area of information management is partly responsible for rumor circulation. When government-provided information is sparse or seems to be obviously inaccurate, people will naturally engage in "blind guessing" about issues that concern them. The government is also at fault for not keeping pace technologically with

society's savvy network users, who continually think of new ways to evade state controls. In addition, laws and regulations for managing information flows are typically behind the times, which makes it difficult to pin the legal costs and consequences of (false) rumors on the particular people or groups who initiated their circulation. Ineffective governance in this area then further emboldens rumormongers in a downward spiral.[77] (Many critics use the "downward spiral" metaphor to suggest where the Internet is leading China.)

4. Relatedly, "the falling public credibility of the government has caused the public's lack of trust to strengthen."[78] The statement is circular, but from the context Jiang appears to be suggesting that falling public credibility fuels rumors—because people distrust government-provided information. Some of the rumors then further worsen the government's credibility in a vicious cycle—or again, a downward spiral.

5. Under the control of the Party's propaganda apparatus, the traditional mass media still have the primary responsibility for dispelling rumors by denying them and presenting the official line on whatever issue is at stake. The mass media may undertake this task energetically, but they have no ability to control information exchanged through the network. Particularly when rumors expand from the Internet to the telephone network, there is effectively no stopping them until people can be convinced (or they decide for themselves) that the rumors are not credible. This is not easy when the Party-state and its mass media are widely perceived as being incompletely honest.[79]

6. Owing to their weakened commitment to discipline in comparison with decades past, Party members and cadres sometimes themselves initiate and circulate rumors as a means of puffing up their own image and self-esteem. A minority of Party members and cadres like to use text messaging to transmit "secret news" that they sometimes acquire from illegal publications originating in China or abroad: "At dinners and cocktail parties they will recklessly discuss, recklessly inquire, and recklessly transmit rumors acquired directly from other people or the Internet." This includes secret information concerning China's top leaders.[80] The secular weakening of Party discipline thus interacts with the advent of the network society to allow information

the Party would prefer not to circulate—and/or that may be false—to flow freely to the point it quickly saturates society.

7. Once Internet opinion leaders, in particular, endorse a rumor, suppressing it can prove almost impossible even if Party-state officials go online expressly for the purpose of denying it. Embedded in the network society is a hierarchical structure of opinion leaders and followers: a structure that emerged spontaneously and "democratically" insofar as followers willingly chose to accept the leaders. When opinion leaders endorse a rumor, the rumor spreads more widely and quickly and with more damaging social consequences. The question then becomes how best to handle the opinion leaders themselves, with the three modal choices being to suppress, malign, or co-opt them. All three tactics are used at various times, but it is never easy to predict the consequences—which sometimes backfire.[81]

8. Occasionally, businesses mobilize people to circulate rumors in pursuit of their commercial interests. For example, they might leak information suggesting that a competitor's products are faulty or tainted. This need not have direct political consequences, but it can fuel panic buying, price increases, and an outraged sense of injustice on the part of the targeted, victimized businesses.[82]

9. "Western hostile forces fabricate and utilize all kinds of rumors to step up their efforts to Westernize and split China," even as Western political leaders "bloviate about 'Internet freedom.'" Jiang repeats the often-heard example of CNN and other Western news media "issuing repeated twisted reports" about the Tibet uprising of March 2008.[83] Here, the obvious question invited by Jiang's assertion—a question raised by his indictment of rumors more generally—is whether the information circulated by CNN and other foreign news media, governments, and NGOs should be considered "rumors" or instead "facts the Party-state's propaganda apparatus would otherwise suppress for dubious reasons."[84]

Underlying all of the concerns about rumors, character assassination, chaos, and the like appears to be a strong conviction in some quarters that the Party-state is *losing control* (to the extent that it ever had substantial control) over the construction of Chinese people's values, norms, and be-liefs. This seems to parallel a concern that the Party is losing control in other realms, too—particularly the economy. In a September 2011 *neibu* analysis, Liu Ruisheng, a researcher in the Chinese Academy of Social Sciences School of Journalism, presents the two forms of hemorrhaging control—over the ideological and the material—as intertwined.[85] Identi-fying the network and the new media as becoming "the most important carriers for constructing social values," Liu finds four chief problems fac-ing China's governing elites as they attempt to cultivate socialist culture under today's radically transformed conditions:[86]

1. The proliferation in new social roles combines with the growing gap between rich and poor to cause a reduction in the willingness of PRC citizens to accept core socialist values. Instead, motivated by a soul-less utilitarianism, they fall into a pattern of worshipping money and indulging in consumerism. Some "special interest groups" cynically promote these tendencies so that they can reap material benefits. Nat-urally, all of this becomes magnified and takes deeper root (particu-larly among young people) as a result of reinforcement by network communication.[87]

2. International relations enters the picture because the CCP must strug-gle to construct its new socialist values "even while it is operating in a condition of being surrounded by American-style values and capi-talist ideology."[88] The CCP's task, Liu believes, is rendered substan-tially more difficult by "the fact" that American and other Western multinational communications and entertainment giants dominate the world's media, including the Internet. Until China can strengthen its own culture industries to the point where they can compete effec-tively with those of the West, there will be no stopping the flood of pernicious Western values into China via the network. Unlike ultra-conservatives, Liu does not seem to think that *all* Western values are inconsistent with core socialist values, but he does think that some of them certainly are. Liu thus frames the problem in terms of nation-states' comparative levels of "discourse power" (an issue discussed in greater detail in Chapter 6).[89]

3. In addition to foreign "hostile forces," there are, inside China, commercial websites, network opinion leaders, hosts of Internet community discussion groups, microblog managers, and individual netizens who act collectively as "anti-China, anticommunist forces" and who use the new media for the targeted purpose of sabotaging the CCP's vast array of sociopolitical objectives, including the inculcation of core socialist values. Less severe critics find that the sheer multiplicity and cacophony of voices inside the network—along with the cynicism of so many network users—are the primary reasons the traditional mass media now find it so difficult to cultivate core socialist values.[90] But Liu contends that, rather than characterizing network discourse as chaotic and cacophonous, it should instead be viewed as *structured* on the basis of a systematic and coherent bias against the CCP. What is more, the groups and individuals articulating this bias possess an awesome degree of "broadcasting power," which they use effectively to subvert the mission of building socialism with Chinese characteristics.[91]

4. The system and methods for disseminating the CCP's core socialist values (which Liu never defines explicitly) are shot through with shortcomings. Liu identifies two such problems as particularly damaging: (a) unlike what he perceives to be the case in the United States, China has no national strategy for constructing and disseminating core values; and (b) whereas the United States is talented at concealing its core values in social science theories, education, religion, and entertainment, China is clumsy and inept, typically foregrounding the ideology by placing it on the surface in a way that turns audiences off.[92]

Yet, perhaps surprisingly, Liu argues that the solution to these problems is for the CCP to *refuse* to change to any significant degree. He recognizes that many people think China should reform or even jettison its ideology and political system to adapt to the increasingly global network society. But Liu counters that "this is an extremely dangerous viewpoint considering its likely consequences for Communist Party governance and social stability." He calls instead for the CCP to "fully utilize the advantages of the Chinese political system" (evidently, its authoritarian nature) to take the initiative and "adjust the Chinese social structure and economic development model" so that the network and the economy "adapt to our ideology," rather than the other way around. Eventually, this would lead to social groups identifying positively with the ideology, after which the use of coercion would no longer be necessary.[93]

Liu professes confidence that this sort of bending of network and market to accommodate ideology can be accomplished. He gives three reasons:

1. The 2008–2009 GFC, he thinks, dealt a serious blow to the West, whereas China emerged from it economically stronger than ever.[94] One consequence is that people in China and throughout the world now celebrate China's "socialist model." The CCP can take advantage of this development to "step up construction of an effective and comprehensive system for constructing and circulating core socialist values."[95]

2. The traditional "mouthpiece" and "eyes and ears" functions of television, radio, film, and print can be resurrected and restored if the media will only expend more time and effort trying actively to help Chinese people solve their real-world, practical problems. Indeed, the media have been engaging in more such activities during recent years, with the result that citizens now view television, radio, film, and print with a greater fondness and respect than in the not-too-distant past. If the outlets could think of newer and even more creative ways to demonstrate their practical usefulness, they would also be in a position to inculcate core socialist values more effectively, counteracting the network's corrosive and demoralizing influence.[96]

3. The Party-state, meanwhile, should vigorously exercise its capacity to (a) tighten control over commercial websites, which Liu thinks have acquired enormous and unjustified influence over Chinese popular culture; (b) hold competitions among media workers to encourage creativity in the methods of disseminating core values—Liu acknowledges that the current methods are often too dull; (c) "guide and protect" online nationalists more effectively—nationalists being useful in the cultivation of socialist values because they tend to be left-wing (in the special Chinese sense); and (d) strengthen audience research so that propagandists can better understand people's psychology and

the conditions under which they are most likely to accept values inculcation. This would allow propaganda messages to be crafted more intelligently and effectively.[97]

Other conservative writers are substantially harsher in tone and refuse to recognize—as does the comparatively sophisticated Liu—that the advent of the network society presents the CCP with unprecedented new challenges in governance. A good example of such a conservative is Li Hong, professor of politics and law at the Communications University of China. Li warns in a vitriolic contribution to *Modern Communication* that if the CCP fails to rein the network in, the same "tragedy" that befell the Soviet Union in 1991 could devastate China. Li considers that undisciplined mass media became a "material and spiritual force" contributing causally and powerfully to the Soviet Union's collapse. He worries that the same thing could happen to the PRC but offers as a solution only three time-worn policy recommendations: prevent U.S. cultural subversion, use the media to cultivate core values among the people, and strengthen teaching and research on the connection between mass media and politics. Li offers no assessment of how these objectives could be attained in the new networked environment.[98]

Somewhat similarly, Huang Weixin and Li Lin, of Qinghua University's School of Communication and Journalism, denounce the new situation in a November 2011 article: "Everyone is worried" about public communication in China because the situation today "is chaotic and confused." It is a challenge to social management, cultural construction, and political stability alike. Huang and Li complain that "a few rightist intellectuals" are taking advantage of the situation by promoting "anti-Party, antisocialist, and anticommunist beliefs" in the form of "Western democracy, liberalism, imperialism, and capitalism."[99] Media workers are "mostly rightists" who, while scheming to promote liberalization, denigrate China's glorious history and even malign the reputation of "the national founder," Mao Zedong. Such people write and act as if, in the sixty-plus years of PRC history, "everything before the Third Plenum of the Eleventh Central Committee [December 1978] was darkness and everything afterward light."[100]

Huang and Li are clearly frustrated and angry, but they offer no solutions for the problems they perceive. This would be difficult because they are angry at so many things: the CCP, for putting economic construction above cultural construction; the West, for introducing nihilism and liberalism to China while monopolizing global discourse power; and more. They are angry at very broad trends in history but vent their frustrations by denouncing the communications system. It seems strongly likely—as many Chinese commentators perceive—that the new networked structure of the system does have significant causal consequences for politics and culture. That, indeed, is a key presupposition of this chapter. But, on another level, the network simply reflects content or conveys messages relating to or servicing larger historical trends. In this situation, Huang and Li can demand only that the CCP recognize the problem of undesirable communications content and get tough.[101] They cannot, however, explain exactly how getting tough could succeed given the logic of network functioning and the CCP's broader strategic objectives, which center on the quest to increase comprehensive national power.[102]

Some other writers dislike the Internet because of the platform it provides for extreme Chinese nationalists to articulate poisonous views and disseminate them to others. A good example of this kind of critic is Wang Jun, associate professor of international relations at the Central Nationalities University. In an October 2010 article in *World Economics and Politics*, Wang first concedes that Internet nationalism helps to expand the space for civil society to influence foreign policy: He seems at pains to prove that he is fully aware of the argument that the Internet can be a force for democratic political change. But he stresses that because nationalism increases tensions between states, Chinese foreign policy elites could never accept Internet discourse as a constructive input to the foreign policy-making process. Consequently, the rise of Internet discourse to high visibility has had the unintended consequence of *impeding* Chinese progress toward democratization. It would be very dangerous for China to get into serious conflict with foreign countries over issues such as the Diaoyu Islands dispute.[103] Yet Internet nationalism drives China precisely in this direction. For this reason, Internet nationalism and the networked public sphere more generally are widely (and correctly, Wang thinks) viewed as forces that must be contained if China is to achieve its developmental goals. Wang clearly sympathizes with those who contend that the Internet is not a platform for encouraging rational debate. He argues that opinions expressed online must therefore be managed, guided, channeled, and/or suppressed by the Party-state—but for the ultimate goal of establishing a more democratic political system and maintaining cooperative relations with foreign states.[104]

Other authors stress that the advent of the network society is problematic because of the ways in which it complicates the CCP's efforts to impose a Chinese identity on "minority nationalities." The rate of Internet and telephone penetration is lower among ethnic minority groups than it is among Han Chinese, but the rate is higher than before and is increasing at a rapid pace. Massive penetration does not in any case seem necessary to activate network linkages among many minority nationalities (within their own groups) because interpersonal networks already flourish beyond the control of CCP cadres.

A Chinese Academy of Social Sciences study group assessed the problem in Xinjiang for a January 2012 *neibu* article.[105] The point of departure was that in 2005 the CCP went on the offensive against "illegal cultural organizations of a religious nature" in Xinjiang but appears to have achieved only mixed success. The study group's task was to find out why and to make recommendations for improvements.

The group discovered that the CCP's primary strategy has been to expand the number of Chinese "cultural stations or offices" (*wenhua zhan* or *shi*) in every county, township, and village of the province.[106] In this, at least, the Party has been successful: The stations and offices are now abundant. However, they (1) lack sufficient high-quality "software" (for example, television programs or films that people actually want to watch, including those with religious content) and (2) are poorly managed. For these reasons the Party has still not been able to "seize the front" in the war to control Xinjiang's culture construction.[107]

On average, the study group notes, each township or village in Xinjiang has 2.5 mosques and one cultural station or office. Most mosques "are used frequently and are managed well" but not so the stations and offices. The "problem," according to the group, is that the mosques serve multiple cultural roles—even serving as places where community disputes can be resolved—and enjoy a legitimacy in these roles deeply rooted in history. From the CCP's perspective, socioeconomic modernization—including the advent of what became the network society—was supposed to solve these "problems." But instead, they seem to be getting worse:

In conducting our investigation and research, we found that traditional culture is especially lively among all of Xinjiang's minority nationalities. Owing to the fact that most of these cultures are closely related to religion and popular culture, the people of minority nationalities frequently find it difficult to make correct assessments, which . . . to a great extent weakens the government's efforts to lead the people to a healthy cultural life. This is especially prominent in south Xinjiang, where large groups of Uighurs live. Many people in south Xinjiang villages operate outside the "mainstream social life" permitted or promoted by the government.[108]

The solution—"what we urgently need to do at the present"—is to "find a point of overlap between the newly established public culture infrastructure [the stations and offices established since 2005] and the traditional cultural infrastructure [the mosques] to achieve an integration of their functions."[109] This, in turn, would require three moves:

1. Switch the focus in CCP cultural construction from hardware (the stations and offices) to software (films and television programs). This recommendation is notable insofar as it suggests a lingering belief in the power of mass media to change a group of people's mind-sets rather easily—or in other words, that the new network society makes little difference. Yet it seems strongly likely that telecommunications network logic is interacting with "traditional" cultural network logic to render the Party-state's work substantially more difficult than in the past.[110]

2. Develop a "new road" in culture management by "guiding the mosques into gradually adapting to the needs of socialist modernization and development with Chinese characteristics." Concretely, this would entail, among other steps, physically relocating the cultural stations and offices from their current locations inside village Party commit-

tee headquarters (not exactly inviting places for most Uighurs) to right next door to the mosques. At the same time, because women and children are not allowed inside the mosques, the CCP could "invite" teachers and lecturers to visit the cultural stations and offices to explain to women and children the basic knowledge associated with CCP-approved religion. The teachers and lecturers could also produce handbooks of basic knowledge so that women and children would be less attracted to underground publications produced and circulated by "extremists."[111]

3. Recognizing the positive contributions that Islam can make to Xinjiang's socialist Chinese modernization, act respectful toward the religion and refrain from attacking it head-on. Concretely, for example, the Party should abandon its policy of blocking retired Uighur cadres from taking part in religious activities when they return to their villages. Instead, the Party should encourage the retired cadres to participate in the activities as a stratagem to increase their local prestige. The cadres would then be in a better position to serve as intermediaries and opinion leaders who could instruct villagers in the realities of the CCP-dominated world outside, while seeming to do so from the inside—the side of the villagers. As the study group summarizes this recommendation: "Use the retired cadres' enlightenment and knowledge to influence the villagers; let them become policy interpreters and cultural activity leaders."[112]

Whether the CCP succeeds in its effort to resocialize Uighurs, Tibetans, and other "minority nationalities" into the ideology it seeks to impose is obviously a critically important question for the PRC's future. The CASS study group evidently spent a great deal of time and energy trying to understand the situation on the ground in Xinjiang before making policy recommendations. The group's assessment—though not surprisingly colored by the expected biases—is more nuanced than the typical assessments of Xinjiang or Tibet problems published in Xinhua reports or in the pages of the *People's Daily*. But, in failing to recognize the current and potential influence of network technologies on identity development, the study group is surely overlooking a critical piece of the puzzle. This would mean that the CCP is likely to be surprised and frustrated by minority nationalities repeatedly in the years ahead, ensuring that occasional violent crackdowns become a permanent part of the landscape. Xinjiang may be particularly explosive because petroleum and natural gas are expected to be piped over it from Central Asia and the Middle East and because the province has its own energy reserves, so critical to China's continued economic growth and its rise in comprehensive national power.

CONCLUSION

With China becoming a network society, governance has unavoidably changed—even as some commentators resist the change and a few go so far as to refuse to recognize the newness of the network society's challenges. The Chinese media can no longer make claims, assertions, and observations without thinking very carefully about the relationship between these statements and reality as perceived by people in society. The "linked-in" Chinese citizen of the twenty-first century is no longer predisposed to believe or even act as if she or he believes official claims, assertions, and observations; today, the Party-state must *persuade*. Undoubtedly in the past, many—possibly most—Chinese people never truly *believed* much of what the CCP was stating, but they were compelled to act as if they believed; this, in turn, reinforced the conviction of ruling groups that they could get away with claiming almost anything through the media, no matter how divorced from reality—or simply not mentioning after a short passage of time such huge events as the Tiananmen uprising and crackdown. From this point forward, however, it seems certain that Party-state assertions will increasingly have to match or at least become substantially more consistent with what Chinese citizens perceive, in person and through the Internet. The critical question then becomes how effectively the CCP will respond to the transformative new demands and adapt to the network society. Three modal possibilities emerge:[113]

1. CCP elites could decisively acknowledge that they cannot effectively control information and images flowing through the network without compromising their other strategic objectives. They might then decide to give up trying to control the flows except in ways practiced

commonly by other states (monitoring for genuine threats to national security, hate speech, child pornography, and other activities universally recognized as criminal or destructive). The problem, of course, is that moving away from the control model could strike some Party leaders as likely to undermine efforts to achieve other strategic goals related to consolidating the national rise and maintaining the Party in power. For example, what if a less-constrained public opinion began to favor abandoning the goal of a nationalistic rise in favor of devoting attention to—and spending resources on—improving the quality of life at home? The possibility of losing effective control over the national agenda is something the CCP (with the PLA) would have to consider very carefully before contemplating a fundamental policy change in the area of media management. The ruling groups would first have to convince themselves that such a change would ultimately work to their benefit—not an easy argument to make. On balance, then, a sudden change in communication strategy (in a liberalizing direction) seems highly unlikely in the near term, even if some in the Party have already calculated that this is a road China must eventually take. "Eventually," though, is in this context a term designed to stall for time: an empty "promise" insofar as it could imply years or even decades into the future.

2. CCP elites could continue in subtle ways to adapt to the network by making minor adjustments that slowly accumulate into big changes but at the same time repress in ways that most other states do not. This is the currently dominant trend, but whether it will prove sustainable as even more people (including disenfranchised groups) secure network access, and citizens become more cynical, is an open and important question. Continuing the current strategy is similar to saying "eventually we will liberalize" because it could be viewed as simply procrastinating on a controversial and difficult decision— "kicking the can down the road." But for the reasons procrastination proves repeatedly popular among almost all governments, in all times and places, it seems the most likely choice here. The question then becomes how long procrastination would remain tenable: whether a

crisis of some sort related to dissenting citizens' use of the network to organize protests or even a large-scale opposition movement could at some point force the issue.

3. Listening to conservatives, CCP elites might decide that the wisest choice would be to stop trying to adapt to the network and instead intensify repression and coercion. Perhaps investment in surveillance technologies and infrastructure would make this a more viable and attractive policy option in the years ahead. But it would seem to be more useful in deterring or punishing people who exchange information and images that the CCP hopes to suppress than in proactively creating a positive new communications environment. The society would almost certainly become sullen and angry if repression were intensified and more rather than less cynical—unless, perhaps, their animus could be redirected outward toward an imagined foreign enemy. Even in that case, inculcating "core socialist values" would become more, not less, difficult. As Fei Aihua, a researcher at the Nanjing Municipal Academy of Social Sciences, argues, intensifying repression (or even continuing the current policies) would actively alienate the general public, as the government (a) ignores the issues people currently consider to be the most important while (b) lecturing the public paternalistically on what people *should* find important. Active alienation increases the prestige of netizens who have a predisposition to "go against the tide."[114] This scenario could then lead the CCP into yet another downward legitimacy spiral, this one entirely of its own making through a misguided policy choice. The scenario would also surely compromise some of the CCP's other long-standing objectives, particularly those related to economic development. It therefore seems unlikely to be adopted in whole, but it could be used sporadically in particular times and places when communication messages come to seem especially dangerous or irritating to Party elites.

Communication is central to all social processes—political, economic, and cultural—and it changes profoundly with the advent of the network society. As networked communication patterns take deeper root in China, critical political changes seem certain to unfold, but they will probably be

evolutionary rather than revolutionary in nature, and they will not necessarily—especially at first—produce outcomes that proponents of political
liberalization and foreign policy moderation would look upon with favor.
Already, it seems obvious that the popular nationalism fuelled partly by
Internet discourse reinforces the hubris of some of the international relations specialists discussed in Chapters 5 and 6. The hubristic IR specialists, in turn, reinforce the popular nationalism—not only by expressing
their views in television interviews but also by hosting popular blogs and
microblogs. Partial liberalization is problematic because the Party-state
would then preferentially repress some groups and individuals more than
others. Liberals and those who call for milder policies toward other Asian
states—including Taiwan—are far more likely to be repressed than the
hubristic nationalists, shielded not only because their policy preferences
are closer than those of the liberals to the preferences of the Party Center
but also because their often outrageous and offensive jingoism allows the
CCP to claim that "it would be dangerous for us to democratize because
then these wild-eyed nationalists would end up in power."

On the other hand, as explained in Chapter 6, the CCP imagines itself
to be in a high-stakes contest with the United States, Japan, and other
democracies for control over the "discourse power" (very similar to "soft
power") that Party propagandists believe potently shapes the thinking of
people throughout the world and consequently plays a critical role in the
rise and fall of great powers. Any closure of the CCP's acknowledged gap
with the United States in soft power would thus be interpreted as both
reflecting the success of China's rise to date and as providing important
if intangible new resources ("hearts and minds") for consolidating and
deepening the rise. But can the CCP increase its soft power if it persists
in its basic repression of the Internet, punctuated by periodic crackdowns
on bloggers? Such repression makes China's political system far less appealing in the eyes of many foreigners—and it was never particularly appealing to begin with. On the other hand, maintaining the capacity to
repress does allow the CCP ready access to the tools it needs to silence
any nationalist who goes too far in expressing hostility toward foreign
countries. This puts the CCP in a quandary. Indeed, it might be the Party's

"master quandary," insofar as determining how to manage the flow of images and information into and through Chinese society—given the unavoidable logic of network functioning—interacts with all of the other dilemmas jammed into the CCP's bulging basket of conundrums, which would include all of the issue areas discussed in this book.

CHAPTER 5

China's Rise: Irreversibly Reconfiguring International Relations?

FOLLOWING THE GFC OF 2008–2009, Chinese foreign and security policies became substantially more "assertive," "aggressive," "muscular," or "robust," particularly in connection with the territorial disputes in the East and South China Seas. The contrast to the 1996–2008 period was striking because, in those years, Beijing struck a generally less belligerent pose—especially in Southeast Asia—in an effort to reassure the Association of Southeast Asian Nations (ASEAN) countries (and certain others) that, guided by a "new security concept" stressing cooperation among states in the pursuit of common objectives, China would rise peacefully and play a constructive role in building a harmonious region and world.[1] All along, however, Beijing continued to increase the budget of the People's Liberation Army (PLA) at annual rates higher than GDP growth, and, in *neibu* and other Chinese-language publications (which foreigners were presumably not expected to read), some Chinese officials and academics frankly acknowledged that the proclamation of a harmony-seeking new approach to international relations was primarily designed for the strategic purpose of increasing soft power; in other words, the "new" security concept remained "old" insofar as it assumed a realist world of hostile states competing with each other for relative power.[2] Nevertheless, Chinese rhetoric and practice—especially in relations with Southeast Asia—both were milder and more restrained during 1996–2008 than either before or after, as the CCP strove to convince the world that China had been a peace-loving, harmony-seeking state for 5,000 years. Loving peace and seeking harmony were presented as predispositions almost hard-wired into China's eons-old national identity.[3]

Rhetoric and practice both changed markedly after the GFC. Countless observers—Chinese and foreign alike—find the PRC's policies of the 2010s to be bolder, brasher, more demanding, and more risk-acceptant, particularly on issues related to China's self-defined "core national interests"—most notably, those associated with the CCP's irredentist territorial claims in the East and South China Seas.[4]

The new assertiveness takes many forms.[5] Suisheng Zhao observed in early 2012 that "China has grown increasingly vocal in protesting and pushing back U.S. naval operations in international waters off its coast. A group of Chinese vessels intercepted an American surveillance ship . . . in the South China Sea in March 2009, although the American navy had routinely deployed the craft to monitor China's military activities." When, in January 2010, the White House announced an arms sales package for Taiwan—consistent with established practice—"the Chinese Foreign Ministry spokesman for the first time threatened to impose sanctions on American companies involved in arms sales."[6]

Carlyle Thayer, a Southeast Asia specialist monitoring the Chinese shift, observes that in 2009 "the South China Sea emerged as a regional hotspot as a result of an increase in China's assertiveness in pressing its sovereignty claims."[7] Reinforcing Thayer's finding, Elizabeth Economy of the Council on Foreign Relations finds evidence of the new toughness in an icy observation made by Chinese Foreign Minister Yang Jiechi at the July 2010 ASEAN Regional Forum. During a tense discussion of the South China Sea disputes, the foreign minister coldly reminded his ASEAN counterparts that "China is a big country, and other countries are small countries, and that's a fact." Economy also details how, in September 2010, a Chinese fishing boat intentionally rammed two Japanese Coast Guard vessels near the disputed Senkaku/Diaoyu islands, prompting Japanese authorities to detain the fishing boat's captain. Far from expressing embarrassment or offering an apology, Beijing instead demanded an apology for itself and flatly refused Japan's request to pay for the damage to the Coast Guard vessels. China also imposed a (temporary) ban on the export of rare earth metals to Japan, causing harm to the Japanese microelectronics industry.[8]

Other manifestations of China's new "forward" policy would include the June 2012 upgrading of Sansha, a tiny town on Yongxing Island in the Paracels, from a county administrative office to a prefecture-level city—with formal responsibility for administering all of the land features and water claimed by Beijing in the South China Sea.[9] Also in June 2012, China outmaneuvered the Philippines in negotiations to end a two-month standoff over the contested Scarborough Shoal (Huangyan Island). Initially, Beijing agreed to an American proposal that both sides first withdraw their fishing and maritime enforcement vessels to reduce tensions. But after the Philippines complied, China reneged, quickly moving its vessels back into the area and then reinforcing its control.[10] Later in 2012, Beijing reacted with fury when Japan's central government announced that it would purchase the largest of the Senkaku/Diaoyu Islands from their private Japanese owners. Fusing legalistic arguments with thinly concealed rage, the PRC launched a multipronged, highly vocal campaign against the Japanese move. The first consequence—albeit probably unintended— was to encourage fringe-group Chinese nationalists to parade through city streets carrying banners calling not only for the return of the islands but also, in some cases, for Chinese men to rape Japanese women, for the PLA to exterminate Japanese "dwarfs" and "wild dogs," and ultimately for China to use its nuclear weapons to wipe the Japanese nation from the face of the Earth. Although only a small minority of Chinese citizens participated in these marches, and many others used microblogs and other outlets to express revulsion at the nationalists' extreme rhetoric, a wider movement to boycott Japanese goods (partly organized through the Internet) proved more popular. It soon succeeded in sharply reducing the export of Japanese goods to China. The Chinese response to the Japanese move seemed disproportionately aggressive because the well-publicized reason Japan's central government decided to buy the islands was to prevent them from falling into the hands of right-wing Japanese nationalists, who probably would have used them to stage provocative acts.[11]

There are other examples of the uncooperative or aggressive turn in Chinese foreign policy. Preferring the term *abrasive* to describe the new approach, Thomas Christensen faults Beijing's refusal to criticize Pyongyang after North Korean forces attacked a South Korean naval vessel (the *Cheonan*) in March 2010, killing dozens of sailors, and then launched another attack in November 2010 on a civilian-populated South Korean island (Yeonpyeong), also causing deaths.[12] Meanwhile, in a February

2010 State Department cable subsequently published by Wikileaks, U.S. Ambassador to China John Huntsman reported that many leading figures in the foreign diplomatic community were becoming increasingly exasperated by China's "newly pugnacious" approach.[13] Senior China analyst Michael Swaine found that the change in China's strategy was widely acknowledged (and supported) by members of China's own attentive public:

Many Chinese observers not only recognize that the Chinese government is becoming more influential and assertive . . . , but regard such a development as entirely unsurprising . . . [They] calmly assert that China has "marched to the center of the world stage" . . . and is more publicly emphasizing the defense of its "core interests" as part of a long-term process of development involving the gradual expansion of Beijing's global power and influence.[14]

Swaine's account of how some Chinese observers are explaining the shift overlaps with the dominant explanation given outside of China. Suisheng Zhao succinctly summarizes this explanation:

Chinese leaders have become increasingly confident in their ability to deal with the West because the Chinese economy rebounded quickly and strongly from the [2008–2009] global downturn. Whilst the crisis severely weakened the major Western powers, . . . China surpassed Germany as the world's largest exporter in 2009 and overtook Japan as the world's second-largest economy in 2010 . . . Confident in the balance of power tilting in its favor, Chinese leaders [now] believe that China has gained more leverage and rights to forcefully safeguard China's core interests rather than compromise them.[15]

Joseph Nye came to a similar conclusion following a series of meetings with Chinese foreign policy analysts in the spring of 2011. Nye reported that his interlocutors all acknowledged the shift in Chinese foreign policy and explained unapologetically that "we were weak [before 2008] but now we are strong." One of the Chinese analysts elaborated that "after the financial crisis, . . . many Chinese came to believe that we [in China] are rising and the US is declining." This, the analyst added, should logically now lead the United States and other countries to abandon their arrogance and begin showing an appropriate degree of deference toward China.[16]

The focus of this chapter is Chinese thinking on the PRC's trajectory in international relations. The hubristic mentality that outside analysts use to explain the shift to a more aggressive foreign policy after 2008 seems difficult to comprehend given the serious economic problems China faces, as identified by the economists discussed in Chapter 2. Although the economists warn that China's rise could stall unless the CCP pursues wrenching reforms, international relations specialists seem mostly to celebrate the inevitable victory of China's rise and on that basis approve of (and even encourage) the aggressive new foreign policy. They also seem uninterested in the potentially transformative implications of a network society coming to embrace all economically developed countries across the globe.

Yet some analysts of the military/strategic and economic realms are more confident than others. The confident analysts argue that China should continue on its current path, which they view as inherently right and reasonable. Continuing on the current path will result in China's rise succeeding as the Party leadership consolidates the great rejuvenation of the Chinese people, or what CCP General Secretary Xi Jinping has been calling since November 2012 "the China Dream."[17] The newly assertive foreign policy suggests that some voices from the Chinese IR world must have been consistently calling for a more muscular foreign policy—an observation easily confirmed through perusal of open publications, some of which are discussed in the following pages. Curiously, though, when it comes to the military/strategic sector, most Chinese analysts publishing in the outlets available (or willing to speak to a foreign researcher) are not as frankly boastful or bombastic as those writing about international cultural or soft-power competitions (discussed in Chapter 6). Analysts of strategic issues are marginally more cautious, possibly because they understand the dangers associated with military conflict. The familiar term *offensive realist*—to be used in Chapter 6—does not seem accurately to capture the posture of even those analysts who encourage the more aggressive foreign policy. This does not make them any less hubristic; rather, as explained in the following discussion, they express their hubris more subtly (with some notable exceptions).

For this reason, instead of using the offensive/defensive realist rubric featured prominently in Chapter 6, for this chapter I want to use a classification scheme that I borrowed from the English School for a 2009 *China Quarterly* article.[18] This scheme still allows for differences among offensive and defensive realists but within a constrained continuum whose *general* rubric would be "moderately-realist to pluralist-rationalist." To the left, this continuum (which ultimately becomes a circle) shades into the direction of imperialistic offensive realism. To the right, it shades into the direction of cooperation-oriented pluralist rationalism: very similar, in key respects, to the neoliberalism of American IR.[19] And, indeed, we find that, although most Chinese analysts of the military-strategic and economic realms—at least in the sample under study—are moderate realists, with some more offensively minded than others, quite a few (in absolute terms) cross the line into pluralist rationalism, proposing not merely a realist caution in dealing with the United States and other great powers but genuinely cooperation-oriented policies.

The key difference between the Chinese scholars clustered at the two ends of the (constrained) spectrum is that those who tend in the direction of pluralist rationalism are *more worried* about the fate of China's rise than those who tend in the direction of imperialistic realism: the hubristic community that is evidently applauding the shift to a more aggressive foreign policy. At first glance, this may seem obvious or even tautological, but it focuses attention on a critical—and surprising—point: A large segment of the Chinese IR community seems (at least as of mid-2013) to have been *almost completely unaware* of the profound economic challenges facing China, difficulties that Chinese economists have been warning about since the mid-2000s. These IR specialists are not alone. A summer 2013 Pew poll found that fully two-thirds of Chinese respondents (from the general public) think China will eventually supplant—or has already supplanted—the United States as the world's leading economic power.[20] Other IR scholars have *heard* there are economic problems but dismiss their importance, even sometimes during interviews with a wave of the hand and a knowing chuckle at how some people (especially, it would appear, gullible foreigners) can be so naïve. Certainly, in my sample, a majority—even a substantial majority—of Chinese IR specialists demonstrate little to no concern about the PRC's economic challenges and do not let the possibility of severe economic difficulties deter them from offering highly optimistic assessments of China's international future. These scholars seem convinced that China is living through a belle époque: a period of spiritual and sensual satisfaction, grounded in material plenty and secured by the steadily growing military power of a country predestined to rise unstoppably. Because of the PRC's glorious, preordained destiny, there is little reason to worry about the current economic situation or possible international conflicts: Problems will work themselves out—just so long as the CCP continues to follow the wise policy course it has pursued in the recent past.

Consequently, the hubris of contemporary Chinese IR specialists emerges as distinctive in that it does not seem self-consciously boastful or strutting—as does the hubris of certain vocal PLA officers or nationalistic public intellectuals. The hubris of contemporary Chinese IR specialists is instead blissfully unaware of the problems and risks China will face if, in fact, it *does* continue on its present course and the economists discussed in Chapter 2 turn out to be right. That the hubris is not boastful or strutting should not be taken to mean that its effect on other countries is benign. Certainly the IR hubris has, through its influence on Chinese policy, harmed the Philippines, Vietnam, and Japan in recent years. Indeed, the insidiousness of this sort of seemingly benign hubris may make it even more damaging over the long run than the willfully aggressive sort of arrogant jingoism that can easily be spotted as problematic and marked as unreasonable. Moreover, the belle époque hubris of most Chinese IR specialists also—obviously—threatens to harm China itself. This is, in fact, the chief danger that IR specialists who tend in a rationalist direction (those who read the economists' warnings) worry about the most. They profess concern that China's blissfully uninformed IR optimists are misleading CCP leaders into overestimating the PRC's strengths and capabilities while misreading what foreign countries are likely to tolerate. The concerned, well-informed minority of Chinese IR specialists want their country to revert to a low profile in international affairs, at least until the national rise is securely consolidated. They reject the claims of the hubristic optimists that the great rejuvenation of the Chinese nation is already a done deal.

MULTIPOLARIZATION

The characteristic expression of realist Chinese optimism is that the world is naturally—almost mystically—trending in the direction of multipolarization; that is, it is being restructured around several distinct power centers rather than just one (unipolarity, which some contend characterized the world for a decade or so after the Soviet Union collapsed) or two (bipolarity, as from 1945 to 1992). Multipolarization is a perceived master trend that Chinese analysts have been writing about since the 1980s, sometimes in conjunction with assessments predicting the inevitability of America's decline.[21] In addition to China, the other poles expected in the world of the future variously include India, Russia, and Europe. Formerly Japan was included on the list, but interview subjects confirmed that Japan was dropped in 2005–2006.[22] The interviewees said that Japan's shrinking population and persistent economic woes meant that it could no longer compete for great power status. One interviewee said that, in addition, Prime Minister Junichiro Koizumi's visits to the Yasukuni Shrine each August from 2001 through 2006 resulted in Japan losing the soft-power component of great power status—or in other words, that it was morally unfit for great power status.[23]

On his ascent to power in 2002, CCP General Secretary Hu Jintao may have tried to suppress discussion of multipolarization as a master trend. Multipolarization implies jostling or even outright conflict among the great powers, but Hu was insisting that China's rise would be peaceful. Starting in 2005, he also began arguing that China would use its comprehensive national power to help build a harmonious world.[24] This led to criticism of the multipolarization concept in the Chinese IR literature. Peking University's Ye Zicheng published a curious example of this phenomenon in a January 2004 article titled "Reflections on the History and Theory of China's Multipolarization Strategy." Ye spends approximately the first 90 percent of the article fulfilling the promises of the title and generally extolling the multipolarization concept, presenting it as wise.

But then, almost at the very end, he suddenly announces that China can, and should, transcend talk of multipolarization and move beyond it. Ye gives four reasons:

1. With its emphasis on conflict among states, polarization is a typically cynical Western concept, which Ye claims was invented by Richard Nixon in 1967. Multipolarization "represents the tendency of Western great powers to dominate international politics. This word, *multipolarization*, is not at all an invention of the Chinese people . . . [Thus], Chinese people should feel no sorrow in abandoning the concept."[25]

2. Multipolarization fails to capture the complexity of both today's world and the world of the future, which is or will be changing constantly as a result of globalization and related trends. "Any single concept we might use" in describing the international system would fail to capture this complexity.[26]

3. Not only does multipolarization imply conflict among the great powers, but it also implies that the great powers are carving out spheres of influence in the Third World as they prosecute their conflicts. China cannot divorce itself from the Third World, with which it has always remained locked in loyal solidarity.[27]

4. Talk of multipolarization is inconsistent with other aspects of China's grand strategy. (This would appear to overlap with Point 3.) In particular, China is a developing country that has always allied itself with other developing countries. But talk of multipolarization implies a world divided neatly into two categories: the poles of power, and the other countries too poor or weak to count as poles of power. Chinese discussions of multipolarization always imply that China will become one of the new poles. This would put China at odds with the Third World, and "China has no need to draw a line between itself and the masses of medium- and small-sized countries."[28]

If Ye's article sounds as if it was revised just before going to press to accommodate the new line on international relations being propagated by Hu Jintao, an August 2004 article in *Studies of International Politics* by two scholars from Central China Normal University is devoted entirely to castigating the multipolarization concept. In "Transcend 'Polarized'

Thinking and Grasp the Fundamental Trend of World Structure," Xia Anling and Hou Jiehui come out swinging against the concept from the start. They first note that "the mainstream viewpoint in our country's scholarly world is that multipolarization is an objective trend; . . . that it will be beneficial to China; and that therefore China should actively promote it."[29] Xia and Hou acknowledge that multipolarization may be an objective trend but stress that it is not the *only* such trend in international relations. Moreover, although multipolarization might well contribute to peace and stability, it could also become a fundamental source of contradictions, conflict, and ultimately war. The concept even fails fully to capture relations between China and the United States, because, although in some ways the United States is an arrogant unilateralist causing problems for China, it is also a weighty member of the world's most important multilateral organizations and therefore a potential PRC partner.[30] Pole talk is problematic, in short, because "it turns the mind away from compromise and cooperation," actively worsening contradictions that might have been solvable before.[31] For this reason, "we should replace the multipolarization strategy with a strategy of great power cooperation."[32]

At first glance, one might be tempted to marvel at how easily Chinese scholars can be convinced by the political authorities to turn on a dime and abandon their intellectual convictions. Both the article by Ye and the article by Xia and Hou emphasize how deeply ingrained the concept of multipolarization is in the Chinese scholarly world before calling for the concept's rejection. The question is, how could analysts who have for many years been portraying multipolarization as the most important objective and thus unavoidable trend in international relations now start thinking or even just talking about something else entirely? It would be one thing to abandon multipolarization as a strategy; quite another to abandon it as an image of the future structuring the context in which China must formulate its strategy.

But not surprisingly, multipolarization as a concept remains alive and well among Chinese analysts, appearing occasionally in articles and books and popping up in discussions even though "we don't have to emphasize the concept as much as we did in the past."[33] The concept could hardly fail to remain alive and well given the overlap in meaning between multipolarization and not-yet-discredited concepts such as China's rise and the China Dream, both of which stress China's return to relative greatness in international affairs. Let us then turn to some of the more recent discussions of multipolarization to frame more clearly how some Chinese thinkers continue to use it to help conceptualize China's rise and its profound implications for the future of world order.

In 2006, Huang Zhengji, a "high-level strategist" with the China International Institute for Strategic Studies, published a book titled *On the Multipolar World*.[34] In this complex and lengthy study, Huang squares the tension between declarations that multipolarization is a Western concept that should be jettisoned because it stresses conflict and power politics with the desirability of using it as an analytical tool. The chief source of conflict in the world today, Huang finds, is U.S. hegemonism (putative unipolarity) and the struggle by Washington and its agents to secure it. Although it may well be true, as all realists emphasize, that "because poles exist, international relations can never be completely just or equal," Huang stresses that some poles are worse than others because "they are incapable of relinquishing hegemonism and power politics." This implies that China's rise must be rocky because the United States will put obstacles in the way of the rise's consolidation—China being the only power with any possibility in the near future of competing with the United States in comprehensive national power terms. Yet it also implies that once China does consolidate its rise and thus locks down the multipolar structure, the PRC could check the United States and thus help to usher in a brand-new epoch of world peace. "Even despite the current state of affairs," Huang avers, "in the end, international justice will defeat hegemonism and power politics."[35]

How will the world navigate to "the end" when justice will prevail? Huang develops his vision of the evolution of international relations in the course of discussing four general characteristics of the multipolar world, which he argues started to emerge in 1992 but still has many decades or more to go before it will be consolidated.

The first characteristic Huang finds is that "the new multipolar world is a world full of struggle and competition." It is a world of approximately 200 nation-states, all different in type of social system, size, national power, level of prosperity, and other key variables. Because all of these states are competing (as realists would hold) to seize advantageous positions, the world can never be quiet and peaceful, at least not at any point in the near future. On the other hand, multipolarization is good for peace insofar as it reduces the probability that *large-scale* conflict will break out.[36] This is a contested issue in IR as a social science, with Kenneth Waltz (among others) famously arguing that multipolar international structures are likely to be *more* war prone than bipolar structures.[37] Huang does not spell out his logic as to why multipolarizing structures should be less war prone, leaving the reader with the impression that the chief reason is that China's rise must inherently be peaceful. If multipolarization is in key respects simply another term for China's rise relative to the United States, then how could the process possibility facilitate war breaking out?

Second, multipolarization today and tomorrow has a cultural characteristic—an assertion that will put Huang even more at odds with mainstream Western realists. The cultural characteristic is that today's and tomorrow's multipolarization is emerging out of a present world that esteems "peace and development," articulated by Deng Xiaoping in the 1980s as foundational to Chinese grand strategy. Peace and development are actually, Huang argues, the eternal demands of the human race, with "advanced personages struggling to achieve them for thousands or even tens of thousands of years." But they only became "an unstoppable trend" after humanity experienced the searing twentieth century and then bipolarity collapsed.[38]

Corresponding as it must to China's rise, future multipolarization "will accompany the *progress* of the human race and society. It will accompany globalization and sustained but still-unbalanced development. It will destroy the old international order, allowing humanity to march toward a new order." The positive and progressive process is already underway, but it will take a very long time to complete: "not less than one or two centuries, perhaps even more."[39] So it is not so much finished multipolarity that should be understood if we want to conceptualize the meaning of China's rise. It is the *process* of multipolarization, given the cultural characteristics of the late twentieth century (when it began).

Third, multipolarization will unfold slowly through three stages of development. In the early stage, which includes the present:

Hegemonism and power politics will still function within certain regions and on certain issues. They will still be a threat to world peace and will particularly victimize the smaller and weaker countries. They could even result in the phenomenon of a certain large country or several large countries banding together to manipulate world affairs. . . . Because hegemonists, terrorists, and certain secessionists and extremists [in Xinjiang? Tibet? Taiwan?] will incautiously use military force and violence, armed conflicts and scattered wars of various sizes will, as in the past, frequently trouble the world.[40]

Many of these conflicts will, however, be trivial from the perspective of the master trend associated with China's rise relative to the United States. Thus, Huang contends that "the most important conflict among the multiple poles will be the conflict between those who want to establish a new international order [for example, China, the leading revisionist power] and those who want to preserve the old international order [the United States]."[41]

In the middle stage (Huang does not specify when it will begin), the basic array of great powers will be set as the international structure completes the reorganization process that began with the collapse of bipolarity in 1992 and the subsequent rise of new countries to great power status. Not only does the power of formerly middle-ranking states increase in this stage, but so does their functional significance in international affairs:

Hegemonism and power politics will increasingly be subject to constraint. International peace will stabilize, and the formation of large-scale conflict situations will become increasingly difficult. Among the various international powers there will be cooperation, on the one hand, but still competition and struggle, on the other. As a result of all these contests, some countries or groups of countries will find their power increasing while others [the United States? Japan?] suffer declines or relative declines. But the basic array of the great powers will be set and not change fundamentally.[42]

This latter point is especially important insofar as it undergirds a key assumption behind most Chinese IR analysts' characterizations of the future and their attempts to define the meaning and nature of China's rise: China can only progress; it can never move backward. Once the rise is consolidated, which it inevitably must be, there can be no decline. Faltering and failing are imaginable (indeed, certain) for the United States and perhaps other powers, but would be unthinkable for China. This poses in stark relief the contradictory developments in demography and the economy that will evidently come as a shock to many Chinese IR scholars, or at least those who evince unchallengeable optimism.

In multipolarization's late stage—which, recall, probably cannot begin for a very long time—"all the countries of the world will have universally achieved development. Politics will tend toward genuine democracy [Huang does not define "false" democracy, but numerous other writers such as Pan Wei have criticized "Western" democracy as false] and the quality of citizens will have greatly been raised. However, development will still be unbalanced, and it will prove impossible to erase the differences among countries in wealth and strength. Multiple poles will continue to exist"—so again, China and the world will not or cannot turn back—"but relations among them will chiefly be characterized by fair competition, compromise, and coexistence. Hegemonism and power politics will fundamentally disappear but not completely disappear; thus, the possibility of warfare cannot be ruled out entirely."[43]

Returning to the main list, the fourth and final core characteristic of multipolarization is that it will function in such a way as to make economic globalization—another "master trend of world development"—more just: "Only in the current stage of world development, with its unjust old international economic order, does globalization cause negative consequences for some less developed countries." Increasingly, after multipolarization gains momentum, economic globalization will become "beneficial to each and every one of the world's nation-states while also helping to promote world peace."[44] The focus on globalization as affecting the nature of multipolarization in the twenty-first century is another factor setting Huang apart from the realists of Western IR.

At some point in the coming years or decades (Huang is not specific as to when), multipolarization will reach a takeoff stage. After that, the substance and tone of international relations will change substantially for the better: "Upholding and protecting all states' legitimate rights will receive universal sympathy and support. Infringing on other states' sovereignty or damaging other states' interests will receive universal sanctioning—even more so when a state threatens the general peace. Dialogue will increase; confrontations will decline."[45] There will still be differences among states and even conflict, but violence will largely be contained. The world will be operating under a completely different set of rules from the set that prevailed in the late twentieth century (when multipolarization began).[46] Note that the critical point is the strong correlation between multipolarization and China's rise or even the successful attainment of the China Dream. Although Chinese analysts assert that there will still be other poles besides the United States and China, they tend to emphasize the importance of the power transition between these two being resolved in a particular way—that is, China satisfying its core national interests without having to fight a large-scale war. Sometimes *multipolarization* seems like a code word for *bi*polarization, even a bipolarization that would eventually lead to China becoming the stronger party relative to the United States. Certainly no Chinese writer ever excludes China from the list of countries that will be poles in the multipolar world of the future. Some might exclude Europe, others Russia, but none ever excludes China.

A more recent publication addressing multipolarization and its significance is *China's Future Direction: Uniting High-Level Policymaking and National Strategic Arrangements*, the May 2009 volume published under the name of the China Future Directions Editorial Group.[47] In the sections of this book discussed in Chapter 2, the authors express concern about China's economic trajectory. But the sections on international relations exude a similar kind of blithe-optimism-bordering-on-hubris that characterizes the confident realist camp in Chinese IR, even though the authors also insist that the rise is far from consolidated (much could still go wrong) and realism cannot fully capture the international relations of today and tomorrow. At the beginning of the forty-three-page "Strategy Section," the authors present a quote from Sunzi's *Art of War*, warning that those who fail to plan for the whole picture will not even be able to plan for a part of it, while those who fail to plan for the long term will not even be able to plan for an hour.[48] This is followed by a quotation from an article in the October 6, 1987, *People's Daily*, in which unnamed experts predict a global economic crisis by century's end. No one should scoff at predictions such as this: China should be ready for anything—and in particular should be ready to take advantage of a global crisis to advance its relative position. That would in turn require putting into place healthy preconditions prior to the crisis.[49] But so far, at least, the CCP has done an excellent job of planning and implementing—preparing for the "what ifs"—in five key respects:

1. Finding "balance"; that is, pursuing stability, reform, and development successfully all at the same time. As long as this continues—and there is no reason to think the situation will change—"China can establish the basis for joining the ranks of the world's most powerful countries."[50]

2. The CCP has also been good at "seizing key opportunities." The authors illustrate by citing the contrary case of the obtuse United States of the 2000s, which defined the primary world problem as fighting terrorism, whereas China sagely defined it as ending poverty. This scored China substantial soft power points in its conflict with the United States.[51] Thus, "seizing opportunities" in international relations means finding ways to elevate China's power and reputation relative to the hegemon. By definition, China's rise implies an increase in PRC power relative to that of the faltering West, especially the United States—and this transition shifted into higher gear during the first decade of the twenty-first century. There is nothing in this writing to suggest recognition of the massive economic problems China now faces, which seem certain to slow the rise—and perhaps even more. Indeed, there is nothing to suggest even recognition of the possibility that the huge stimulus program put into place at the time of writing—a stimulus so widely praised for its boldness—could itself serve to propel China straight into an economic morass. There is also nothing to suggest recognition that the advent of a network society potentially threatens to undermine political stability insofar as it challenges CCP control.

3. At its best, the CCP has been successful at testing its larger initiatives first in smaller experiments; then, after that, once the kinks have been ironed out, implementing the experiments successfully over larger areas.[52] The authors do not seem especially concerned that this approach is on the verge of being abandoned, and yet it does seem to have been abandoned—at least temporarily—with the adoption of the 2008 stimulus. It might also have been abandoned in the approach to solving conflicts with Japan and Southeast Asian countries over territorial disputes, unless the assertive/aggressive new policy that emerged after 2009 was itself only a regional experiment in preparation for a more assertive policy on a larger geographical or functional plane.

4. The Party has also shown deftness and wisdom in its strategy of doing the easy things first and saving the more difficult tasks for later, after experiences have been accumulated and the country has become stronger. "The early successes create new situations that pave the way for later successes";[53] in the process, they help the Party and people to discover a distinctive China model or China Road: "The content of the Road will be revealed, and in that way reinforce our confidence and determination to continue to advance along this Road—without a doubt meaningful not only to ourselves but also to international society."[54]

5. The Party was right in its decision to eschew "setting up a separate stovepipe" in international relations; that is, it was right in deciding instead to follow the "Burkean" approach (they cite Burke approvingly) of making use of existing institutions to advance China's rise and waiting until later to try to reform these institutions: "We should do our utmost to make use of the current system and in the process gradually try to reform it—or cause it to change—to serve our modernization."[55] The context of this comment suggests that some elites might have been arguing at the time that China *should* be pushing for more substantial change in international institutions. But the Future Directions Editorial Group thinks caution should continue to be the watchword and that there would be little reason to promote substantial change as long as China can continue to derive benefits from current arrangements.

Even though CCP leaders have been wise and China has enjoyed re-markable successes, the authors warn that the situation could at some point change for the worse. The new world order, though it tends toward multipolarization—an unalloyed good—is also unsettled, or "plastic," with consequently the potential for many things to go wrong and to do so at inopportune moments. The world seems in a constant state of consoli-dating that never quite crystallizes. The many unknown and unknowable variables affecting the global trajectory could at any point combine in unpredictable ways to present obstacles to China as it struggles to con-tinue its ascent. On the whole, however, it is still possible to identify three dominant international tendencies that are likely to continue in the years and decades ahead and try to bend these tendencies to China's purposes:

1. "World integration is strengthening at the same time as the influence of the international system on individual countries is increasing. All individual countries must adapt to the constraints imposed by the inte-grated world system and in that way [*only* in that way] seize advantages for one's own nation."[56] The international structure—which is thicker than the term *multipolarity* can convey (the authors thus sometimes use the term *integrated multipolarity*, hinting, perhaps, at recognition of the network society's importance)—becomes more restrictive; yet still, the clever country can exercise agency within the structure to fulfill its national interests. Integration need not imply intermeshed with others to the point of losing one's own national distinctiveness. It also does not mean fully trapped. China the nation-state will con-tinue to enjoy room for maneuverability and can chart its own course. What is more, integration on balance creates a beneficial situation for China because it also constrains the United States. Consequently, "it would be quite difficult for the future world to develop according to the designs of some single country or single force, even if the country were to use extreme measures while it exercises superpowerful eco-nomic and military might."[57]

2. Tighter world integration in the context of multipolarization also means that the issue-areas in which states' interests overlap or clash are *both* bound to increase, meaning that the great powers, in particular, will

have to devote extensive energy to finding ways to compromise and work through their differences.[58] This is a function of international relations becoming more "complex." The complexity is positive, insofar as the new interconnections it fosters will help further integration among states before multipolarization can play this role. At present, it is still too early in the multipolarization process for anything like the logic prevailing under bipolarity to integrate international society; thus, two decades after the Soviet Union's collapse, the world has still not "embarked upon a new track."[59] This challenges China because it cannot simply sit back and wait for multipolarization to unfold. It must help to make it happen in a way consistent with China's national interest as defined by the CCP Center: "In the realm of strategy, China must recognize the new complexity and cultivate the ability to make good use of it."[60]

3. Though pursuing the national interest at the lowest possible cost will always be the foundation of China's international strategy, Chinese policy makers must also cultivate suppleness and sophistication and not commit to an overly crude or thoughtless variant of realism. Statements such as "those who are not our friends are our enemies," "the absence of cooperation is conflict," and "the absence of victory is defeat" are "already less and less appropriate. Today, fixing one's national identity requires realizing the national interest but also cultivating appropriate flexibility."[61] At the same time, "in exploring the future role of what a rising China will be, or how it will realize its interests, we cannot overrely strictly on a realist perspective. In today's world, we cannot rely purely on realism or any other particular theory" to explain the functioning of the international system.[62] Instead, policy makers should examine problems, each one on its own, and gradually accumulate knowledge.

This approach would ultimately remain consistent with realism insofar as it takes for granted China's national interests in any given situation and avoids problematizing or politicizing the nature of these largely CCP-given (and thus politically constructed) objectives. But problematizing Party policies is not to be expected in a Party-backed publication.

The recommended approach is noteworthy for its injunction to recognize the complexity associated with current and future multipolarization and not expect charting China's course to be an easy task guided by a list of core national interests and a playbook from realism. Some claim, the authors note, that "the torch of history" has already passed from the United States to China—aided partly by the global financial crisis and Washington's folly in Iraq. But the authors caution that it is still too early to make such a claim. Readers should be aware that China will continue to face "obstacles, blockages, and traps" along with "difficulties, troubles, and criticism."[63] It will take continued cleverness and wisdom for the country to realize a successful rise, yet there is no reason to expect that continued cleverness and wisdom will be absent.

Whereas *China's Future Direction* generally exudes optimism and at some points borders on hubris, a 2011 article by Yin Chengde, a researcher at the China Institute for International Studies, crosses the border unapologetically.[64] The task Yin sets for himself is to identify the effects of the global financial crisis on international relations. The summary effect, he finds, is that the crisis "sped the trend of multipolarization" now developing "to an unprecedented degree."[65] The reason, Yin argues, is the close relationship between the financial crisis and America's decline, in a context in which China responded effectively to the crisis by putting into place the 2008 stimulus. Yin identifies three ways in which the U.S. decline was intensified by the crisis. The first concerns GDP. Yin calculates that the United States produced 33 percent of the world's goods and services in the year 2000 but only 22 percent in 2010. He calculates that the U.S. contribution to global *growth* in 2010 (he does not discuss global growth in 2000) was "only around 10 percent," which put the United States "very far behind China. America's role as the chief engine of the world economy is already a thing of the past."[66] Second is the dollar's decline relative to other currencies during the 2000s, a development that, Yin contends, "signals the decline of U.S. hegemonism."[67] Third is "the serious fall in American soft power and international influence," which Yin does not document but conveys as a well-known fact.[68]

Yin sounds alternately angry and celebratory in proclaiming that the GFC conclusively rebutted the end-of-history thesis, which is now consequently dead. There are three reasons: (1) The crisis discredited "the Western liberal economic model," which will sound surprising to the Chinese economists championing that model, as discussed in Chapter 2; (2) the U.S.-led West is now completely frustrated by its inability to force other countries to accept democracy as the only universally valid political model (this evidently a function more of the war in Iraq than the financial crisis and subsequent recession); and (3) China's road and model "are radiating a strong and powerful life force," which intrinsically challenges the end-of-history thesis.[69] It should be obvious that Yin and other writers articulating similar points of view do not object to history ending as such. They only object to history ending with the U.S.-led West on top of the international system, and at the center of world history, as opposed to sharing the starring role with other states and civilizations or even yielding it completely to China.

Yin may be at the extreme of hubris (for IR scholars), but numerous other analysts display an unshakeable confidence in the sustainability of China's rise. Indeed, some of the scholars interviewed in 2011–2012 observed the optimism among their peers and found it remarkable. One such scholar dates ultraconfidence to the conjunction of the GFC with the 2008 Olympics. He thinks confidence is much more prevalent among academic and other elites than the general public, which would be the first to experience economic, environmental, and other problems.[70] This scholar is himself aware of the economic difficulties and worries that "8 percent growth" has become inscribed into the national identity, at least as imagined in the intellectual world and the world of officials. He suspects that confidence could survive a short slowdown to perhaps 7 percent growth, but any sustained slowdown at 5 percent or lower would deal a psychological blow to national elites.[71]

Another scholar argued that the Party would have only itself to blame for any political instability resulting from an economic slowdown. He traces "economism—the conviction that all problems throughout the country can and will be solved by economic growth"—to Deng Xiaoping's approach to governance.[72] This scholar believes the reason Beijing so frantically and hastily launched its 2008 stimulus was that top leaders cannot imagine any approach to solving problems other than political repression and economic growth. Correspondingly, they think that if growth stalls, problems will explode. Any sort of reform could only be carried out if growth remained strong: "If it were to fall much below 8 percent, the leaders would probably become anxious again and resort to their old habit" of using stimulus and investment to return growth to the levels society now expects.[73]

One of the colleagues of these two scholars exemplified almost perfectly the overlap between blithe optimism and potentially incautious realism. This scholar is strongly supportive of the CCP and confident in its leadership. He argues that CCP elites are united, intelligent, and foresightful. They "have a plan and know what needs to be done. And they always tell us the plan in advance" so there will be no surprises.[74] This scholar is not worried that the CCP could ever make any fundamental mistakes or that it would be too stubbornly ossified or beholden to bureaucratic or political-economic interest groups to make quick changes when they become necessary. For example, he is not in the least concerned that the one-child policy combined now with the urban coastal preference for fewer children will get China into trouble demographically and then economically.[75] It is not merely that the scholar thinks the CCP could handle a shift to a substantially older population structure. His confidence is deeper than that. He does not even think the structure will become older and thereby present the Party with a challenge. He believes that the traditional Chinese preference for large families will always ensure against excessive aging of the population or population shrinkage. I pointed out to him that some of China's own demographers argue that it is already too late—that the population has already begun to age substantially and will begin to shrink in 2026. He (politely) responded that "foreigners don't always understand China" and said it would be a simple matter for the Party, if it deemed such a move necessary, to abolish the one-child policy and get the Chinese people to start reproducing again. The key point that foreigners fail to grasp is that "Chinese peasants will always be Chinese peasants," even after they move to the cities. Thus, all the migrant workers of recent years can easily be convinced to start having more children when it becomes necessary. I repeated in response that not only foreign but also Chinese demographers were worried that such a logic would no longer hold, and that, even if the Party suddenly ended the policy tomorrow and people responded with alacritous reproduction, there would still be twenty years of labor shortages ahead. But he did not seem to want to continue the discussion about demography.[76]

Instead, he turned to prospects for political change. The scholar thinks that China should not pursue "Western democracy" (again, he was very polite in saying so) but instead "rule of law with Chinese characteristics." This and the process of "political institutionalization" remain on schedule and should be achievable by 2050, which is the Party's current goal.[77] Much more so than democratization—which could be destabilizing—political institutionalization and implementation of the rule of law with Chinese characteristics would help China to become an even more reliable partner in international affairs. There is absolutely zero chance, the scholar contends, that China could ever become a threat to other countries as its rise continues. Given that it has never threatened other countries in the past, why would it do so in the future? If only foreigners would understand this fact, they could respond more effectively to China's rise and make it work for them. The scholar finds that China has always taken a "harmony is precious, but only harmony in diversity [*he wei gui, he er bu tong*]" approach to international relations: This is a slogan the CCP began promoting in the mid-2000s to suggest a pluralist-rationalist approach to foreign affairs; that is, that China would pursue harmonious relations with other countries but would never band together with them for the purpose of trying to establish a community of solidaristic states. This scholar fully accepts the formulation and argues that it is the key reason there is no doubt that China's approach to international relations will not evince the realist concern to increase power relative to other states but instead will exemplify the rationalist or neoliberal concern that "all sides win" in the interactions among states. This would, in fact, become China's chief contribution to world history: It will change the nature of international relations by supplanting the West's realism with China's own harmony is precious, but only a harmony-in-diversity approach.[78]

In response to my suggestion that perhaps China promotes harmony now because it is still relatively weak and that it could become more ambitious and assertive when its power increases, the scholar replied that "this is impossible because China isn't like the United States." For example, "China is now friendly to Vietnam" in ways the Soviet Union and the United States never were in the past. "We can give Vietnam and other neighboring countries advice, but unlike the United States, we won't insist that they take it."[79] What was rather surprising about this observation was that the scholar offered it right at the same time as Sino-Vietnamese relations were worsening substantially owing to China's increasing aggressiveness in the South China Sea. The scholar could only imagine China behaving in a friendly manner with neighboring countries, with Western states behaving arrogantly. The same sort of logic applied to Sino-Indian relations, then also in the process of worsening. The scholar said that "if there were only two countries in the world, China and India would get along fine." Unfortunately, there are also the United States and Japan, two countries that are trying to use India to check China's rise. "There is no basic reason for China and India not to get along." And in the end, they *will* get along as they draw on their ancient wisdom and the Indians come to realize that the United States and Japan are only manipulating them for their own dubious and selfish purposes.[80]

Another scholar interviewed a year later in another city was more subtle. This scholar—also friendly, hospitable, and polite—was researching how the United States succeeded in implementing the Monroe Doctrine in the Western hemisphere. The motivation was that he hoped China could adopt a similar approach in twenty-first-century Asia. The scholar calculated that the United States could not have risen to become a global power if it had not first established a "leading position" in the Americas. China now wants to establish an analogous leading position in Asia. It, too, needs to exercise authority over neighboring states at some point in the future to become a global power.[81] When challenged with the observation that possibly Asia today is different in key respects from the Americas of the nineteenth century, the scholar acknowledged that "China can't go as far as the United States." He said he imagines that even after China establishes its leading position, the West will still have a role to play in Asia, certainly in the area of trade. The scholar received a grant for his research project from the Party-run Chinese Academy of Social Sciences.[82]

Other realist scholars recognize the many challenges that China faces—economically and otherwise—but on balance view the future in a positive light. Reflecting on the challenges leads these scholars to reject hubris even as they profess an ultimate optimism. In January 2011, for example, Chairman Ma Xiaotian of the China Institute for International Strategic Studies published an article in *The Study Times* (a publication of the Central Party School) analyzing the international problems that China must resolve in the years leading up to 2020. Ma discusses the Taiwan issue (China must continue to exercise patience), territorial disputes, assorted U.S. demands, terrorism, and the aftereffects of the global financial crisis. Although managing these problems will not be easy, Ma professes a cautious optimism, citing six core reasons:

1. Even though it will always be obstreperous and irritating to some extent, the United States is likely to maintain a cooperative attitude toward China in the years ahead and emphasize the importance of dialogue in resolving disputes. This is because Washington recognizes that the United States and China are bound together economically. American elites understand that common interests between the two countries are continually increasing. Beyond economic issues, the United States and China share regional and global responsibilities in combatting terrorism, blocking the proliferation of weapons of mass destruction, and other "hot-topic issues." Interdependence and a sense of having to shoulder great power responsibilities will not be enough to guarantee a cooperative attitude on the part of the United States, but it should create important preconditions for cooperativeness.[83]

2. Although it is true that some countries are worried about China's rise and how China might behave in the future, it is also important to recognize that Chinese influence throughout the world continues to increase. This is not necessarily because of soft power; it is primarily because so many other countries can benefit materially from China's economic successes. Ma finds that whereas China contributed only 2.3 percent to global economic growth in 1978, by 2010 it was contributing 20 percent.[84] Moreover, China has done a good job of translating its economic accomplishments into positive feeling in foreign states, by

fostering mutually beneficial and cooperative exchanges. So success-ful has China been diplomatically in recent years that Ma concludes "even if the United States were to decide that it wants to try to contain China, it would find itself isolated and helpless and would itself become regarded as destructive of a good situation."[85] Ma does not address the possibility of an economic slowdown, but his logic would seem to suggest that if China were to stop contributing substantially to global growth, then suddenly its diplomatic position would weaken. Perhaps in such a scenario there would still be goodwill toward China as a re-sult of the mutually beneficial exchanges of the past, but the goodwill would not be as solid or reliable as before. China's diplomatic corps would have to scramble to work with unusual energy and creativity to maintain Chinese influence abroad. But an economic slowdown is not something that Ma anticipates.

3. On the whole, Ma finds China's relations with immediately neighboring countries to be stable and expects that China will be able to maintain this advantageous security situation indefinitely. There is no denying that "a few complications" appeared in 2010 (Ma does not name any), but these should not prove serious enough to affect the overall positive situation. Some neighboring countries remain suspicious of China, but they are not likely to band against it. The simple reason is that the countries' economic dynamism and physical (military) security dic-tate prudence in dealing with the PRC.[86] Thus, based on Ma's logic, a faltering Chinese economy could cause these neighboring states to start behaving less prudently—and yet they would still have to worry about Chinese military might. Even if China's rise were to slow, the PRC would continue to wield substantially more material power than ever before in history.

4. Although the weaknesses of the world economy will certainly pose problems for China, on the whole Ma thinks that "the opportunity to realize stable and relatively fast economic development remains."[87] Here it becomes clear that Ma has either not read the Chinese econo-mists' criticisms or else has read the criticisms but rejects them. He does not address the substance of the criticisms in this article. He cites no Chinese economist but does cite with approval some of the

numerous foreign entities that were predicting China would have the world's largest macroeconomy by 2030.[88] Ma himself considers that China will exercise unspecified "advantages of late developing countries" throughout the 2010s and will achieve rapid economic growth through reliance on new industries, especially green industries. But he does not give a reason for his optimism nor spell out his logic. Although Ma does not display hubris as some Chinese IR scholars do, he does seem typically to be relying in his forecast on an assumption about economic dynamism that may no longer be tenable in the years and decades ahead. He may be among the IR specialists likely to be caught off-guard or even stunned by a sustained slowdown.

5. Indeed, Ma feels sufficiently confident about China's economic performance to declare that "international society's identification with our country's development model increases by the day, corresponding to increases in our country's soft power."[89] Gone is the time when Westerners could boast that history has ended and the American model has emerged victorious. Now Westerners and others will have to take the Chinese model seriously, and they do. This is the core reason that Ma is confident China will be able to resolve its international problems to its advantage in the period leading up to 2020.[90]

6. Finally, high-quality CCP governance ensures that the domestic situation will continue to provide a firm foundation for economic and social development: "The Party continues to accumulate rich experience in managing our country and handling crises. The Party's abilities in these areas have strengthened as it digests the experiences." Ma acknowledges that the effective administration he perceives depends partly on economic performance, but, again, he does not expect economic performance to flag: "We have a strong domestic market with huge potential; our people show increasing inventiveness in science and technology; the adjustment of the economic structure continues gradually to advance; thus, it is entirely possible to maintain relatively high-speed and stable economic development" and on that basis for "elements in society causing disorder to be controlled" by the increasingly skilled Party-state.[91] Although undoubtedly CCP officials have amassed substantial experience in how to control a society being transformed

by technological advance and partial economic marketization, it remains unclear how effectively it could govern in a context in which economic growth suddenly and "surprisingly" stalls for many years as the network society takes deeper root. The economists discussed in Chapter 2 certainly do not share Ma's optimism that "the adjustment of the economic structure [by which he appears to mean the shift to domestic consumption-led growth] continues gradually to advance." Indeed, this core structural imbalance worsened in 2012–2013.[92]

Not all Chinese realists are equally sanguine about the PRC's future prospects. There may be a strong correlation between realism and optimism, but the relationship is far from lawlike. A good illustration of how even offensive realists can sometimes feel anxiety about China's trajectory is an article appearing in the February 2012 issue of *Theoretical Trends*, a *neibu* journal. Written by Jing Linbo, an associate director of the Chinese Academy of Social Sciences' National Academy of Economic Strategy, this article offers a strongly realist analysis of how U.S. international strategy changed after 2001 and the ways in which the new American strategy threatens China. Author Jing differs from the hubristic realists in declining to celebrate the long U.S. wars in Iraq and Afghanistan. He does not seem to think that on balance the United States lost ground internationally as a result of these wars. Although America may have taken some hits to its soft power, it also accumulated substantial war-fighting and threat-mitigating experiences of a sort that China could barely conceive. Consequently, Jing worries that the United States has become an even more formidable potential foe of China—even if the Great Recession did set it back economically. Jing is not one to think that China can relax and enjoy a belle époque of automatic development and security enhancement in the coming years. He recommends that China implement five changes in its approach to designing security strategy to ensure that the United States and other challengers will not be able to exploit Chinese weaknesses and block the national resurrection:

1. Start investing more financial and human resources into researching national security strategy so that the gap with the United States in such expenditure is closed.[93] Although many Chinese realists seem im-

plicitly to assume not only that the economy will continue to flourish but also that the bounteous new economic resources will flow almost automatically (on the basis of wise Party leadership) to where they should flow to increase Chinese power—the ultimate objective—Jing is not certain. He declines, however, to specify precisely in what areas the new expenditures should be made.

2. Rationalize and perfect the coordination mechanisms among the various Chinese bureaucracies responsible for assessing national security conditions and formulating the policies to respond to those conditions.[94] Jing hints at significant problems in Chinese attempts to coordinate "economic, military, religious, ideological, and Internet strategies" in the effort to assemble an integrated grand strategy.[95] Automatic economic development—the certainty of 8 percent growth—could not, even if it were possible, ensure national security if Party elites are incapable of managing the security bureaucracies effectively.

3. Foster improved linkages between strategic research institutes and the state and military bureaucracies executing policy.[96] Although most of the influential research institutes are "owned" by state and military bureaucracies, others are semi-"autonomous" (from the state and military, though presumably not the Party), even though often staffed by retired PLA professors and officers. Jing evidently believes that these research institutes often produce insightful and creatively ingenious work that too often goes ignored in policy-making circles. Why should a society invest in such activities if the research results will not even be used?

4. Do a better job of integrating research into how to solve short-term problems with medium- and longer-term strategic objectives—and also study those grander objectives more systematically.[97] In particular, focus on how possible short-term moves either would or would not support medium- and longer-term goals and ambitions and how potential foes—especially the United States—might take advantage of the negative consequences of certain short-term moves. Jing offers this advice twice, in two separate sentences, which suggests that he believes Chinese strategy is presently often shortsighted in approach,

failing to imagine the possibly negative consequences of various moves several or more years into the future.[98] But, as with his other suggestions, Jing declines to provide illustrations, preferring an elliptical approach that might reflect the dangers associated with explicitly pointing out shortcomings in the military-strategic sector. His article does, however, effectively communicate alarm about China's current trajectory and invites readers to view with skepticism not only frank hubris but also the more soothing sort of blithe optimism associated with much Chinese realism.

5. Go on the offensive in public relations and soft power initiatives with the United States. Jing makes a boldly directly statement: "We must strengthen our influence in all spheres of American life."[99] The statement is bold (less so in a *neibu* journal, perhaps) insofar as Jing is calling in effect for Chinese intervention in domestic U.S. affairs. But this, too, appears to be a result of his concerns about Chinese complacency. Jing seems to be trying to shake his readers into realizing that in the realm of soft power, China is making very little progress vis-à-vis the United States, certainly inside the United States itself. In this formulation, even if the material rise could somehow be relied on to succeed automatically, there would be no guarantee that material power could be transformed into soft power.

CAUTIOUS PLURALIST RATIONALISTS

The Chinese analysts who cross the line into pluralist rationalism are even less sanguine about the PRC's prospects for consolidating the national rise than the moderate realists. The rationalists are not necessarily deeply pessimistic or profoundly worried, but they are more willing to acknowledge the possibility that things could go wrong for China, either for economic or other reasons. This indeed may be a key factor explaining why they promote a rationalist approach. The classical realists of the West may have recommended prudence in foreign policy, but realism in a Chinese context often comes across—at least in discourse, if not always in practice—as bellicose. In portraying international relations as an arena of struggle in which good (China) and evil (Japan, often the United

States, and others) are clearly demarcated, Chinese realists convey an image of interstate interactions as a dangerous moral contest but with a preordained conclusion: China's glorious ultimate victory. Given that the positive conclusion is preordained, it is almost logical for Chinese realists to find signs of victory—perhaps even imminent victory—within the swirling vortex of otherwise confusing international events. This seems to be a key reason the realists play down the problems China is facing, while at the same time exaggerating the problems faced by states and other actors they consider to be China's enemies. Some evidently find it impossible to imagine a serious economic slowdown or China becoming mired in a middle-income trap. Xi Jinping's China Dream rhetoric surely reinforces this predisposition, which could well lead to the realists being shocked and disappointed if a sustained slowdown does materialize.

Were that to happen, the realists *could* try activating the "China-as-perennial-victim" narrative to acknowledge the stall in China's rise but shift the blame for the country's difficulties onto the West, Japan, and/or other perceived or constructed enemies.[100] Nevertheless, if the realists' promise of inevitable success comes to be seen as demonstrably empty, the realists will find themselves "on the ropes" politically and be forced to contend for policy makers' attention with another cluster of analysts who forthrightly acknowledge China's problems and the possibility the national rise could falter. In recognition of Chinese weaknesses, these analysts—the pluralist rationalists—oppose the post-2009 increased aggressiveness and promote instead a genuinely more cooperative approach (moving beyond the plane of rhetoric) to international relations, whether in the area of security, economics, or culture.

How influential are the rationalists? While it would be impossible to specify with precision, there seems no doubt that they had the ear of policy makers when Hu Jintao was CCP general secretary. This is suggested not only by the ubiquity of rhetoric declaring that China's rise would be peaceful and that it hoped to build a harmonious world. The influence of the rationalists (or at least rationalism as a worldview) is also suggested by the specific actions Chinese policy makers took as they moved to integrate China into the world economy; foster educational and cultural exchanges; work with the United States and other powers in fighting terrorism, piracy, and the proliferation of weapons of mass destruction; and take other cooperative steps. Although, obviously, China has not always behaved cooperatively—especially to the degree that foreign states would like—it has behaved cooperatively to a point, and probably far more so than Chinese realists (certainly the imperialistic-realists, to use the English School terminology) would like. When the PRC state takes actions of a cooperative sort or in recognition of international norms, the moves will often have been influenced by rationalist logic, except in the absurdly circular sense that "everything a state does must be in the national interest (as defined by realists) or else it would have made other moves." Consequently, rationalism is an approach to international relations that must be considered as a potentially important factor in shaping China's trajectory, even if realism seems ultimately more potent.

PRC Vice Minister of Foreign Affairs Cui Tiankai articulated an official rationalist view consistent with Hu Jintao's doctrine of harmony on the eve of the fortieth anniversary of the Shanghai Communiqué (February 1972), which signaled the formal beginning of U.S.–China diplomatic rapprochement. In 2012, Cui published an article in *International Studies*, a leading Chinese IR journal, making recommendations for moving China and the United States further in the direction of "cooperative and partnerlike relations."[101] Cui argues that in all of the key issue-areas facing the two countries and the world as a whole, China and the United States must deepen their degree of "trust," a key component of the "foundation" for a cooperative, partnerlike relationship. Trust is essential, Cui contends, because at present, every time a small problem develops between the two countries, "some people" (Cui does not name names) start to question the entire relationship. To survive endless rounds of such questioning, the relationship must be built on the more solid foundation of deepening trust.[102]

But to be sure, realist concerns are not entirely absent from Cui's thinking; thus, trust can be built only on the basis of "two especially important preconditions" being met:

1. Both sides must earnestly respect the core national interests of the other, not only in talk but also in action. Cui specifies unification and terri-

torial integrity as the bottom-line Chinese core national interests—a formulation that suggests the United States must first accept the CCP's expansive territorial claims if trust is to be established.[103] Here is an example not only of realism but even imperial-leaning realism insofar as it requires the United States to accept Chinese irredentism, even if the consequence is that Washington must alienate its Asian allies, particularly Japan and the Philippines.

2. Both sides—but evidently the United States especially—must thoroughly, objectively, and realistically recognize the strategic intentions of the other side for what they truly are. By this Cui seems to mean that the United States must recognize that China is genuinely serious about rising peacefully (assuming its claims regarding core national interests are accepted) and should therefore not treat China as an enemy.[104] Cui does not say what Chinese analysts might now be misunderstanding about American intentions and how the Chinese side must therefore also change, but the context of his article suggests that he does think PRC scholars should do more to emphasize the positive elements of American global leadership for China's rise: the ways in which this particular hegemon (in the neutral, social-science sense) has been beneficial to China whereas other potential hegemons might have posed more serious problems. Emphasizing factors such as these would go a long way toward promoting the desired trust.[105]

The promotion of trust—a hot topic in recent years—was in 2010 subjected to an almost mocking critique by archrealist Yan Xuetong. In the journal *World Economics and Politics,* Yan ridiculed what he called "the doctrine of false friends," meaning the rhetoric in U.S.-China relations that the two countries should strive to become friends or even already are friends.[106] Yan finds that, in reality, the two countries have fundamentally conflicting national interests rooted in the structural fact that one is the hegemon and the other a rising challenger. As a result, problems and frictions will inevitably appear and reappear, yet politicians and pundits are constantly—and foolishly—wringing their hands and lamenting that the "friendship" is in trouble. This leads to summits and other events at which the friendship is proclaimed to be restored, very soon after which it starts to fray again as the problems stemming from structural reality naturally reappear. This dynamic creates unreasonable expectations, so that when the next set of problems crops up, observers and policy makers are even more disappointed than they would have been were it not for the illusions created by the doctrine of false friends. Commentators express surprise and concern, worrying about "what is going wrong" even though the problems are completely to be expected. Lamentation itself then fuses into the structure so that relations become worse than the structure would otherwise dictate. The solution, Yan argues, is for the two countries to stop overselling the idea of friendship and start instead to identify more areas of common interest.[107] Trust is unnecessary for a positive relationship between two great powers when the powers share common interests.

One rationalist who thinks in contrast that trust is critical is the well-known IR scholar Wang Jisi, Dean of Peking University's School of International Studies. With Kenneth Lieberthal of the Brookings Institution, Wang coauthored a widely circulated publication in the spring of 2012 arguing forcefully in favor of enhancing Sino–U.S. trust.[108] Here, however, I focus on an article Wang published for Chinese audiences in 2011, an article in which he vigorously championed the continuing relevance for Chinese foreign policy of Deng Xiaoping's 1989 injunction that China should bide its time in international affairs while keeping a low profile and making steady progress toward achieving significant goals.[109] Wang begins by trying to debunk the myth propounded by many Chinese realists that China will soon surpass the United States in comprehensive national power. If the realists are exaggerating Chinese strengths, then continuing to maintain a low profile would be China's only sensible course. It is important to emphasize that in wading into this debate Wang was not merely indulging in an academic exercise. By 2011, the Chinese shift to a more aggressive posture over territorial disputes was in full swing and surely was inconsistent with Deng Xiaoping's injunction. Wang was criticizing a risky strategic policy shift that held critical implications for the trajectory of China's rise.

Wang proceeded painstakingly in making his case. He rejected the idea that China will soon surpass the United States and argued instead that it has not even surpassed Japan or the EU in terms of comprehensive national power.[110] How could this be so? After all, Chinese GDP eclipsed that of Japan in 2010 as the PRC became the world's second-largest economy—on top of which China possesses nuclear weapons. Certainly this is true, Wang concedes, but the Japanese quality of life, cultural and educational attainments, level of science and technology development, and degree of national unity—all rooted in a democratic political stability that had defied two decades of economic stagnation—far outpace Chinese accomplishments in these areas. Much the same could be said for most EU countries. Consequently, it is "a completely unrealistic way of thinking" to conceive China as having already surpassed Japan and Europe and being likely to surpass the United States in ten to twenty years, the argument Wang identifies other Chinese elites as making. In contrast, Wang contends that at best China should be identified as "the world's strongest developing country,"[111] a formulation that allows for the possibility that success in development is still far from certain. Wang's rationalism can accommodate the possibility that China could get stuck in a middle-income trap. Very few realists seem willing to accept this possibility.

Second, Wang finds China to be mired in a geopolitical predicament likely to present PRC leaders with vexing strategic challenges for many years to come. He recognizes that China is now at the center of an increasingly well-integrated Asian economic order—a fact that realists trumpet with pride. But Wang emphasizes that economic centrality is not sufficient to confer military security on China. The problem is that economic integration notwithstanding, China has no formal military allies among Asian countries and is embroiled in serious (and worsening) territorial disputes with Japan, India, Vietnam, and the Philippines. The international security architecture of economically Sino-centric Asia paradoxically remains U.S.-centric, based on the hub-and-spoke model of bilateral security relationships the United States has had in place for decades and that it began to reinvigorate in 2010.[112] Not only does this basic contradiction negatively affect Chinese security directly, but it also implies that China cannot purport to speak on the world stage for all of Asia—as (Wang believes) France and Germany sometimes do for Europe and Brazil for Latin America. The situation is embarrassing, but more seriously it undermines PRC soft power.[113]

Third, China is almost isolated on the world stage ideologically. The PRC is one of only a very small number of states still ruled by a Communist Party and is in addition somewhere on the path of a reform-and-opening process whose end goal is uncertain. This implies a fundamental political insecurity. The country is also not yet unified: National integrity is thus threatened. The economic development to date has caused social instability and environmental destruction, and efforts to improve the economic development model are not yet succeeding.[114]

All of these interrelated weaknesses restrict China's ability to act as a major player in international relations. For this reason, Wang strongly criticizes those who contend that Deng Xiaoping's "keep a low profile" instruction is out of date. Some Chinese elites in 2009–2011 were calling for a more forward policy on territorial and other issues, risking conflict with the United States. Wang warns that China must not behave confrontationally with the United States at this point in its development. He rejects the arguments of Chinese intellectuals and media commentators expressing overoptimism about China's relative international position. Their views "are alarming and need to be rectified," Wang contends, because China is not yet sufficiently strong to risk a major conflict.[115] Wang also criticizes the nationalists who were, in 2011 (before Xi Jinping co-opted and modified the idea), promoting a China Dream. Wang argues that what China needs at present is to improve the Chinese people's welfare, proceeding modestly and prudently. Instead, China Dream promoters were at the time vaingloriously striving to build "the tallest, the biggest, the strongest, the most expensive, the fanciest"—pursuing the relative gains that all realists champion instead of the absolute gains or improvements that neoliberal or rationalist states pursue in cooperation with other states. "We should not be trying to surpass the United States," Wang writes. "We should be trying to surpass ourselves."[116]

To be sure, Wang concedes that China need not behave as timorously as in 1989–1992, the period initially covered by Deng's injunction to keep a low profile. In connection with this observation, Wang makes two points that further illuminate his rationalism:

1. In 1989–1992, China's overwhelmingly top foreign policy concern was responding effectively to pressures in the post-Tiananmen period from the U.S.-led West; generally, this required adopting a conciliatory policy. Today, however, the PRC has a substantially broader foreign policy perspective and more complex and varied national interests. It would not be sensible for the Party-state to act equally cautiously in dealing with all of these issues. When China faces urgent challenges such as the global financial crisis or global warming, it must act with bold assertiveness. On other issues, however, there is no need for urgency, particularly when boldly assertive actions could lead to the risk of military conflict with other powerful states.[117]

2. Playing up the "keep a low profile" slogan in the media or official foreign policy statements is itself a bad idea. The reason is that the "bide our time" segment of the slogan has negative connotations. Wang notes that Deng did not initially intend the slogan to be read or heard by foreigners. By 1996, however, it was appearing regularly in Chinese newspapers and magazines. Particularly since 2000, the slogan has increasingly been analyzed and picked apart by foreign observers. Wang is fully aware that in some foreign societies the "bide our time" phrase can be taken to mean, "Let's bide our time until we're in a stronger position, after which we can settle old scores." He says that the phrase can be understood this way in China itself, especially when applied to interpersonal relations. Consequently, it is little wonder that some foreigners would find the "keep a low profile" phrase alarming.[118]

Another reason to stop talking about the slogan publicly is that it arouses unreasonable expectations inside China itself. Chinese audiences hear the slogan today, and some respond: "But we're strong now. Why should we wait any longer to settle old scores?" Yet China is *not* as strong now as many nationalists believe—and certainly it is not (to Wang) sufficiently strong to pursue irredentist claims or the rest of the nationalist agenda aggressively. Emphasizing Deng Xiaoping's slogan can only frustrate popular expectations, creating unnecessary headaches for policy makers as they struggle to guide public opinion and craft a rational security strategy.[119]

Wang concludes by recommending that China (1) realize the true spirit of the "keep a low profile" injunction by pursuing a "modest and prudent" foreign policy, which would have the effect of reassuring foreigners and convincing other countries of the reasonableness of China's limited and perfectly justifiable claims regarding core national interests; and (2) correctly understand and convey that China's long-term strategic objectives *must* be centered on pursuing development for the Chinese people, a task that for many years into the future will require a peaceful strategic environment, particularly in Asia itself.[120]

Another scholar who rebuts the confident realists—although less forcefully than Wang Jisi—is Yang Jiemian, President of the Shanghai Institute for International Studies. In 2012, Yang published an article in *International Studies* criticizing those who argue that the GFC and wars in the Middle East and Central Asia spell the final decline of U.S. hegemony. Although conceding that these developments did deal serious blows to the United States, Yang finds enduring strengths in American society. He points particularly to (1) science and technology, especially computer- and communications-related science and technology and industries associated with the life sciences; (2) the enormous American demand for consumption, which Yang estimated at US$9 trillion annually—surely the envy of a country like China straining to make a shift to consumption-led growth; and (3) the prodigious U.S. capacity to "determine the flow of resources globally," which Yang attributes to thirty or so U.S.-registered multinational corporations (which he does not identify).[121]

Yang is, however, upset by the renewed U.S. focus on Asia-Pacific security affairs, which President Barack Obama put into place after 2009—the so-called pivot in response to increasing Chinese assertiveness on territorial issues. Although Yang does not see the United States as being on the verge of collapse, he does find that the events of the 2000s weakened the hegemon and its Western allies; thus, "One incontestable fact is that the political and economic systems of the Western countries are now facing increasingly powerful pressures to reform."[122] These developments, coupled with China's undeniable successes, lead Yang to conclude that the United States should behave more humbly than in decades past. He seems not a little irritated that the United States would have the audacity to reassert itself in the Asia-Pacific area given that there is no doubt American power relative to China's is now at its lowest point in history, even though in absolute terms the United States remains substantially more powerful than the PRC.[123] The United States, Yang thinks, should acknowledge the shifts of recent years by treating China with greater respect and behaving more circumspectly in the Asia-Pacific area. The U.S. refusal to adjust its posture is obnoxious—and yet Yang still recognizes that "although the U.S. at present faces all manner of real and long-term difficulties, it continues to possess significant advantages in the areas of comprehensive national power, politics, military affairs, culture, management, and science and technology. We must acknowledge this point as we comprehensively and objectively assess U.S. influence on the international system."[124] The time is not yet right, Yang is cautioning, for China to abandon rationalist prudence under the false assumption that its day in the sun relative to the United States has finally dawned.

Another scholar writing in 2012 was equally concerned as Yang Jiemian and Wang Jisi that some Chinese IR analysts are exaggerating U.S. weaknesses. Zhang Wenzong, a specialist on U.S. affairs at the China Institute of Contemporary International Relations, argues in an open journal article that despite America's numerous problems—and Zhang discusses a number of them in detail—U.S. society retains formidable strengths.[125] Even with regard to the problems, Zhang finds the United States displaying an impressive determination to transcend its difficulties and reinvigorate the economy, political system, and culture. Zhang develops a meticulously researched rejoinder to the hubristic community, arguing that overstating U.S. weaknesses and recommending a more muscular Chinese approach could prove to be extremely costly. Although it is always possible the United States has begun tumbling into a long-term decline, the evidence is far from conclusive. China could well be making a huge mistake if it decides to found its international strategy for the next decade on the assumption that the power transition is trending unmistakably in China's favor.

Director Huang Ping of the Institute of American Studies at the Chinese Academy of Social Sciences is yet another scholar who warns against overstating America's international decline. Writing in a *neibu* journal,

Huang in November 2011 cautioned his Chinese readers that no matter whether the question is energy and other natural resource reserves, underlying economic strength, attractiveness to foreign direct investors, population growth, population structure, technical innovativeness, education quality, or military power, the United States continues to boast extraordinary strengths. Even the country's persistent trade deficit can be explained partly as a function of the awesomely voracious American consumer demand. The only serious problems facing the United States, Huang finds, are (1) the mounting public debt, and (2) the pathological political culture engendered by Republican–Democratic contestation. But even these problems he does not consider to be devastating.[126] He concludes that "the United States still has the most comprehensive national power of any leading state."[127] It does not appear to be declining in any actionable sense, and for this reason China must reevaluate its strategic options more carefully.

One of the scholars interviewed in May 2012 concurred that more caution is warranted and in particular that the robust new Chinese maritime strategy is deeply problematic. This scholar argues that the root problem is that CCP leaders are abusing the concept of core national interests. The scholar notes that in a white paper on peaceful development issued in September 2011, the PRC State Council identified six core national interests: state sovereignty, national security, territorial integrity and national reunification, China's political system as defined by the Constitution, overall social stability, and the basic safeguards for ensuring sustainable economic and social development.[128] The scholar rejects such a capacious definition of core national interests and contends that, instead, there should be only one such interest: upholding CCP rule over China indefinitely. Identifying all of the other desiderata as core national interests and pursuing them as such could paradoxically work to weaken or undermine the Party's leadership, because they imply the Party making ambitious promises that it cannot possibly succeed in fulfilling.

For this reason, the scholar argues that all of the currently specified core national interests except maintenance of the Party's leadership role should be reclassified as "legitimate interests." The special characteristic of legitimate interests is that they must meet the criterion of being consistent with the U.N. Charter, to which China willingly acceded.[129] The scholar finds all six so-called core national interests as fully consistent with the Charter. But he argues that not even unification with Taiwan should at present be defined as a core national interest because China lacks the diplomatic and military strength to force the issue. If China tried to use its military might in the near future to compel Taiwan into accepting a settlement, the United States would surely respond with force, and China would be defeated. Such a colossal miscalculation and failure would, the scholar expects, spell the end of CCP rule. By the 2020s, the balance of power in the Taiwan Strait might well have changed in China's favor; if so, then the leaders could think about redefining Taiwan's unification as a core national interest. For now, however, China should more cautiously identify it as merely a legitimate interest.[130]

By the same logic, however, the scholar judges that China might well declare that its claims to parts (at least) of the South China Sea are a core national interest. The reason is that, unlike in the case of Taiwan, the PRC is fully capable of enforcing some of its maritime claims without igniting self-destruction. The only problem, the scholar notes, is that the "nine-dashed line" by which successive Chinese governments have, since 1947, signaled their claim to most of the sea implies that China should possess nearly all of it, both the land features and the water: "This wasn't the original intention and shouldn't (even by implication) be what China claims today." Instead, China should stake its claim to (and define as a core national interest) all the islands and rocks—inhabitable or otherwise—in the sea, and twelve miles of water around them. Then it should define as "important" interests 200 miles of water surrounding only the genuinely inhabitable islands. The remainder—although it may not amount to much—should be acknowledged by Beijing as being "high seas." Although such a move would largely be symbolic, because it would still suggest that China claims vast swathes of the sea—most, in fact, of what is suggested by the nine-dashed line—it would still signal to the Americans and other commercial powers the reasonableness of China's claim. The foreigners would then have less reason to oppose China's stance—although their allies in the region might certainly complain.[131]

Even though this idea seems transparently sensible to the scholar he does not expect CCP leaders to embrace it: "No one in China these days would be willing to say that parts of the South China Sea are high seas. No one wants to be the traitor who suggests backing down." Consequently, the scholar finds it unsurprising that the United States and other great powers would view Beijing's current claim as unreasonable (he is far less sympathetic to the objections of Vietnam and the Philippines). "Between you and me," he said, "the nine-dashed line was in any case only drawn hurriedly and at random" by the Republic of China (ROC) government in the late 1940s. It has no intrinsic special meaning. And yet China now seems committed to taking control of everything inside the nine-dashed line as a core national interest. This, the scholar concludes, is dangerously overambitious.[132]

Sometimes Chinese analysts identify the machinations of smaller powers rather than ever-present U.S. arrogance as posing the greatest potential to destroy U.S.–China relations. Teng Jianqun, a researcher at the China Institute for International Studies, develops such a line of argument in a 2011 article in *International Studies*. Teng's concern is to warn Chinese leaders specifically about how North Korea could drag China into an unwanted conflict with the United States, whereas Japan could drag the Americans into an unwanted conflict with China.[133] Writing in the months following North Korea's March 2010 attack on the South Korean naval vessel *Cheonan*, an attack that killed forty-six sailors, and its November 2010 shelling of Yeongpyeong Island, which killed four civilians, Teng devotes most of his attention to the unpredictable and violent Pyongyang regime. He worries that China and the United States might expend great efforts to improve their relationship only to have all the hard work dashed by misbehaving and irresponsible client states with serious repercussions for the overall structure of world order. The leaders of great powers must constantly be reminded of this possibility and communicate with each other before taking actions that could prove rash.[134] Teng is warning that it would be easy for China–U.S. relations to deteriorate rapidly in the absence of intelligent, firm, and patient leadership. Although analogizing Japan to North Korea is obviously dubious, the main point is that Teng is a rationalist fully on board with the "peace and development" line inherited from Deng Xiaoping. He favors caution and prudence in foreign policy but recognizes that, even if the rising and currently dominant powers behave wisely, world order could still come unglued as a result of the actions of irresponsible third parties. This differs from many realist formulations insofar as the United States is not automatically cast as a villainous behind-the-scenes manipulator of most important events.[135]

THE LIMITS OF RATIONALISM
AND THE ROAD AHEAD

It can be seen that even these Chinese forays into pluralist rationalism retain important realist elements. The concept of a heroic Chinese nation-state, which will always be menaced by foreigners, repeatedly recurs in the writings of international relations analysts (though they are less likely to invoke such imagery in interviews with foreign academics). Even scholars who may not hold such views seem pressured to acknowledge their centrality and the national interests to which they give rise in making policy recommendations. For this reason we might expect that rationalism can act as a brake on Chinese policy but probably cannot supplant realism as the fundamental driver of policy. The question then becomes whether the more aggressive sort of imperialistic-realism will determine policy or the more moderate versions that sometimes seem difficult to distinguish from rationalism. There is no easy way to answer this question. The answer partly depends on the degree to which Chinese policy-making communities can be socialized into norms of cooperation with foreign powers and the use of nonviolent means to settle disputes. In Chapter 6, I show how most Chinese IR writers (in my sample, at least) view international culture (the source of norms) as a zone of contestation or even a battleground with the West.

Such an orientation suggests that socialization is not going to be an easy process and may, in fact, never succeed. Certainly there is no justification in thinking that it will succeed automatically and thus that there is little reason to be concerned about the post-2008 shift to a more assertive foreign policy. A sustained economic slowdown could force China to become more cautious, but it might also suggest to the more ambitious realists that the country should move quickly to achieve its core territorial objectives before the window of opportunity closes. Realists might also blame foreign countries for China's economic predicament, further fueling international tensions. In short, it is not easy—based on the materials analyzed for this book—to imagine China shifting in the direction of a fundamentally more cooperative foreign policy in the years immediately ahead. Yet, at the same time, the persisting influence of the rationalists discussed in this chapter—and the economic and political liberals discussed in previous chapters—does give grounds for optimism that militarized conflict is not inevitable and that the PRC state's posture could slowly change. But change would be necessary to ensure against conflict because current trends in thinking and the post-2008 foreign policy shift contain many worrisome features.

CHAPTER 6

Competing with the West on the "Cultural Front" in International Relations

PROBABLY THE CENTRAL QUESTION OF CONCERN to analysts and policy makers who study China's trajectory is whether the PRC's national rise will be peaceful, given the logic of power transitions.[1] Would a transfer of global preeminence from the United States to China more closely resemble the processes that led to the peaceful handoff from Great Britain to the United States after World War I or the violent rises of Germany and Japan in the first half of the twentieth century?

One key factor determining whether a transition will be peaceful is the relative satisfaction of the rising power with the international status quo and overall course of the transition.[2] The presumption of this chapter is that if a rising power's (and certainly China's) foreign policy elites perceive *culture* on the international level—the globally prevalent pattern of values, beliefs, norms, and symbolic structures—as a zone of cooperation with the dominant state and its allies, rather than a zone of contestation, the rising power will probably be satisfied, and the transition is more likely to be peaceful. Countries in the dominant coalition will have played a central role in forming the global cultural order. This was certainly true for the United States in the twentieth century. Whether the issue is Washington's role as chief architect of the system-defining international regimes put in place in the years following World War II or Hollywood's (and, more recently, Silicon Valley's) dominant position in shaping global popular culture and the architecture of the worldwide network society, the United States and its allies have indisputably been central to creating the "ideational order" into which China began rising in the 1990s. If Chinese elites now perceive this side of international relations to be benign or helpful for China's rise, the rise is more likely to be peaceful and free of large-scale conflict.

If, on the other hand, Chinese elites perceive globally prevalent culture in adversarial or conflictual terms, there is heightened reason to be concerned that the transition will turn violent. Probably nothing is more productive of conflict when securitized than culture. Consider a politically authoritative Chinese definition of the concept:

Culture is the real, lived experiences and feelings in people's internal life-worlds; their thinking patterns, value standards, and emotional tendencies; it manifests itself in human activities and the material objects they create . . . [Culture] indicates people's thoughts and rational concepts, their knowledge and technical capacities, morality and beliefs, arts and imagination. Society is a living organism; . . . culture is the brain, the soul . . . We [Communist Party elites] must "construct the brain."[3]

CCP elites might decide that opening China to relatively unfettered flows of culture from abroad would be useful for strengthening the country. The PRC has already come a strikingly long way in this direction since the days of Mao Zedong. The Party evidently values China's deep enmeshment in the global economy (although there is the counterforce of economic nationalism). Its leaders might adopt a similar attitude and similar policies toward global cultural flows. If they were to do so, we might conclude that elite Chinese thinking on culture in international relations is trending in a rationalist or neoliberal (in the IR sense) direction, which would give grounds for optimism concerning the power transition.[4] To the extent these putative neoliberal conceptions of culture reflected the deeper construct of the identity of the Chinese state, we might even confidently expect substantially more cooperative policies from China across a variety of issue-areas in the years ahead and the power transition to be productive of a larger-scale global peace.

On the other hand, it is possible that Chinese thinking on global culture could exemplify the adversarial or conflictual presuppositions normally associated with realism. This, too, might reflect the deeper construct of state identity and to that extent make it less likely that China's rise would be smooth and trouble free.[5] But the specifics of the assumptions are important. A realist approach might assume conflict but not the inevitability of violent disruption, because some forms of realism prescribe prudence in foreign policy along with the rational adjustment of interests in the face of demands from other states. This is why not all scholars holding a predominantly realist view are consistently pessimistic about China's rise.[6] Robert Ross, for example, argued in 2009 that the United States and China have arrived at a stable security arrangement in Asia based on Chinese domination of the East Asian mainland and U.S. domination of the East Asian littoral.[7] Peace results not because of interdependence, participation in regimes, or common identities but because power is balanced. In the same spirit, Thomas Christensen offers that a robust U.S. security role in Asia can paradoxically work to elicit cooperative Chinese behavior across a broad range of policy issue-areas: "A firm security posture toward China would not only hedge against a potential turn for the worse in Chinese domestic politics and foreign policy; it would also help shape long-term Chinese political and diplomatic evolution in directions that reduce the likelihood of unwanted conflict and instability."[8]

Analogously, not all scholars predominantly influenced by neoliberalism are consistently optimistic. For example, Susan L. Shirk worries that if the United States and Asian countries were to abandon their policies of engagement, burgeoning Chinese nationalism could combine with dysfunctional political institutions to lead China into an unreasonably threatening stance. In this formulation, China's state identity is portrayed as not inherently cooperative. Whether it will become cooperative depends on the policies of other powerful players in interaction with domestic Chinese political dynamics.[9] Similarly, Deborah Welch Larson and Alexei Shevchenko use social identity theory to assess the implications of China's rise (and Russia's possible return) for great power cooperation. They conclude that China (and Russia) are unlikely to challenge the international status quo if the United States acknowledges and accepts as legitimate their efforts to compete creatively for soft-power status by presenting alternative developmental models. If, in contrast, the United States refuses to respect these efforts, the two states will probably become uncooperative as their power increases. Behavior is thus presented as shaped more by context than by intrinsic identity.[10]

OBJECTIVES

The point of this chapter is to advance the debate on the potential peacefulness of China's rise in the coming ten to fifteen years by assessing whether culture in Chinese writing on foreign and security policy is presented as a zone of cooperation with other states (particularly powerful states) or a zone of contestation. To what degree is this the case, and with what logic and implications for the power transition (assuming it continues)? What explains the specific hallmarks of elite Chinese thinking on culture in international relations? How culture is treated is important for categorizing the Chinese state's identity in an international context because of the lower likelihood that attitudes and policies toward the cultural sector (as opposed to the military and economic sectors) could be attributed to international structures, including balances of power (globally and regionally), alliance systems, regimes and institutions, and hard geographical facts. Finding that Chinese elites tend to frame problems in the military and economic sectors in realist terms—as discussed in Chapter 5—is obviously important but cannot reliably tell us as much as we would like to know about state identity over multiple issue-areas because a substantial proportion of China's posture in these sectors flows from the situational factor of structure.[11] The cultural sector is quite different. In this relatively unregulated and unstructured realm, institutions to govern interaction are underdeveloped, and states must determine for themselves what policies to pursue. Some states' elites might perceive world politics fundamentally as a clash of civilizations and act accordingly, trying to maximize their soft power aggressively. Others, although not unconcerned with soft power, might expect to gain from opening up their borders to relatively unfettered cultural exchanges. Although some particular forms of exchange (such as trade in certain information technologies or mass media products, or broadcasting from the geosynchronous orbital belt) are governed by regimes, cultural interactions in the broader sense are too multifaceted and diverse to be contained by international structures and often too abstract to be measured or even perceived clearly. Because state policies in this vital area are thus relatively unstructured by international institutions—unlike key aspects of policy in the military and economic sectors—the choices a state makes in the cultural sector can shine a light on critical dimensions of the state's identity, which in interaction with structural factors will shape its overall security posture.

There is also a kind of "crucial case" logic at work in this issue-area. Because cultural interaction does not present direct material threats to a state's security, it should be relatively safe for a nation-state's elites to express positive, cooperative attitudes toward other states in cultural interaction. If instead they portray interaction even in the cultural sector in adversarial terms, then it seems strongly likely they would view military and economic relations in such terms. It would be odd if they portrayed cultural interactions in adversarial terms but military and economic relations in cooperative terms.

PREVIEW

The record, it transpires, is clear: Policy-oriented Chinese elites are widely convinced that the PRC is locked in a realist competition with the United States and the broader West not only in military and economic affairs but also for the power to shape construction of Chinese culture and the mentalities of people in China and other societies. This struggle is imagined to be one of the key components of a larger contest to determine China's developmental course—the nature and meaning of its rise—and, as a result, the next stage of world history. Rare is the Chinese author publishing on questions of culture in international relations who does not frame the problem in this way. Indeed, the framework seems to structure or reflect the mentalities of Chinese decision makers as they contemplate not only culture policy itself but also military and economic policy. Chinese analysts tend to present all three of these as intrinsically interconnected. The viewpoint crystallized in September 1997 when the final report of the Fifteenth Communist Party Congress announced that "a socialist culture with Chinese characteristics can be an important force for consolidating and motivating all of China's ethnic groups, an important indicator of comprehensive national power"—the first time, according to a Chinese historian, that the Party linked state-directed cultural development to increasing comprehensive national power.[12]

The potential usefulness of culture to any state determined to increase its relative power is implicit in the Chinese definition of the concept given earlier, which concludes that "society is a living organism; . . . culture is the brain, the soul . . . We [Communist Party elites] must 'construct the brain.'"[13] Although it would be impossible, in this view, for a society to stand outside of its body to construct its own brain, leading members of a vanguard Leninist political party can imagine themselves trying to do precisely that: remaking China so that it can be guided toward a future of perpetually increasing wealth and relative power in competition with foreign states. The essential precondition for success is that the vanguard party must retain control over cultural construction. If it loses control to foreign states in what Chinese elites consider to be the intensely competitive arenas of international relations, the Party would no longer be able to direct China's development. Instead, control would fall into the hands of foreign states—most likely the United States, because that is the country Chinese analysts regularly insist is striving to consolidate world hegemony. Should Washington secure control over the direction of China's cultural development, U.S. power would increase to dizzying heights. China would lose its distinctive identity and eventually be vanquished.

Publicly, Chinese writers often call for building a harmonious world, but in their Chinese-language books and articles, which they presumably do not expect foreigners to read, most express deep skepticism that the world can be anything other than conflict ridden, even in the realm of culture.[14] Such thinking seems to undergird the PRC's policy toward Google and other foreign Internet firms, malware circulation, Internet surveillance, the Great Firewall, and other familiar elements of the Chinese policy stance toward international cultural flows and the global network society. The flows can be allowed unimpeded if (and only if) they hold the promise of strengthening China or at worst having a neutral effect. Otherwise, the flows must be regulated tightly or suppressed. At the same time, China must work diligently to increase its own cultural appeal so that it can compete with the United States and broader West for influence over third countries.

The main disagreement among Chinese elites centers on whether they view contests in the cultural sector in offensive or defensive terms.[15] The clear parallel is with general offensive and defensive realism. As Mearsheimer explains the distinction:

Offensive realism parts company with defensive realism over the question of how much power states want. For defensive realists, the international structure provides states with little incentive to seek additional increments of power; instead it pushes them to maintain the existing balance of power. Preserving power, rather than increasing it, is the main goal of states. Offensive realists, on the other hand, believe that status quo powers are rarely found in world politics, because the international system creates powerful incentives for states to look for opportunities to gain power at the expense of rivals, and to take advantage of those situations when the benefits outweigh the costs. A state's ultimate goal is to be the hegemon in the system.[16]

Chinese offensive cultural realists view the world as dangerous but believe that China's rise has advanced to the point it can compete confidently with other states and expand Chinese cultural influence abroad. The game is realist, but China can now play it more successfully, which means that it should become substantially more assertive. Defensive realists worry that continued American cultural and soft-power advantages keep China locked in a precarious strategic position. They are pessimistic even about prospects for China's rise continuing, and in that respect they more closely resemble the moderate realists or even the rationalists discussed in Chapter 5. Linking cultural power to material power, the defensive realists worry that the United States and broader West are daily waging a cultural war to subvert China and undermine its rise.

The final category of analysts (to be discussed first) might be called "realist empiricists." These social scientists focus on measuring relative cultural power carefully—but they also fully to accept the realist framework, which assumes mutually suspicious states as the irreducible, core actors in a world political system laden with conflict because of international anarchy.

REALIST EMPIRICISTS: COUNTING WHO'S AHEAD

Perhaps the leading practitioner of the empiricist approach is archrealist Yan Xuetong, Director of the International Problems Research Institute at Qinghua University. With Xu Jin, a PhD student, Yan in 2008 published an article in *Contemporary International Relations* quantitatively and qualitatively comparing Chinese and American soft power.[17] The authors' primary conclusion was that, by 2007, China had increased its soft power to around one-third that of the United States, whereas prospects were good that it could close the gap even further in the years ahead if the CCP leadership adopted wise policies.

Yan and Xu consider that soft power can be disassembled into three distinct components: international attractiveness (of the overall national development model, the political-economic system, and the culture); international mobilization capacity (good strategic relationships as a basis for diplomatic efforts to influence formation of international rules of the game without resorting to violence); and domestic mobilization capacity (ability to motivate and organize society's upper- and lower-level strata for the purpose of attaining collective goals without using force). "The problem is that in a situation in which the international [normative] environment and China's [political] system both do not change, on what basis could the attractiveness of China's system increase" in the eyes of foreigners? Some scholars suggest not worrying about the problem of China's political system being unattractive and simply focusing efforts on promoting Chinese culture abroad. But Yan and Xu see the contradiction between Chinese politics and global norms and values as serious; moreover, there is not much the CCP can do about this problem in the short term, because "cultural attractiveness and its ability to spread are the natural cumulative results of long-term development. National policy can have only a minuscule effect on increasing the international attractiveness of a country's culture."[18]

Yet Yan and Xu do offer four proposals for painstakingly increasing Chinese soft power, step-by-step. First, the CCP should open the channels of public discussion to ensure that Party cadres and the general public are all aware China will need more than economic growth to secure lasting national power. Cadres and citizens alike must come to realize that some of their less-attractive practices (political and cultural) must change if China's rise in cultural terms—essential to consolidating the military and economic rise—is to succeed.

Second, China should continue to promote the harmonious world concept first articulated by CCP General Secretary Hu Jintao in April

2005.[19] This, Yan and Xu believe, can increase the legitimacy of China's international strategy as it becomes richer and more powerful militarily. China can position itself as something of a golden-mean country: lodged between developed and developing, democratic and authoritarian, religious (Confucian) and nonreligious. Strategically categorizing China in this way should increase its appeal to numerous different kinds of countries and enhance its capacity to mobilize international coalitions for supporting policies that would strengthen the Chinese relative position.

Third, the CCP should reconsider its strategy of not forming international alliances. Such a strategy sharply limits China's international mobilization capacity. China should instead form alliances with "more countries" (an increase in quantity) and "better countries" (an increase in quality). (Yan and Xu do not name the potential partners they have in mind.) It should especially form good military-strategic relations with neighboring countries.

Fourth—and clearly as a long-term endeavor—China should work harder to achieve domestic fairness and justice, the key to achieving the goal of building a harmonious society. One reason this is important for soft power and Chinese cultural influence is that a higher degree of fairness and justice would increase *internal* mobilization capacity. Although China may be a long way from building a harmonious society in any absolute sense, Yan and Xu note that the key for soft power competition is how domestically harmonious China will be relative to its chief international rival, the United States. And here they think prospects are reasonably bright: China has a fair chance of surpassing the United States in domestic fairness and justice and, as a result, "to greatly increase the international attractiveness of the Chinese national model."[20]

In a 2009 interview, Yan elaborated on these points while making the realism at the root of his thinking more explicit.[21] He complained that China is unlikely to make any major strides in increasing its soft power until significant progress is achieved in reducing the negative externalities associated with Chinese-style economic growth: "A country in which everyone high and low considers making money to be the loftiest pursuit is a country that will not be respected in international society." This seemed crucial. But Yan argued that the *best* way to increase Chinese soft power is "very explicitly to use our own policy choices to tell international society in the clearest terms that our policies will firmly proceed from the principle that we first protect the Chinese national interest and only secondarily consider what effects our policies might have on the global realm." Only countries that faithfully fulfill their responsibilities to themselves first will be in a position to shoulder global responsibilities. And the CCP's core responsibility in governing China—the focus of all its policies—must be to "realize the dignity of the Chinese people." Economic growth alone is insufficient to the task: "Only an increasingly powerful state can realize the Chinese people's dignity."[22] This is because dignity is impossible for a people who cannot satisfy their territorial claims or otherwise defend themselves in the face of exploitation by foreigners.

Another example of a realist empiricist approach is "Constructing China's Cultural Attractiveness to Neighboring Countries," contributed by Yao Qin—then a researcher at the Shanghai Academy of Social Sciences—to a 2006 edited volume.[23] Yao acknowledges that China has in recent years accumulated some successes in constructing cultural attractiveness. The CCP launched its Confucius Institutes (CIs) program in 2004 to promote Chinese culture abroad, and this contributed to a worldwide "Chinese language fever" that purportedly led to 40 million foreigners studying Mandarin by 2006[24]—as the CCP planned to establish CIs in 500 cities worldwide by 2020.[25] In recent years, meanwhile, Chinese film directors, actors, athletes, and architects have become famous and admired personages worldwide. China has even produced—at least in the minds of some foreigners—an alternative development model, the "Beijing consensus" (a concept invented by Joshua Cooper Ramo), which "may not be compatible with the concrete national conditions of every single country" but nevertheless "provides to numerous developing countries a completely new development path to reflect on as a reference."[26]

But, like Yan Xuetong and Xu Jin, Yao stresses China's relative cultural weakness—the areas that it desperately needs to improve to compete effectively with the West. He cites data indicating that, in 2004, Chinese individuals and entities bought the publishing rights to import 4,068 books from the United States, 2,030 books from the United Kingdom, and 694 books from Japan. In turn, American, British, and Japanese individuals and institutions bought the publishing rights to import only, respectively, fourteen, sixteen, and twenty-two books from China. (These figures do not include pirated books, for which the magnitude of discrepancy is undoubtedly much greater.)[27] This is the problem of the so-called cultural deficit, which numerous Chinese analysts lament as a major brake on the expansion of Chinese influence abroad. The cultural deficit also has a qualitative dimension. Although the books Chinese import from the West and Japan typically cover topics related to science, technology, economics, business, and public administration, the (few) books Westerners and Japanese import from China cover traditional Chinese medicine, martial arts, literature, and other relics of a premodern culture. Yao considers this to be a serious problem. Foreigners may admire imperial China's accomplishments from centuries past, "but toward contemporary China, [they] harbor doubts and suspicions."[28]

Yao contends that unless contemporary China can increase its international attractiveness, the country's rise in military and economic terms will be viewed with alarm by other states. This could have two dangerous consequences. First, neighboring states might decide to increase their own military power and/or form defensive alliances against China. Yao mentions (without providing a detailed citation) a 2005 public opinion poll that found 37.7 percent of South Koreans believed that, within ten years, China would become Korea's biggest international threat.[29]

Second, the U.S. hegemon could try to choke off a potentially menacing China's rise before it can build the momentum necessary to ensure success. These two points are interrelated, because if China could increase its cultural attractiveness to neighboring countries, "then even if the existing hegemon decided to choke off China's rise, it would lack the ability."[30] On the other hand, if neighboring countries do not find China attractive, they could become amenable to forming an alliance with the United States to pursue containment. As a result, whether China can increase its cultural power is perceived as a matter likely to have tangible consequences for the country's strategic position. Arguably, China was making substantial progress in this direction in the years leading up to the 2008 Beijing Olympics and may have made even more progress by hosting that event and the 2010 Shanghai World Expo successfully. But it still had a long way to go before it could surpass the United States or even Japan and Europe.

Much the same pessimism or at least caution is expressed by Yu Xintian (Shanghai Institute for International Studies) in a 2011 article in *International Studies*. Yu's main point of contention is that despite China's world-historic economic transformation, which most foreigners find dazzling and impressive (even considering the heavy costs), China will still find it impossible to increase cultural influence abroad until it first makes fundamental improvements to the culture at home. Yu argues that Chinese culture was severely damaged during the Cultural Revolution and since then has been twisted further by materialism and "the worship of gold." It is true that the situation is improving, as more Chinese people pay attention to cultivating "civilized" thoughts and behaviors. But Yu's core argument is that China still has such a long way to go in improving its internal culture that it should not expect soft power internationally to come easy. If it does come, it will only be after the cultural reconstruction efforts at home start to take deeper root. Nor would resurrecting Confucianism serve as a shortcut to soft power success. Yu agrees with Yao Qin that emphasizing ancient Chinese culture is not an especially useful tack for China to take. What foreigners focus on is present-day Chinese culture. Only to the extent that Confucianism (or other ancient thought systems and practices) can be seen as manifest in contemporary culture will trumpeting it internationally serve to increase Chinese soft power or cultural influence.[31]

On the other hand, Yu thinks that China does possess an essential culture hundreds or even thousands of years old and that this culture is fundamentally good: a useful foundation on which to build soft power. She cites as an illustration the voyages of Zheng He from 1405 to 1433. Yu finds that these voyages were completely peaceful and that they suggest or even mandate the inherent peacefulness of contemporary China's rise.[32] Because of this inherent peacefulness, even though Yu warns that China needs a cultural renaissance, she also strongly approves going ahead and trying now to propagate the notion of timeless Chinese goodness. This is because, whenever China makes such a move, friendly countries (she offers Malaysia as an example) feel motivated to echo and reinforce the PRC claims, which then has the effect of counteracting the negative propaganda that enemies of China are constantly circulating.

What is important to underscore is how Yu portrays the CCP as locked in a competition with hostile foreigners to define the Chinese identity or characterize the meaning of Chinese rise. Even though in other publications[33] Yu sometimes comes close to sounding like an IR rationalist or neoliberal in stressing the importance of cooperation with foreign states, ultimately she subscribes to the common view held among Chinese analysts that interactions among states should be modeled as a realist struggle. Yu does allow that China still has much to learn from foreign societies (and foreign societies from China)—and that, indeed, the necessary internal renaissance will be possible only if China remains open to "globalization, modernization, and informationalization."[34] But the point and purpose of the civilizational renaissance will be to increase Chinese power relative to the power of foreign states.

Yu's commitment to a realist worldview is also implicit in her rejection of the concept of "universal values" and counterproposal that all the world's countries—or at least all the world's *powerful* countries (the poles that would constitute a multipolar world)—are essentially distinct and must insist on remaining that way. Although conceding that it would be a mistake to overemphasize diversity or plurality among nation-states— and criticizing China for too often stressing diversity and plurality at the expense of unity with foreign societies—Yu concludes that the concept of universal values is, as presently conceived, bankrupt. She cites some unnamed "European scholars" as calling universal values into question because they equate to West-centrism—which, Yu continues, increasingly more of the world's people can no longer accept as a result of the severely painful experience of the 2008–2009 GFC.[35] Although some might argue that the global financial crisis resulted from the *incomplete implementation* of the democratic concepts at the core of "universal values" (banks were not transparent in packaging securities; big bankers exercised huge untoward influence over the U.S. Congress via powerful lobbies and campaign donations; and so forth), Yu suggests that anything emerging from the West—perhaps especially the bad things—should be considered the core of West-promoted universal values. Many Chinese elites share in such a view. For those concerned with increasing relative Chinese soft power, it seems critically important to denigrate the West because the West is the main challenger to China in the realist international game.

As with Yu Xintian, another scholar not so interested in quantitatively measuring China's relative soft power but instead in stressing that Chinese culture must always be distinctive from (and in some ways superior to) Western cultures is Xu Chongwen, a senior scholar at the Chinese Academy of Social Sciences. Writing in the *neibu* policy journal *Leadership Reference*, Xu in a pair of articles takes up the controversial topic of the China model but addresses it in a more subtle and logically consistent manner than Pan Wei (discussed in Chapter 3). Xu's formulation sounds more similar to that of Yu Keping (also discussed in Chapter 3) than it does to Pan's because Xu stresses that the model is constantly in the process of being formed on the basis of practical Chinese experience. At the same time, however, it is also constantly being reformulated through both exchanges and competition with the West.[36]

Xu emphasizes the special problem China faces in that it has been struggling to realize its model during a world-historical juncture in which the West continues to possess enormous advantages in material and ideational power. There is no doubt to Xu that China remains far behind the West—especially the United States—in soft power. But unlike Yan Xuetong, Xu does not seem overly confident that China can, through pursuing internal reforms, surpass the United States at any time soon. Yan portrays the two countries as competing in what ultimately is a neutral context in which the rules have been set objectively so that the meritorious country stands a fair chance of winning. In contrast, Xu perceives the very context of the competition to be structured in favor of the currently dominant power. It will be difficult enough in such a setting to construct a viable and defensible Chinese model, let alone a model that could actually supplant the models propagated by the dominant Western states. There are two dimensions to the difficulty: (1) designing and putting into place the model's concrete institutional practices and (2) defining what the institutional practices add up to—what the model actually *means* in a context in which the West still dominates. Because the West, through discourse, enjoys the power to accept, reject, ridicule, despise, and so on, China has a tortuous route to take unless it is willing to surrender to Western dominance and give up the struggle.[37]

But Xu and most other Chinese writers who publish in the outlets surveyed for this book regard surrender as unthinkable. In trying to increase China's soft power, they are fighting for far more than the ability to score points against Western countries in diplomatic spats. They are fighting for the power to recast world history. They evidently would like to write a new history in which not the West but China is featured at the center—as the primary actor leading humankind in the direction of perpetual progress. The contest is thus enormously significant to these Chinese elites because it defines the very purpose of the Chinese renaissance associated with the country's material rise: a central component of the China Dream. It is another reason—perhaps the fundamental reason—democratization must be rejected.[38] Democratization would imply succumbing to the West's ideational hegemony and thus the disappearance of China as an essentially distinctive entity with the qualities necessary to supplant the West and achieve world centrality.[39]

Xu Chongwen dates the emergence of talk about the China model to the early Deng Xiaoping years—a significant point from the perspective of trying to understand Chinese perceptions of the PRC's developmental trajectory because it implies that, from the start, Deng and his lieutenants never accepted the possibility that reform and opening would eventually result in China becoming just another industrialized democracy. Of course rejecting democratization was already implicit in the Four Cardinal Principles, which Deng first articulated in March 1979. But the Four Cardinal Principles were defensive: an effort to specify what China would *not* become. The debate over the China model was from the beginning exploratory: devoted to generating a consensus (at least among CCP elites) on what China positively *should* become.

Xu ignores the so-called Sinification of Marxism under Mao and dates the China model debate from May 31, 1980, when Deng Xiaoping gave a speech in which he argued that China should not demand that other countries (developed or developing) follow "the Chinese model of revolution." This was during a time when the CCP was winding down support for Third World revolutionaries in Southeast Asia and other parts of the world. Deng contended that the people of those countries must find their own pathways to the future just as China eventually had to carve a path different from that of the Soviet Union.[40]

Two years later—on September 1, 1982, at the opening ceremony of the Twelfth Party Congress—Deng announced that China would continue to blaze a trail of its own to find a distinctive path not only to socialism but also to modernization: a path rooted in China's actual conditions, not based on off-the-shelf models borrowed from foreign countries. To be sure, the experiences of other countries could be studied, and those foreign practices that seemed suited to Chinese conditions could be borrowed and tested experimentally. But the key point was to reject mindless commitment to ideological dogmatism (of whatever stripe—except the Four Cardinal Principles) and slowly nurture the China model into being through bold but pragmatic experimentation. To Xu Chongwen, then, "without a doubt, Deng Xiaoping's thesis forms the foundation for the systematic discourse on the China model."[41]

Although Deng himself did not establish explicit boundaries for the discussion (beyond the Four Cardinal Principles), Xu derives two boundaries both from Deng's original formulation and the continuing ideational contest with the United States and the broader West. First, Xu insists on the essential, eternal differences among all countries, or at least among all *important* countries, by which he means the great powers. Xu proclaims as a given that "there is no unchanging development model in the world suitable for all times and places; China will have its own distinctive model."[42] This statement is more profound that it might first appear. On the surface, Xu is rejecting the possibility of "universal values" emanating from the more enlightened corners of the West and now other places and whose proponents insist that they apply to China as to every other country. This is obviously important, but there is another dimension to Xu's comment. He is suggesting that the applicability of so-called universal values will be limited not only in space (to certain countries) but also in time (from roughly the early twentieth century until the success of China's rise, which means the realization of the Chinese renaissance and crystallization of the Chinese model). To some people in the West, history seems to have ended with the consolidation of Western world dominance—this is a point made by philosopher Stephen Toulmin and various writers in IR when they contend that out of the Enlightenment emerged a widespread belief in the West that people were now living in an eternal present, one in which progress would continue to unfold but no fundamental, genuinely Earth-shaking new developments would be possible.[43] Such a complacent ahistoricism was reinforced by Western victories in the horrific struggles of World War I and World War II and the less-horrific but still costly and demoralizing Cold War. But to Xu, once the rise of China succeeds, and with it a genuinely compelling new China model, the historical phase of Western world dominance will end and along with it the largely unquestioned (or questioned, but ineffectively) hegemony of Western discourse. This is when China will achieve recentering in world history. It is the ultimate meaning of China's rise, the point and purpose of accumulating wealth and power.

Xu's second guiding principle for developing the China model is related to the first but is more metaphysically ambitious. Xu wants to explain exactly *why* there can be no universally valid model that all powerful countries must follow. To achieve this goal, he delves into evolutionary theory and argues that "the basic special characteristic of humanity as a species and what causes civilizations to progress is plurality or diversity in the world, a principle that naturally we must try to respect."[44] To Xu's mind, trying to go against the grain of this inherent (and inherently positive) plurality would at best be doomed to failure and at worst could cause serious problems and tensions of a sort that would retard human progress. Xu cites Jiang Zemin as arguing this point at a U.N. heads-of-state meeting on September 6, 2000. Jiang said at the meeting that fundamental diversity among human societies (including diversity among political systems) is precisely what drives human progress, just as competition among organisms in nature drives biological progress. Xu interprets Jiang as having meant that because such competition is a fundamental natural process, in the end it *must* be respected. It is a natural biological law. To be sure, China or some other non-Western countries might try to adhere to so-called universal (actually, Western) values, but in the end they will unavoidably fail. To Xu, then—following Jiang (and others)—China could never become a country like the United States or other Western democracies because that would be inconsistent with the fundamental principles of the universe. Knowing this, it would at best be foolhardy to accept Western political and other institutions uncritically and try to make them work in China. At worst, it would be criminal because of the genuine harm such mindlessly wanton borrowing could cause.[45]

This is why China must continue pragmatically to explore for its own road, developing over time a compelling China model that will close the gap between Western and Chinese soft power. And yet it is clear that Xu and other writers want to do more than just close the gap. They want to take the lead—essential if China is to achieve world recentering. The problem is that there is nothing in evolutionary metaphysics to mandate that one organism or another should be destined to establish a dominant position over all other organisms of its kind. Xu, Jiang, and the others do not seem at first glance to have a theoretical justification for why China's rise must inevitably succeed. On closer examination, however, a justification emerges. Because China is now the second superpower—and is committed to resisting universal values (at least in the realm of politics)—it is the only power standing in the way of the victory of universal American dominance. It is, in other words, the only international actor striving heroically to prevent the Americans and their Western and other allies from trying to violate the laws of nature in a way likely to produce disaster by insisting that every country become institutionally and, in key respects, culturally alike. This makes China's rise and renaissance—the nurturing of a new China model— important not only for China itself but for the entire world. In some ways we might even say that in the minds of some Chinese thinkers it makes the success of China's rise to be of almost cosmic significance, because by resisting the West China is upholding the laws of nature. This is an exceptionally important public good that China is providing to the world. And China provides the good not selfishly, so that other countries will imitate the China model once it crystallizes into a shining new alternative to "Western democracy." China provides the good so that the world can be made safe for all countries to discover their own models—which would not be possible if the Americans were to consolidate the ideational hegemony that has accompanied their rise to world military and economic supremacy.

DEFENSIVE REALISTS: PROTECTING
THE CHINESE "NATIONAL SPIRIT"

In 2006, the China Political Thought Work Research Committee joined with the CCP Central Propaganda Department Political Thought Work Research Institute to produce an edited volume on China's "national spirit"—aimed at providing a clear and simple conceptual explanation for Party members of the importance of protecting and nourishing this spirit. From the start, the book suggests that the spirit is under threat and that the Party has the responsibility to protect it by providing "cultural security, . . . [which] is a kind of infrastructural national security."[46] The book's chief purpose is to explain the importance of the national spirit and how Party members can go about nourishing and protecting it in the face of foreign threats.

It is important to note that the spirit—which "penetrates every aspect of the nation's life and culture, and expresses itself through every kind of concrete, living formation" (including myths, music, literature, and outstanding personages)—consists of only good characteristics and fine human qualities *that strengthen the nation-state.* In contrast, "those forms of thought and consciousness that are inconsistent with the whole nation's fundamental interests and desires, and that damage the nation's unity, cannot represent the national spirit . . . Those forms of thought and consciousness that block the nation's development and that are negative do not belong in the category of the national spirit."[47] This would seem to be essential because Party elites are here identifying those aspects of national identity that the CCP is striving to cultivate. As a vanguard Leninist party, the CCP would not cultivate anything it perceived to be bad or pernicious. But this allows the Party, in effect, to invent and essentialize a national spirit by using its power to determine the content. The national spirit then becomes the set of cultural characteristics (including "patriotism, diligence, courage, and truth seeking") the CCP is trying to encourage among Chinese citizens so that it can achieve its domestic and international political objectives.[48]

As long as the national spirit is safe and secure, the country will eventually become wealthy and strong. In the words of another author concerned with similar problems, "We must influence and change people's internal life-worlds for the purpose of realizing an internal rise" to ensure the success of the national rise.[49] The spiritual trumps the material—at least to these officials working in the Party's propaganda system: "As long as a nation has a spirit that is willing to struggle sooner or later it will become capable of changing its poverty-stricken condition." On the other hand, "if a nation lacks the willingness to struggle, it cannot stand among the ranks of the world's [leading] nations." The reason is that "contemporary international competition includes not only economic, science and technology, military, and other forms of material power competition, but also the thought, cultural, and other hidden-in-the-background forms of spiritual power competition." Nations must continually advance culturally, or they will fall behind. Nourishing the national spirit is the key to progress and ultimate victory.[50] The spirit is "a stimulating power that directs the nation to pursue its goals and objectives as well as a centripetal psychological force that brings the whole body of the nation's individual members together, uniting the national will." Its most important function is "to establish a spiritual homeland for the nation." And it has a racial dimension with potentially important implications for international relations because the CCP attempts to appeal to ethnically Chinese citizens of other countries: "As descendants of the Yellow Emperor, no matter in what corner of the world we may find ourselves, we all have, from our innermost hearts, boundless hopes for the fatherland, and project on it a rich, aching longing for home."[51]

But the book's authors worry that China's national spirit is under threat from Western cultural penetration. This threat takes four forms: (1) the "Davos crowd" of global business elites, "carrying their cell phones and talking about tricks of the business trade in English"; (2) the "professorial club" of transnational intellectual elites, "who start from Western conceptual presuppositions and go around discussing such topics as feminism and environmental protection"; (3) McDonald's culture, which hooks young people in particular—not only on fast food but also on Western clothing, popular music, and holidays (with Valentine's Day viewed as especially pernicious); and (4) the "gospel faction of new religious culture," in which "numerous Asians"—in China and elsewhere—"find themselves attracted by the relatively relaxed and open new American religions" and then start attending church services. China's struggle against these trends "has become unusually fierce" in recent years because of the deepening of globalization. Globalization and American power are thus presented as intrinsic threats to the Chinese national spirit, which these authors believe must be protected and nurtured to consolidate and give meaning to the military and economic rise.[52]

Another author—a specialist on ethnic minorities—addressed the issue of the specific content of Chinese culture that must be protected in a January 2012 article for the *neibu* journal *Leadership Reference*. He Xingliang, of the CASS Institute of Nationalities, identifies seven binary distinctions between Western and Chinese civilizations that, he believes, lead to the derivation of seven dimensions of an essential Chinese culture:

1. Although Western civilization stresses the relationship between humans and the natural world, Chinese civilization stresses the relationship between humans and humans: ethics, morality, norms, character, and self-cultivation: "From beginning to end, Chinese civilization stresses people."[53] Although He does not specify how exactly Western civilization is threatening Chinese human-centeredness, he appears to be responding to the charge that China's political system does not protect human rights. He is suggesting that there is a higher human-centeredness in China far more profound than the West's mere concern for human rights, falsely claimed to be valid universally.

2. Chinese civilization possesses an integrity and unity that should not be jettisoned casually in favor of a claimed Western universalism. He contends that Chinese civilization has continued unbroken for many thousands of years, "the only ancient civilization to be preserved right up to today."[54] Although the West has constantly been buffeted by wars, national disintegration, and cultural turmoil, China has not changed substantially, He finds, over several millennia. This raises the question of how the West could then constitute such a serious threat. If in the past China always succeeded in absorbing and Sinifying foreign invaders, why would a strong contemporary China not be able to dispatch the West? He does not address this question. He seems

implicitly to think that the myth of unbroken continuity can no longer be maintained under today's conditions. Even if in the past it was never true to begin with, control over education and (to a lesser extent) information flows allowed elites to maintain the fiction. The network society and globalization generally make this no longer possible.

3. Chinese civilization has always consisted of many cultures, languages, religions, and ethnic groups. All these elements have always integrated harmoniously into a single, overarching Chinese culture. This essential characteristic is related organically to China's inherent ability to absorb and Sinify the best elements of foreign cultures.[55] For this reason, by implication, if China is failing to integrate different groups harmoniously, it will also face challenges absorbing the best elements of foreign cultures (and vice versa).

4. Chinese civilization has always evinced a tendency for its originally distinct component parts (groups and individuals of different religions, languages, and ethnicities) gradually to converge on an acceptance of common ethics, values, and life goals.[56] As with the similar point 3, He does not explain how this tendency is under threat from the West and globalization. His primary objective is to clarify the lines between China and the West: to reinforce in his readers' minds the notion that China is essentially distinctive in ways very much worth preserving.

5. Claims He: Chinese culture is introverted; Western culture is extroverted. Thus, Chinese culture seeks stability, balance, and harmony whereas Western culture seeks constant turbulence and change. As expressed in international relations, this tendency means that Chinese people seek peace because they hate war and always adopt a purely defensive strategic posture. Western people, in contrast, are inherently expansionist (as a reflection of Western culture) and see war fighting as a natural and normal part of the process of trying to dominate and control others. Thus, the Western strategic posture is always offensive as it values taking the initiative and striking first.[57] The question raised by such a characterization—a question He leaves hanging—is how China can protect itself given such a contrast in the character of its civilizational adversary. How can China, in the course of its rise,

maintain the purity of its international posture and yet avoid being vanquished by the inherently aggressive West?

6. Contrary to some popular misconceptions, Chinese culture has always possessed a great and generous capacity to absorb positive influences from abroad, which is why China today readily allows religious freedom. China also always accepts the positive elements of foreign cultures and pursues peaceful coexistence with other nation-states on the basis of friendliness and mutual respect.[58] Although, on the one hand, He is thus clearly brushing aside the possibility that China could ever be unreasonable in international affairs, let alone menacing to others, he may at the same time be trying to suggest that Chinese foreign policy should remain consistent with China's essence. In other words, he may be arguing against nationalists that accepting the positive elements of foreign cultures and pursuing peaceful coexistence would be a more complete expression of essential Chineseness than trying to isolate China from global cultural flows or bullying the country's smaller Asian neighbors. Ultimately, therefore, he may be taking a position consistent with a cooperative China but a China that nevertheless remains fundamentally distinct from other countries and does not converge with them on the norm of what a desirable political system for all advanced countries should be.[59]

7. Finally, He finds that Chinese culture is inherently "open."[60] Although this may seem inconsistent in key respects with the assertion in Point 5 that China is introverted, it also seems related to the likely strategy behind Point 6 of asserting as an essential characteristic any proclivity that He would like to see nurtured or maintained. He does not want China to close off; he supports the reform-and-opening general line. Thus, he suggests by implication that those who call for protecting China excessively from foreign influences are, in a misguided quest to defend the Chinese essence, paradoxically violating one of the key components of that essence. What is noteworthy is that He feels compelled to take this stand—which suggests that those who worry about the problems caused by reform and opening are far from an insignificant force in Chinese politics.

Participants in a December 2006 Beijing conference on the subject of "Cultural Construction and National Security" evince similar concerns in their published speeches and papers. This conference was the fifth in a series of quasi-academic conclaves cosponsored by the National Security Policy Committee, the Chinese Policy Sciences Research Association, Peking University, and the Chinese Association for the Promotion of International Friendship. Some 150 dignitaries attended, drawn from national-level ministries and commissions, social science research institutes, universities, and the culture and media industries. Vice Chairman Xu Jialu of the Standing Committee of the National People's Congress was selected to give the keynote address.

Xu devoted his remarks to warning his audience about the threat posed to contemporary Chinese culture by the United States.[61] "The core of a national culture"—its basic structure—consists of four elements, Xu argues: worldviews, values, ethics, and aesthetics. The surface of this structure is where some people naïvely assume that it is safe to engage in exchanges with foreigners. This is where analysts locate such practices as Chinese people "wearing Western clothing, eating McDonald's or KFC, wanting to live in large houses, or being told by the media they should aspire to buy their own car." Even though these all seem to be innocuous surface phenomena, "over time, they will start to penetrate the middle of the structure." The state might try to shape people's tastes and consumption patterns, but if its efforts are halfhearted or fail for other reasons, eventually the base of the structure (the location of such core values as individual life objectives and the root sources of meaning) will become infected. Xu criticizes "consumptionism—the constant demand for more, bigger, prettier, fancier" and associates the sociopolitical dissatisfaction that it breeds with the West. He becomes palpably agitated in tone and claims that many people with PhDs in Beijing and Shanghai commit suicide because the essence of Chinese culture is being annihilated: "With America at its core, the West's intentional cultural penetration" aims to destroy China.[62]

It is significant that Xu presents the United States as the driving force behind this subversion because the United States is the hegemon that China would supplant if its power transition succeeds. Xu portrays American culture as profoundly dangerous—far more dangerous than the cultural penetration of other Western countries. He quotes some unnamed European academic visitors to China disparaging American culture—and then he quotes an unnamed French professor as denying that America even *has* a culture. But Xu does not go quite so far. He concedes that America has a culture but one that it is dangerously destructive: "The powerful culture that I am chiefly talking about here is American culture; it poses a serious challenge to our traditional values."[63]

At the same conference, two People's Liberation Army (PLA) researchers, Zhang Haisheng and Liu Xifeng, presented a paper on the subject of "Nine Great Challenges Our Country's Cultural Security Currently Faces."[64] Some of these challenges are familiar; others less so. What is significant is that PLA officers at a semiacademic conference would pronounce on matters of culture and define challenges presented to Chinese culture as national security threats.

The nine challenges that Zhang and Liu identify are as follows:

1. Westernization, because Western countries, especially the United States, actively "scheme to use the Western and U.S. economic model, political system, and values to control the globe."[65]
2. Splittism, which contradicts a purported essential Chinese tendency for many thousands of years to seek unity. Splittism on the part of Taiwanese, Tibetans, and Uighurs is fueled and encouraged by the West, through its promotion of "so-called human rights, liberty, democracy, and equality."[66] The PLA's chief mission is to prevent splittism, which these authors identify as partly driven by intentional Western (especially U.S.) cultural subversion.
3. The threat of being marginalized in the global media and culture industries: "Based on its great economic and technological power, the U.S.-led West is occupying the thought and culture fronts, squeezing the living and development space for our country's national culture."[67] The militarization of the language reflects culture's securitization.
4. The "poisoning" of Chinese culture said to be pursued intentionally by the United States. Zhang and Liu quote without citation a purported "CIA document" that proclaims a strategy of "doing our utmost to

use materialism to entice and spoil China's youth; encourage them to belittle, denigrate, and more openly oppose the ideology and education they originally received, especially Communist doctrines. Cultivate their interest in pornography and provide them with opportunities to consume it. Further encourage them to engage in licentious sexual behavior. Make them no longer consider superficiality and vanity to be shameful. Certainly destroy the spirit they formerly emphasized of perseverance in the face of adversity."[68]

5. The pluralization of ideology, which threatens the centrality of Chinese Marxism; that is, CCP-mandated orthodoxy: "Any country, no matter how many different ideologies it may have, can only have one ideology that serves to guide thought."[69]

6. The perceived Western determination to encourage the rise of a Chinese middle class and a new social elite. This takes the form of first enticing talented Chinese people to take managerial jobs in foreign-invested firms and then "putting great effort into using Western values, political views, democratic thinking patterns, and styles of life to influence, conquer, and control these people, causing them to 'become slaves' and then representatives of Western thought and culture."[70]

7. Culture's commodification in the global market economy. Although market competition and exchange can help fuel economic development, "they also cause people's utilitarian consciousness to strengthen, leading to the worship of money, extreme self-regard, and extreme individualism," all of which undermine the socialist values of collectivism and "looking on helping others as a joy."[71]

8. China's backwardness in the area of socioeconomic "informationalization" (application of information technology to socioeconomic processes). Unless China can deepen informationalization relative to the United States and other foreign states, it will not be able to consolidate cultural security or compete internationally for influence: "The higher the level of informationalization, the stronger a society's cultural power—and the easier it is in international competition to occupy the dominant position."[72] This is obviously true for the PLA and its affiliated enterprises as the core "system" (*xitong*) supplying Chinese security, but it is also true for China's telecommunications

and mass media industries. Zhang and Liu find that "75 percent of the world's television program creation and production activities are controlled by the United States." This gives the hegemon enormous advantages in cultural competition and clearly threatens China's "information security."[73]

9. The need to absorb more effectively and digest the admittedly positive culture that sometimes originates abroad and enters China. This is a problem of state boundary maintenance. No digestion takes place when a society imports culture indiscriminately. Such absorption will be incomplete or have toxic effects. Those who promote "complete Westernization" (no one is named) are misguided. China must improve its capacity to "distinguish the beautiful from the ugly and not simply pursue the fashionable."[74]

Yet another analyst—in another venue—expresses greater concern about America's intellectual hegemony than its influence over popular culture. Zheng Yongnian, a PRC-born academic now chairing the East Asian Institute at the National University of Singapore, frequently publishes in Chinese journals, including *neibu* journals. In October 2007, he wrote a short piece titled "Urgently Prevent the Americanization of Chinese Thought Patterns" for the *neibu* publication *Internal Reference Materials on Reform*.[75] Zheng worries that "the American IR discourse has become the mainstream Chinese discourse in international relations research"—decidedly a problem, he says, because in the American IR theory that emerged under U.S. world hegemony, "there are only limitless power struggles among states. This kind of American thinking directly influences the U.S. government's foreign policy."[76] When the PRC makes questionable moves internationally—such as sometimes "with neighboring countries or with African countries"—it is precisely, Zheng believes, because of the pernicious American influence on Chinese IR scholars, who in turn help to shape Beijing's foreign policies. Chinese impulses are pure; when China behaves improperly, it is because the Chinese essence has been poisoned by American badness. Zheng warns that "the Americanization of Chinese thinking patterns" could thus lead China to denigrate and bully weaker countries, which in turn would undermine the PRC's long-term strategic interests. Zheng acknowledges that "China is currently in the process of rising and [therefore] must study other countries." But he worries that "if we lose our subjectivity and allow our thinking patterns to become Americanized or Europeanized, it will be very difficult for China to become a truly great power, especially a sustainably great power."[77]

Some other scholars express pessimism about China's potency in cultural competition but do not blame the West. They blame China's own shortcomings, particularly the CCP's failure to deepen its economic reforms of the 1980s and 1990s. In the *neibu* journal *Internal Reference Materials on Reform*, Zhan Jiang of the Beijing Foreign Studies University discusses frankly how the entrenchment of state-linked special economic interests in China's media and Internet sectors could undermine the country's cultural appeal. Already Zhan finds Chinese media content to be vapid, officious, and propagandistic. Increasing dominance of central-state-owned enterprises in the media and Internet sectors suggest that this problem will only get worse. The effect would be more damaging than simple solidification of the status quo in China's international image. Propagandistic content could make the image intrinsically worse as it corrodes what is good in Chinese culture.[78] *Internal Reference Materials on Reform* is known as a liberal journal. Zhan appears to be couching his appeal to deepen political-economic reforms in a patriotic call to increase Chinese cultural influence abroad. That he considers such a tactic to hold promise suggests the centrality of realism and nationalism (a desire to increase Chinese relative power) in the minds of readers, which for *neibu* journals would be other Chinese elites.

OFFENSIVE REALISTS: CHINA'S TIME HAS COME

Especially in recent years, as China's rise in material terms has continued without apparent interruption, some analysts have taken to expressing strong optimism about prospects for Chinese cultural influence expanding abroad. These writers argue that it will be necessary for China to increase its cultural power for the material rise to be consolidated. Almost always, they phrase the problem in realist terms—a realism filtered through Leninism and (perhaps) imperial China's distinctively hierarchical conceptions of world order.

The Chinese analysts' frankness of language can sometimes be surprising. Take, for example, a book with the innocuous-sounding title *Cultural Diplomacy: A Media Studies Interpretation*, by Li Zhi, a philosopher teaching international relations at the Communication University of China, where many of China's elite journalists train. In the book—which was published in 2004 by the prestigious Peking University Press—Li makes a number of boldly direct statements. He writes that the primary reason a state should try to project its culture abroad is "to change other states . . . to infect, affect, and influence [foreign] people's beliefs and value preferences . . . to alter the target state's attitudes, decisions, and policies until finally they will benefit our own state's national interest." Sometimes this requires either stretching the truth or telling outright lies: "To maximize the effect, a state might conceal some unfavorable facts or even provide false information that aims at enticing other states to focus, understand, and remember the points we are promoting while ignoring others." But this approach does not entail shutting China off from foreign cultural influences; on the contrary: "We must learn the barbarians' advantageous techniques for the purpose of checking the barbarians" (*shi yi chang ji yi zhi yi*).[79]

A related argument is developed by the dean of Renmin University's School of Journalism in a 2011 article for *Renmin Zhengxie Bao*, a publication of the Chinese People's Political Consultative Conference. Zhao Qizheng titles his article "Dialogue with the Global," which on first glance would appear to hold the promise for containing a multifaceted examination of the myriad ways in which China wrestles with global and international cultures. Almost immediately, however, Zhao lets on that his intent is less intellectually ambitious when he *defines* having a "dialogue with the global" as China pursuing its public diplomacy objectives more effectively; thus, the dialogue becomes a monologue in which China carefully monitors the responses of foreign actors to make certain they are receiving the proper message. There is no reason for China to change (to any fundamental extent) as a result of this "dialogue"; the purpose is "to influence foreign countries to improve their policies toward China."[80] Nor, to that extent, is the "dialogue" imagined to be with the global. It is instead with the international: the society of states. The global realm is not even imagined as possible (for Zhao) because ultimately every individual or group belongs to, and represents, some country, which can either be friendly or hostile toward China. Correspondingly, the CCP is free to mobilize Chinese individuals and groups (inside government or out) to tell foreigners how China really is, counter foreign misunderstandings or mischaracterizations, and help China to realize its CCP-defined national interests.[81]

The chief—or at least a core—purpose behind this expansion of cultural or soft power abroad would be to realize the unification of Taiwan. PLA professor Niu Hanzhang argued in a 2007 publication that "the historical experiences of the world's rising powers tell us that a nation's unification is a prerequisite to its rise . . . What national unification can bring is stabilization of the political system, normalization of social life, development of the quality of economic production, flourishing of cultural construction, and elevation of the level of harmony in domestic affairs— which, in turn, enhance the nation's ability to resist external challenges."[82] Given the importance of Taiwan's unification to consolidation of China's rise, Niu thus decides that he must warn Taiwanese people of the dangers entailed in resisting unification. In a classic realist statement, Niu channels Thucydides in offering the Taiwanese a stark choice: Either "(a) rein your horse in at the precipice, cease 'Taiwan independence' separatist activities, acknowledge that both sides of the Strait belong to one China, and work to promote the development of cross-Strait relations; [or] (b) continue single-mindedly on your lonely course, insanely plot to separate Taiwan from China, and, in the end, play with fire and get yourself burned."[83]

Other writers suggest that China could extend its cultural influence far beyond Taiwan and that the CCP should correspondingly expand Chinese ambitions. In a 2008 article on "China's Geocultural Strategy," analysts Pan Zhongqi (Fudan University) and Huang Renwei (Shanghai Academy of Social Sciences)—Shanghai scholars with reputations as liberals—develop the decidedly realist concept of "geocultural strategy," analogous to geopolitical strategy in stressing tough, realist competitions among states operating on a geographical plane in the realm of culture.[84] Geocultural strategy "refers to the integrated, comprehensive conceptualizing that guides a country when, under specific historical

conditions, and from the perspective of geocultural space, it comprehensively utilizes all manner of cultural techniques and resources for the
purpose of facing a core challenge or threat and protecting the national
interest."[85] Pan and Huang proceed from Samuel Huntington's presuppositions in *The Clash of Civilizations*, along the way renaming Huntington's "Confucian civilization" as "Chinese civilization" (*Zhonghua
wenming*) without discussing the complications.[86] Consistent with many
other Chinese writers and with CCP orthodoxy, Pan and Huang write
that Chinese civilization and several others are currently under threat
from American hegemonism. This is central to their ultimately optimistic argument: "From the perspective of geographical space, the chief
geocultural conflicts and threats China faces are at the global level. The
adversary with which Chinese culture is most likely to engage in direct
conflict is Western culture, especially American culture. At the level of
the Asian region and immediately surrounding areas, there is no similar
geocultural threat facing China."[87]

But, unlike other Chinese writers worried about cultural competition,
Pan and Huang are confident that China can ultimately prevail. The key
reason is that China "has already begun to manifest the beginnings of a
renaissance." Not only has it "successfully established an excellent international image as a responsible, constructive, and predictable country,
but it has also given the world a new development model and new value
perspectives." These successes lead the authors to propose that, in the
great geocultural competitions of the present and future, China should
self-confidently try to expand its cultural influence abroad—particularly
in what Pan and Huang find to be the culturally weak zones of Africa,
Latin America, and Central Asia.[88] On the one hand, these areas urgently "need to strengthen their own cultures' special characteristics; on
the other hand, they must borrow from and make use of non-American
cultural power" to resist U.S. hegemony. They are too weak to resist on
their own. "Chinese culture's great capacity and relative acceptability
can provide an important basis and guarantee for the expansion of Chinese culture's latent space into these regions," a kind of "go West" policy
that would take advantage of the African, Latin American, and Central
Asian countries' perceived cultural weakness to expand Chinese influence,

albeit "helping" the African, Latin American, and Central Asian countries in the process.[89]

It might even be possible for China to expand culturally into areas very close to home. Pan and Huang observe that Asia since the end of the Cold War has experienced a cultural revival, which pivots on "an Asian values perspective different from the West's cultural relativism." The reason for the revival's success, they say, is the salutary influence of "traditional Chinese Confucian culture," which experienced a renaissance after the CCP launched reform and opening in the late 1970s. Confucianism's prominent role in the pan-Asian cultural revival now affords China with an excellent geocultural opportunity. It has produced a situation in which "the Japanese cultural zone, Hindu cultural zone, and Islamic cultural zone are all potential spaces into which China might expand its cultural influence." Even though these neighboring civilizations all differ markedly from China, "they are also strongly interdependent with Confucian culture and share a common interest in resisting the West's cultural invasion." In addition, "no matter whether to strengthen their own special characteristics or to respond to the expansion of American cultural imperialism, these cultures must all borrow from the power of Confucian culture."[90]

Such statements are remarkable for the worldview they reveal. First, Pan and Huang—leading and influential scholars regarded as liberals—in this case present international relations as a global, zero-sum struggle pitting civilization against civilization; or more precisely, pitting "the U.S.-led West" against everyone else. Second, they are convinced that people in other civilizations view the world in similar terms and are, like China, trying to find ways to resist the imposition of Western cultural hegemony. But most remarkable of all is their conviction that people in these other civilizations—especially Africa, Latin America, and Central Asia but also Japan, India, and the broader Islamic world—want and *need* Chinese Confucian cultural assistance to resist the U.S.-led West.[91]

Pan and Huang make four policy recommendations that they hope CCP leaders will adopt as they take up the challenges of pursuing geocultural expansion. First, China should increase its cultural attractiveness by "Sinifying Marxism" and promoting development, stability, and harmony as "universal values." This seems to be an obligatory statement aimed at signaling that the authors accepted Hu Jintao's call for building a harmonious world.[92]

Second, although resisting American cultural imperialism, "China must avoid clashing with American culture directly, to prevent Chinese culture from coming to be regarded in the United States as an enemy." Instead, China should resist by promoting the harmonious diversity of world cultures as a contrasting principle to American hegemonism, while at the same time "developing latent geocultural space to promote China's own political values and correctly interpreting China's development model for the world."[93]

Third, China should "promote the Asian region's geocultural integration" by expending effort first to specify the cultural commonalities among Asian countries and then "use [these] Asian cultural commonalities to oppose American cultural hegemonism while at the same time striving to eliminate the negative influence of Asian nationalisms"—including Chinese nationalism, which helps give rise to China threat theories and consequently hinders the PRC's rise.[94] Pan and Huang do not explain how—practically or doctrinally—China could unite the highly distinctive Buddhist, Islamic, Hindu, Shinto, Christian, and other peoples/regions of Asia under a single geocultural umbrella, nor why these myriad peoples would be willing to go along with the plan. The authors seem to assume that (1) Confucianism, somehow, forms the basis of all Asian cultures and (2) all Asian peoples will eventually (but sooner rather than later) perceive the imperative necessity of waging a struggle to drive out destructive American cultural hegemonism. But they can only achieve this historically all-important task if they unite under Chinese leadership.

Finally, China should "consolidate the immediately surrounding geocultural space by making peoples in the Great Chinese Confucian Cultural Circle [including Taiwanese] more willing to regard China as the nucleus." This strategy would require, among other things, "putting effort into solving the problem of differences in cultural recognition between Taiwan and the mainland" so that unification can be achieved.[95] Under Ma Ying-jeou, the Republic of China openly embraces the PRC as a *cultural* brother, which justifies the KMT's willingness to set unification as an ultimate goal. Cross-Strait popular cultural exchanges have also increased substantially since 2008, partly by political design, partly in response to market signals. However, it is far from clear whether Taiwanese (and, increasingly, the people of Hong Kong) are "willing to regard China as the [cultural] nucleus." Entertainers often pay lip service to such demands to avoid exclusion from the Chinese market, but what they think privately may be quite something different.

One of the academic elites interviewed for this research exuded an optimism similar to that of Pan and Huang concerning Chinese prospects for prevailing in cultural competition—but for different reasons.[96] This analyst believes that in future years and decades, the great powers—especially the United States and China—will still compete as realists would hold. But instead of competing militarily they will compete through soft power, by trying to appeal to what the analyst believes is the (already) globally shared value of "reasonableness." With the deepening and widening of the network society worldwide, states will come under greater scrutiny from their own and other states' publics, leading unavoidably to increases in transparency. In this way, the analyst believes, public participation in the global decision-making processes of international relations will increase. At first, this could cause some states to adopt *less* reasonable or even belligerent foreign policies. Nationalists in China and elsewhere could put pressure on their leaders to act tough with other states. But this will be a transitional period during which states learn to manage public opinion more effectively. Over the following two decades, the foreign policies of all the great powers will become increasingly prudent and moderate. Intensification of interdependence will convince states and publics alike that settling disputes through violence is irrational.

Still, the scholar believes that, even in this type of world, states will compete for power relative to other states. The only difference—and it is an important one—is that they will compete using persuasion rather than violence. Ultimately, in this kind of game, "China will win the competition with the United States." The reason is twofold. First, "the United States is perceived as too selfish, arrogant, and presumptuous." China is not. Its low-key posture will give it a significant advantage in future soft-power contests.

Second, the authoritarian political system affords China important competitive advantages. It will allow the CCP to effect a smoother, less troubled transition to the new political order in which the public participates extensively: "China's leaders can afford to take the long view; they aren't always reacting to changes in public opinion." Because the CCP will take a relatively cool, levelheaded approach to foreign affairs, it can appeal to the desire of people throughout the world for reasonableness on the part of the great powers in their interactions with other states. In contrast, the unstable and emotional United States will find itself in the position of having to adapt to a new international society that in the area of culture will be led by China.

Two younger analysts interviewed jointly in a different city made similar points.[97] One said that "China's biggest challenge over the next thirty years will be to construct a development model appropriate for the Third World—a model emphasizing environmental protection and resource conservation." The Western model no longer works: Humanity would run out of resources if everyone worldwide tried to emulate the lifestyles of people in the West. But this creates an opportunity for China in the area of cultural competition. "Now the West is teaching China, but in thirty years China will be teaching others," especially (but not exclusively) the developing countries. These analysts believe that people throughout the world who are dissatisfied with U.S. leadership *want* China to develop an alternative model, and that Chinese elites feel pressured to answer the call. It is a kind of historical responsibility that must be fulfilled and that will have the effect of reinforcing China's rise in material and cultural terms: "We have to solve China's own problems first, but we feel the expectation to become a leading nation. China is the big story in the world media; this increases the pressure. To offer an alternative development model is something we must do to satisfy the demands of the global community. The world welcomes and benefits from China's rise."

Another scholar phrased the matter in sharper tones, saying that the CCP is determined to increase its "discourse power" (*huayuquan*) in global affairs and that, after it succeeds, no longer will the foreign powers mock and ridicule China for its troubling human rights record, its sometimes poor quality or contaminated exports, pollution, copyright infringements, and so forth. Foreigners will no longer ridicule China, both because Chinese performance in these areas will have improved and because the PRC will have too much power to criticize it without inviting dangerous consequences.[98]

Somewhat similarly, China Foreign Affairs University professor Zhu Liqun dismisses the IR concept of state socialization as unacceptably West-centric in a 2012 article first published in *Foreign Affairs Review*.[99] Zhu does not reject the concept entirely; rather, he contends that the socialization process China is undergoing is two-way socialization, not a unidirectional socialization in which China becomes more like the Western countries that currently dominate international society. As recently as the early 2000s, most Chinese writers seemed reluctant even to acknowledge the existence of a rules-governed international society as opposed to a violence-prone international *system* whose constituent state units would sometimes play by rules but only to the extent that the outcomes of such moves would serve the most powerful states' national interests.[100] Zhu—writing as Chinese power continued rapidly to mount—had no trouble acknowledging the existence of an international society, but he locates agency for helping to shape its rules and guiding principles to China as well as the West and other industrialized democracies: "As China participates in this society it ceaselessly reflects on what it experiences and responds with counterthinking and creativity in a way that influences the society, propelling it in the direction of becoming more just, rational, and orderly."[101] Zhu finds that in focusing on this phenomenon—in breaking free of the idea of a passive China mindlessly receiving socialization—the world makes three important discoveries:

1. "China and the international system mutually influence each other, are functionally integrated, mutually adapt to each other, and mutually change in response to the other."[102] This is very different, Zhu contends, from the currently dominant view of socialization, "which emphasizes the path of influence from the center to the periphery; for example, developing countries completely accepting the norms propagated by the system's core countries, wantonly abandoning their former international status in the process of yielding to socialization."[103] With

its increasing power, China does not intend to yield to socialization in this way. It intends instead to resist the imposition of Western norms and consequently reshape international society to the point that it becomes more rational, reasonable, and just. There is no possibility of the PRC accepting socialization to the point that China undergoes a painful and humiliating transmogrification at the level of core identity. Through resisting—and reconstituting international society—China makes the world a better place for all developing countries.

2. IR specialists on state socialization tend to overgeneralize, primarily because they work at too grand a level of theory. The field urgently needs more case studies (for example, of China's approach to socialization) to enrich understanding of the process by demonstrating the ways in which it varies by state. Up to the present, the theory has tended to ignore world diversity (*shijie de duoyangxing*): divergent state approaches stemming from different national conditions, historical backgrounds, geographical circumstances, and citizens' perspectives.[104] What makes Zhu's formulation novel in a Chinese context is that earlier writers tended to emphasize how world diversity—presented as a fact of nature—precluded the sheer possibility of international society (in any meaningful sense) taking shape: Any drive to institutionalize an international society was likely to be a dangerous ploy by some hegemony-seeking state to consolidate its world dominance. Now, as China becomes more powerful, imagining the reality of an international society becomes a safer proposition—possibly because China could well become one of the two main powers competing to shape the world's new order. To this extent, the desideratum of world diversity does not literally mean taking joy or finding benefit in all countries celebrating their differences but instead means acknowledging the goodness for everyone inherent in the CCP successfully defending China's essential differences from the West—for example, its distinctive political system.

3. Some international norms are more important than others—more powerful in their ability to constitute or reconstitute because of the ways in which they affect people's thinking patterns. Zhu does not specify

exactly what norms he has in mind, but he does say that China's decision in the late 1970s to pursue reform and opening—which has led to China increasing its comprehensive national power and entering into the two-way socialization process—is in the process of reshaping these profound constitutive norms. This is because the awesome reality of China's rise combined with the two-way socialization process that the rise makes possible have together fundamentally altered the ways in which aware people throughout the world think.[105] Particularly the peoples of developing countries now find it possible to imagine all manner of different futures: No longer must they morosely acquiesce to a future that entails inevitably becoming like the West. China's rise and its consequent reshaping of the rules of international society liberate the world's peoples from the shackles of dreary subservience within a U.S.-centered Western world order. As a result, China's twenty-first-century recentering in world history opens a revolutionary new epoch of emancipation within the human experience. What is good for the CCP, in short, is good for all of humankind.

SUMMARY AND CONCLUDING POINTS

In numerous articles published in *neibu* policy and high-level academic journals—and books or book chapters published by leading presses—very few Chinese analysts take a position on culture in international relations at variance from ultimately realist positions. Most Chinese writers depict the world as inherently conflict ridden in the realm of culture, with the ideational fault lines reinforcing lines of military and economic conflict. The major cleavage among Chinese analysts is whether they think China is now in the ascendant and therefore should assert itself more muscularly in cultural competitions with the West or is weak and under grave threat.[106] All of this has critical implications for understanding the trajectory of China's rise.

Particularly important is the question of whether the PRC's policies in the military and economic sectors might become even more assertive in the years and decades ahead if the rise continues and China's power relative to international military, economic, and social structures increases. If the conclusions of this chapter are accurate, then increasing Chinese power relative to structures could lead CCP decision makers to calculate that because they have now become even less constrained by structural factors, they can more easily afford to behave less cooperatively in various policy arenas in those cases in which uncooperative policies would be consistent with how the CCP defines China's national interests.

Of course this possibility assumes that the findings of this chapter reflect a core dimension of Party-state identity and that this identity is not limited strictly to the culture/soft power realm. If the construct is a deeper identity and not ephemeral or more limited mentalities, then it would be less likely to change through international interdependence, globalization, (relatively one-way) socialization to international society, and so forth. A deeper identity *might* change but the process would be slow and tortuous. The socialization pathways identified by Alastair Iain Johnston in 2008 do not negate the possibility that socialization of the PRC state has a limit, which may be one of the reasons that Johnston himself declined to state explicitly that his research gives solid grounds for thinking that China's rise will inevitably be peaceful:

I am making more limited claims—albeit within the context of hard or least likely cases—about how under certain conditions certain parts of the decision-making process have been weaned away from realpolitik calculations of maximizing relative power. Put differently, there is now greater tension within the PRC's overall diplomatic thinking and practice between harder realpolitik and softer realpolitik than ever before. But I am not arguing that multilateralism, say, has supplanted realpolitik as the predominant ideational construct behind China's foreign policy.[107]

The cost of acting on realist impulses to exploit power advantages in the military and economic sectors should prove higher than in the cultural sector. But not always, given that much of what counts as a cost in international relations depends on the values and perceptions of state decision makers. For example, the CCP might be willing to take big risks in the area of military security for the purpose of defending a national identity (cultural construct) that insists Taiwan, the Senkaku/Diaoyu Islands, and most of the South China Sea become integral parts of the PRC. As a result, it would not be surprising to see other states intensify their efforts to strengthen international structures (the balance of power, alliance systems, economic regimes such as the WTO, antiproliferation regimes, and so on) in tandem with increases in PRC hard and soft power. The post-2010 U.S. "pivot" may be just the beginning.

The rise of China, assuming it continues, will be an enormously important, world-historical event. It would be difficult to exaggerate the significance of the rise for both the Chinese people's quality of life and for the power transition in international relations. Assuming the Chinese state's root identity and/or strategic culture are realist (which is not to suggest that the identity *completely* rejects cooperation or the mutual adjustment of interests)—as revealed not only in Beijing's on-the-ground behavior but also in Chinese analysts' writing on strategy and soft power—it seems likely that Chinese leaders will continue (perhaps increasingly) to justify policy moves and stratagems that take full (cynical) advantage of China's increasing power advantages over vulnerable and weak adversaries such as Vietnam and the Philippines. Certainly this has been the trend since 2009. In the face of such worrying moves, it would be only logical—consistent with centuries or even millennia of international relations practice—for other states to redouble their efforts to strengthen the full array of international structures that could be used to constrain the CCP's options and "sandbox" its more aggressive moves so that any damage they might cause to international institutions and norms could be contained. Probably there are, in absolute terms, quite a few citizens of China who would support constraining and sandboxing the CCP's international behavior. Chinese citizens have little to no influence over foreign and security policies. Yet if the CCP miscalculates or overplays its hand, the resulting blunders could lead the country's people to peril.

CHAPTER 7

China: Unstoppably Rising, or
Perched on the Edge of a Crisis?

IN THIS BOOK, I HAVE SURVEYED a large variety of Chinese and, to a lesser extent, foreign writings on the question of China's possible futures, in the specific issue-areas of the economy, domestic politics, media and social structure, and international relations. The many different authors of these numerous and diverse writings offer a huge number of subtle and nuanced observations—so many, in fact, that collating, summarizing, and generalizing to find "dominant strands of thinking" seems almost brutal. Nevertheless, I want to make such an attempt in this concluding chapter to help readers tie the divergent strands together and cultivate a sense of what to watch for next in China's development.

First, however, let us review the summary conclusions of each individual chapter.

Chapter 1

The roots of the contemporary fascination with predicting the future can be traced to the Western Enlightenment of the eighteenth century and the Romantic movement of the nineteenth century. Fascination with the future became deeply embedded in the social sciences, to the point that some sociologists and political scientists began to insist that predicting and even controlling future events should be regarded as reasonable objectives. Thus, Carles Boix and Susan C. Stokes claim in a widely cited *World Politics* article that "we have shown that economic development both causes democracy and sustains it,"[1] suggesting the inevitability of democratization and its consolidation in a country like China, with its stunning (to date) record of economic success. Based on a similar logic, Henry S. Rowen predicted in 2007 that China would be "partly free" by 2015 and "a country correctly classed as belonging to the Free nations of the earth" by 2025.[2] Rowen's logic is rooted in an economic determinism similar to that of Boix and Stokes. He explains that, except for the big oil exporters, all countries with a per capita GDP of US$8,000 or more (measured in terms of purchasing power parity) were—by 2007—at least partly free.

Meanwhile, to proponents of the democratic peace, China's democratization would be a decidedly positive development from a normative point of view, because it would suggest the near-impossibility of the United States and China going to war with each other to resolve the power transition—assuming the two countries could pass peacefully through the stage during which China *moves* from authoritarian to democratic, given that the democratization process itself can paradoxically make a country more likely to go to war.[3] On the other hand, to a realist like John Mearsheimer, war or something very close to it is unavoidable no matter what kind of political regime China ends up with:

My argument is that if China continues to grow economically, it will translate that economic might into military might, and it will become involved in an intense security competition with the United States, similar to the security competition that existed between the United States and the Soviet Union during the Cold War. That intense security competition, in my opinion, is unavoidable.

Why do I say that? Because all states like to be regional hegemons, they like to dominate their backyard and make sure that no other state can interfere in their backyard.

If China becomes a hegemon in Asia, it also becomes on the global level a peer competitor with the US. I believe that the US will go to great lengths to make sure China does not become a peer competitor. It will go to great lengths to contain China and cut China off at the knees. The US has a long and clear record of not tolerating peer competitors in either Asia or Europe.[4]

Examples of this sort of certainty in social science predictioneering could be multiplied. But the point of Chapter 1 was to argue that ever-changing political and social realities are normally far too complex or chaotic to capture with overly parsimonious theories, especially predictive theories. Sociologists and other analysts working in "futures studies" arrived at this conclusion decades ago, but their work tends to be ignored by political scientists and members of the commentariat who publish sometimes sensationalistic op-eds on the implications of China's rise. To be sure, predictioneering can be valuable for shaping research agendas. Everyone who works on China, in whatever capacity, will be enriched by thinking through the arguments of Mearsheimer, Rowen, Boix and Stokes, and the other confident prognosticators mentioned at various points throughout this book. In the end, however, we have to recognize that all of these models are likely to fall short when matched against the messy reality of China's hugely complex and frequently shifting apparent trajectory. This is why viewing China on its developmental path as constantly being pulled and tugged in differing directions by competing "attractors"—a concept invented by chaos and complexity theorists to explain the dynamics of nonlinear systems—is likely to prove a more accurate approach to conceptualizing and mapping the range of the PRC's possible future states.

Chapter 2

Chinese economists seem to be deeply worried about the PRC's economic trajectory. Different analysts focus on different dimensions of the problem, but almost all converge on the conclusion that the Party-state must resume liberalizing economic reforms for China to escape its predicament of overrelying on wasteful investment to ensure economic growth. Here is an instance in which perceptions probably correspond closely to material reality: Chinese economists surely know their system well; meanwhile, by now, most foreign economists seem to agree that China is certain to face slowing growth in the years ahead, even though they differ on how sharp and sustained the expected slowdown is likely to be. Even if shifting to a sustainable, domestic-consumption-led growth model can be accomplished within a few years (which would be miraculously rapid), China would then face a deeper problem almost certain to sap economic dynamism: the rapidly aging population structure and the corresponding shrinking workforce. There is simply no way for China to escape the challenges posed by these ironclad demographic facts over the next two decades or more. An aging and then (after c. 2026) declining population imply that China's "rise"—which suggests a rapid ascent up the ranking tables of the world's most powerful countries—*must* slow substantially and probably to the point that people will stop using the rise metaphor. No matter what, of course, China will still have the world's second-largest economy at the time, and it could still eventually surpass the United States. It will remain vastly wealthier in absolute terms than ever before in history. The quality of life of the Chinese people will surely continue to improve, assuming that households can consume more and that wealth/income inequality as well as environmental destruction are addressed effectively. China would continue to possess the military and economic power to threaten its neighbors and even the United States should its leaders decide to take that dangerous route.

Chapter 3

The "decisions" announced at the end of the Third Plenum of the Eighteenth CCP Central Committee in November 2013 (discussed in detail in the following pages) suggest the real possibility that China's leaders will heed the warnings of the economists and resume some form of economic liberalization in the years ahead. Consequently, it seems reasonable to conclude that the overwhelmingly critical discourse of the economists is, as an attractor, already pulling China back in the direction of liberalizing economic reforms.

On the other hand, the situation regarding political change is murkier. Chinese economists agree on what needs to be done in their sector, but political analysts do not express anything close to a similar degree of unanimity on the question of the PRC's political trajectory: what it appears to be now versus what they think it should be. In particular, political commentators, unlike their economic counterparts, do not insist unanimously that liberalization and democratization must take place or else China's rise will be at risk. They do not strongly (or even weakly) warn against signs of tightening authoritarianism under Xi Jinping or the crackdown on Internet discussions, tougher policies in Tibet and Xinjiang, and so on. Most of the political analysts who agreed to interviews say they definitely want liberalization and are cautiously optimistic that eventually it will come about. But political analysts willing to be interviewed by a foreign researcher are likely to be more liberal in their political inclinations than the modal Chinese political analyst.

Liberal political sentiment is also often expressed in blogs and micro-blogs—to the consternation and irritation of the CCP. But relatively rare is the Chinese analyst willing to write in establishment print publications that she or he wants or expects (genuine) liberalization and/or democratization in the PRC. Especially rare is the scholar who expresses such views in *neibu* journals. It certainly is possible that at some point the CCP will decide that the economic liberalization necessary to rekindle strong GDP growth and achieve other economic objectives will require a measure of political liberalization. But there has been no sign of this so far; indeed, the other big news to emerge from the November 2013 Third Plenum was that China would establish a new "National Security Council" with responsibilities somewhat akin to those of the U.S. Department of Homeland Security, though presumably with a heavier emphasis on domestic repression.[5] Given that the new agency's formation was announced at the economic reform plenum, it is possible that Xi and his advisers decided that a period of wrenching economic transition would require *less*, not more, political liberalization; in other words, it might require intensified repression to ensure that opponents of reform—those who would probably lose—would be in no position to block it.

Chapter 4

The biggest wildcard affecting China's trajectory across multiple sectors is communication and the deepening of the network society. Probably the network society is the biggest wildcard affecting *all* countries' trajectories: It is new everywhere, and no one has a firm sense of what its vastly complex long-term implications might be. Arrival of the network society to China is comparable to the partial economic reform and opening China has experienced (with the attendant pathologies), as well as the changing demographic structure, insofar as it represents an ironclad material change that there can be no escaping. The only (huge) question is: What exactly does this fact mean? Where exactly is the network society leading China as an attractor, and how does it interact with changes in non-communication-specific sectors, given that communication is central to all social processes? Some of the Chinese analysts discussed in

Chapter 4 argue in summary fashion that the network society will strengthen a tendency toward political liberalization and eventual democratization. But others contend in sharp contrast that the Internet in particular is in the process of ripping the body politic apart.

Consequently, unlike the economists who generally favor liberalization, China's communication specialists are strongly divided over how to manage the new communication networks. There is no unified discourse in communications that could act as an attractor pulling China in an easily mapped direction. If one or the other camp in this debate should eventually "win" in the eyes of policy makers, its members could become significantly influential. They might be able to influence policy over the network society's evolving shape and dynamics, in the direction of either loosening or of tightening controls. But then the secondary and tertiary consequences in multiple dimensions of social life would be left to play out in ways exceptionally difficult to anticipate. For now and the immediate future, the Party-state seems strongly likely to follow a middle course in which it retains tight controls without at the same time squeezing the life out of the Internet and choking off its contributions to economic growth and social dynamism. The middle course (which is the current course) should allow proponents of limited political liberalization—as well as, at the other extreme, hard-core leftists and nationalists—to continue to propagate their views and attempt to mobilize wider public support.

Chapter 5

The striking fact about the foreign policy discourse on China's trajectory is that the PRC's international relations specialists seem mostly to be unaware of the serious challenges their country faces economically and demographically. Consequently, most IR scholars exude a blithe optimism that resembles the complacent mentalities of French elites during the belle époque period (1871–1914): Everything is working wonderfully, and nothing could ever go seriously wrong. On the basis of such overconfidence, Chinese IR realists—who are in the overwhelming majority—support the post-2008 foreign policy line, which many or even most of China's neighbors experience as unreasonable. Some Chinese IR specialists recognize that the PRC is still weak in key respects (for example, soft power) and may become even weaker still relative to the United States and Japan if the economy slows substantially. But these IR specialists are in the minority. Most Chinese foreign policy analysts seem to support the CCP's tougher post-2008 line, believing that (1) China's claims are inherently reasonable, and (2) because the success of China's rise is preordained, it does not particularly matter much what foreign countries think about Chinese reasonableness. The foreigners will eventually have no choice but to give in and accept China's transcendently right demands. They will have to come to their senses. But when they do, they can count on China's historically deep-rooted magnanimity to ensure that they will share in the bountiful benefits of the belle époque.

The problem with this view is that, if China's own economists are right, the belle époque cannot last. A large proportion of the Chinese foreign policy community would then be in for a substantial shock. Included would be not only academics but also those policy makers in the foreign policy establishment who decided it would be consistent with the national interest to pursue a more assertive foreign policy after 2008 because America's decline had finally begun. In society, the nationalists who use the Internet to disseminate their aggressive and hyperconfident views are also going to be in for a shock. Of course some nationalists and leftists have all along criticized the inequality engendered by Chinese-style economic growth. But to pursue the bellicose foreign policy they demand, China would have to remain exceptionally dynamic economically. It would have to draw on vast reserves of creativity, initiative, and morale among the Chinese people sufficient to withstand the counterblows that ultra-aggressiveness would invite from the United States, Japan, and other countries. Whether nationalists or even the substantially milder hubristic realists of the academic and foreign policy-making worlds would passively accept a stagnating economy could well become an urgent political question at some point during the next five to ten years. It is easy to imagine the frustration of these groups' overdeveloped expectations causing serious political disaffection in a society continually being transformed by the Internet and related communications technologies. But whether frustration and anger would then lead the realists or the nationalists to reduce their support for an ambitious foreign policy is far less certain. They might blame foreign countries for China's problems or calculate that an even more aggressive stance (for example, seizing control over energy reserves and fisheries in the East and South China Seas) could be the key to economic rejuvenation.

Chapter 6

Analysts of Chinese soft power and the cultural side of international relations are divided between pessimists who fret that China could be vanquished by the awesomeness of American ideational power and optimists who think that, in contrast, American culture is a paper tiger that China could defeat if it first expands its cultural influence into weak areas (whose people will happily accept it) and strengthens the PRC's culture industries. The soft-power optimists thus take an implicitly mixed position on the question of the network society. On the one hand, they would agree with liberals that wider diffusion of the Internet and continued technological transformations in the communications realm are unalloyed goods because they can strengthen society (through "informationalization") and security institutions such as the PLA.

On the other hand, their reasons for thinking this are themselves out of touch with network society logic. The reasons implicitly assume that the Party-state can continue to control a Chinese society being transformed by network logic and direct it toward achieving CCP-defined objectives. The soft-power optimists imagine that via informationalization, the ongoing communications revolutions can ignite sustained increases in the PRC's comprehensive national power. They ignore the potential for the network society to empower all (or most) groups and individuals linked to the network as nodes that can initiate and circulate their own interpretations and analyses of events—a potential that, in turn, could undermine unity and in that way reduce comprehensive national power. To this extent, the soft-power optimists would ultimately favor the state trying to regulate the network more rigorously and use it to increase China's relative power internationally. This might work to some extent, but it would also have the effect of sharpening tensions between the controllers and those on the network who chafe at the restrictions and deny the CCP's right to shape definitions of political reality. Even the online nationalists—natural allies of the cultural offensive realists—sharply criticize the authorities and reject their attempts at manipulation. As Internet participation continues to expand and eventually encompasses the currently disenfranchised members of the lower classes, online discourse could become even more subversive and challenging for the Party-state to repress. If rebellious online communities begin increasingly to evolve into angry social groups, China's soft power will likely suffer—unless the CCP learns the value of trying to channel such dissent through newly liberalized political institutions.

REDUCING COMPLEXITY TO TWO "DOMINANT STRANDS OF THINKING"

If there is to be a summary conclusion, by this point it should be obvious: Some Chinese writers—highly accomplished men and women who contribute to policy debates—are convinced that China must change and change quickly or else face a severe crisis. Economists, in particular, are almost unanimous in warning that the CCP must resume substantive, even though wrenching, economic reforms as soon as practically possible or else the rise of China will stall, stop, or go into reverse. The country could walk mindlessly into a middle-income trap; it could even—should the property bubble collapse—suffer an economic collapse of the sort that drove Japan, after 1990, into two decades of stagnation (to be precise, 1 percent average annual GDP growth), after which no one ever again discussed the rise of Japan. Moreover, any sustained Chinese stagnation—which would be aggravated by deleterious demographic trends—would begin well before the PRC attained anywhere near the levels of per capita income Japan had already achieved by 1990. Thus, any cessation or sharp, sustained slowdown in Chinese GDP and income growth would make solving all of China's other problems (related to the environment, public health, the educational system, corruption, crime, and more) incalculably more difficult. This would obviously be an unmitigated disaster—yet as the discussion in Chapter 2 makes clear, numerous Chinese economists are warning that it is a very real, even imminent, possibility.

In striking contrast, most (though not all) Chinese international relations specialists seem completely, perhaps even willfully, oblivious to the dangers that so concern the economists—"willfully" because, when confronted in interviews with some of the evidence the economists put forward, the IR specialists *consistently* reject the evidence without even reflecting on it. As explained in Chapter 5, many of these IR specialists, in their writings, evince an almost mystical belief in the inevitability of China's rise, coupled with the certainty of America's decline. To these observers, the GFC and subsequent Great Recession, coming on the heels of the U.S. military debacle in Iraq, evidently served as almost cosmic signals that the great recentering of China in world history, which so many IR analysts have been predicting for decades, was finally beginning in earnest. At last, a future of international justice was coming clearly into view—the light at the end of a long, dark tunnel—and no amount of nitpicking or faultfinding by captious and pedantic, insignificant, and small-minded economists (let alone visiting foreign researchers who annoyingly reiterate the economists' critiques) could stand in the way of the historically almighty Rise of China, which absolutely was destined to succeed; which no force could stop; and which would be good for all of humankind.

So jarring are the differences between these two dominant views that one of this book's anonymous reviewers suggested it would be reasonable to conclude that there are two fundamentally different, completely disjointed Chinas floating in the minds of PRC elites. What is more, in the light of all the evidence the economists marshal to make their sobering case, the IR specialists—or at least the majority who champion the grand inevitability of China's rise—appear to be "unhinged," the reviewer stated: effectively, *out of touch* with the fundamental Chinese realities on which the success or failure of the rise must unavoidably rest, no matter how strong the analyst's beliefs. (*Beliefs* seems the appropriate term because an alternative such as *studied conclusion* would imply that the hubristic IR specialists had actually weighed carefully what the economists were saying.)

What is especially alarming about the "unhinged" beliefs of the heedlessly optimistic Chinese IR scholars is suggested most forcefully by *other* Chinese IR scholars: the minority (including Wang Jisi, Yang Jiemian, and others) who *do* evidently read the economists and take their warnings seriously. This minority directly charges the hubristic, sometimes unabashedly nationalistic IR scholars with *directly encouraging* and perhaps even *fueling* the aggressive turn in foreign policy after 2008—which the moderate minority views as gravely irresponsible, because, as the solidly documented concerns of the economists make clear, China is not yet in a sufficiently powerful position relative to the United States, Japan, and other states to take such huge risks in international relations, even though the risks may be aimed at achieving glorious ends such as reunification of the imagined national territory. The boldly aggressive moves in the East and South China Seas championed by hubristic IR specialists—and backed by their supporters in the PLA and the Party-state—threaten to start fires that China will probably prove incapable of containing; in a worst-case scenario, the fires could engulf the PRC and put an end to its rise through devastating defeat in warfare as opposed to the mere economic stagnation about which economists are warning.

These two, wildly divergent China's were fully on display in November 2013. First, on November 12, the Party Center concluded the Eighteenth Central Committee's Third Plenum by issuing its sixty-point "Resolution Regarding Certain Important Issues on the Question of Comprehensively Deepening [Economic] Reform." This document, though not as obviously or incontestably committed to liberalizing economic reforms as it was sometimes portrayed as being, nevertheless did clearly indicate that the Party Center acknowledged and accepted the veracity of almost all of the critiques being offered by the economists discussed in Chapter 2, as well as countless others—the consensus, in effect (perhaps not completely, but very nearly so) of the Chinese economics profession. Most prominently, the Center pledged in the sixty points to shift to a system in which (relatively unfettered) market functioning becomes the primary mechanism by which the allocation of resources is determined. The Center also pledged to increase transparency in economic policy making, create a more level playing field for the private enterprises that must compete with SOEs, reduce inequality, close the gap between city and countryside, and much more. To be sure, it also made abundantly clear that SOEs would continue to play prominent roles in the economy—and the dominant roles in certain strategically critical sectors and/or in the provision of public goods.

The "Resolution" is not *radically* reformist. It does not propose a massive reallocation of wealth from SOEs to households, which might be the only way to achieve a shift to domestic-consumption-driven growth without suffering a dangerous and debilitating recession. The document is also long on slogans, short on policy specifics (ironing out the details would be left to a leading small group); this naturally invites the question of whether the policies that ultimately emerge will prove as bold as the document seems to promise. Yet, on the whole, there can be no denying that the rhetoric and substance of the "Resolution" are strongly reformist. The drafters even make it a point to reject the neoleftist insistence that the first thirty years of the PRC (the Maoist decades) contributed just as much to China's rise as the second thirty years. Instead, the drafters ignore Mao and proclaim Deng Xiaoping's reform-and-opening policies of 1979 and beyond "a great new revolution" reflecting "enormous political courage" and "an historically unprecedented, powerful [reformist] determination."[6]

Relentlessly rousing and upbeat in tone, the document does not discuss the difficulties China's economy will inevitably face even *if* all of its implied liberal promises are implemented.[7] For example, if the market—dominated by a private sector facing hard-budget constraints—were to become the decisive mechanism determining the allocation of resources, aggregate investment would immediately plunge because of China's enormous productive overcapacity, throughout multiple sectors. Given that the contribution of investment to GDP in China stands at world-historic highs, transitioning to market-directed investment allocation would almost certainly result in an initial collapse of GDP growth and probably also a contraction in existing GDP, reflecting the "creative destruction" of excessive capacity. Unemployment would then increase, meaning that in absolute terms if not necessarily as a percentage of GDP, consumption would almost certainly fall. *Eventually*, if all the reforms were diligently pursued in the face of furious opposition from special interest groups, the economy could return to balanced growth—on a much healthier and more sustainable track. But this is assuming the Party-state can defeat the special interests and maintain sociopolitical order during the unavoidable period of intense turmoil that would surely accompany the transition. Anticipating this turmoil may be one reason the Party Center announced at the Plenum that it would establish the new "National Security Council," whose functions would include domestic security. The Council would be headed by Party General Secretary Xi Jinping.[8]

On the one hand, one would not expect a document of this nature to dwell on the negative and thus alarm its intended audiences. A "doom and gloom" document would fail to rally support for the reforms, particularly if it openly acknowledged the heavy short- and medium-term pain the reforms must inflict. The problem is that the excessively upbeat tone of the document—even as it proclaims an intention to pursue fundamental reforms (which obviously implies recognition that something must be seriously wrong with China's economy)—feels in key respects forced, false, and artificial. And the reason for this, in turn, may be that Xi Jinping had already decided twelve months earlier (in November 2012) to ally himself with those who profess optimism about China's future; hence, his co-optation and reconfiguration of the superoptimistic "China Dream" discourse.[9] Secondly, Xi may have been seeking to avoid alienating the hubristic IR optimists, who, as we have seen, cannot be convinced that there is anything seriously wrong with China's economy. These people—who, based on the post-2008 foreign policy shift, are powerful—would presumably reject any document that accentuated the negative as distorted, defeatist, and going against the tide of history. Xi cannot afford to alienate the architects of the aggressive new foreign policy, which began well before his ascension to power. So the document resulting from the Third Plenum calls for reforms so profound as to suggest serious dysfunctions in the Chinese economy, yet expresses the call in a tone of confident, sunny optimism that implies that nothing could stop the reforms from succeeding in an almost completely cost-free way. The reforms may well be pursued, reflecting a bottom-line realism in Xi's worldview. But the document promising the reforms is sufficiently dishonest about the serious nature of China's difficulties that the hubristic IR optimists are still permitted to delude themselves that the rise is not threatened. This must have been the trade-off to which Xi agreed. Perhaps he believes it himself. It is impossible to say with any certainty.

Barely a week after issuing its reformist "Resolution," the CCP—on November 23, 2013—suddenly announced another initiative with entirely different implications. It declared the establishment of a provocative new Air Defense Identification Zone (ADIZ) over most of the East China Sea, overlapping in certain places with comparable zones declared in decades past by Japan, South Korea, and Taiwan. China's new ADIZ would require all aircraft—military and civilian—intending to enter the zone first to identify themselves to PRC military authorities (and thus, in effect, seek their permission to enter)—or else risk unspecified negative consequences (though Beijing was quick to offer reassurances that no civilian aircraft would face the risk of being shot down).[10] Immediately, Japan and the United States declared that their military aircraft would not respect the zone—although civilian aircraft would be instructed to abide by Beijing's demands. Both Tokyo and Washington challenged the zone almost immediately, pointedly dispatching military aircraft into the ADIZ without first giving notification. Beijing responded only verbally. Soon, however, the CCP began floating the possibility that it would take the even more provocative step of establishing an ADIZ over the much vaster South China Sea: airspace through which countless civilian and military aircraft, from multiple nations, fly day and night, 365 days a year. Both the logistical and political challenges of administering a South China Sea ADIZ would be formidable. Nevertheless, a researcher at the PLA Naval Academy, Senior Colonel Li Jie, told a foreign journalist in February 2014 that "the establishment of another ADIZ over the South China Sea is necessary for China's long-term national interest."[11] Once again, the United States registered its strong objections.

Consequently, despite its mounting economic difficulties, China's heedless post-2008 hubris continued unabated and even became bolder and riskier. It was difficult to comprehend how, in the minds of Chinese elites, including (presumably) the nation's highest policy makers, the "two Chinas"—one facing the prospect of economic stagnation or decline, the other soaring inexorably ever upward in an unstoppable rise—could peacefully coexist. Yet, clearly, they did. The juxtaposition of the East China Sea ADIZ declaration with the reformist "Resolution" issued at the Third Plenum suggests that any cognitive dissonance elites might have experienced in trying to reconcile the two China's was resolved by the *tone* of the "Resolution." Deploying the relentlessly upbeat tone allowed the Party Center to square the circle, by acknowledging that, yes, it is true: China faces serious economic problems—but these can, without question, easily be solved by means of reforms that cannot fail because the success of China's rise is inevitable. Just how many perceptive and nonsense-intolerant Chinese leaders would have had their cognitive dissonance becalmed by the "Resolution" (its content and tone) is questionable. But adopting a tone that contradicted the content may have been the only option available for securing the support for the reforms to go forward. Perhaps they can only go forward just so long as the hubristic nationalists are also permitted, simultaneously, to continue to aggressively pursue the PRC's irredentist claims by means of the abrasive and hyperconfident post-2008 foreign policy.

The vastly more positive outcome—for China, its neighbors, and the world at large—would have been for the expansionists to back down and acknowledge that China's current economic and other problems are far too severe to justify making such risky foreign policy moves. If China could rebalance and restructure its economy first—an inevitably painful process—then perhaps, eventually, the irredentist agenda could be taken up again. But this was not the deal that resulted. Consequently, the hubristic IR expansionists may well be setting themselves up for a crushing setback. Assume, for the moment, that the economists are right. After all, they certainly document their case with far more attention to factual detail and logical argumentation than do the confident IR specialists, who tend to assert or proclaim rather than demonstrate. If the economists are right, then even if the Xi Jinping government implements the reforms highlighted in the Third Plenum's "Resolution," the Chinese economy will suffer several years (or more) of low or declining growth—probably punctuated by periods of contraction. Under the circumstances of a sputtering economy, the PRC's bellicose posturing of recent years will no longer be tenable. In aggregate terms, China would still possess formidable power with which to bully its neighbors. But it could appear desperate or even ridiculous in the process—depending on how bad the economic situation became—and as a consequence would suffer a debilitating loss of prestige. This, in turn, would presumably come as shock to the hubristic foreign policy strategists, something like a bolt from the blue blow to the head. They would suffer from all the complications that follow in the wake of rising expectations suddenly being frustrated. But whether this would convince them humbly to climb down or lash out even more aggressively is impossible to say, though critically important—because the eventual (and probably sooner rather than later) frustration of the hubristic nationalists' sky-high expectations seems a high-probability development. Containing their anger may be yet another function envisioned for the new National Security Council, given its coequal responsibility for domestic stability. Surely Xi Jinping understands that, if the reforms proceed, the hubristic nationalists cannot be permitted to lash out when China goes through its painful period of rebalancing and restructuring. The pain—the trauma—would be magnified enormously if, at the same time, hubristic foreign policy strategists were given free rein to heighten tensions with foreign powers. Who would tolerate their excessive territorial claims, menacing threats, and gratuitous insults in the event China were to sink into an extended economic malaise?

THE POSSIBILITY FOR THINKING TO CHANGE

If the primary presupposition of this book is that how a country's elites think about the national trajectory is likely to exert a powerful independent effect on what the trajectory eventually becomes—at least to the extent that elite thinking is unified—then is it possible Chinese thinking will change for other than endogenous reasons? Recall first that only in the issue-areas of the economy and foreign policy is Chinese elite thinking fairly unified (and even in these areas there are still significant divisions). Elites are sharply at odds over how best to shape the political system and what the future of politics is likely to become, as well as the optimal approach to take in regulating the network society based on what it might be leading to (democratization? a debilitating downward cultural spiral?). *The core strand that seems to unify, however tenuously, thinking across the issue-areas is commitment to the national rise in absolute and relative power terms as unquestionably desirable and justified.* All readers of this book will be well aware that such thinking has deep roots in modern China history, dating back to the nineteenth-century concern to nurture wealth and strength to fight off barbarian invaders and restore the Sino-centric world order. Such thinking—which probably resonates throughout most of the Han Chinese population—is unlikely to change. But what if a contradiction developed between achieving the Chinese dream of wealth and strength and continuing the CCP's monopoly on political power?

This is an issue that Chinese elites have not had to face in well over a generation, since the advent of Deng Xiaoping's reform and opening policies. But depending on how successfully the Party manages the unavoidable transition to a slower rate of growth, it may well become an issue that elites have no choice but to confront at some point during the next decade. Endogenously, then, Chinese elites might well decide that nothing should supersede the goals of attaining wealth and strength, not even the Four Cardinal Principles of Deng Xiaoping (as enunciated in March 1979 and then written into the PRC Constitution), which specify the Party's monopoly on power and authority to determine the country's guiding ideology as bedrock principles.[12] At the same time, elites and the general public continue constantly to be bombarded with *exogenous* messages from the global culture telling them that an authoritarian political system is illegitimate for a leading power of the twenty-first century, and that China must, and will, inevitably change. Elites could, in their own minds, rather easily reject this logic and resist global culture's socializing pressures when the PRC state was "flying high" and China's economy was growing at double-digit rates.[13] They may find it significantly more difficult to resist in the event of a sustained economic slowdown. They might even decide more affirmatively that political liberalization could become a core part of the solution for China as it seeks to return to the track of a rising great power. Of course it would be one thing for academic and (possibly) business elites in the private sector to come to this conclusion and quite another for the Party Center to go along with it. The point is that changing assessments of what it will take for China to resume and then consolidate the rise could cause shifts in thinking on politics and culture management (including via the Internet) to the point that elite assessments become relatively unified and then act as an attractor reinforcing the economists' discourse and pulling China in the direction of political liberalization.

As ever, material interest groups would challenge this tendency and seek to block fundamental change. But it matters when a country's academic elites and public intellectuals all start to agree that fundamental change is necessary. In a climate in which elite and public opinion becomes increasingly loud and hostile toward maintaining the political status quo, material interest groups would find it tougher to hold the line. They would especially come under strong pressure were elements in the PLA—the bastion of realist foreign policy—to decide that whatever it takes to revive economic growth must be risked because for the rise in material power terms to stop would mean the loss of absolutely everything.

Notes

PREFACE

1. Overholt (1993).

2. Some expect that the two countries' nuclear arsenals will decisively ensure that the transition—assuming it continues—remains peaceful, through the logic of mutual deterrence.

3. See Chapter 3 on political change and Chapter 4 on China's metamorphosis into a "network society."

4. For a wonderfully rich description and analysis of the *plurality* of Chinese dreams, as articulated by China's "citizen intellectuals," see Callahan (2013).

5. Bueno de Mesquita (2009). (I discuss his book at length in Chapter 1.)

6. See Zhu Xufeng (2009) and Jakobson and Knox (2010).

7. This model of Chinese governance is similar to Kjeld Erik Brødsgaard's (2012) "fragmented integration" model of how the Party-state (loosely) governs the PRC's powerful state-owned enterprises (SOE)—although Brødsgaard emphasizes the Party's power to appoint key SOE personnel.

8. "Ideological and Theoretical Basis of the CPC" (2007).

9. Cardoso (2005), pp. 23–24.

10. For a magnificent and comprehensive overview of CCP media-control strategy, see Yuezhi Zhao (2008).

CHAPTER I

1. See Baumer (1977), pp. 26–46, 140–159, 258–267, and 402–416.

2. Lombardo (2006), p. 117.

3. Bell (2003), p. 11; emphasis added. Also see Scott (1999) and Migdal (2001).

4. Lombardo (2006), pp. 5–108.

5. Allen (1939), pp. 332–333.

6. Lombardo (2006), p. 118.

7. Bell (2003), p. 36.

8. Ibid., pp. 75–97.

9. Ibid., pp. 75–76.

10. Bueno de Mesquita (2009), p. xiv.

11. Ibid., pp. xv–xix; quotations on p. xv and p. xix.

12. Ibid., p. xv.

13. Ibid., p. xix.

14. Wendt (1999), p. 231; emphasis added.

15. Bueno de Mesquita (2009), p. 87.

16. Ibid., p. 87.

17. For some examples of these kinds of predictions, see Mann (2007).

18. One laudable exception would be Rowen (2007).

19. Bueno de Mesquita (2009), p. 172; and see pp. 173–202 for the predictions.

20. Ibid., pp. 179–180.

21. Ibid., p. 225.

22. On the dangers of assuming the inevitability of ingenuity, see Homer-Dixon (2000).

23. Bueno de Mesquita (2009), p. 221.

24. Ibid.

25. Ibid., pp. 215–216.

26. See ibid., p. 217.

27. BDM (2009) does acknowledge offhandedly at one point that "we will want to take more seriously the predictions closer in than farther out, since a great deal can happen between now and 2130" (p. 219). But he does not examine this critical problem systematically.

28. Staley (2007), p. 17.

29. Ibid., pp. 6–7.

30. Ibid., pp. 12–13.

31. Ibid., p. 12.

32. Ibid., p. 12.

33. I write about this category in Lynch (2006).

34. Kiel and Elliott (1997), p. 1; also see Gleick (1987), Rihani (2002), and Orrell (2007).

35. See Chapters 3 and 4 on the potential for democratization and Chapters 5 and 6 on the international power transition.

36. Staley (2007), pp. 9–10 (emphasis added). Sensitivity to initial conditions is conceptually similar to "path dependence." As defined in an influential article by Paul A. David, path-dependent social dynamics

> . . . refer to systems of human social interaction whose motions remain under the influence of conditions that are themselves the contingent legacies of events and actions played out within each system's history . . . The events in question sometimes will be recent or obtrusive enough to be salient in the collective cultural identity of the society, . . . [but] in other cases the critical events will have taken place in a past so remote that it has slipped from the conscious memories of the actors. (David, 2007, p. 93)

37. Rihani (2002), p. 78.

38. Ibid., p. 79.

39. Ibid.

40. Staley (2007), p. 35.

41. Bell (2003), p. 82; emphasis added.

42. To some unmeasureable extent, the material attractor also helps shape the elite images attractor, but the reverse is equally true. Neither is fully reducible to the other; both have autonomous force.

43. Zheng Wang (2012) and Gries (2004).

44. Christopher Hughes (2011) argues that in recent years the new nationalism has fused with the geopolitical perspective on international relations so long prominent—or even dominant—in Chinese IR studies. The result, Hughes argues, is to make the contemporary PRC increasingly resemble prewar Japan or prewar Germany in foreign policy rhetoric and sometimes practice. Hughes does not predict that China will inevitably embark on a course of violent expansionism, but he does demonstrate that worldviews in China—including popular worldviews—are not consistently trending in the liberal direction that celebrants of global integration or the inevitability of democratization following economic development would expect.

CHAPTER 2

1. Steinfeld (2010), p. 25.

2. Ibid., p. 125.

3. Ibid., p. 69.

4. There were, to be sure, a few notably important exceptions to the dominant trend. Among the most prominent dissenters were Michael Pettis, Patrick Chovanec, Victor Shih, and the political economist I discuss next, Yasheng Huang. At the time, even I—though certainly not prominent, nor a specialist in political economy—had already shifted to the bearish camp. For example, I argued in the October 1, 2009, *Far Eastern Economic Review* that "as the Chinese Communist Party celebrates the People's Republic's 60th anniversary, China's economy is in trouble . . . No matter what, China's growth rate—and, by extension, its 'rise'—must now slow. The only uncertainty is by how much and for how long" (Lynch, "The Next Chinese Revolution," 2009). The reason I came to this conclusion was not only that I had been reading the insightful and genuinely bold works of Pettis, Chovanec, Shih, Huang, and the tiny minority of other skeptics; I had also been reading Chinese economists, in early preparation for writing this book. As detailed later in this chapter, Chinese economists have been consistently pessimistic since at least the mid-2000s.

5. A mild recession began in December 2007; it only became "great" as a result of the GFC.

6. Cited in "U.S. Global Investors" (2012). Also reflecting the dramatic reversal in foreign confidence was the performance of the Shanghai stock exchange. After the market effectively collapsed over the course of 2008—primarily as a result of CCP efforts to deflate what it decided were asset bubbles in equities and housing—the Shanghai market bounced back to become one of the world's best performers in 2009. The index peaked (post-GFC) at 3,454 on July 1, 2009. But then it began a long, inexorable decline, punctuated by occasional rallies. The market closed at 2,004 on March 10, 2014, only marginally higher than its post-GFC low-point of 1,979, reached on June 24, 2013. (See the *New York Times*, "Analysis Tools," 2014)

7. Huang (2008), p. 239.

8. Ibid.

9. Ibid., p. 286.

10. Yao Yang (2010), p. 14.

11. See Joseph Fewsmith's (2011) discussion of the debate over the "China model."

12. "Zhonggong Zhongyang" (2013).

13. For a thoroughly comprehensive assessment of the Chongqing model, see Philip C. C. Huang (2011).

14. See Chapter 1 for an explanation of attractors.

15. Note the convincingly documented contention of Carl Walter and Fraser Howie, in *Red Capitalism*, that reforms in the strategically central financial sector stopped cold in the mid-2000s, paving the way for discipline in the system to collapse after the CCP launched its monetary stimulus program in 2008–2009. See Walter and Howie (2011), especially pp. 111–142.

16. Zhou Ruijin (2009). Not all analysts agree that China has a problem with special interest groups. For example, Professor Yao Yang (2010) of Peking University contends that China has a "neutral government," by which he means "a government that does not represent the interests of any particular interest group, and that is not captured by any

interest group . . . A neutral government pays more attention [than captured governments] to the integrated overall and long-term interest" of the whole society (pp. 17–18).

17. Zhou Ruijin (2009), p. 34.

18. Ibid.

19. Ibid.

20. Ibid.

21. Ibid., p. 35.

22. Ibid.

23. Zhongguo Weilai Zouxiang Editorial Group (2009).

24. "Renmin Chubanshe."

25. A book of this nature, covering multiple policy issue areas, would have taken at least a year to research, write, vet, edit, and publish.

26. See the following discussion.

27. Ward (2014).

28. National Bureau of Statistics of China (2014); also see Mackenzie, "China Is Having a Credit Fueled Non-Recovery" (2013); Mackenzie, "China's Massive Credit Dependency" (2013); and Ford (2013).

29. Country Analysis Unit (2013); no pagination provided.

30. See Country Analysis Unit (2013), Mackenzie, "China Is Having a Credit Fueled Non-Recovery" (2013), Mackenzie, "China's Massive Credit Dependency" (2013), and Ford (2013).

31. Xiao Gang (2012).

32. Zhongguo Weilai Zouxiang Editorial Group (2009), p. 133.

33. Ibid. This calculation is high compared to others; for example, Ye Tan (2009), an economics journalist, reports in a *neibu* article that consumption as a percentage of GDP "unprecedentedly" fell from 46.4 percent in 2000 to 35 percent in 2007, "a new low" (p. 43). Ye's numbers are closer to those seen most often. Unfortunately, it is quite common in Chinese academic books and articles for authors to report data without citing original sources.

34. Zhongguo Weilai Zouxiang Editorial Group (2009), p. 134.

35. For a comprehensive and sobering assessment of China's overinvestment and underconsumption imbalance, see Pettis, *Avoiding the Fall* (2013).

36. Zhongguo Weilai Zouxiang Editorial Group (2009), p. 173. Certainly Chinese households are wealthy in aggregate terms. Credit Suisse (2010) calculated in October 2010, using data issued prior to the explosion in house prices, that Chinese household wealth had reached US$16.5 trillion, third in the world behind Japan (US$21 trillion) and the United States (US$54.6 trillion).

37. Zhongguo Weilai Zouxiang Editorial Group (2009), p. 134. (Also on underconsumption, see Chi Fulin, 2010.) It is important to underscore that the authors are talking about consumption as a percentage of GDP, not absolute levels of consumption—which for many products and services continue to grow robustly. The authors are concerned that as a central component of aggregate demand, consumption growth will be insufficient to support increasing levels of productive capacity (including employment) or even existing levels of productive capacity. This, in turn, would present China with the dilemma of trying to fill the demand gap by either increasing investment (leading to even more productive capacity), increasing government spending, and/or increasing exports—any of which would either exacerbate existing problems or prove impossible to implement. The only

other alternative would be to accept the need for China to undergo a painful process of "decapacitization" (*quchanyehua*), which by definition would mean a sustained recession as well as the ominous prospect of a downward deflationary spiral. (See ibid., pp. 172–173.)

38. Ibid., p. 135. For a rich discussion of the relationship between economic growth and natural resource utilization, see Roumasset, Burnett, and Wang (2008).

39. U.S. Energy Information Administration (2013); no pagination provided.

40. The world's leading foreign specialist on China's severe environmental degradation is Elizabeth Economy. See, in particular, Economy (2004) and Economy (2007).

41. Zhongguo Weilai Zouxiang Editorial Group (2009), p. 135. Also see CASS economist Jin Zhouying's (2010) call for establishing a "Genuine Progress Indicator" (GPI) to replace GDP. The GPI would take into account environmental destruction.

42. See this chapter's dedicated section on "Inequality." Lower- and middle-income households everywhere have a higher propensity to consume any additional increases in income they might receive than their wealthier counterparts. This is because lower- and middle-income households chronically suffer the frustrations of "pent-up demand," whereas wealthier households eventually run out of things to buy.

43. Zhongguo Weilai Zouxiang Editorial Group (2009), p. 134.

44. Ibid., p. 135. Banks and SOEs have what the authors call a "big brother, little brother relationship" (ibid., p. 136). This is undoubtedly one reason that corporate debt as a percentage of GDP rose from about 94 percent in 2007 to 125 percent in 2012. See Rabinovitch (2013) and Steger (2013).

45. Zhongguo Weilai Zouxiang Editorial Group (2009), p. 135.

46. Also see Haggard and Huang (2008).

47. Tsai (2004).

48. Zhongguo Weilai Zouxiang Editorial Group (2009), p. 136. The book's authors are also concerned about mounting public debt—and they were writing this *before* the explosion in local government debt that resulted from the post-GFC stimulus program. The stimulus probably resulted in total government debt as a percentage of GDP rising from 57 percent in 2005 to 78 percent in 2012. See Chen Long (2013). By mid-2014, total debt in China—public and private—soared past the alarming level of 250 percent of GDP, reflecting public and private entitites borrowing ever more to pay off earlier loans, or to speculate in real estate. See Holliday (2014).

49. Zhongguo Weilai Zouxiang Editorial Group (2009), p. 135. See the section on demography and population policy later in the chapter.

50. Chang Xinghua and Li Wei (2009). Also on this problem, see Hung Ho-feng (2009).

51. Chang Xinghua and Li Wei (2009), p. 5.

52. The full list of countries and regions (besides China) in the sample includes the Eurozone (collectively), Japan, South Korea, Canada, Mexico, the United States, the Czech Republic, France, Germany, Italy, the Netherlands, Poland, Spain, the United Kingdom, Australia, and New Zealand.

53. Chang Xinghua and Li Wei (2009), p. 5.

54. In 2000, the Chinese state's expenditures on "social guarantees" (*shehui baozhang*) amounted to only 3.31 percent of GDP, but by 2006 they had increased to 5.28 percent of GDP. By comparison, Chang Xinghua and Li Wei (2009) calculate that even in the United States—not one of the topmost social welfare states—welfare expenditures amounted in 2006 to 12 percent of GDP (p. 7).

55. Ibid., p. 6. Also on the meagerness of Chinese income redistribution schemes, see Han, Wei, and Mok (2011) and Solinger and Hu (2012).

56. Some writers think it would not be a good idea to change the situation too soon. Mao Zhenhua (2009) of Renmin University (apparently he has also worked in the private sector) warns that rebalancing the economic structure too quickly could lead to the growth rate falling precipitously, causing additional problems. Mao coins a slogan: "Adjust the structure while the growth rate is kept high" (p. 26). Mao believes that China can grow at an average annual rate of 8.2 to 8.8 percent from 2013 through 2022 and 7.3 to 7.6 percent from 2023 through 2032 (p. 24). It is rare for a Chinese economic analyst to make such concrete predictions for two decades into the future. It is also rare for an economic analyst to exude such optimism.

57. Chang and Li (2009), p. 7.

58. Zhang Monan, "Zhongguo jingji fusu" (2009), p. 20. Economics journalist Ye Tan (2009) counters those who suggest that consumption of luxury goods by the wealthy can contribute significantly to growth. She argues that when the wealthy compete to consume luxury goods conspicuously, the economy and society are more likely to be malfunctioning in significant respects than sustainably developing (p. 43).

59. Zhang Monan, "Zhongguo jingji fusu" (2009), pp. 20–21; quotation on p. 21.

60. Zhang Monan, "Yingxiang weilai" (2009).

61. Wang Jian (2010), of the China Society of Macroeconomics, calculates that to pay off their personal debts, U.S. households will have to reduce their consumption by, on average, 10 percent a year, indefinitely into the future. This would have hugely negative repercussions for aggregate demand (and, therefore, employment and production) (pp. 11–15).

62. Zhang Monan, "Zhongguo jingji fusu" (2009), pp. 19–21; quotation on p. 21. Indeed, China's average annual export growth rate has been steadily sliding ever since a temporary bounce-back in 2010 (Mackenzie, "Why China's June Trade Data," 2013) In 2014, as reported by Bloomberg, "Exports for January and February combined [even] *declined* 1.6 percent, the most for that period since 2009, according to previously released data, and compared with a 23.6 percent gain a year earlier" ("China's Exports Unexpectedly Drop," 2014, emphasis added). No longer could China be characterized as an "export-led-growth economy." To be sure, the huge and (at least until 2014) still growing—albeit at much lower rates—volume and value of exports was still critical to maintaining the existing structure of GDP. But the contribution of net exports to GDP *growth* slowly shriveled to near-insignificance by 2013–2014.

63. Liu Jiejun (2010), p. 29.

64. Ibid.

65. Ibid., p. 30.

66. Ibid., p. 31. Liu also warns that another side of export-reliance—accumulation of foreign exchange reserves—is dangerous because, over the long term, decline in the value of foreign currencies relative to the renminbi seems inevitable (p. 32.) This view is shared by, among others, Yu Yongding (2010). But the view is not universally held. Wang Jian (2010) of the China Society of Macroeconomics expects the dollar (he does not discuss the euro or the yen) to restrengthen in the late 2010s as the world economy gradually recovers (pp. 14–15).

67. International Monetary Fund (2012); no pagination provided.

68. Zhang Monan, "Zhongguo jingji fusu" (2009), p. 21.

69. According to Rio Tinto calculations, to meet this demand, China's steel foundries (the ones already in existence and the many new ones hastily constructed) increased their production from about 350 million metric tons in 2005 to almost 700 million metric tons in 2012. Yet they were still operating at only 82 percent of capacity. See Albanese (2012), p. 21.

70. A Pivot Capital Management report (2009) on "China's [2009] Investment Boom" concludes that given the country's level of economic development and its existing stock of infrastructure, investing in conventional rail capacity makes good economic sense. The same, however, cannot be said for investing in high-speed rail, airports, bridges, and certain other types of infrastructure. I am grateful to Michael Pettis for drawing this report to my attention.

71. Gao Shangquan (2010), p. 33.

72. Ibid., pp. 33–34.

73. Ibid., p. 34.

74. See Naughton (2007), pp. 430–441; also see Wong and Bird (2008).

75. Gao Shangquan (2010), p. 34.

76. Ibid.

77. Zhongguo Shekeyuan Jingjixuebu (2010). The individual members of the study group are not identified.

78. Ibid., pp. 8–9.

79. Magnus (2011).

80. Quoted in Mackenzie, "China's Massive Credit Dependency" (2013).

81. The CCP Center may have committed itself to this goal at the November 2013 "Third Plenum," but the degree of commitment will not become clear until implementation of the Plenum's promises begins. (See Zhonggong Zhongyang, 2013.)

82. Zhongguo Shekeyuan Jingjixuebu (2010), p. 9. The group was also concerned that in response to the GFC, Chinese local governments, enterprises, financial institutions, and households had all increased their debt loads. Consequently, they must deleverage because too much debt will cause latent financial risks to accumulate. On the other hand, they must deleverage *gradually* because suddenly cutting spending to pay off debts would result in a negative shock to aggregate demand (pp. 9–10).

83. Stephens (2013).

84. Bloomberg News (2011), Burkitt and Page (2011), and Page (2011). For deep background, see Wang Feng and Mason (2008) and Wang Feng (2011).

85. Stephens (2013) (emphasis added).

86. Zhang Yi (2010), p. 78.

87. See the following section on "Urbanization and the Property Bubble."

88. Zhang Yi (2010), p. 77.

89. Ibid., p. 78.

90. Hu told a meeting of Party leaders that China would "stick to and improve its current family planning policy and maintain a low birth rate" (Page, 2011). Pressure to stay the course comes primarily from the Family Planning Commission, which administers a powerful bureaucracy of 500,000 officials (Interviews). For a detailed discussion of this point, see Wang Feng (2011).

91. Zhang Yi (2010), pp. 78–79.

92. Ibid., p. 81. Zhang is also concerned about the sex imbalance in China's population structure, noting that in 2007 there were only 100 girls reported born for every 120 boys (pp. 79–80).

93. Wang Guixin, "Renkou laolinghua" (2010); also see Wang Guixin, "Jinkuai" (2010).

94. Wang Guixin, "Renkou laolinghua" (2010), pp. 228–229.

95. Ibid., p. 229.

96. If, that is, they can find affordable housing. See the following section on "Urbanization and the Property Bubble."

97. Ibid., p. 230.

98. Ibid., pp. 230–231. Wang suggests that the "younger elderly" (aged sixty-five through seventy) could also be encouraged to do more to help themselves, perhaps by continuing to work for a few more years (health permitting).

99. Ibid., p. 231.

100. Fan et al. (2010), p. 19. As explained by the *China Daily* in March 2011: "At present, China adopts a differentiated retirement age policy. The regulations stipulate a retirement age of 60 for male managerial personnel and technicians, 55 for their female counterparts, and 55 for male laborers and 50 for their female counterparts" (Xinhua, 2011).

101. Fan et al. (2010), p. 19.

102. Ibid.

103. Ibid., p. 20.

104. Ibid.

105. Ibid.

106. Ibid.

107. Ibid., p. 21.

108. Zhou Tianyong (2010). On ascending to the premiership in March 2013, Li Keqiang began forcefully articulating this case and charting plans to make it happen (Li Keqiang, 2013).

109. Zhou Tianyong (2010), p. 9. Zhou avoids addressing the issue of concern to Fan and his coauthors concerning the possibility of diminishing productivity returns resulting from rural-to-urban migration.

110. As noted in the opening paragraphs of the section on demography, the 2010 census takers found that only 49.68 percent of Chinese people were then living in cities, a significantly lower proportion than most observers had predicted (see note 75). One scholar calculates that China's urbanization rate slowed from 5 percent in the 1980s to 4 percent in the 1990s and then to 2 percent in the 2000s—precisely the opposite of what those who place their hopes in urbanization as the key to future economic growth would hope—and expect—to see (Wang Xiaochang, 2010, pp. 101–102). Looking ahead, Renmin University economist Mao Zhenhua argues in a *neibu* report that the steep-slope phase of China's urbanization process has ended for good. He summarizes his concern about this development by noting the unfortunate coincidence that "the urbanization dividend has ended right at the same time as the demographic dividend" (Mao Zhenhua, 2009, pp. 24–25).

111. Zhou Tianyong (2010), p. 10.

112. Ibid.

113. Ibid.

114. Ibid. Otherwise, the country will chronically overproduce, and eventually its leaders will have to decide whether to accept the pain inevitably associated with reducing surplus capacity or else make policy changes so that the overproduced goods can more easily be exported to other countries, forcing *them* to reduce productive capacity.

115. Ibid., p. 11.

116. Ibid., pp. 11–12.

117. Yin Zhongli (2010).

118. Ibid., pp. 29–30. Also see Adams (2009) and Gibson (2009).

119. Yin Zhongli (2010), p. 30.

120. Ibid., pp. 30–31. Also see Naughton (2007), pp. 430–441; Wong and Bird (2008); and Oi et al. (2012).

121. Yin Zhongli (2010), p. 31.

122. Ibid., p. 30.

123. Ibid., p. 32.

124. Wang Lina (2010), p. 105.

125. See "Lack of Funding Threatens China's Affordable Housing Plan" (2011).

126. Wang Xiaochang (2010). Wang makes an unsettling assertion concerning the relationship between high housing prices and a society's urbanization rate: "Under a regime of high house prices, there will not be any additional urbanization" (p. 102.)

127. Ibid., pp. 101–103.

128. Yi Xianrong (2010), director of the CASS Institute of Financial Development, worries that high housing costs will have multigenerational consequences. If families must pay huge proportions of their income on housing, they will have correspondingly less to spend not only on consumer goods but also on their children's educations, broadly defined. They may even have to pass mortgage debt on to their descendants. People who cannot afford a house at all will have no choice but to live in substandard conditions, a situation that itself will have negative consequences for the next generation. Inequality can become deeply ingrained as class divisions crystalize (p. 94). On this broad and critically important issue—inequality, class crystallization, and class consciousness—see Guo (2012) and Solinger (2012).

129. Wang Xiaochang (2010), p. 100.

130. Ibid. Two other researchers, Wang Lishan and Liu Xiaoyan, note that from November 2008 through December 2009, Chinese banks issued a total of 10.84 trillion yuan in new credit (Wang Lishan and Liu Xiaoyan, 2010, p. 15).

131. Wang Xiaochang (2010), pp. 100–101. It was also, of course, only because of excessive money and credit expansion that China experienced the massive surge of investment in 2009, leading directly to the accumulation of debt witnessed in the years since.

132. Cao Jianhai (2010), p. 109.

133. See "Index Mundi."

134. Cao Jianhai (2010), p. 110.

135. Ibid., pp. 111–113. Based on a Credit Suisse analysis, real estate investment as a percentage of GDP reached 13.8 percent in 2012, rising from 13 percent in 2011. As finance and economics reporter Zhang Monan (2013) notes, the comparable figures in the United States, Spain, and Ireland just before their property bubbles collapsed in the mid- to late 2000s were all *less* than 13 percent. This would suggest that a collapse of the Chinese property bubble could do far more damage to China's economy than the catastrophic collapse of the American bubble did to the economy of the United States.

136. Wang Lina (2010), p. 105. Wang is, however, one analyst who also stresses the role of temporary supply-side factors contributing to the 2009 bubble. She writes that when the GFC hit in late 2008, Chinese property developers stopped work on most new projects and even temporarily suspended work on projects in progress. This resulted in the number of new units going up for sale in 2009 increasing by only 16.1 percent, "the lowest increase in a decade." In contrast, following the government's extraordinary money and

credit expansion, the total amount of residential space sold increased by 43 percent—and more than 50 percent in certain top-tier cities. In this kind of market, prices would obviously have nowhere to go but up (pp. 104–105).

137. See Huang Xiaohu (2010). Huang, an economist with the China Institute of Land Surveying and Planning, finds that the real estate bubble further fuels "the imbalance between accumulation and consumption" and leads to "enormous waste" as artificially high profits from investing in the industry attract resources away from sectors where they could optimally be invested.

138. Zai Fu (2010).

139. Ibid., p. 24.

140. Ibid.

141. Ibid.

142. Ding Yuanzhu (2010), pp. 95–99.

143. Shih (2011) and Chovanec (2011).

144. Chen Zhi (2010).

145. Ibid., p. 1.

146. Ibid.

147. See Pettis (2013), chapters 3 and 5.

148. See "Insight" (2011) for a typical example of this kind of argument.

149. Chen Lixin (2009), p. 21. In 2010, the government raised the required down payment for the purchase of additional homes beyond the primary residence. But, even after this reform, it was quite possible that purchasers could borrow the down payment funds from sources other than the mortgage-issuing bank. For example, they could turn to entities in the shadow banking sector.

150. Ibid., p. 22.

151. Ibid., pp. 20–22. The Soufun 100 cities property price index rose at a rapid rate from mid-2009 through mid-2011. It then declined from July 2011 to July 2012, when it began rising again and eventually—by July 2013—reached a new high. (See Noble, 2013).

152. Ma Guangyuan (2014).

153. Ibid.

154. Wang Zhanyang (2010), p. 61. An analyst interviewed in Shanghai in May 2012 confirmed that, according to internal reports he had seen, the Gini coefficient had surpassed 0.5—"but the leaders don't want us to talk about it publicly" (Interview 431). Wang Zhanyang (2010) worries that the only reason Western countries were able to resume growing after World War II was that, in response to the Great Depression, they redistributed wealth using Keynesian and quasi-socialist policies (p. 60). Also see Chen Jia, reporting in the May 12, 2010, *China Daily* that China's Gini Coefficient had reached 0.47.

155. Zheng Gongcheng (2010).

156. On this point, see Hung Ho-feng (2009).

157. Zheng Gongcheng (2010), p. 64.

158. Ibid. Qinghua University history professor Qin Hui argues provocatively in a *neibu* journal that Chinese officials actively conspire with both foreign and domestic capital to keep wages repressed. He says that one part of the solution is to allow workers—especially migrant workers—to bargain collectively with their potential employers. Inequality would still be a problem "but absolutely would be less of a mess than the way things are now" (Qin Hui, 2010; quotation on p. 36).

159. Zheng Gongcheng (2010), p. 64.

160. Ibid., p. 65.

161. Ibid.

162. Ibid., p. 69.

163. Ibid., p. 65.

164. Ibid. On the increases in mass incidents (riots, strikes, protests, and so on), see Tong Yanqi and Lei Shaohua (2010).

165. Zheng Gongcheng (2010), pp. 65–66.

166. Ibid., p. 66.

167. Liu Shangxi (2010), p. 11.

168. Ibid.

169. Ibid., p. 12.

170. Song Xiaowu (2009). Also see Fang Cai, Albert Park, and Yaohui Zhao (2008).

171. Song Xiaowu (2009), p. 1.

172. Ibid., p. 2.

173. According to Song, the salaries-and-wages share of GDP in 1980 was 17 percent; in 1990, it was 15.8 percent; in 2005, it was 10.8 percent; and in 2007 it rose a bit to 11.3 percent (ibid., p. 2).

174. Ibid., pp. 2–3.

175. Ibid., pp. 2–3. Song calls for developing the *service industries* to reduce unemployment and inequality. He finds that in the 1980s, the number of Chinese people employed in the service industries increased by 116 percent; in the 1990s, by 65 percent; but then from 2001 through 2008, they increased by only 30 percent. The proportion of the population employed in the service industries remained frozen at 30 percent for almost a decade, just as the production value of the service industries as a proportion of GDP remained frozen for a decade at 40 percent. By comparison, Song notes that in the United States, Japan, and Europe, services in the late 2000s contributed close to 70 percent of GDP (p. 3). Being "frozen" in so many ways, China cannot be said to be "moving" in the right direction. This concern is shared by the authors of Zhongguo Weilai Zouxiang Editorial Group (2009), pp. 169–174.

176. Song Xiaowu (2009) estimates that up to 75 million Chinese people were out of work and looking for jobs in 2009: 30 million migrant workers and 45 million registered urban residents (p. 1). Because the official Chinese unemployment figures paint a strikingly different picture, Song calls toward the end of his article for the government to begin computing and openly distributing accurate unemployment data comparable to the data provided by other countries. He contends that this is important because China's ultimate goal should be not to increase GDP for its own sake, but instead to improve the people's livelihood (p. 6).

177. Maocan Gao (2011); also see Emily Hannum et al. (2008).

178. Stanley Rosen's calculations (private communication, November 23, 2011).

179. Hong Chengwen (2010).

180. Ibid., p. 235.

181. Song Xiaowu (2009), p. 1. Also see Zhu Min (2009).

182. Hong Chengwen (2010), pp. 235–236.

183. This point is argued by numerous authors and was suggested by some interview subjects. It seems to be accepted widely as a "social fact."

184. Ibid., pp. 237–239.

CHAPTER 3

1. For the most compelling and vigorously argued case, see Gilley (2004).

2. Nathan (2003).

3. Nathan (2009).

4. On the Party's creative adaptability, see Dickson (2008).

5. O'Brien (2011), pp. 535–541.

6. Exploring this possibility systematically but not quite committing himself to such an optimistic conclusion is Johnston (2008).

7. See Lynch (2007).

8. For a widely cited argument that economic development "causes" (in the strong sense of the term) democratization, see Boix and Stokes (2003).

9. Diamond (2012), p. 12. Also see Diamond (2003) and Guobin Yang (2009).

10. Diamond (2012), pp. 12–13.

11. See Lynch (2006) and Lynch (2007).

12. For a good illustration of the latter argument, see Zeng Ke (2010). Zeng contends, in short, that "what New China has [already] implemented is the most thorough and complete people's democracy" (p. 156).

13. For a thorough overview of the Western debate on the possibilities of a China model, see Suisheng Zhao (2010).

14. It is critical in a study of this nature to focus on mainstream scholars such as Yu, whose potential for influence is suggested by the fact that he holds a position with an important Party think tank and is still allowed to publish in *neibu* journals; correspondingly, it seems less critical to focus on well-known but evidently less politically acceptable intellectuals such as those associated with *Yanhuang Chunqiu*, to say nothing of imprisoned or exiled dissidents such as Liu Xiaobo and Yu Jie. It would perhaps be more normatively satisfying to focus on "deep" liberals, but they do not have the political influence at this point to justify it. Willy Lam (2012) quotes Yu Jie as saying after his January 2012 expulsion from China that one of his jailers had boasted: "As far as we, the state security [apparatus], can tell, there are no more than 200 [liberal] intellectuals in the country who oppose the Communist Party and are influential."

15. Interview 427. The Internet's contributions to the new societal pluralism are discussed in Chapter 4.

16. Ibid.

17. Ibid.

18. Interview 430.

19. Ibid.

20. Interview 428. The scholar is referring to risk aversion in domestic politics. On the CCP's risk-*seeking* of recent years in international security relations, see Chapters 5 and 6.

21. Ibid.

22. Ibid.

23. "Renmin Chubanshe."

24. Zhongguo Weilai Zouxiang Editorial Group (2009).

25. Ibid., pp. 180–181. The group also cites the rise of Hitler as an example of the horrors that can occur when a political system still "not ready" for democracy nevertheless attempts to put a democratic system in place (pp. 186–187).

26. Ibid.

27. Ibid., p. 183. As an anonymous reviewer of this book pointed out, the CCP is ignoring the possibility that only by first putting democratic institutions into place could Chinese citizens develop the "rational" habits of behavior and mind that would, in turn, eventually help the new institutions to flourish. The atmosphere associated with the CCP's brand of uncompromisingly oppressive, post-"socialist" authoritarianism is not conducive to nurturing the habits and mentalities of a democratic civil society.

28. For a detailed discussion of this issue, see Chapter 6.

29. Zhongguo Weilai Zouxiang Editorial Group (2009), pp. 187–190.

30. Ibid., pp. 190–191. For the concept of the "third wave," see Huntington (1991).

31. Zhongguo Weilai Zouxiang Editorial Group (2009), p. 191.

32. Ibid., p. 190.

33. Ibid., p. 191.

34. Ibid., p. 192.

35. Ibid.

36. Ibid., p. 194.

37. Ibid.

38. Ibid., p. 196.

39. On this point, also see the discussion in Chapter 5 on the "inevitable" trend of multipolarization.

40. Ibid.

41. Ibid., p. 197.

42. Ibid.

43. Ibid., pp. 198–200.

44. Ibid., pp. 199–200.

45. Ibid., pp. 200–201; quotation on p. 201.

46. Xiao Gongqin (2009).

47. On this point, also see Zhou Ruijin (2009).

48. Xiao Gongqin (2009), pp. 120–126.

49. Ibid., p. 121.

50. Ibid., p. 126.

51. Interview 432.

52. Ibid.

53. Xiao Gongqin (2009), pp. 220–221.

54. Interview 432.

55. Xiao Gongqin (2009), pp. 221–222.

56. Interview 432. On the Guangdong model, see Lam (2012). On the battered Chongqing model, see Su Wei, Yang Fan, and Liu Shiwen (2011).

57. Interview 432.

58. Ibid.

59. Xiao Gongqin (2012), p. 23.

60. Ibid.

61. Ibid., pp. 26–27.

62. Interview 432.

63. Ibid.

64. Wang Yukai (2010), p. 146.

65. Ibid.

66. Ibid., pp. 146–147. See the more detailed discussion of inner-Party democracy in the following section on liberal images of China's political future.

67. Pan Wei (2010), pp. 1–2.

68. Ibid., p. 5.

69. Ibid., p. 8.

70. Ibid., pp. 6–7.

71. Ibid., p 7.

72. Some foreign observers would argue that this package of controls increases Chinese competitiveness *unfairly*; that is, that it is protectionist. Some Chinese economists would argue that protectionism in the end can only hurt China because it encourages the flow of production resources into those areas of activity in which China lacks a comparative advantage.

73. Ibid., p. 7.

74. This is a point that Michael Pettis stresses repeatedly in his blog and newsletter. Also see Pettis (2013).

75. Pan Wei (2010), p. 7.

76. Ibid., pp. 7–8.

77. Ibid., pp. 8–9.

78. Ibid., p. 6.

79. Ibid., p. 11.

80. Ibid., p. 12.

81. Ibid.

82. Ibid.

83. Ibid., p. 13.

84. Ibid.

85. Ibid., pp. 13–14.

86. Pan Wei (2003) and Huntington (1991).

87. Pan Wei (2003), p. 2.

88. Ibid., p. 6.

89. Ibid., p. 12; emphasis added.

90. Ibid., p. 28.

91. He Xuefeng (2010), pp. 233–235.

92. He (2010) cites the example of the Great Leap Forward as evidence for how well this system can work in an economic crisis (p. 235).

93. Ibid., p. 235.

94. Ibid., p. 237.

95. Ibid., pp. 237–238.

96. Hu Shuli (2012) and "Live Report" (2012).

97. Yu Keping (2006).

98. Subsequently, he posted the critique on his blog. See Yu Keping, "Zhongguo moshi" (2010).

99. Yu does not, however, mention Pan or any other proponent of the China model by name.

100. Yu Keping, "Zhongguo moshi" (2010).

101. Yu Keping, "Minzhu zhengzhi" (2010).

102. Ibid., p. 157.

103. Ibid.

104. The ones I have read, at least.

105. Yu Keping (2005), pp. 4–9.

106. Han Yunchuan (2009). Han does not argue that the existence of these errors is the only reason reform is blocked. He also identifies "authoritarian traditions" (in the political culture) and "obstacles posed by special interest groups" as key problems (p. 15).

107. Ibid., pp. 15–16.

108. Ibid., p. 16.

109. Ibid.

110. Ibid.

111. Ibid.

112. Ibid.

113. Qin Xiao (2010).

114. Qin Xiao (2007).

115. Ibid., p. 1.

116. Ibid.

117. Ibid., p. 2.

118. Ibid.

119. For an overview of this debate, see Qi Jianmin (2011).

120. Qin Xiao (2007), p. 2.

121. Ibid., p. 3.

122. Ibid.

123. Ibid., p. 3.

124. Xu Yaotong (2009), p. 23.

125. Ibid.

126. Ibid.

127. Ibid., pp. 23–24.

128. Ibid., p. 24.

129. Ibid.

130. Ibid.

131. Ibid.

132. On the pluralization of culture, see Chapter 4.

133. For excellent English-language analyses of the Chongqing model, see Bo Zhiyue and Chen Gang (2009), Godement et al. (2011), Philip Huang (2011), and Garnaut, *The Rise and Fall of the House of Bo* (2012).

134. Su Wei, Yang Fan, and Liu Shiwen (2011), p. 2. Yang Fan, an economist, was always somewhat troubled by Bo's brutal crackdown on organized crime and his attempt to revive some of the trappings of "Red culture." On February 20, 2012, following the arrest of Bo's lieutenant, Wang Lijun, Yang wrote in his blog that the Chongqing model should be reevaluated, and that a group of dozens or even hundreds of impartial intellectuals and other public figures should be formed to go to the city and study the model objectively. Depending on the results of this investigation, Chongqing authorities should abandon those aspects of the model found to be wrong, while they should reinforce and further develop those aspects found to be right ("Ting Bo xuezhe zhuan xiang," 2012). I am indebted to Ho-fung Hung for calling Yang's proposal to my attention. Yang's "second thoughts" had been brewing for many months. See Garnaut (2011).

135. Su Wei, Yang Fan, and Liu Shiwen (2011), pp. 233–241.

136. Ibid., p. 232.

137. Ibid., pp. 234–235.
138. Ibid., pp. 231–254.
139. Ibid., p. 235.
140. Quoted in ibid., pp. 204–206.
141. Ibid., p. 206–207 (emphasis added).
142. Ibid., pp. 203–204.
143. Ibid., pp. 147–158.
144. Ibid., pp. 168–169.
145. Ibid., p. 169.
146. Ibid. It bears stressing, however, that Chongqing never went so far as to suggest giving the villagers ownership rights to the land they farmed, which was far larger in area than the land occupied by villager houses. Such a radical reform—promoted by some liberal economists (see Chapter 2)—would have profoundly altered power relations in the countryside and substantially improved the villagers' lot when they moved to the cities. But it seems never to have been on Bo Xilai's agenda.
147. Su Wei, Yang Fan, and Liu Shiwen (2011), pp. 163–167.
148. Ibid., p. 166.
149. Ibid., p. 167.
150. Ibid., p. 25.
151. "Former Chongqing Police Chief" (2011).
152. Su Wei, Yang Fan, and Liu Shiwen (2011), p. 26.
153. Ibid., pp. 27–30.
154. Ibid., pp. 51–58.
155. See the discussion in Chapter 7 of the November 2013 "Third Plenum."

CHAPTER 4

1. Li Wenge et al. (2011), p. 38.
2. Ibid., pp. 38–39.
3. Ibid., p. 41.
4. Ibid., pp. 42–43.
5. Reported in Liu Baohua (2012), p. 11.
6. Ibid.
7. Reported in Wang Yukai (2011), p. 18.
8. See, for example, Guobin Yang (2009). Yang finds that "popular demands for government transparency, accountability, and citizens' rights to know act [via the Internet] as countercurrents against control" (p. 62.) Also see Yuezhi Zhao (2008), especially pp. 245–338, and Lynch (1999).
9. Brady (2008), pp. 186–202.
10. Castells (2005), pp. 7–13; emphasis added.
11. For an authoritative but concise Chinese-language overview of the PRC communication system's chief characteristics prior to the advent of the network society, see Jing Xuemin (2012). Jing is a professor and Director of the Political Communication Research Institute at the Communications University of China.
12. Castells (1997), pp. 470–471.
13. See, for example, Cheng Yuhong and Zeng Jingping (2011), pp. 110–111. Cheng and Zeng are humanities professors at the Beijing University of Posts and Telecommunications. Also see Fang Xingdong, Zhang Jing, and Zhang Xiaorong (2011). Fang teaches

at the Zhejiang University School of Management; Zhang and Zhang both work for the Beijing Internet Lab, a private company.

14. On the *People's Daily's* overall adaptation to the Internet era, see Xu Guangpu and Wu Huifan (2012).

15. Cheng Yuhong and Zeng Jingping (2011), p. 111. Microblogs (*weibo*) are similar to Twitter.

16. Liu Baohua (2012). For more specifically on mass media versus telecommunications in a Chinese context, see Yang Fengjiao (2011), pp. 114–117.

17. Liu Baohua (2012), p. 11.

18. Ibid., p. 13. As expressed by another observer: "In the network era, everyone can become a channel for disseminating news . . . Everyone has a microphone in front of them" (Chen Lidan, 2011, p. 113).

19. Liu Baohua (2012), p. 13.

20. Ibid.

21. Ibid.

22. This claim is obviously in some tension with Liu's earlier assertion that the status of individuals is problematic once they become (potentially) mere points on the network.

23. Ibid., pp. 13–14.

24. Ibid., p. 14.

25. Ibid., pp. 14–16.

26. Ibid., p. 15.

27. Cheng Yuhong and Zeng Jingping (2011), p. 111.

28. Ibid., pp. 110–111.

29. Ibid., p. 110.

30. Ibid..

31. Ibid., p. 111.

32. Ibid.

33. For a compelling foreign analysis of the Chinese Party-state's efforts to prevent the Internet from being used to organize collective action, see King, Pan, and Roberts (2012).

34. Nie Chenxi (2011).

35. Ibid., p. 11.

36. Ibid.

37. See Chapter 6 for a discussion of how some international relations analysts express alarm that these values are being poisoned by the influx of foreign culture: a national security threat.

38. Nie Chenxi (2011), p. 11.

39. Ibid., p. 12.

40. Ibid.

41. Ibid., pp. 12–13.

42. For more on soft power and culture, see Chapter 6.

43. See Xie Yungeng and Xu Ying (2011).

44. Jiang Shenghong (2011), p. 21.

45. Wang Yukai (2011), p. 21. In January 2010, some 13 percent of Chinese netizens used microblogs; by June 2011, about 40 percent did so (p. 22).

46. Jiang Shenghong (2011), p. 22.

47. Cao Jingsong (2011), p. 60.

48. Jiang Shenghong (2011), p. 22.

49. Ibid.

50. Cao Jingsong (2011), p. 60.

51. Jiang Shenghong (2011), p. 22.

52. Ibid., p. 23; and Chen Lidan (2011), p. 112.

53. Cao Jingsong (2011), pp. 60–61.

54. Cao Jingsong (2012).

55. Ibid., p. 49.

56. Wang Yukai (2011), pp. 21–24.

57. On "panopticonism" and social control, see Foucault (1995), pp. 195–230.

58. Wang Yukai (2011), p. 24.

59. Ibid.

60. Xie Yungeng and Xu Ying (2011), p. 78.

61. Zhu Huaxin, Dan Xuegang, and Hu Jiangchun (2011), p. 15.

62. Ibid. See Chapter 2 on the post-GFC housing bubble.

63. Ibid., pp. 16–17.

64. Gu Liping (2011), pp. 113–115.

65. Ibid., pp. 114–115.

66. Ibid., p. 115.

67. Ibid., pp. 115–116.

68. Ibid., p. 116.

69. Ibid.

70. Ibid.

71. Jiang Shenghong (2012).

72. Ibid., p. 22.

73. Ibid., pp. 22–23.

74. In August 2011, Peking University communications scholar Hu Yong criticized a CCP antirumors campaign, arguing, among other things, that the term *rumor* carries an inherently negative connotation that implies those who would circulate uncertain information are evil people motivated solely to cause trouble: damaging reputations and instigating social turmoil. Hu counters that rumors often begin innocently in response to people's legitimate quest for information in an environment in which the government maintains a long list of "sensitive topics" that must never be discussed. In the midst of another CCP antirumor campaign in 2013—part of a general crackdown on microbloggers—the University of Hong Kong's China Media Project reprinted the Hu Yong interview. See Bandurski (2013).

75. Jiang Shenghong (2012), pp. 24–25.

76. Ibid., p. 25.

77. Ibid., pp. 25–26.

78. Ibid., p. 26.

79. Ibid., pp. 26–27.

80. Ibid., p. 27.

81. Ibid.

82. Ibid., pp. 27–28.

83. Ibid., p. 28. The irony is that this, itself, was a rumor: CNN personnel acknowledge having made some mistakes in their initial, hurried quest to gather and broadcast reliable information. But they flatly deny "issuing repeated twisted reports," particularly

as part of some organized campaign "to Westernize and split China" (personal communications with CNN and other foreign reporters, 2010–2012).

84. Echoing, to a degree, Hu Yong (the Peking University scholar who criticizes the CCP's antirumors campaigns), Professor Chen Lidan (2011) of Renmin University argues that rumors—including, presumably, rumors circulated by foreigners—would not have nearly as large an audience in China if the government were doing a better job of being transparent, thorough, and honest and if it were addressing more effectively the anxiety-causing concrete problems faced by Chinese people (pp. 110–111). Two Jinan University researchers, Dong Tiance and Wang Junlin (2011), make a similar point.

85. Liu Ruisheng, "Xin meiti" (2011).

86. In another article published about the same time, Liu argues that the Internet and broader network have become "the biggest and most important battlefield in cultural construction." See Liu Ruisheng, "Dangqian wangluo wenhua" (2011); quotation on p. 15. Warfare metaphors are common in CCP commentary on media and culture (and much else).

87. Liu Ruisheng, "Xin meiti" (2011), p. 12.

88. See Chapter 6.

89. Liu Ruisheng, "Xin meiti" (2011), pp. 12–13. In one respect, at least, the CCP has made significant strides in counteracting the infusion of Western culture into China in recent years: control of satellite television receiving dishes. This was a big "problem" in the 1990s and the early 2000s. Individuals and owners of apartment complexes would purchase the dishes illegally and use them to receive all manner of television broadcasts, including from foreign sources. But as Sun Wusan of the Chinese Academy of Social Sciences explains in a richly detailed 2012 report, based on extensive fieldwork, nowadays most people use illegal satellite dishes to watch CCTV offerings, which have improved markedly in quality. Consequently, few local governments see much reason to expend time and effort trying to stop people from buying and installing the dishes, even though technically the behavior is illegal. See Sun Wusan (2012).

90. On cynicism, see the article on "trick playing" by Zhao Chenchen and Wu Yumin (2011). "Trick playing" is an inexact translation of the term *egao*. Zhao and Wu define this phenomenon (which they date from the early to mid-2000s) as circulating through the network texts, photographs, video clips, and cartoons designed to convey subversive, sardonic, or bitterly ironic perspectives on contemporary PRC life. The goal is to "deconstruct the 'normal' . . . *Egao* is a new expression of historical and cultural nihilism" (p. 112).

91. Liu Ruisheng, "Xin meiti" (2011), p. 13.

92. Ibid.

93. Ibid., pp. 13–14. For a case study of how the city of Ningbo tries to control network content, in line with some of Liu's logic, see Jiang Weiping (2011).

94. This perception is, of course, at great variance from the views of most Chinese economists. See Chapter 2. But also see the discussion in Chapter 5 of the numerous Chinese international relations specialists who agree with Liu and who argue, in addition, that the "serious blow" the West received probably amounted to a death blow.

95. Liu Ruisheng, "Xin meiti" (2011), p. 14.

96. Ibid.

97. Ibid.

98. Li Hong (2011).

99. Huang Weixing and Li Lin (2011), pp. 40–41.

100. Ibid., p 43. Also see Pan Wei's analogous assessment of the Mao era, discussed in Chapter 3.

101. Ibid., pp. 44–46.

102. For another conservative critique—more elaborate but still not offering solutions—see Sun Yaoliang (2011). Sun is a lecturer in the Central Party School's Department of Philosophy and is secretary of Peking University's Institute of Hominology (the latter word being the university's translation of the term *renxue*). On increasing comprehensive national power, see Chapters 5 and 6.

103. See Chapter 5.

104. Wang Jun (2011), pp. 5–9.

105. Zhongguo Shekeyuan (2012). The members of the study group are not identified.

106. Xinjiang is technically an "autonomous region" (though it is not actually autonomous) or "province-level unit." I use the term *province* here only for the sake of convenience.

107. Ibid., p. 11.

108. Ibid., p. 12.

109. Ibid.

110. Ibid., pp. 14–15.

111. Ibid., p. 15.

112. Ibid., p. 16.

113. For a related argument, see Fei Aihua (2012).

114. Ibid., p. 64.

CHAPTER 5

1. On the new security concept, see Gill (2007). Toward Japan and Taiwan, Beijing continued throughout 1996–2008 to take a tough and uncompromising approach—even as trade, investment, and "people-to-people" exchanges increased. (On Japan, see Green. 2003, pp. 77–109; on Taiwan, see Lynch, 2006, pp. 181–206.) However, open bellicosity toward Japan did not begin until c. 2010; meanwhile, Taiwan under Ma Ying-jeou, first elected president in March 2008, avoided the CCP's post-2009 anger and associated punitive acts by opting for a strategy of appeasement (Bush, 2013). Relations with South Korea were generally quite strong during 1996–2008, marred in a serious way only by the Koguryo dispute. Relations with North Korea, however, were troubled because of Pyongyang's refusal to pursue PRC-style reform and opening, and then—beginning in 2006—its determination to proceed with a nuclear weapons development program. (On China's relations with the two Koreas, see Snyder, 2009.)

2. See Lynch, "Chinese Thinking" (2009).

3. I discuss these claims in greater in detail in Lynch (2006) and Lynch, "Chinese Thinking" (2009).

4. Chinese media reports sometimes explicitly identify the disputed territories of the East and South China Seas as integral to China's core national interests, but Party and government leaders have been more circumspect in using such terminology.

5. Alastair Iain Johnston questions how new and assertive the new assertiveness really is. He eventually decides that China was, often enough, equally or more assertive—sometimes almost belligerent—prior to 2009, even during the period of the 1996–2008 new security concept. Johnston concedes that the PRC became more assertive in the South and East China Seas after 2009, but not in other parts of the world. Still, to Johnston (2013), the Chinese moves were relatively benign and probably were taken in response to

provocative moves by Vietnam and the Philippines. Michael D. Swaine and M. Taylor Fravel (2011) make a similar case (but also see footnote 14). Notably in contrast, however, Michael Yahuda (2013), writing in the *Journal of Contemporary China* (*JoCC*), argues vigorously that the new Chinese assertiveness is far from illusory. *JoCC* editor Suisheng Zhao (2013) takes a position similar to Yahuda's, expressing his conviction that Chinese policies are becoming increasingly aggressive and even "strident."

6. Suisheng Zhao (2011–2012), pp. 40–41.

7. Thayer (2011), p. 555.

8. Economy (2012), pp. 52–59.

9. "Sansha" (2012).

10. Heydarian (2012).

11. Branigan (2012).

12. Christensen (2011).

13. Reported in MacAskill (2010).

14. Swaine (2010).

15. Zhao (2011–2012); emphasis added.

16. Nye (2011). Nye's findings and those of Zhao and others receive strong theoretical reinforcement from the conclusions of Yuan-Kang Wang in his 2011 study, *Harmony and War.* Wang contends that, over the centuries, Chinese leaders have tended to adopt aggressive foreign policies when they believe their country enjoys relative power advantages. When, in contrast, they consider China to be relatively weak, they propose peace-and-harmony-seeking "Confucian" approaches. Wang thus explains Beijing's emphasis on the "new security concept," "peaceful rise," and "harmonious world" from 1996 to 2008 as a function of Chinese strategists perceiving their country as weak relative to the United States. Wang would predict that if Chinese decision makers now calculate that China holds a relative power advantage over the United States, Beijing's foreign policy will become even more ambitious and aggressive. See Yuan-Kang Wang (2011), especially pp. 181–209.

17. See "Building the 'China Dream'" (2013). I am indebted to Victoria Hui for bringing this source to my attention.

18. Lynch, "Chinese Thinking" (2009).

19. The "pluralist" dimension of this rationalism indicates the conviction—shared by the overwhelming majority of Chinese analysts—that although states (power centers) may come increasingly to cooperate in international affairs, they will never dissolve together into a community of highly like-minded states and form a "solidarist" world. Chinese analysts seem almost universally to believe that although solidarism may come into force in parts of the world, such as Europe, it will never take root in the world as a whole—regardless of the advent of the network society and other profound changes. Certainly a solidaristic world will never include China. The world in which China will realize its dream(s) will always remain pluralist, with states differing fundamentally from each other in institutions and culture even as they learn to interact more cooperatively in pursuit of common interests. See Lynch, "Chinese Thinking" (2009).

20. Atlas (2013).

21. See Wang Jisi (2003).

22. Interviews 401 and 413.

23. Interview 413.

24. See Gill (2007), pp. 1–136.

25. Ye Zicheng (2004), p. 21.

26. Ibid.

27. Ibid, p. 22.

28. Ibid

29. Xia and Hou (2004), p. 20.

30. Ibid.

31. Ibid., p. 16.

32. Ibid., p. 20.

33. Interview 406.

34. Huang Zhengji (2006). The book itself includes no biographical information on Huang, but his affiliation is provided on a number of websites.

35. Ibid., p. 235.

36. Ibid.

37. Waltz (1979).

38. Huang Zhengji (2006), p. 236.

39. Ibid.; emphasis added.

40. Ibid.

41. Ibid., p. 238.

42. Ibid., pp. 236–237.

43. Ibid., p. 237.

44. Ibid.

45. Ibid., p. 243.

46. Ibid., pp. 245–249.

47. Zhongguo Weilai Zouxiang Editorial Group (2009).

48. Ibid., p. 86.

49. Ibid.

50. Ibid., p. 90.

51. Ibid., pp. 48–52 and 90.

52. Ibid., p. 90.

53. Ibid., p. 91.

54. Ibid., p. 87. Also see Pan Wei's discussion of the China model in domestic Chinese politics and the economy in Chapter 3.

55. Zhongguo Weilai Zouxiang Editorial Group (2009), p. 91.

56. Ibid., p. 44.

57. Ibid., p. 45.

58. Ibid.,, pp. 45–46.

59. Ibid., p. 46.

60. Ibid.

61. Ibid., p. 47.

62. Ibid.

63. Ibid., pp. 57–58.

64. Yin Chengde (2011).

65. Ibid., p. 38.

66. Ibid.

67. Ibid., p. 39.

68. Ibid.

69. Ibid., p. 45.

70. Interview 427.

71. Ibid.
72. Interview 428.
73. Ibid.
74. Interview 429.
75. Ibid. See Chapter 2 on problems related to the population structure.
76. Ibid.
77. Ibid.
78. Ibid.
79. Ibid.
80. Ibid. In contrast, China's own India specialists—including the sophisticated scholar in Interview 434—are fully aware that Indians have their own perspectives on relations with China and cannot easily be manipulated by outside powers.
81. Interview 433.
82. Ibid.
83. Ma Xiaotian 2011, p. 10.
84. Ibid.
85. Ibid.
86. Ibid.
87. Ibid., pp. 10–11.
88. Ibid., p. 11.
89. Ibid.
90. Ibid.
91. Ibid.
92. See Pettis, "What's in a Number?" (2013).
93. Jing Linbo (2012), p. 27.
94. Ibid.
95. Ibid.
96. Ibid.
97. Ibid., p. 28.
98. Ibid.
99. Ibid.
100. On the China-as-victim narrative as an integral component of Chinese nationalism, see Gries (2004) and Zheng Wang (2012).
101. Cui Tiankai (2012), p. 1.
102. Ibid., p. 2.
103. Ibid.
104. Ibid.
105. Also see State Councilor Dai Bingguo's 2010 article in *The Contemporary World*, in which he argues that "common interests have become broader and wider [in international relations] while the problems states must join together to solve have become increasingly numerous. The desire of states to cooperate in order to realize mutual benefit has grown stronger" (p. 3).
106. Yan Xuetong (2010), p. 19.
107. Ibid., pp. 19–34.
108. Lieberthal and Wang (2012). Yan Xuetong criticized the Lieberthal–Wang argument in June 2013 (though not identifying the two authors by name), using the same logic he developed in the 2010 article (Yan Xuetong, 2013).

109. Wang Jisi (2011). For an illuminating English-language discussion of Deng's dictum, see Yong Deng (2008), especially pp. 41–45.

110. Wang Jisi (2011), p. 3.

111. Ibid.

112. Mastanduno (2003) and Saunders (2013).

113. Wang Jisi (2011), p. 4. On this point, also see Dong Xiaodan (2011), an econo-mist who proposes in a *neibu* article the use of investment to build "strategic economic bridges" to Africa, developing Asia, and the southwest Pacific.

114. Wang Jisi (2011), p. 4.

115. Ibid., pp. 5–6.

116. Ibid., p. 7.

117. Ibid., p. 6.

118. Ibid.

119. Ibid.

120. Ibid., p. 7.

121. Yang Jiemian (2012), p. 52.

122. Ibid., p. 54.

123. Ibid.

124. Ibid., p. 60.

125. Zhang Wenzong (2012), pp. 8–14.

126. Huang Ping (2011), pp. 35–38.

127. Ibid., p. 41.

128. The white paper is available online. See "Information Office of the State Coun-cil" (2011).

129. Analogously, the scholar argues that China must do a better job in protecting the full array of human rights. The U.N. Charter mandates that member states uphold not only social and economic but also civil and political rights. The CCP does not currently uphold such rights in China, the scholar states straightforwardly, and this situation must be rectified (Interview 431).

130. Ibid. The scholars in interviews 428 and 432 made similar points; clearly, some Chinese political scientists are far more patient on the Taiwan issue than others.

131. Ibid.

132. Ibid. For illuminating English-language analyses of these issues, see Swaine and Fravel (2011) and Thayer (2011).

133. Teng Jianqun (2011). Another scholar worries that rootless Chinese soldiers sta-tioned in border regions (particularly near Russia) could precipitate conflicts with neighboring foreign states, after which the PRC would be compelled to intervene, even if Beijing would much prefer to maintain peaceful relations with the neighboring country (Interview 421).

134. Teng Jianqun (2011), pp. 6–8.

135. Also see Wu Xinbo (2011), who promotes building a prosperous and peaceful community of Asia-Pacific states in the years leading up to 2020 but does not go so far as to suggest the states should try to integrate into a solidarist international community.

CHAPTER 6

Portions of this chapter appear in Daniel C. Lynch, "Securitizing Culture in Chi-nese Foreign Policy Debates: Implications for Interpreting China's Rise." *Asian Survey*,

Vol. 53, No. 4 (July–August 2013), pp. 629–659. Reproduced by permission of The Regents of the University of California.

1. See Kugler and Organski (1993), Kugler and Lemke (2000), Levy (2008), and Friedman (2011).

2. On this question, see—in addition to the citations in note 1—Lemke (1997) and Feng Yongping (2006).

3. Yao Guohua (2006), p. 17. Chinese elites also frequently express the view that cultures are contained by the boundaries corresponding to states. As one informant insisted in an interview: "There are basically only national cultures" (Interview 417).

4. Influential scholars who appeared (at least at the time they were writing) to be optimistic about the potential peacefulness of China's rise included Oksenberg and Economy (1999), Lampton (2001), Johnston (2003), Medeiros and Fravel (2003), and Gill (2007).

5. John J. Mearsheimer (2001) lucidly details the pessimistic structural realist case (pp. 360–402). However, Mearsheimer does not believe that variation in state identity or elite attitudes toward global culture could give grounds for expecting different outcomes from a power transition. He thinks that all rising powers are fundamentally the same—as are the currently dominant powers not willing to tolerate a challenger.

6. See Aaron L. Friedberg's (2005) discussion of "realist optimists" and "liberal pessimists" (especially pp. 24–33).

7. Ross (2009) does acknowledge that "the Taiwan Strait remains a contentious region because it is the one region in East Asia where there are serious conflicts of interest and where each of the great powers exercises relatively equal and stable influence" (p. 82).

8. Christensen (2006), p. 83. Also see Ikenberry (2008).

9. Shirk (2007).

10. Larson and Shevchenko (2010). Elsewhere, Alastair Iain Johnston develops a state socialization model by analyzing how China's adherence to international security regimes between 1980 and 2000 led to a micro-socialization of Chinese diplomats and specialists. This socialization may have produced (or reflected) a change in the identity of the Chinese state itself into a more cooperative formation. See Johnston (2008), especially pp. 1–44 and 155–196.

11. On China's cultural framing of military issues in realpolitik terms—at least during certain periods of history (the tendency is not necessarily immutable)—see Johnston (1995, 1998) and Pillsbury (2000). But also note Andrew Scobell's (2003) argument that although there clearly is a realpolitik dimension to Chinese strategic culture, there is also a harmony-oriented Confucian dimension.

12. Zhang Fengqi (2009), pp. 29–30. Ironically, this was also the time period in which the Party-state unveiled the cooperation-oriented "new security concept" designed to reassure neighbors of an increasingly powerful China's benign intent. See Gill (2007), pp. 1–120, and Goldstein (2001).

13. Yao Guohua (2006), p. 17.

14. Examples of publications that call for harmony while on the surface downplaying realist themes include Ding Xiaowen (2005), Yu Xintian (2005, 2010), Fan Jianzhong (2007), and Mao Feng (2007). But even these works end up revealing core realist presuppositions. For example, Mao Feng (2007) writes that China should "carry out a strategic civilizational dialogue to propagate the viewpoint of 'harmonious humanism,' and in that way establish China's image as a harmonious country, reducing international suspicions and worries about China's rise" (p. 41). The emphasis here is on instrumentally promoting

the image of harmony rather than the reality—the purpose being to improve China's reputation and thereby facilitate its rise.

15. In this respect, my findings differ from those of Tang Shiping, who wrote in 2008 that "China has decisively evolved from an offensive realist state under Mao Zedong to a defensive realist state under Deng Xiaoping and thereafter . . . China is unlikely to revert to the offensive realism mindset in its past." In fact, the policy discussions on culture and security analyzed for this chapter make clear that Chinese offensive realism is alive and well.

16. Mearsheimer (2001), p. 21.

17. Yan Xuetong and Xu Jin (2008).

18. The scholar in Interview 420 also acknowledged that the unattractive nature of China's political system limited the country's cultural influence internationally. But he worried that "tinkering with the [Chinese] political system could lead to disaster"; therefore, "international society will ultimately have to accept China's system."

19. For a history of this concept, see Li Qi et al. (2007), especially pp. 13–17 and 96–97.

20. Yan Xuetong and Xu Jin (2008), p. 29.

21. Yan Xuetong, interviewed by Sun Modi (2009), p. 5.

22. Ibid.

23. Yao Qin (2006).

24. Ibid., p. 118.

25. "China's Confucius Institutes" (2013). The analyst in Interview 404 explained that the thinking behind the CIs was that "if other countries can better understand Chinese history and culture, they will realize there is little possibility China could ever become a threat or pose a danger" because it has always been inherently peaceful—except when menaced by foreigners.

26. Yao Qin (2006), p. 119. For a thoughtfully critical Chinese assessment of the Beijing consensus concept, see Xie Lizhong (2010) and Ke Huaqing (2010). The subjects in interviews 400, 401, 406, 420, and 423 all criticized the Beijing consensus as a model, arguing that China's experiences are unique and cannot easily be replicated by other developing countries.

27. Yao Qin (2006), p. 121.

28. Ibid., p. 129.

29. Ibid., p. 126.

30. Ibid.

31. Yu Xintian (2011), pp. 16–17.

32. Yu's take on Zheng He is consistent with what Geoffrey Wade characterizes as the "orthodox or traditional view . . . within the Chinese traditions." In contrast, Wade (2004) argues—based on exhaustive research—that the voyages "were military missions with strategic aims . . . [The] history of the Zheng He voyages is replete with violence as the eunuch commanders tried to implement the Ming emperor's requirements" (quotations on pp. 2, 12, and 13).

33. For example, Yu Xintian (2005).

34. Yu Xintian (2011), p. 17.

35. Ibid., pp. 18–19.

36. Xu Chongwen (2010, 2011).

37. Ibid.

38. Xu Chongwen (2011), pp. 3–4. Also see Chapter 3.

39. See Lynch (2006).

40. Xu Chongwen (2011), p. 5.

41. Ibid.

42. Ibid., p. 6.

43. Toulmin (1990).

44. Xu Chongwen (2011), p. 7.

45. Ibid., pp. 7–10.

46. Zhongguo Sixiang Zhengzhi (2006), p. 2. The scholars in Interviews 407, 411, 412, and 413 also all made the point that they considered China to be culturally weak in an international context, though they did not use the term *national spirit*.

47. Ibid., p. 20. Also on this point, see Mao Feng (2007).

48. The special term for the *negative* qualities of a people that the CCP tries to suppress is "the national psychology" (Zhongguo Sixiang Zhengzhi, 2006, pp. 22–25).

49. Yao Guohua (2006), p. 17.

50. Zhongguo Sixiang Zhengzhi (2006), p. 14. Or, as one interview subject explained: "There is no way that China can become a leading country until the quality of its people is uplifted and the culture is improved" (Interview 408).

51. Zhongguo Sixiang Zhengzhi (2006), quotations on pp. 11, 12, 14, 15, and 27.

52. Ibid., p. 4.

53. He Xingliang (2012), p. 21.

54. Ibid.

55. Ibid., p. 22.

56. Ibid.

57. Ibid.

58. Ibid., p. 23.

59. On this point, also see Lynch, "Chinese Thinking" (2009).

60. He Xingliang (2012), p. 23.

61. Xu Jialu (2007).

62. Xu finds that American presidents and entertainment executives even mockingly boast about their ability to subvert Chinese culture (Ibid., p. 19).

63. The scholar in Interview 418 argued that *all* Western countries have collectively threatened Chinese culture in myriad ways for 120 years.

64. Zhang Haisheng and Liu Xifeng (2007).

65. Ibid., p. 64.

66. In the *neibu* publication *Internal Circulation Reference*, even the Vice Chairman of the Chinese Calligraphers Association, Shao Bingren, takes up this security concern by contending that "at present, the 'three independence' forces [in Taiwan, Tibet, and Xinjiang], . . . in scheming to split the country apart, have all selected differing forms of cultural splittism as a part of their strategies" (Shao Bingren, 2006, p. 6.)

67. Zhang Haisheng and Liu Xifeng (2007), p. 65. Also see Chapter 4 on the network society.

68. Ibid., pp. 65–66. Calligrapher Shao Bingren (2006) warns that, when looking into history, "We can see very clearly that invasions damaging or aiming to damage other sovereign countries' national security always, while invading politically, militarily, and economically, [first] carry out carefully planned cultural invasions . . . and in this way achieve their objectives" (p. 6).

69. Zhang Haisheng and Liu Xifeng (2007), p. 66.

70. Ibid., p. 67.

71. Ibid.

72. Ibid., p. 68. More broadly on informationalization, see Zhongguo Shekeyuan (2009).

73. For Chinese approaches to information security, see Wang Qingdong (2004); Chen Xinxin (2005); Zhongguo Faxuehui (2005); Cao Zelin (2006), especially pp. 113–147; and Gao Wanglai (2011). Also see Chapter 4.

74. Zhang Haisheng and Liu Xifeng (2007), p. 68.

75. Zheng Yongnian (2007).

76. Another scholar claimed that "the West is obsessed with power, especially military power, but Chinese leaders and responsible intellectuals hardly ever think about it" (Interview 404).

77. Zheng Yongnian (2007), pp. 40–41. For a related argument, see Xiao Gang and He Changhua (2010).

78. Zhan Jiang (2010). Also see Xu Chongwen (2010).

79. Li Zhi (2004); quotations on pp. 45, 53, and 175.

80. Zhao Qizheng (2011), pp. 3–4.

81. Ibid., pp. 4–6.

82. Niu Hanzhang (2007), p. 365.

83. Ibid., p. 368. Richard Bush argues in his masterful assessment of the future of China–Taiwan relations that by mid-2013, all of the easier issues (the "low-hanging fruit") had been resolved. But that left the difficult matters, especially in military–political affairs. Because the difficult matters implicate the ultrasensitive question of Taiwan's de facto autonomous status, given that the CCP continues to insist on unification as Taiwan's only future "choice," Bush worried that the surface calm in cross-Strait relations that prevailed from May 2008 (when Ma Ying-jeou took office) to early 2013 could quickly evaporate if Beijing were to become impatient and decide to abandon the "paradigm of mutual persuasion" of recent years, moving instead to a more coercive stance consistent with the harsh warnings of Niu Hanzhang. (See Bush, 2013.)

84. Pan Zhongqi and Huang Renwei (2008). Many Chinese analysts promote a geopolitical perspective on international relations; for example, Zhang Wenmu (2004), Guo Xuetang (2006), and Lin Limin (2010).

85. Pan Zhongqi and Huang Renwei (2008), p. 44.

86. Huntington (1996).

87. Two other analysts claim that South Korea poses a cultural threat because its Christian missionaries are carrying out a planned penetration of China; however, the missionaries ultimately propagate "the U.S.-led Western countries' so-called values of liberty, democracy, and equality" (Li Wen and Li Yongchun, 2010, p. 45.)

88. In the same vein, Shanghai scholar Zhu Majie (2005) writes that rising states' soft power possesses an *inherently* expansive nature: It cannot be contained by borders or boundaries, and it propels individuals and societies in new directions not easily anticipated or predicted. Because of this expansive nature, "within international society, when multiple countries' forms of soft power intermingle, competition and contestation are unavoidable, and as a result the generation of friction and conflict are inevitable" (p. 72).

89. Anticipating Pan and Huang, retired general Li Jijun—a pioneer in the study of Chinese strategic culture—gave a paper at the December 2006 "Cultural Construction and National Security" conference in which he proposed that China should "consolidate its strategic relationships with Africa and Latin America" in the process of "raising China's strategic posture vis-à-vis the United States and Europe." Li argued that such a

strategy would clarify the point that, whereas hegemonists see the world through the lens of clashes of civilization, China promotes harmony among civilizations (Li Jijun, 2007; quotation on p. 27.)

90. Pan Zhongqi and Huang Renwei (2008), p. 47.

91. Also on these themes, see Tao Wenzhao (2009); Zheng Bingwen, "Wo guo zai La Mei fazhan liyi de xuanze" (2010), pp. 39–44; and Zheng Bingwen, "Quebao ziyuan anquan" (2010). These three articles all reveal varying degrees of offensive realism in Chinese thinking about cultural relations with other civilizations.

92. Pan Zhongqi and Huang Renwei (2008), p. 48.

93. Ibid.

94. Ibid., p. 49.

95. Ibid.

96. This and the immediately following paragraphs are based on Interview 421.

97. Interview 410.

98. Interview 422.

99. Zhu Liqun (2012).

100. Lynch (2006).

101. Zhu Liqun (2012), p. 20.

102. Ibid.

103. Ibid., pp. 20–21.

104. Ibid., p. 22.

105. Ibid., p. 23.

106. Curiously, few if any Chinese analysts argue that China could one day find itself under threat culturally (and in other ways) precisely *because* it is now in the ascendant—and actively using its increased relative power to push an irredentist agenda. Already China's new assertiveness seems to be stimulating formation of a countercoalition. It is possible the coalition could one day find it strategically beneficial to try to to subvert China culturally—or more likely, try to subvert CCP cultural orthodoxy.

107. Johnston (2008), p. xxvii.

CHAPTER 7

1. Boix and Stokes (2003), p. 545.

2. Rowen (2007), p. 38.

3. Russett (1993).

4. "Conversation with John Mearsheimer" (2002).

5. Perlez (2013).

6. Zhonggong zhongyang (2013).

7. Ibid.

8. Perlez (2013).

9. See the Preface.

10. "Announcement" (2013).

11. Quoted in Keck (2014).

12. Deng Xiaoping (1979).

13. Lynch (2006, 2007).

Glossary of Chinese Terms

bian lao bian fu (边老边富) Get old and rich at the same time.

biaotai (表态) Express support for a policy line; display the politically correct attitude.

chengguan (城管) Low-level municipal functionaries who "regulate," often harshly, street sellers.

cheng xiang tongyi (城乡统一) The city and countryside fuse together.

cong zhong xinli (从众心理) Conformist psychology; follow-the-herd mentality.

danwei (单位) Work unit.

diduan (低端) "Low-end," as in less skilled and/or poorly paid laborers.

dipiao jiaoyisuo (地票交易所) Land coupon exchange market.

duoyuan xiandaixing (多元现代性) Pluralistic modernity.

Fanfou (饭否) China's first microblog service, which debuted in May 2007.

fu buzhang (副部长) Vice minister, used even for certain *provincial* level Party officials.

guanxi (关系) Connections; networks of friends, relatives, and associates.

Guojia Xingzheng Xueyuan (国家行政学院) Chinese Academy of Governance.

guojinmintui (国进民退)) Advance of the state, retreat of the private.

he wei gui, he er bu tong (和为贵, 和而不同) Harmony among diverse units is precious and to be valued; sameness is not.

huayuquan (话语权) Discourse power.

hukou (户口) Residency permit; "license" to reside in a particular city or other locale.

kuaikuai (块块) Province-level bureaucratic entities; contrast with *tiaotiao*.

linglei xiandaixing (另类现代性) Modernity of a different kind or distinctive sort.

luan (乱) Sociopolitical (in this context) chaos or disorder.

minben (民本) People-based; taking the people's interests as (the government's) primary concern.

minsheng gongcheng (民生工程) The project of establishing the people's livelihood.

neibu (内部) Internal-circulation-only: a category of PRC publications.

quchanyehua (去产业化) "Decapacitization"; reducing productive capacity.

renxue (人学) "Hominology," or "the study of people," a discipline distinctive to societies influenced by the Soviet Union.

shehui baozhang (社会保障) Social (security) guarantees, provided by the state.

shijie de duoyangxing (世界的多样性) World plurality; diversity among nation-states.

shiye danwei (事业单位) Cause-oriented or public-goods-providing unit or organization.

shi yi chang ji yi zhi yi (师夷长技以制夷) "Learn the barbarians' advantageous techniques for the purpose of checking the barbarians," a slogan originating in the mid-nineteenth century.

tiaotiao (条条) Vertical bureaucratic hierarchies originating in Beijing; contrast with *kuaikuai*.

tudi guanli fa (土地管理法) Land Management Law.

weibo (微博) Microblogs.

wenhua zhan, shi (文化站，室) Cultural stations and cultural offices.

xiandaixing bentuhua (现代性本土化) Localization of modernity.

xitong (系统) Vertical bureaucratic hierarchical "system"; relate to *tiaotiao*.

yi fu yang lao (以富养老) Use wealth to support the old.

Bibliography

Adams, Bill. "Macroeconomic Implications of China's Urban Housing Privatization, 1998–1999." *Journal of Contemporary China*, 18(62), November 2009, pp. 881–888.

Albanese, Tom. *Rio Tinto: 2012 interim results.* Melbourne, Australia: Rio Tinto, [August 8] 2012. Retrieved on March 20, 2014, from http://s3.amazonaws.com/ zanran_storage/asx.com.au/ ContentPages/2562436886.pdf#page=22.

Allen, Frederick Lewis. *Since Yesterday: The 1930s in America.* New York: Harper and Row, 1939.

"Analysis Tools." *New York Times*, 18 March 2014. Retrieved on March 18, 2004, from http://markets.on.nytimes.com/research/stocks/tools/analysis_tools.asp?symbol=586621.

"Announcement of the Air Defense Identification Rules for the East China Sea Air Defense Identification Zone of the P.R.C." Xinhua, November 23, 2013. Retrieved on February 14, 2014, from http://news.xinhuanet.com/english/china/2013-11/23/c_132911634.htm.

Atlas, Terry. "China Seen Surpassing the U.S. as Superpower in Polling." Bloomberg News, July 18, 2013. Retrieved on July 18, 2013, from www.bloomberg.com/news/2013-07-18/china-seen-surpassing-the-u-s-as-superpower-in-polling.html.

Bandurski, David. "Are Rumors Really So Bad?" Interview with Hu Yong; reprinted from the August 12, 2011, issue of *Time Weekly*. China Media Project, August 27, 2013. Retrieved on February 24, 2014, from http://cmp.hku.hk/2013/08/27/33907/.

Baumer, Franklin L. *Modern European Thought: Continuity and Change in Ideas, 1600–1950.* New York: Macmillan, 1977.

Bell, Wendell. *Foundations of Futures Studies: History, Purposes, and Knowledge.* Volume 1. New Brunswick, NJ: Transaction Publishers, 2003.

Bloomberg News. "China Faces Upgrade-or-Die Deadline as Supply of Labor Dwindles." *Bloomberg BusinessWeek*, August 29, 2011.

Bo Zhiyue and Chen Gang. "Bo Xilai and the Chongqing Model." *East Asian Policy* 1(3), July/September 2009, pp. 42–49.

Boix, Carles, and Susan C. Stokes. "Endogenous Democratization." *World Politics* 55 (July 2003), pp. 517–549.

Brady, Anne-Marie. *Marketing Dictatorship: Propaganda and Thought Work in Contemporary China.* Lanham, MD: Rowman & Littlefield, 2008.

Branigan, Tania. "China and Japan Relations Tense after Standoff over Disputed Islands." *The Guardian*, September 14, 2012. Retrieved on October 23, 2012, from www.guardian.co.uk/world/2012/sep/14/china-japan-senkaku-diaoyu-islands.

Brødsgaard, Kjeld Erik. "Politics and Business Group Formation in China: The Party in Control?" *The China Quarterly*, Vol. 221 (September 2012), pp. 624–648.

Bueno de Mesquita, Bruce. *The Predictioneer's Game: Using the Logic of Brazen Self-Interest to See and Shape the Future.* New York: Random House, 2009.

"Building the 'China Dream' for the Great Chinese Rejuvenation." *People's Daily*, April 1, 2013, p. 1. Translated in two parts by the China Elections and Governance blog,

April 4, 2013 (http://chinaelectionsblog.net/?p=21354) and April 15, 2013 (http://chinaelectionsblog.net/?p=21399). Retrieved on June 14, 2013.

Burkitt, Laurie, and Jeremy Page. "China's Population Is Aging Rapidly." *Wall Street Journal*, April 28, 2011. Retrieved on November 27, 2011, from http://online.wsj.com.

Bush, Richard C. *Uncharted Strait: The Future of China-Taiwan Relations*. Washington, DC: Brookings Institution Press, 2013.

Callahan, William A. *China Dreams: 20 Visions of the Future*. New York: Oxford University Press, 2013.

Cao Jianhai (曹建海). "Fangdichan zhengce zhiding xu jinshen qianxing" ("房地产政策制定须谨慎前行") ["We must proceed cautiously in setting policy for the real estate industry."] In Renmin Luntan Zazhi, ed., *Shijie Da Qushi yu Weilai 10 Nian Zhongguo Mianlin de Tiaozhan* (世界大趋势于未来10年中国面临的挑战) [*World Megatrends and Challenges China Will Face in the Coming Decade*] (Beijing: Chang'an Chubanshe, [May] 2010), pp. 109–113.

Cao Jingsong (曹劲松). "Zhengfu jigou weibo yu guan-min jiaoliu chuangxin" ("政府机构微博与官民交流创新") ["Government agencies' microblogs and the remaking of relations between officials and the public"]. *Xiandai Chuanbo* (现代传播) [*Modern Communication*], No. 178 (May 2011), pp. 59–63.

———. "Zhengfu xingxiang weihu de zhanlue juece" ("政府形象维护的战略决策") ["Strategic decision-making to uphold the government's image"]. *Xiandai Chuanbo* (现代传播) [*Modern Communication*], No. 186 (January 2012), pp. 48–51.

Cao Zelin (曹泽林). *Guojia Wenhua Anquan* (国家文化安全轮) [*National Cultural Security*]. Beijing: Junshi Kexue Chubanshe, 2006.

Cardoso, Gustavo. "Societies in Transition to the Network Society." In Manuel Castells and Gustavo Cardoso, eds., *The Network Society: From Knowledge to Policy* (Washington, DC: Center for Transatlantic Relations, 2005), pp. 23–76.

Castells, Manuel. *The Information Age: Economy, Society, and Culture, Volume II: The Power of Identity*. Malden, MA: Blackwell Publishers, 1997.

———. "The Network Society: From Knowledge to Policy." In Manuel Castells and Gustavo Cardoso, eds., *The Network Society: From Knowledge to Policy* (Washington, DC: Center for Transatlantic Relations, 2005), pp. 3–22.

Chang Xinghua and Li Wei (常兴华, 李伟). "Wo guo guomin shouru fenpei geju de guoji guancha" ("我国国民收入分配格局的国际观察") ["The structure of our country's income distribution from an international perspective"]. *Gaige Neican* (改革内参) [*Internal Reference Materials on Reform*] No. 631 (October 20, 2009), pp. 5–7; *neibu faxing*.

Cheng Yuhong and Zeng Jingping (程玉红, 曾静平). "Lun xuni wangluo shehui dui wo guo zhengzhi fazhan de yingxiang" ("论虚拟网络社会对我国政治发展的影响") ["The virtual network society's influence on our country's political development"]. *Xiandai Chuanbo* (现代传播) [*Modern Communication*], No. 182 (September 2011), pp. 110–113.

Chen Jia. "Country's Wealth Divide Past Warning Level." *China Daily*, May 12, 2010. Retrieved on November 27, 2011, from www.chinadaily.com.cn/china/2010-05/12/content_9837073.htm.

Chen Lidan ((陈力丹). "Liuyan, yijian de liutong yu Web 2.0 huanjing" ("流言, 意见的流通与 Web 2.0 环境") ["The circulation of rumors and opinions and the Web 2.0 environment"]. *Xiandai Chuanbo* (现代传播) [*Modern Communication*], No. 185 (December 2011), pp. 110–115.

Chen Lixin (陈丽新). "Dui dangqian wo guo fangdichan paomo chengyin de renshi" ("对当前我国房地产泡沫成因的认识") ["Recognizing the reasons behind the formation of our country's current property bubble"]. *Jingji Yaocan* (*经济要参*) [*Essential Economic Reference Materials*] No. 1883 (November 24, 2009), pp. 19–23; *neibu* faxing.

Chen Long. "Why Is China Auditing Local Government Debt Again?" Institute for New Economic Thinking, July 29, 2013. Retrieved on March 17, 2014, from http://ineteconomics.org/china-economics-seminar-0/why-china-audit-local-government-debt-again.

Chen Xinxin (陈新欣). "Wanshan wo guo xinxi neirong chanye he shichang de jianguan tixi" ("完善我国信息内容产业和市场的监管体系") ["Perfect our country's supervision and management system for the information-content industries and markets"]. 领导参阅 (*Lingdao Canyue*) [*Leadership Reference*] 339 (February 25, 2005), pp. 9–11; *neibu* faxing.

Chen Zhi (陈植). "Chengtou 'juneiren' zishu difang rongzi pingtai fengxian" ("城投'局内人'自述地方融资平台风险") ["An insider's account of the risks involved with local finance platforms"]. *Gaige Neican* (*改革内参*) [*Internal Reference Materials on Reform*] No. 649 (April 2. 2010), pp. 1–4; *neibu* faxing.

Cheng Yuhong and Zeng Jingping (程玉红, 曾静平). "Lun xuni wangluo shehui dui wo guo zhengzhi fazhan de yingxiang" ("论虚拟网络社会对我国政治发展的影响") ["The virtual network society's influence on our country's political development"]. *Xiandai Chuanbo* (*现代传播*) [*Modern Communication*], No. 182 (September 2011), pp. 110–113.

Chi Fulin (迟福林). "Di erci gaige yu fazhan fangshi zhuanxing" ("第二次改革与发展方式转型") ["The second phase of reform and transformation of the development model"]. In Yuan Xucheng (袁绪程), ed., *Weilai 30 Nian: Zhongguo Gaige Dashi* (*未来30年: 中国改革大势*) [*The Next 30 Years: Megatrends in China's Reform*]. Beijing: Kexue Chuban She [Science Press], [March] 2010, pp. 80–84.

"China's Confucius Institutes to Reach 500 Global Cities by 2020." Xinhua, March 11, 2013. Retrieved on March 21, 2013, from http://news.xinhuanet.com/english/china/2013-03/11/c_132225228.htm.

"China's Exports Unexpectedly Drop." Bloomberg News, March 8, 2014. Retrieved on March 8, 2014, from www.bloomberg.com/news/2014-03-08/china-feb-exports-unexpectedly-fall-18-1-imports-rise-10-1-.html.

Chovanec, Patrick. "Chinese Banks Are Worse Off Than You Think." *Wall Street Journal*, July 21, 2011. Retrieved on November 27, 2011, from http://online.wsj.com.

Christensen, Thomas J. "The Advantages of an Assertive China: Responding to Beijing's Abrasive Diplomacy." *Foreign Affairs*, Vol. 90, No. 2 (March/April 2011). Retrieved on October 11, 2012, from www.brookings.edu/research/articles/2011/03/china-christensen.

———. "Fostering Stability or Creating a Monster? The Rise of China and U.S. Policy toward East Asia." *International Security* 31(1), Summer 2006, pp. 81–126.

"Conversation with John Mearsheimer" (Mearsheimer interviewed by Harry Kreisler). Institute of International Studies, University of California (Berkeley), April 2002. Retrieved on July 1, 2013, from http://globetrotter.berkeley.edu/people2/Mearsheimer/mearsheimer-con0.html.

Country Analysis Unit, Federal Reserve Bank of San Francisco. "Shadow Banking in China: Expanding Scale, Evolving Structure." *Asia Focus*, April 2013. Retrieved on February 15, 2014, from www.frbsf.org/banking-supervision/publications/asia-focus/2013/april/shadow-banking-china-scale-structure/asia-focus-shadow-banking-in-china.pdf.

Credit Suisse. "Press Release: Global Wealth," 8 October 2010. Retrieved on November 27, 2011, from www.credit-suisse.com/news/en/media_release.jsp?ns=41610.

Cui Tiankai (崔天凯). "Jiandingbuyi tuijin Zhong Mei hezuo huoban guanxi" ("坚定不移推进中美合作伙伴关系") ["Resolutely promote cooperative and partnerlike China–U.S. relations"]. *Guoji Wenti Yanjiu* (*国际问题研究*) [*International Studies*] 2012 (2), pp. 1–5.

Dai Bingguo (戴秉国). "Jianchi zou heping fazhan daolu" ("坚持走和平发展道路") ["Uphold the principle of peaceful development" (title as translated by author)]. *Dangdai Shijie* (*当代世界*) [*The Contemporary World*] 2010 (12), pp. 4 –8; reprinted in *Zhongguo Waijiao* (*中国外交*) [*China's Foreign Affairs*] 2011 (3), pp. 1–7.

David, Paul A. "Path Dependence: A Foundational Concept for Historical Social Science." *Cliometrica: The Journal of Historical Economics and Econometric History* 1(2) (Summer 2007), pp. 91–114.

Deng Xiaoping. "Uphold the Four Cardinal Principles." *People's Daily*, March 30, 1979. Retrieved on August 2, 2013, from http://english.peopledaily.com.cn/dengxp/vol2/text/b1290.html.

Deng, Yong. *China's Struggle for Status: The Realignment of International Relations.* Cambridge, UK, and New York: Cambridge University Press, 2008.

Diamond, Larry. "China and East Asian Democracy: The Coming Wave." *Journal of Democracy* 23(1), January 2012, pp. 5–13.

———. "The Rule of Law as Transition to Democracy in China." *Journal of Contemporary China* 12 (Issue 35), May 2003, pp. 319–331.

Dickson, Bruce J. *Wealth into Power: The Communist Party's Embrace of China's Private Sector.* Cambridge, UK, and New York: Cambridge University Press, 2008.

Ding Xiaowen (丁孝文). "'Zhonghe' sixiang yu Zhongguo waijiao" ("'中和'思想与中国外交") ["'Zhonghe' thinking and Chinese diplomacy"]. *Guoji Wenti Yanjiu* (*国际问题研究*) [*International Studies*], May 2005, pp. 28–31.

Ding Yuanzhu (丁元竹). "Gei fangjia wenti yige geng quanmian de shuofa" ("给房价问题一个更全面的说法") ["Developing a more comprehensive explanation for the housing price problem"]. In Renmin Luntan Zazhi, ed., *Shijie Da Qushi yu Weilai 10 Nian Zhongguo Mianlin de Tiaozhan* (*世界大趋势与未来10年中国面临的挑战*) [*World Megatrends and Challenges China Will Face in the Coming Decade*] (Beijing: Chang'an Chubanshe, [May] 2010), pp. 95–99.

Dong Tiance and Wang Junlin (董天策, 王君玲). "Wangluo quntixing shijian yanjiu de jinlu, yiti yu shijiao" ("网络群体性事件研究的金鹿, 一体与视角") ["Research perspectives on network mass incidents"]. *Xiandai Chuanbo* (*现代传播*) [*Modern Communication*], No. 181 (August 2011), pp. 23–28.

Dong Xiaodan (董筱丹), ed. "Chonggou Zhongguo zhanlue huixuan kongjian." ("重构中国战略回旋空间") ["Reconstruct the operating space for Chinese strategy"]. *Gaige Neican* (*改革内参*) [*Internal Reference Materials on Reform*], No. 700 (April 29, 2011), pp. 15–17; *neibu* faxing.

Economy, Elizabeth C. "The Great Leap Backward? The Costs of China's Environmental Crisis." *Foreign Affairs* 86(5), September/October 2007, pp. 38–59.

———. *The River Runs Black: The Environmental Challenge to China's Future.* Ithaca, NY, and London: Cornell University Press, 2004.

———. "Time for a Strategic Reset." *Americas Quarterly*, Vol. 6, No. 1 (Winter 2012), pp. 52–59. Retrieved on October 11, 2012, from http://americasquarterly.org/economy.

Fan Jianzhong (范建中). "Jianshe hexie shijie: yu Xifang quanqiuzhuyi lilun bu tong de zhuzhang" ("建社和谐世界：与西方全球主义理论不同的主张") ["Establishing a harmonious world: a proposal that differs from the West's globalism"]. In Liang Shoude and Li Yihu (梁守德，李义虎), eds., *Quanqiuhua yu Hexie Shijie* (全球化与和谐世界) [*Globalization and a Harmonious World*] (Beijing: Shijie Zhishi Chubanshe, 2007), pp. 244–251.

Fan Yan, Cheng Dinghua, Zhang Zhi, and Du Haibin (范妍，程定华，张治，诸海滨). "Renkou jiegou jiang xitongxing yingxiang Zhongguo chanye jieguo" ("人口结构将系统性影响中国产业结构") ["The demographic structure will systematically influence China's industrial structure"]. *Gaige Neican* (改革内参) [*Internal Reference Materials on Reform*] No. 653 (April 30, 2010), pp. 19–21; *neibu* faxing.

Fang Cai, Albert Park, and Yaohui Zhao. "The Chinese Labor Market in the Reform Era." In Loren Brandt and Thomas G. Rawski, eds., *China's Great Economic Transformation* (Cambridge, UK, and New York: Cambridge University Press, 2008), pp. 167–214.

Fang Xingdong, Zhang Jing, and Zhang Xiaorong (方兴东，张静，张笑容). "Jishi wangluo shidai de chuanbo jizhi yu wangluo zhili" ("即时网络时代的传播机制与网络治理") ["The mass communication mechanism and network control in the age of the instant network"]. *Xiandai Chuanbo* (现代传播) [*Modern Communication*], No. 178 (May 2011), pp. 64–69.

Fei Aihua (费爱华). "Xin meijie beijing xia de zhengfu yulun yindao" ("新媒介背景下的政府舆论引导") ["Government guidance of public opinion in the context of the new media"]. *Xiandai Chuanbo* (现代传播) [*Modern Communication*], No. 186 (January 2012), pp. 62–65.

Feng Yongping. "The Peaceful Transition of Power from the UK to the US." *Chinese Journal of International Politics* 1(1), 2006, pp. 83–108.

Fewsmith, Joseph. "Debating 'the China Model.'" *China Leadership Monitor* No. 35 (September 21, 2011), pp. 1–7.

Ford, William. "It's Doom and Gloom for China's Big Four Lenders." Durham University Investment and Finance Group, November 17, 2013. Retrieved on March 20, 2014, from http://duifg.com/its-doom-and-gloom-for-chinas-big-four-lenders/.

"Former Chongqing Police Chief Wen Qiang Executed." *People's Daily*, July 7, 2010. Retrieved on March 12, 2012, from http://english.peopledaily.com.cn/90001/90776/90882/7056102.html.

Foucault, Michel. *Discipline and Punish: The Birth of the Prison*, 2nd ed. Translated by Alan Sheridan. New York: Vintage Books, 1995.

Friedberg, Aaron L. "The Future of U.S.–China Relations: Is Conflict Inevitable?" *International Security* 30(2), Fall 2005, pp. 7–45.

Friedman, Edward. "Power Transition Theory: A Challenge to the Peaceful Rise of World Power China." In Herbert S. Yee, ed., *China's Rise: Threat or Opportunity* (London and New York: Routledge Books, 2011), pp. 11–32.

Fung, Esther. "Chinese Property Prices Record First Fall Since Cooling Campaign." *Wall Street Journal*, November 20, 2011. Retrieved on November 27, 2011, from http://online.wsj.com.

Gao Shangquan (高尚全). "Zhuanbian jingji fazhan fangshi keburonghuan" ("转变经济发展方式刻不容缓") ["Transforming the economic development model brooks no delay"]. In Yuan Xucheng (袁绪程), ed., *Weilai 30 Nian: Zhongguo Gaige Dashi* (未来30年：

中国改革大势) [*The Next 30 Years: Megatrends in China's Reform*]. Beijing: Kexue Chuban She [Science Press], [March] 2010, pp. 33–37.

Gao Wanglai (高望来). "Xinxi shidai Zhong-Mei wangluo yu taikong guanxi tanxi" ("信息时代中美网络与太空关系探析") ["Information age U.S.–China relations in cyberspace and outer space"]. *Meiguo Yanjiu* (美国研究) [*American Studies*] 2011(4), December 5, 2011, pp. 62–76.

Garnaut, John. "Bo Paints the Town Red, Invokes Mao and Jails Gangsters." *The Age*, August 7, 2011. Retrieved on March 12, 2012, from www.theage.com.au/world/bo-paints-the-town-red-invokes-mao-and-jails-gangsters-20110806-1igi7.html.

———. *The Rise and Fall of the House of Bo: How a Murder Exposed the Cracks in China's Leadership*. New York: Penguin, 2012.

Gibson, Neil. "The Privatization of Urban Housing in China and Its Contribution to Financial System Development." *Journal of Contemporary China*, 18(58), January 2009, pp. 175–184.

Gill, Bates. *Rising Star: China's New Security Diplomacy*. Washington, DC: The Brookings Institution, 2007.

Gilley, Bruce. *China's Democratic Future: How It Will Happen and Where It Will Lead*. New York: Columbia University Press, 2004.

Gleick, James. *Chaos: Making a New Science*. New York: Penguin Books, 1987.

Godement, Francois et al. "China Analysis: One or Two Chinese Models?" Asia Centre, European Council on Foreign Relations, November 2011. Retrieved on March 18, 2013, from www.ecfr.eu/page/-/China_Analysis_One_or_two_Chinese_models_November2011.pdf.

Goldstein, Avery. "The Diplomatic Face of China's Grand Strategy: A Rising Power's Emerging Choice." *The China Quarterly* 168 (December 2001), pp. 835–864.

Green, Michael J. *Japan's Reluctant Realism: Foreign Policy Challenges in an Era of Uncertain Power*. New York: Palgrave, 2003.

Gries, Peter Hays. *China's New Nationalism: Pride, Politics, and Diplomacy*. Berkeley and Los Angeles: University of California Press, 2004.

Gu Liping (顾理平). "Lun xuni renqun de pansuixing xingwei" ("论虚拟人群的叛逆性行为") ["The rebellious behaviour of virtual communities"]. *Xiandai Chuanbo* (现代传播) [*Modern Communication*], No. 181 (August 2011), pp. 113–116.

Guo, Maocan. "The Consequences of Educational Expansion in Reforming China." Newsletter of the Weatherhead Center for International Affairs, Harvard University (26:1), Fall 2011. Retrieved on November 23, 2011, from www.wcfia.harvard.edu/misc/publications/ centerpiece /fall11_vol26_no1/feature_guo.html.

Guo Xuetang (郭学堂). "Liangtiao diyuan zhengzhi min'gan didai tiaozhan Zhongguo waijiao" ("两条地缘政治敏感地带挑战中国外交") ["Two geopolitically sensitive regions challenge China's diplomacy"]. *Neibu Canyue* (内部参阅) [*Internal Circulation Reference*] 817 (June 30, 2006), pp. 43–48; *neibu faxing*.

Guo, Yingjie. "Classes without Class Consciousness and Class Consciousness without Classes: The Meaning of Class in the People's Republic of China." *Journal of Contemporary China*, 21(77), September 2012, pp. 723–739.

Haggard, Stephan, and Yasheng Huang. "The Political Economy of Private Sector Development in China." In Loren Brandt and Thomas G. Rawski, eds., *China's Great Economic Transformation* (Cambridge, UK, and New York: Cambridge University Press, 2008), pp. 337–374.

Han Yunchuan (韩云川). "Fang'ai zhengti gaige de renshi wuqu" ("妨碍整体改革的认识误区") ["Errors in recognition that block reform of the political system"]. *Gaige Neican* (改革内参) [*Internal Reference Materials on Reform*] 2009 (26), pp. 15–16; *neibu* faxing.

Han, Zhaozhou, Zhangjin Wei, and Vincent Wai-Kwong Mok. "Empirical Study on Minimum Wage Level in China: The ELES Approach." *Journal of Contemporary China*, 20(71), September 2011, pp. 639–657.

Hannum, Emily, Jere Behrman, Meiyan Wang, and Jihong Liu. "Education in the Reform Era." In Loren Brandt and Thomas G. Rawski, eds., *China's Great Economic Transformation* (Cambridge, UK, and New York: Cambridge University Press, 2008), pp. 215–249.

He Xingliang (何星亮). "Yao zhongshi he baohu Zhonghua wenming de dutexing" ("要重视和保护中华文明的独特性") ["We must take seriously and protect the special characteristics of Chinese civilization"]. *Lingdao Canyue* (领导参阅) [*Leadership Reference*] 588 (January 25, 2012), pp. 21–26.

He Xuefeng (贺雪峰). "Cheng xiang eryuan jiegou shi Zhongguo moshi de hexin he jichu" ("城乡二元结构是中国模式的核心和基础") ["The two-pillared city-countryside structure is the nucleus and foundation of the China model"]. In Pan Wei [潘伟] and Ma Ya [玛雅], eds., *Renmin Gongheguo Liushi Nian yu Zhongguo Moshi* (人民共和国六十年与中国模式) [*Sixty Years of the People's Republic and the Chinese Model*] (Beijing: Sanlian Shudian, [February] 2010), pp. 233–238.

Heydarian, Richard Javad. "China Splits Philippine Politics." *Asia Times*, October 10, 2012. Retrieved on October 15, 2012, from www.atimes.com/atimes/Southeast_Asia/NJ10Ae02.html.

Holliday, Katie.. "China's Debt Soars to 250% of GDP." CNBC, July 21, 2014. Retrieved on October 19, 2014, from www.cnbc.com/id/101854344#.

Homer-Dixon, Thomas. *The Ingenuity Gap: Facing the Economic, Environmental, and Other Challenges of an Increasingly Complex and Unpredictable Future.* New York: Knopf, 2000.

Hong Chengwen (洪成文). "Daxuesheng jiuye kunnan chengyin fenxi" ("大学生就业困难成因分析") ["Analyzing the reasons college graduates have difficulties finding work"]. In Renmin Luntan Zazhi, ed., *Shijie Da Qushi yu Weilai 10 Nian Zhongguo Mianlin de Tiaozhan* (世界大趋势于未来10年中国面临的挑战) [*World Megatrends and Challenges China Will Face in the Coming Decade*] (Beijing: Chang'an Chubanshe, [May] 2010), pp. 235–239.

Hu Shuli. "Inside Lianghui: A Memorable Press Conference." *Caixin Online*, March 15, 2012. Retrived on March 16, 2012, from http://english.caixin.com/2012-03-15/100368871.html.

Huang, Philip C. C. "Chongqing: Equitable Development Drive by a 'Third Hand?'" *Modern China* 37 (November 2011), pp. 569–622.

Huang Ping (黄平). "Meiguo de liliang bianhua: shinian lai de yixie guiji." ("美国的力量变化: 十年来的一些轨迹") ["Changes in American power: trends over the past ten years"]. *Lingdao Canyue* (领导参阅) [*Leadership Reference*], No. 582 (November 25, 2011), pp. 33–48; *neibu* faxing.

Huang Weixing and Li Lin (黄卫星，李淋). "Wenhua zijue yu dangqian wo guo yulun yindao" ("文化自觉与当前我国舆论引导") ["Cultural self-consciousness and our country's present guidance of public opinion"]. *Xiandai Chuanbo* (现代传播) [*Modern Communication*], No. 184 (November 2011), pp. 40–46.

Huang Xiaohu (黄小虎). "Dapo zhufang gongji de longduan geju" ("打破住房供给的垄断格局") ["Smash the monopolistic situation in residential housing supply"]. *Gaige Neican* (改革内参) [*Internal Reference Materials on Reform*] No. 642 (February 5, 2010), pp. 2–4; *neibu* faxing.

Huang, Yasheng. *Capitalism with Chinese Characteristics: Entrepreneurship and the State.* Cambridge, UK, and New York: Cambridge University Press, 2008.

Huang Zhengji (黄政基). *Lun Duoji Shije* (论多极世界) (*On the Multipolar World*). Beijing: People's Liberation Army Press, 2006.

Hughes, Christopher. "Reclassifying Chinese Nationalism: The *Geopolitik* Turn." *Journal of Contemporary China*, 20(71), September 2011, pp. 601–620.

Hung Ho-feng. "America's Head Servant? The PRC's Dilemma in the Global Crisis." *New Left Review* 60 (November–December 2009), pp. 5–25.

Huntington, Samuel P. *The Clash of Civilizations and the Remaking of World Order.* New York: Simon and Schuster, 1996.

———. *The Third Wave: Democratization in the Late Twentieth Century.* Norman: University of Oklahoma Press, 1991.

"Ideological and Theoretical Basis of CPC." *China Daily*, July 10, 2007. Retrieved on February 9, 2014, from www.chinadaily.com.cn/china/2007-07/10/content_5424228.htm.

Ikenberry, G. John. "The Rise of China and the Future of the West: Can the Liberal System Survive?" *Foreign Affairs* 87(1), January/February 2008, pp. 23–37.

Index Mundi. "China Inflation Rate (Consumer Prices)." Retrieved on October 10, 2014, from www.indexmundi.com/china/inflation_rate_ (consumer_ prices).html.

Information Office of the State Council [People's Republic of China]. White Paper: China's Peaceful Development. Reprinted on the website of *China–U.S. Focus*, September 6, 2011. Retrieved on June 27, 2013, from www.chinausfocus.com/library/government-resources/chinese-resources/documents/white-paper-chinas-peaceful-development-september-2011/.

"Insight: Deflating China's Housing Bubble." Reuters, October 7, 2011. Retrieved on November 27, 2011, from www.reuters.com/article/2011/10/07/us-economy-china-property-idUSTRE7960D720111007.

International Monetary Fund. *People's Republic of China: 2012 Article IV Consultation.* Washington, DC: International Monetary Fund, 2012.

Jakobson, Linda, and Dean Knox. *New Foreign Policy Actors in China* (SIPRI Policy Paper No. 26). Stockholm: SIPRI, 2010.

Jiang Shenghong (姜胜洪). "Dangqian wangluo yaoyan chuanbo de tedian, chengyin, ji duice" ("当前网络谣言传播的特点，成因，及对策") ["Network rumor circulation: special characteristics, causes, and policy recommendations"]. *Lingdao Canyue* (领导参阅) [*Leadership Reference*], No. 597 (April 25, 2012), pp. 22–31; *neibu* faxing.

———. "Wo guo 'weibo wenzheng' de fazhan zhuangkuang yu wanshan lujing" ("我国 '微波问政'的发展状况与完善路径") ["The development of 'microblog political participation' in our country and the way to perfect it"]. *Lingdao Canyue* (领导参阅) [*Leadership Reference*], No. 575 (September 15, 2011), pp. 21–26; *neibu* faxing.

Jiang Weiping (姜卫平). "Wangluo shehui guanli chuangxin yao jiaqiang wangshang yulun jianguan he yindao" ("网络社会管理创新要加强网上舆论监管和引导") ["Innovation in management of the network society will require strengthening the supervision and guidance of online public opinion"]. *Lingdao Canyue* (领导参阅) [*Leadership Reference*], No. 578, October 15, 2011, pp. 8–13; *neibu* faxing.

Jing Linbo (荆林波). "Meiguo quanqiu zhanlue de tiaozheng ji qishi." ("美国全球战略的调整及启示") ["Adjustments in the U.S. global strategy and what they imply"]. *Lilun Dongtai* (理论动态) [*Theoretical Trends*], No. 1913 (February 10, 2012), pp. 21–31; *neibu* faxing.

Jing Xuemin (荆学民). "Lun Zhongguo tese zhengzhi chuanbo zhanlue yanjiu de shidai beijing yu xianshi yiyi" ("论中国特色政治传播战略研究的时代背景与现实意义") ["The background and contemporary significance of research into political communication with special Chinese characteristics"]. *Xiandai Chuanbo* (现代传播) [*Modern Communication*], No. 187 (February 2012), pp. 62–66.

Jin Zhouying (金周英). "Jianli wo guo zhenshi jinbu zhibiao (GPI) xitong de duice silu" ("建立我国真实进步指标[GPI]系统的对策思路") ["Some thoughts on establishing a national Genuine Progress Indicator (GPI)."] *Lingdao Canyue* (领导参阅) [*Leadership Reference*], No. 524 (April 15, 2010), pp. 19–22; *neibu* faxing.

Johnston, Alastair Iain. "China's Militarized Interstate Dispute Behaviour, 1949–1992." *The China Quarterly* 153 (1998), pp. 1–30.

———. *Cultural Realism: Strategic Culture and Grand Strategy in Chinese History.* Princeton, NJ: Princeton University Press, 1995.

———. "How New and Assertive Is China's New Assertiveness?" *International Security* 37(4) (Spring 2013), pp. 7–48.

———. "Is China a Status Quo Power?" *International Security* 27(4), Spring 2003, pp. 5–56.

———. *Social States: China in International Institutions, 1980–2000.* Princeton, NJ: Princeton University Press, 2008.

Ke Huaqing (柯华庆). "Jianshi 'Beijing gongshi'" (检视 '北京共识') ["Examining 'The Beijing Consensus'"]. *Gaige Neican* (改革内参) [*Internal Reference Materials on Reform*] 657 (June 4, 2010), pp. 30–33.

Keck, Zachary. "PLA Officer: China Must Establish South China Sea ADIZ." *The Diplomat*, February 22, 2014. Retrieved on March 22, 2014, from http://thediplomat.com/2014/02/pla-officer-china-must-establish-south-china-sea-adiz/.

Kiel, L. Douglas, and Euel Elliott. "Introduction." In L. Douglas Kiel and Euel Elliott, eds., *Chaos Theory in the Social Sciences: Foundations and Applications* (Ann Arbor: The University of Michigan Press, 1997), pp. 1–29.

King, Gary, Jennifer Pan, and Molly Roberts. "How Censorship in China Allows Government Criticism but Silences Collective Expression." Working Paper, 2012. Retrieved on August 17, 2012, from http://j.mp/LdVXqN.

Kugler, Jacek, and Douglas Lemke. "The Power Transition Research Program: Assessing Theoretical and Empirical Advances." In Manus I. Midlarsky, ed., *Handbook of War Studies II* (Ann Arbor: The University of Michigan Press, 2000), pp. 129–163.

Kugler, Jacek, and A .F. K. Organski. "The Power Transition: A Retrospective and Prospective Evaluation." In Manus I. Midlarsky, ed., *Handbook of War Studies* (Ann Arbor: The University of Michigan Press, 1993), pp. 171–194.

"Lack of Funding Threatens China's Affordable Housing Plan." *People's Daily*, June 29, 2011. Retrieved on November 27, 2011, from http://english.peopledaily.com.cn/90001/90776/90882/7424118. html.

Lam, Willy. "China's Liberals Keep the Flame Alive." *Asia Times*, February 10, 2012. Retrieved on February 12, 2012, from www.atimes.com/atimes/China/NB10Ad01.html.

Lampton, David M. *Same Bed, Different Dreams: Managing U.S.–China Relations, 1989–2000.* Berkeley and Los Angeles: University of California Press, 2001.

Larson, Deborah Welch, and Alexei Shevchenko. "Status Seekers: Chinese and Russian Responses to U.S. Primacy." *International Security* 34 (4), Spring 2010, pp. 63–95.

Lemke, Douglas. "The Continuation of History: Power Transition Theory and the End of the Cold War." *Journal of Peace Research* 34(1), 1997, pp. 23–36.

Levy, Jack S. "Power Transition Theory and the Rise of China." In Robert S. Ross and Zhu Feng, eds., *China's Ascent: Power, Security, and the Future of International Politics* (Ithaca, NY, and London: Cornell University Press, 2008), pp. 11–33.

Li Hong (李宏). "Sulian jieti de chuanmei yinsu ji qi jiaoxun" ("苏联解体的传媒因素及其教训") ["The mass media variable in the collapse of the Soviet Union and its lessons for China today"]. *Xiandai Chuanbo* (现代传播) [*Modern Communication*], No. 177 (April 2011), pp. 30–33.

Li Jijun (李际均). "Baquanzhuyi de zhengti weixie yu Zhongguo de zhanlue xuanze" ("霸权主义的整体威胁与中国的战略选择") ["The comprehensive threat from hegemonism and China's strategic options"]. In Ba Zhongtan (巴忠倓), ed., *Wenhua Jianshe yu Guojia Anquan* (文化建设与国家安全) [*Cultural Construction and National Security*] (Beijing: Shishi Chubanshe, 2007), pp. 25–29.

Li Keqiang. "Li Keqiang Expounds on Urbanization." *Qiushi* [*Seeking Truth*], Fall 2012. Translated and excerpted by China.org.cn on 26 May 2013. Retrieved on July 30, 2013, from www.china.org.cn/china/2013-05/26/content_28934485.htm.

Li Qi et al. (李琪等). *Zhongguo Heping Fazhan yu Zhongguo Gongchandang* (中国和平发展与中国共产党) [*China's Peaceful Development and the Chinese Communist Party*]. Beijing: Chinese Communist Party Central Party School Press, 2007.

Li Wen and Li Yongchun (李文，李咏春). "Hanguo Jidujiao tuanti mouhua dui wo guo de shentou" ("韩国基督教团体谋划对我国的渗透") ["South Korea's Christian groups are scheming to effect a penetration of our country"]. *Lingdao Canyue* (领导参阅) [*Leadership Reference*] 527 (May 15, 2010), pp. 43–45; *neibu faxing*.

Li Wenge et al. (李文革). "Wo guo wei chengnian ren hulianwang yunyong qushi ji duice" ("我国未成年人互联网运用趋势及对策") ["Trends in juvenile Internet use in our country and appropriate policy responses"]. *Lingdao Canyue* (领导参阅) [*Leadership Reference*], 2011 (19), No. 568 (July 5, 2011), pp. 38–44; *neibu faxing*.

Li Zhi (李智). *Wenhua Waijiao: Yizhong Chuanboxue de Jiedu* (文化外交：一種傳播學的解讀) [*Cultural Diplomacy: A Media Studies Interpretation*]. Beijing: Peking University Press, 2004.

Lieberthal, Kenneth, and Wang Jisi. "Addressing U.S.–China Strategic Distrust." John L. Thornton China Center (The Brookings Institution) Monograph Series Number 4 (March 2012).

Lin Limin (林利民). "Shijie diyuan zhengzhi xin bianju yu Zhongguo de zhanlue xuanze" ("世界地缘政治新编剧于中国的战略选择") ["Recent changes in the geopolitical situation and China's strategic choices"]. *Xiandai Guoji Guanxi* (现代国际关系) [*Contemporary International Relations*] 246 (April 2010), pp. 1–9.

Liu Baohua (刘保华). "Hulianwang shidai de gonggong yulun yindao" ("互联网时代的公共舆论引导") ["Guiding public opinion in the Internet age"]. *Lilun Dongtai* (理论动态) [*Theoretical Trends*], No. 1914 (February 20, 2012), pp. 11–17; *neibu faxing*.

Liu Jiejun (柳茂君). "Renminbi shengzhi li yu jiuzheng jingji shiheng" ("人民币升值利于纠正经济失衡") ["Revaluation of the renminbi would be advantageous for rectifying economic imbalanced"]. *Gaige Neican* (改革内参) [*Internal Reference Materials on Reform*] No. 649 (April 2, 2010), pp. 29–32; *neibu faxing*.

Liu Ruisheng (刘瑞生). "Dangqian wangluo wenhua jianshe cunzai de wenti yu duice" ("当前网络文化建设存在的问题与对策") ["Problems and solutions in present-day network cultural construction"]. *Lingdao Canyue* (领导参阅) [*Leadership Reference*], 2011 (27), No. 576 (September 25, 2011), pp. 3–7; *neibu* faxing.

———. "Xin meiti shidai goujian shehuizhuyi xin jiazhiguan de wenti yu duice" ("新媒体时代构建社会主义核心价值观的问题与对") ["Problems and solutions in constructing new socialist values in the age of new media"]. *Lingdao Canyue* (领导参阅) [*Leadership Reference*], No. 597 (September 25, 2011), pp. 12–14; *neibu* faxing.

Liu Shangxi (刘尚希). "Zhongguo jingji de cuiruoxing: fei liangxing xunhuan" ("中国经济的脆弱性: 非良性循环") ["The fragility of China's economy: non-virtuous cycles"]. *Gaige Neican* (改革内参) [*Internal Reference Materials on Reform*] No. 160 (April 9, 2010), pp. 11–13; *neibu* faxing.

"Live Report: Premier Wen Meets the Press." *China Daily*, March 14, 2012. Retrieved on March 16, 2012, from www.chinadaily.com.cn/china/2012npc/2012-03/14/content_14833430.htm.

Lombardo, Thomas. *Contemporary Futurist Thought*. Bloomington IN and Milton Keynes, UK: AuthorHouse, 2006.

Lynch, Daniel C. *After the Propaganda State: Media, Politics, and "Thought Work" in Reformed China*. Stanford, CA: Stanford University Press, 1999.

———. "Chinese Thinking on the Future of International Relations: Realism as the *Ti*, Rationalism as the *Yong*?" *The China Quarterly*, No. 197 (March 2009), pp. 87–107.

———. "Envisioning China's Political Future: Elite Reponses to Democracy as a Global Constitutive Norm." *International Studies Quarterly* 51(3), September 2007, pp. 701–722.

———. "The Next Chinese Revolution." *Far Eastern Economic Review*, October 1, 2009. Retrieved on March 18, 2014, from www.cfr.org/china/feer-next-chinese-revolution/p20337.

———. *Rising China and Asian Democratization: Socialization to "Global Culture" in the Political Transformations of Thailand, China, and Taiwan*. Stanford, CA: Stanford University Press, 2006.

———. "Securitizing Culture in Chinese Foreign Policy Debates: Implications for Interpreting China's Rise." *Asian Survey*, Vol. 53, No. 4 (July–August 2013), pp. 629–659.

MacAskill, Ewen. "Wikileaks Cables: 'Aggressive' China Losing Friends around the World.'" *The Guardian*, December 4, 2010. Retrieved on October 11, 2012, from www.guardian.co.uk/world/2010/dec/04/wikileaks-embassy-cables-diplomacy-china.

Mackenzie, Kate. "China Is Having a Credit-Fueled Non-Recovery." *FT Alphaville*, April 15, 2013. Retrieved on April 15, 2013, from http://ftalphaville.ft.com/2013/04/15/1459132/china-is-having-a-credit-fuelled-non-recovery/..

———. "China's Massive Credit Dependency." *FT Alphaville*, January 21, 2013. Retrieved on April 15, 2013, from http://ftalphaville.ft.com/2013/01/21/1345542/chinas-massive-credit-dependency/.

———. "Why China's June Trade Data Are Almost Unremittingly Bad." *FT Alphaville*, July 10, 2013. Retrieved on March 21, 2014, from http://ftalphaville.ft.com/2013/07/10/1562432/why-chinas-june-trade-data-are-almost-unremittingly-bad/.

Ma Guangyuan. "Prepare for Pop of Property Bubble." *China Daily*, March 29, 2014. Retrieved on March 31, 2014, from http://usa.chinadaily.com.cn/opinion/2014-03/29/content_17388933.htm.

Ma Xiaotian (马晓天). "Bawo zhanlue jiyu qi de shidai neihan, mingque women de lishi shiming he dandang" ("把握战略机遇期的时代内涵，明确我们的历史使命和担当") ["Grasping the connotation of strategic opportunities, clarifying our historical mission and duty" (title as translated by author)]. *Xuexi Shibao* (学习时报) [*The Study Times, a publication of the Central Party School*], January 17, 2011, no pagination given for original; reprinted in *Zhongguo Waijiao* (中国外交) [*China's Foreign Affairs*] 2011 (3), pp. 8–12.

Magnus, George. "China's central bank is new key player." *Financial Times*, May 16, 2011. Retrieved on November 27, 2011, from www.ft.com.

Mann, James. *The China Fantasy: How Our Leaders Explain Away Chinese Repression.* New York: Viking Penguin, 2007.

Mao Feng (毛峰). "Peiyu daguo shidai de wenhua" ("培育大国时代的文化") ["Nurture a culture for the great power epoch"]. *Gaige Neican* (改革内参) [*Internal Reference Materials on Reform*] 562 (December 1, 2007), pp. 38–41; *neibu* faxing.

Mao Zhenhua (毛振华). "Ci gaosu shiqi de Zhongguo jingji zengzhang xu bawo liu da pingheng shu" ("次高速时期的中国经济增长需把握六大平衡术") ["Six important balancing techniques that must be grasped in order to ensure China's growth in the slower-speed era"]. *Gaige Neican* (改革内参) [*Internal Reference Materials on Reform*] Nos. 629–630 (October 1, 2009), pp. 24–26; *neibu* faxing.

Mastanduno, Michael. "Incomplete Hegemony: The United States and Security Order in Asia." In Muthiah Alagappa, ed., *Asian Security Order: Instrumental and Normative Features* (Stanford, CA: Stanford University Press, 2003), pp. 141–66.

Mearsheimer, John J. *The Tragedy of Great Power Politics.* New York and London: W. W. Norton & Company, 2001.

Medeiros, Evan S., and M. Taylor Fravel. "China's New Diplomacy." *Foreign Affairs* 82(6), November/December 2003, pp. 22–35.

Migdal, Joel S. *State in Society: Studying How States and Societies Transform and Constitute One Another.* Cambridge, UK, and New York: Cambridge University Press, 2001.

Nathan, Andrew J. "Authoritarian Impermanence." *Journal of Democracy* 20(3), July 2009, pp. 37–40.

———. "Authoritarian Resilience." *Journal of Democracy* 14(1), January 2003, pp. 6–17.

National Bureau of Statistics of China. "Statistical Communiqué of the People's Republic of China on the 2013 National Economic and Social Development." February 24, 2014. Retrieved on March 22, 2014, from www.stats.gov.cn/english/ PressRelease/201402/ t20140224_515103.html.

Naughton, Barry. *The Chinese Economy: Transitions and Growth.* Cambridge, MA: The MIT Press, 2007.

Nie Chenxi (聂辰席). "Shenru bawo meiti huanjing bianhua, buduan tigao yulun yindao nengli" ("深入把握媒体环境变化，不断提高舆论引导能力") ["Profoundly grasp changes in the media environment and endlessly raise our ability to guide public opinion"]. *Lilun Dongtai* (理论动态) [*Theoretical Trends*], No. 1908 (December 20, 2011), pp. 11–16; *neibu* faxing.

Niu Hanzhang (牛汉章). "Shixi haixia liang'an de yitihua qushi ("实习海峡两岸的一体化趋势") ["Analyzing the trend of integration across the Taiwan Strait"]. In Liang Shoude and Li Yihu (梁守德，李义虎), eds., *Quanqiuhua yu Hexie Shijie* (全球化与和谐世界) [*Globalization and a Harmonious World*] (Beijing: Shijie Zhishi Chubanshe, 2007), pp. 360–369.

Noble, Josh. "China: property prices rising (again)." *Financial Times*, May 20, 2013. Retrieved on March 3, 2014, from http://blogs.ft.com/beyond-brics/2013/05/20/china-property-prices-rising-again/#axzz2wTWpF2am.

Nye, Joseph S. Jr. "U.S.–China Relationship: A Shift in Perceptions of Power." *Los Angeles Times*, April 6, 2011. Retrieved on October 12, 2012, from http://articles.latimes.com/2011/apr/06/ opinion/la-oe-nye-china-20110406.

O'Brien, Kevin J. "Studying Chinese Politics in an Age of Specialization." *Journal of Contemporary China* 20 (Issue 71), September 2011, pp. 535–541.

Oi, Jean C., et al. "Shifting Fiscal Control to Limit Cadre Power in China's Townships and Villages." *The China Quarterly*, Vol. 221 (September 2012), pp. 649–675.

Oksenberg, Michel, and Elizabeth Economy. "Introduction: China Joins the World." In Oksenberg and Economy, eds., *China Joins the World: Progress and Prospects* (New York: Council on Foreign Relations, 1999), pp. 1–41.

Orrell, David. *The Future of Everything: The Science of Prediction*. New York: Basic Books, 2007.

Overholt, William H. *The Rise of China: How Economic Reform Is Creating a New Superpower*. New York: W.W. Norton, 1993.

Page, Jeremy. "China's One-Child Plan Faces New Fire." *Wall Street Journal*, April 29, 2011. Retrieved on November 27, 2011, from http://online.wsj.com.

Pan Wei (潘维). "Minzhu mixin yu Zhongguo zhengti de qiantu" ("民主迷信与中国政体的前途") ["Democratic superstitiousness and the future of China's government"]. *Xianggang Chuanzhen* (香港传真) [*Hong Kong Fax*], 27 February 2003, pp. 1–51; *neibu* faxing.

———. "Zhongguo moshi" ("中国模式") ["The China model"]. In Pan Wei [潘维] and Ma Ya [玛雅], eds., *Renmin Gongheguo Liushi Nian yu Zhongguo Moshi* (人民共和国六十年与中国模式) [*Sixty Years of the People's Republic and the Chinese Model*] (Beijing: Sanlian Shudian, [February] 2010), pp. 1–23.

Pan Zhongqi and Huang Renwei (潘忠岐, 黄仁伟). "Zhongguo de diyuan wenhua zhanlue" ("中国的地缘文化战略") ["China's geocultural strategy"]. *Xiandai Guoji Guanxi* (*Contemporary International Relations*) 2008 (1), pp. 44–49.

Pei, Minxin. *China's Trapped Transition: The Limits of Developmental Autocracy*. Cambridge, MA: Harvard University Press, 2006.

Perlez, Jane. "New Chinese Panel Said to Oversee Domestic Security and Foreign Policy." *New York Times*, November 13, 2013. Retrieved on March 21, 2014, from www.nytimes.com/2013/11/14/world/asia/national-security-committee-china.html?_r=0.

Pettis, Michael. *Avoiding the Fall: China's Economic Restructuring*. Washington, DC: Carnegie Endowment for International Peace, 2013.

———. "What's in a Number? In China, Not Much." Bloomberg News, July 22, 2013. Retrieved on July 24, 2013, from www.bloomberg.com/news/2013-07-21/what-s-in-a-number-in-china-not-much.html.

Pillsbury, Michael. *China Debates the Future Security Environment*. Washington, DC: National Defense University Press, 2000.

Pivot Capital Management. "China's Investment Boom: The Great Leap into the Unknown." Monaco, October 2009.

Qi, Jianmin. "The Debate over 'Universal Values' in China." *Journal of Contemporary China* 20 (72), November 2011, pp. 881–890.

Qin Hui (秦晖). "Laogong wenti bu yi huibi gonghui" ("劳工问题不宜回避工会") ["In considering the labor question, we cannot avoid the topic of unions"]. *Gaige Neican*

(改革内参) [*Internal Reference Materials on Reform*] No. 649 (April 2, 2010), pp. 34–36; *neibu* faxing.

Qin Xiao (秦晓). "Hou weiji shiqi de Zhongguo jingji—zhengce xuanze yu fusu guanli" ("后危机时期的中国经济—政策选择与复苏管理") ["China's economy in the post-crisis period: policy choices and managing the recovery"]. In Yuan Xucheng (袁绪程), ed., *Weilai 30 Nian: Zhongguo Gaige Dashi* (未来30年: 中国改革大势) [*The Next 30 Years: Megatrends in China's Reform*]. Beijing: Kexue Chuban She [Science Press], [March] 2010, pp. 96–109.

———. "'Zhongguo xiandaixing fang'an' qiujie" ("'中国现代性方案'求解") ["Solution to 'the case of China's modernness'"]. *Gaige Neican* (改革内参) [*Internal Reference Materials on Reform*] 2007 (34), pp. 1–3; *neibu* faxing.

Rabinovitch, Simon. "China's Debt in Charts." *Financial Times*, August 28, 2013. Retrieved on February 28, 2014, from www.ft.com/intl/cms/s/0/e76db82e-0a4d-11e3-aeab-00144feabdc0. html#slide3.

"Renmin Chubanshe." Baidu Baike [encyclopedia entry]. Retrieved on March 17, 2013, from http://baike.baidu.com/view/37406.htm.

Rihani, Samir. *Complex Systems Theory and Development Practice: Understanding Non-Linear Realities*. With a Foreword by Hernando de Soto. London: Zed Books, 2002.

Ross, Robert S. "The U.S.–China Peace: Great Power Politics, Spheres of Influence, and the Peace of East Asia." In Robert S. Ross, ed., *Chinese Security Policy: Structure, Power, and Politics* (London and New York: Routledge, 2009), pp. 70–86.

Roumasset, James, Kimberly Burnett, and Hua Wang. "Environmental Resources and Economic Growth." In Loren Brandt and Thomas G. Rawski, eds., *China's Great Economic Transformation* (Cambridge, UK, and New York: Cambridge University Press, 2008), pp. 250–285.

Rowen, Henry S. "When Will the Chinese People Be Free?" *Journal of Democracy* 18(3), July 2007, pp. 38–52.

Russett, Bruce M. *Grasping the Democratic Peace*. Princeton, NJ: Princeton University Press, 1993.

"Sansha New Step in Managing South China Sea." *Global Times* [editorial], June 25, 2012. Retrieved on September 18, 2012, from www.globaltimes.cn/NEWS/tabid/99/ID/716822/Sansha-new-step-in-managing-SChina-Sea.aspx.

Saunders, Philip C. "The Rebalance to Asia: U.S.–China Relations and Regional Security." *INSS Strategic Forum*, August 2013.

Scobell, Andrew. *China's Use of Military Force: Beyond the Great Wall and the Long March*. Cambridge, UK, and New York: Cambridge University Press, 2003.

Scott, James C. *Seeing Like a State: How Certain Schemes to Improve the Human Condition Failed*. New Haven, CT, and London: Yale University Press, 1999.

Shao Bingren (邵秉仁). "Hongyang chuantong youxiu wenhua, quebao guojia wenhua anquan" ("弘扬传统优秀文化, 确保国家文化安全") ["Promote outstanding traditional culture to guarantee national cultural security"]. *Neibu Canyue* (内部参阅) [*Internal Circulation Reference*] 841 (December 22, 2006), pp. 3–10; *neibu* faxing.

Shih, Victor. "China Needs a Credit Crunch." *Wall Street Journal*, June 29, 2011.

Shirk, Susan L. *China: Fragile Superpower*. Oxford, UK, and New York: Oxford University Press, 2007.

Snyder, Scott. *China's Rise and the Two Koreas: Politics, Economics, and Security*. Boulder, CO: Lynne Rienner, 2009.

Solinger, Dorothy J. "The New Urban Underclass and Its Consciousness: Is It a Class?" *Journal of Contemporary China*, 21(78), November 2012, pp. 1011–1028.

Solinger, Dorothy J., and Yiyang Hu. "Welfare, Wealth, and Poverty in Urban China: The *Dibao* and Its Differential Disbursement." *The China Quarterly*, Volume 211 (September 2012), pp. 741–764.

Song Xiaowu (宋晓梧). "Tiaozheng shouru fenpei jiegou cujin jiuye" ("调整收入分配结构促进就业") ["Adjust the structure of income distribution to stimulate increases in employment"]. *Gaige Neican* (改革内参) [*Internal Reference Materials on Reform*] No. 626 (September 11, 2009), pp. 1–6; *neibu* faxing.

Staley, David J. *History and Future: Using Historical Thinking to Imagine the Future.* Lanham, MD: Lexington Books, 2007.

Steger, Isabella. "Distressed Debt Investors Eye Asia." *Wall Street Journal*, August 7, 2013. Retrieved on March 17, 2014, from http://blogs.wsj.com/moneybeat/2013/08/07/distressed-debt-investors-look-toward-asia/.

Steinfeld, Edward S. *Playing Our Game: Why China's Rise Doesn't Threaten the West.* Oxford and New York: Oxford University Press, 2010.

Stephens, Craig. "China's Baby Boom Mirage." *MarketWatch*, August 11, 2013. Retrieved on August 13, 2013, from www.marketwatch.com/story/chinas-baby-boom-mirage-2013-08-11.

Su Wei, Yang Fan, and Liu Shiwen (苏伟，杨帆，刘士文). *Chongqing Moshi* (重庆模式) [*The Chongqing Model*]. Beijing: China Economic Publishing House, 2011.

Sun Wusan (孙五三). "Jiceng 'cun cun tong' jianshe zhong de mubiao zhihuan" ("基层 '村村通'建设中的目标置换") ["A replacement of the objectives in the base-level 'all villages interlink' project"]. *Xiandai Chuanbo* (现代传播) [*Modern Communication*], No. 186 (January 2012), pp. 36–41.

Sun Yaoliang (孙要良). "Xuanchuan jianxing shehuizhuyi hexin jiazhiguan ying bawo de wuzhong guanxi" ("宣传践行社会主义核心价值观应把握的五重关系") ["The five relationships that we must seize in order for propaganda to realize socialist core values"]. *Lilun Dongtai* (理论动态) [*Theoretical Trends*], No. 1904 (November 10, 2011), pp. 21–31; *neibu* faxing.

Swaine, Michael D. "Perceptions of an Assertive China." *China Leadership Monitor*, No. 32 (Spring 2010), pp. 1–19. Retrieved on October 11, 2012, from http://carnegie endowment.org/ files/CLM32MS1.pdf.

Swaine, Michael D., and M. Taylor Fravel. "China's Assertive Behavior, Part Two: The Maritime Periphery." *China Leadership Monitor*, No. 35 (2011), pp. 1–29. Retrieved on October 11, 2012, from http://carnegieendowment.org/files/CLM35MS.pdf.

Tang Shiping. "From Offensive to Defensive Realism: A Social Evolutionary Interpretation of China's Security Strategy." In Robert S. Ross and Zhu Feng, eds., *China's Ascent: Power, Security, and the Future of International Politics* (Ithaca, NY, and London: Cornell University Press, 2008), pp. 141–162.

Tao Wenzhao (陶文昭). "Zhongguo moshi de Feizhou xiaoying" ("中国模式的非洲效应") ["The China model's African effect"]. *Guoji Wenti Yanjiu* (国际问题研究) [*International Studies*] 2009(1), pp. 37–41.

Teng Jianqun (滕建群). "Lun Zhong-Mei guanxi zhong de di san fang yinsu" ("论中美关系中的第三方因素") ["On the role of third parties in China-US relations"]. *Guoji Wenti Yanjiu* (国际问题研究) [*International Studies*] 2011 (1), pp. 5–10.

Thayer, Carlyle L. "China's New Wave of Aggressive Assertiveness in the South China Sea." *International Journal of China Studies*, 2(3), December 2011, pp. 555–583.

"Ting Bo xuezhe zhuan xiang; chang chong gu 'Chongqing Moshi.'" ("挺薄学者转向 倡重估'重庆模式'") ["Bo-supporting scholar changes direction; calls for re-evaluating 'Chongqing Model.'"] *Duowei Xinwen* [多维新闻], February 22, 2012. Retrieved on February 23, 2012, from http://china.dwnews.com/news/2012-02-22/58612882.html.

Tong Yanqi and Lei Shaohua. "Large-Scale Mass Incidents in China." *East Asian Institute Background Brief*, No. 520, April 15, 2010.

Toulmin, Stephen. *Cosmopolis: The Hidden Agenda of Modernity*. Chicago: The University of Chicago Press, 1990.

Tsai, Kellee S. *Back-Alley Banking: Private Entrepreneurs in China*. Ithaca, NY, and London: Cornell University Press, 2004.

U.S. Energy Information Administration. "Energy Outlook 2013." Report Number DOE/EIA-0484 (2013); released July 25, 2013. Retrieved on March 20, 2013, from www.eia.gov/forecasts/ieo/world.cfm.

U.S. Global Investors. "Heart of China Bull Beats Strong." *Frank Talk: Insight for Investors*, January 30, 2012. Retrieved on March 8, 2004, from www.usfunds.com/investor-library/frank-talk/heart-of-china-bull-beats-strong/#.UyjF2dyCmPA.

Wade, Geoffrey. "The Zheng He Voyages: A Reassessment." Asia Research Institute, National University of Singapore. Working Paper Series No. 31 (October 2004.

Walter, Carl E., and Fraser J. T. Howie. *Red Capitalism: The Fragile Financial Foundation of China's Extraordinary Rise*. Singapore: John Wiley & Sons (Asia), 2011.

Waltz, Kenneth N. *Theory of International Politics*. New York: McGraw-Hill, 1979.

Wang Feng. "The Future of a Demographic Overachiever: Long-Term Implications of the Demographic Transition in China." *Population and Development Review* (Brookings Institution), Volume 37 (March 2011).

Wang Feng and Andrew Mason. "The Demographic Factor in China's Transition." In Loren Brandt and Thomas G. Rawski, eds., *China's Great Economic Transformation* (Cambridge, UK, and New York: Cambridge University Press, 2008), pp. 136–166.

Wang Guixin (王桂新). "Jinkuai ba jiejue laolinghua wenti zuowei guojia zhanlue" ("尽快把解决老龄化问题作为国家战略") ["Urgently start regarding the problem of the population aging as a national strategic question"]. In Renmin Luntan Zazhi, ed., *Shijie Da Qushi yu Weilai 10 Nian Zhongguo Mianlin de Tiaozhan* (世界大趋势于未来10年中国面临的挑战) [*World Megatrends and Challenges China Will Face in the Coming Decade*] (Beijing: Chang'an Chubanshe, [May] 2010), pp. 219–221.

———. "Renkou laolinghua tiaozhan yu laoyousuoyang" ("人口老龄化挑战与老有所养") ["The challenges of an aging population and sustaining the old"]. In Renmin Luntan Zazhi, ed., *Shijie Da Qushi yu Weilai 10 Nian Zhongguo Mianlin de Tiaozhan* (世界大趋势于未来10年中国面临的挑战) [*World Megatrends and Challenges China Will Face in the Coming Decade*] (Beijing: Chang'an Chubanshe, [May] 2010), pp. 222–232.

Wang Jian (王建). "'Shi er wu' qijian bing fei da kai guomen de hao shihou" ("'十二五时间并非大开国门的好时候") ["The period of the 12th five year plan will not be a good time to increase China's opening to the outside world"]. *Gaige Neican* (改革内参) [*Internal Reference Materials on Reform*] No. 638 (January 8, 2010), pp. 11–15; *neibu* faxing.

Wang Jisi (王缉思). "Meiguo baquan de luoji" ("美国霸权的逻辑") ["The Logic of American Hegemony"]. *Meiguo Yanjiu* (美国研究) [*American Studies Quarterly*), 2003, 17(3), pp. 7–29.

———. "Zhongguo de guoji dingwei wenti yu 'tao guang yang hui, you suo zuo wei' de zhanlue sixiang" ("中国的国际定位问题与 '韬光养晦, 有所作为' 的战略思想") ["The international positioning of China and the strategic principle of 'keeping a low profile while getting something accomplished'" (as translated by journal)]. *Guoji Wenti Yanjiu* (国际问题研究) [*International Studies*], 2011 (2), pp. 4–9; reprinted in *Zhongguo Waijiao* (中国外交) [*China's Foreign Affairs*] 2011 (7), pp. 3–7.

Wang Jun (王军). "Wangluo minzuzhuyi, shimin shehui, yu Zhongguo waijiao" ("网络民族主义，市民社会，与中国外交") ["Internet nationalism, civil society, and Chinese foreign relations"]. *Zhongguo Waijiao* (中国外交) [*China's Foreign Affairs*] 2011(1), pp. 5–11.

Wang Lina (汪利娜). "Zhengfu ying qizhi xianming dali fazhan kezhifu zhufang" ("政府应旗帜鲜明大力发展可支付住房") ["The government should take a clear-cut stand and go all out in developing affordable housing"). In Renmin Luntan Zazhi, ed., *Shijie Da Qushi yu Weilai 10 Nian Zhongguo Mianlin de Tiaozhan* (世界大趋势于未来10年中国面临的挑战) [*World Megatrends and Challenges China Will Face in the Coming Decade*] (Beijing: Chang'an Chubanshe, [May] 2010), pp. 104–108.

Wang Lishan and Liu Xiaoyan (王位山，刘小燕). "Da liang xindai toufang dui yinhangye de yingxiang" ("大量信贷投放对银行业的影响") ["The influence on the banking industry of the huge issuance of new credit"]. *Gaige Neican* (改革内参) [*Internal Reference Materials on Reform*] No. 640 (January 22, 2010), pp. 15–17; *neibu* faxing.

Wang Qingdong (王庆东). "Guanzhu wangluo shidai de guojia anquan" ("关注网络时代的国家安全") ["Focus on national security in the Internet age"]. *Neibu Canyue* (内部参阅) [*Internal Reference Materials on Reform*] 698 (February 6, 2004), pp. 24–28; *neibu* faxing.

Wang Xiaochang (王小广) [interviewed]. "Ruhe lishun fangjia yu chengshihua zhi jian de guanxi" ("如何理顺房价与城市化之间的关系") ["How to regulate effectively the relationship between housing prices and urbanization"]. In Renmin Luntan Zazhi, ed., *Shijie Da Qushi yu Weilai 10 Nian Zhongguo Mianlin de Tiaozhan* (世界大趋势于未来10年中国面临的挑战) [*World Megatrends and Challenges China Will Face in the Coming Decade*] (Beijing: Chang'an Chubanshe, [May] 2010), pp. 100–103.

Wang, Yuan-Kang. *Harmony and War: Confucian Culture and Chinese Power Politics.* New York, Columbia University Press, 2011.

Wang Yukai (汪玉凯), interviewed by [Renmin Luntan journalist] Gao Yuan (高源). "Kekongxing zhengzhi gaige shi zui jia xuanxe" ("可控性政治改革是最佳选择") ["Controllable political reform is the best choice."] In Renmin Luntan Zazhi, ed. *Shijie Da Qushi yu Weilai 10 Nian Zhongguo Mianlin de Tiaozhan* (世界大趋势于未来10年中国面临的挑战) [*World Megatrends and Challenges China Will Face in the Coming Decade*]. Beijing: Chang'an Chubanshe, [May] 2010, pp. 145–147.

———. "Wangluo shehui yu gongmin canyu" ("网络社会与公民参与") ["The network society and citizen participation"]. *Lilun Dongtai* (理论动态) [*Theoretical Trends*], No. 1908 (December 20, 2011), pp. 17–24; *neibu* faxing.

Wang Zhanyang (王占阳), interviewed by Zhou Xiaoyan (周晓燕). "Fenpei zhidu gaige bu neng xiao da xiao nao le" ("分配制度改革不能小打小闹了") ["Reform of the distribution system should not be small-scale"]. In Renmin Luntan Zazhi, ed., *Shijie Da Qushi yu Weilai 10 Nian Zhongguo Mianlin de Tiaozhan* (世界大趋势于未来10年中国面临的挑战) [*World Megatrends and Challenges China Will Face in the Coming Decade*] (Beijing: Chang'an Chubanshe, [May] 2010), pp. 59–62.

Wang, Zheng. *Never Forget National Humiliation: Historical Memory in Chinese Politics and Foreign Relations.* New York: Columbia University Press, 2012.

Ward, Simon. "Chinese Economy Sluggish but Hard Landing Risk Contained." *Money Moves Markets*, March 10, 2014. Retrieved on March 20, 2014, from http://money movesmarkets.com/ journal/?currentPage=2.

Wendt, Alexander. *Social Theory of International Politics*. Cambridge, UK, and New York: Cambridge University Press, 1999.

Wong, Christine P. W., and Richard M. Bird. "China's Fiscal System: A Work in Progress." In Loren Brandt and Thomas G. Rawski, eds., *China's Great Economic Transformation* (Cambridge, UK, and New York: Cambridge University Press, 2008), pp. 429–466.

Wu Xinbo (吴心伯). "Cujin Zhong Mei zai Ya Tai diqu de liangxing hudong" ("促进中美在亚太地区的良性互动") ["Advance increasingly positive China–U.S. interactions in the Asia-Pacific region"]. *Guoji Wenti Yanjiu* (国际问题研究) [*International Studies*] 2011 (5), pp. 56–66.

Xia Anling and Hou Jiehui (夏安凌，侯杰辉). "Chaoyue 'jihua' siwei, bawo shijie geju de jiben quxiang" ("超越'极化'思维，把握世界格局的基本取向") ["Transcend 'polarized' thinking and grasp the fundamental trend of world structure."] *Guoji Zhengzhi Yanjiu* (国际政治研究) [*Studies of International Politics*], No. 93 (August 2004), pp. 15–21.

Xiao Gang. "Regulating Shadow Banking." *China Daily*, October 12, 2012. Retreived on January 31, 2014, from www.chinadaily.com.cn/opinion/2012-10/12/content_15812305 .htm.

Xiao Gang and He Changhua (肖刚，何广华). "Qiangzhi waijiao: Xifang guojia junshi waijiao de hexin neihan" ("强制外交: 西方国家军事外交的核心内涵") ["Power politics: the essence of Western countries' military diplomacy"]. *Zhongguo Waijiao* (中国外交) [*China's Foreign Affairs*] 2010 (3), pp. 31–37.

Xiao Gongqin (萧功秦). "Chongjian gongmin shehui: Zhongguo xiandaihua de lujing zhiyi" ("重建公民社会: 中国现代化的路径之一") ["Reconstructing civil society: one pathway to China's modernization"]. *Tansuo yu Zhengming* (探索与争鸣) [*Exploration and Free Views*], No. 271 (May 2012), pp. 23–33.

———. *Zhongguo de Da Zhuanxing: Cong Fazhan Zhengzhixue Kan Zhongguo Biange* (中国的大转型: 从发展政治学看中国变革) [*China's Great Transformation: Examining Chinese Changes from the Perspective of Political Development Studies*]. Beijing: New Star Press, 2009.

Xie Lizhong (谢立中). "Beijing Gongshi: Zhongguo jingyan de lishi zongjie, haishi Zhongguo fazhan de weilai zhanlue" ("北京共识: 中国经验的历史总结, 还是中国发展的未来战略") ["The Beijing Consensus: A summation of China's historical experience, or a strategy for China's future development"]. *Zhongguo Waijiao* (中国外交) [*China's Foreign Affairs*] 2010 (5), pp. 14–19.

Xie Yungeng and Xu Ying (谢耘耕，徐颖). "Weibo de lishi, xianzhuang yu fazhan qushi" ("微博的历史，现状与发展趋势") ["The history, current circumstances, and development trends of microblogs"]. *Xiandai Chuanbo* (现代传播) [*Modern Communication*], No. 177 (April 2011), pp. 75–80.

Xinhua. "58% of Chinese Favor Same Retirement Age for Men, Women." *China.org.cn*, March 30, 2011. Retrieved on November 27, 2011, from www.china.org.cn/ china/2011-03/30/ content_22251668.htm.

Xu Chongwen (徐崇温). "Jianchi tuijin Zhongguo moshi de huayu tixi" ("坚持推进中国模式的话语体系") ["Unyieldingly promote systematic discourse on the China model"]. *Lingdao Canyue* (领导参阅) [*Leadership Reference*] 572 (August 15, 2011), pp. 3–16.

———. "You guan Zhongguo moshi de ruogan wenti") ("有关中国模式的若干问题") ["Regarding several problems with the Chinese model"]. *Lingdao Canyue* (领导参阅) [*Lingdao Canyue*] 517 (February 5, 2010), pp. 3–7; *neibu* faxing.

Xu Guangpu and Wu Huifan (徐光谱，吴惠凡). "Cong 'dang de ermu houshe' dao 'gongzhong huayu pingtai'" ("从 '党的耳目喉舌' 到 '公众话语平台'") ["From 'ears, eyes, and mouthpiece of the Party' to 'platform for public discourse'"]. *Xiandai Chuanbo* (现代传播) [*Modern Communication*], No. 186 (January 2012), pp. 23–29.

Xu Jialu (许嘉璐). "Lun guojia wenhua anquan wenti" ("论国家文化和安全问题") ["On the problem of national culture and security"]. In Ba Zhongtan (巴忠倓), ed., *Wenhua Jianshe yu Guojia Anquan* (文化建设与国家安全) [*Cultural Construction and National Security*] (Beijing: Shishi Chubanshe, 2007), pp. 4–24.

Xu Yaotong (许耀桐). "Fazhan dang nei minzhu de genben he zhang'ai" ("发展党内民主的根本和障碍") ["The foundation for—and obstacles to—developing inner-Party democracy"]. *Gaige Neican* (改革内参) [*Internal Reference Materials on Reform*] 2009 (36), December 8, 2009, pp. 22–24; *neibu* faxing.

Yahuda, Michael. "China's New Assertiveness in the South China Sea," *Journal of Contemporary China* 22(81), 2013, pp. 446–459.

Yan Xuetong (阎学通). "Dui Zhong Mei guanxi bu wendingxing de fenxi" ("对中美关系不稳定性的分析") ["Analyzing instability in China-US relations"]. *Shijie Jingji yu Zhengzhi* (世界经济与政治) [*World Economics and Politics*], 2010 (12), pp. 4–30; reprinted in *Zhongguo Waijiao* (中国外交) [*China's Foreign Affairs*] 2011 (4), pp. 19–34.

———. "Let's Not Be Friends." *Foreign Policy* [online], June 6, 2013. Available at www.foreignpolicy.com/articles/2013/06/05/lets_not_be_friends_us_china_trust.

Yan Xuetong (阎学通), interviewed by Sun Modi (孙墨笛). "Chongsu guojia xingxiang de xin siwei" ("重塑国家形象的新思维") ["A new way of thinking on how to recast the national image"]. *Zhongguo Waijiao* (*China's Foreign Affairs*) 2009 (10), p. 5.

Yan Xuetong and Xu Jin (阎学通, 徐进). "Zhong-Mei ruan shili bijiao" ("中美软实力比较") ["A comparison of Chinese and American soft power"]. *Xiandai Guoji Guanxi* (现代国际关系) [*Contemporary International Relations*] 2008 (1), pp. 24–29.

Yang Fengjiao (杨凤娇). "Wangluo yulun de jiazhi faxian: chuantong meiti ruhe miandui wangluo yulun" ("网络舆论的价值发现: 传统媒体如何面对网络舆论") ["Discovering the values of network opinion: how traditional media should face network opinion"]. *Xiandai Chuanbo* (现代传播) [*Modern Communication*], No. 182 (September 2011), pp. 114–117.

Yang, Guobin. *The Power of the Internet in China: Citizen Activism Online*. New York: Columbia University Press, 2009.

Yang Jiemian (杨洁勉). "Meiguo shili bianhua he guoji tixi chongzu" ("美国实力变化和国际体系重组") ["Changes in U.S. power and the reorganization of the international system"]. *Guoji Wenti Yanjiu* (国际问题研究) [*International Studies*] 2012 (2), pp. 51–61.

Yao Guohua (姚国华). "Goujian minzu wenhua zhanlue kaituo fazhan xin geju" ("构建民族文化战略开拓发展新格局") ["A strategy of constructing national culture for opening up a new situation in development"]. *Neibu Canyue* (内部参阅) [*Internal Circulation Reference*] 836 (November 17, 2006), pp. 17–21; *neibu* faxing.

Yao Qin (姚勤). "Yingjian Zhongguo dui zhoubian guojia de wenhua qinheli" ("营建中国对周边国家的文化亲和力") ["Construct China's cultural attractiveness to neighboring countries"]. In Huang Renwei (黄仁伟), ed., *Guoji Huanjing yu Zhongguo de Heping*

Fazhan (国际环境与中国的和平发展) [*The International Environment and China's Peaceful Development*] (Beijing: Shishi Chubanshe, 2006), pp. 117–135.

Yao Yang (姚洋). "Jingjixue jiaodu de Zhongguo jingyan" ("经济学角度的中国经验") ["The Chinese experience from the perspective of economics"]. In Pan Wei [潘伟] and Ma Ya [玛雅], eds., *Renmin Gongheguo Liushi Nian yu Zhongguo Moshi* (人民共和国六十年与中国模式) [*Sixty Years of the People's Republic and the Chinese Model*] (Beijing: Sanlian Shudian, [February] 2010), pp. 14–18.

Ye Tan (叶檀). "Shechi xiaofei pengzhang yinhan juda weiji" ("奢侈消费膨胀隐含巨大危机") ["The explosion of luxurious consumption conceals a huge crisis"]. *Gaige Neican* (改革内参) [*Internal Reference Materials on Reform*] No. 631 (October 20, 2009), pp. 42–43; *neibu* faxing.

Ye Zicheng (叶自成). "Dui Zhongguo duojihua zhanlue de lishi yu lilun fansi" ("对中国多极化战略的历史与理论反思") ["Reflections on the History and Theory of China's Multipolarization Strategy"]. *Guoji Wenti Luntan* (国际问题论坛) [*International Review*], 2004 (1), pp. 4–23.

Yi Xianrong (易宪容). "Fangchan paomo daozhi weiji de Zhongguo jingshi" ("房产泡沫导致危机的中国警示") ["Warning to China: the housing bubble is leading to a crisis"]. In Renmin Luntan Zazhi, ed., *Shijie Da Qushi yu Weilai 10 Nian Zhongguo Mianlin de Tiaozhan* (世界大趋势于未来10年中国面临的挑战) [*World Megatrends and Challenges China Will Face in the Coming Decade*] (Beijing: Chang'an Chubanshe, [May] 2010), pp. 93–94.

Yin Chengde (尹承德). "Jinrong weiji yu shijie geju de xin bianhua" ("金融危机与世界格局的新变化") ["The global financial crisis and new changes in world structure"]. *Guoji Wenti Yanjiu* (国际问题研究) [*International Studies*] 2011 (2), pp. 38–45.

Yin Zhongli (尹中立). "Tudi jiage niuqu shi wo guo jingji jiegou shiheng de guanjian yinsu" ("土地价格扭曲是我国经济结构失衡的关键因素"). *Lingdao Canyue* (领导参阅) [*Leadership Reference*] No. 526 (May 5, 2010), pp. 29–33; *neibu* faxing.

Yu Keping (俞可平). "Minzhu shi ge hao dongxi" ("民主是个好东西") ["Democracy is a good thing"]. *People's Daily Network* (人民网), December 28, 2006. Retrieved on March 18, 2012, from http://theory.people.com.cn/GB/49150/49152/5224247.html.

———. "Minzhu zhengzhi gaige di yu gongzhong yuqi: di er bufen" ("民主政治改革低于公众预期: 第二部分") ["Political reform is not up to public expectations: part one."] In Renmin Luntan Zazhi, ed., *Shijie Da Qushi yu Weilai 10 Nian Zhongguo Mianlin de Tiaozhan* (世界大趋势于未来10年中国面临的挑战) [*World Megatrends and Challenges China Will Face in the Coming Decade*]. Beijing: Chang'an Chubanshe, [May] 2010), p. 157.

———. "Shehui gongping he shanzhi shi jianshe hexie shehui de liang kuai ji shi" ("社会公平和善治是建设和谐社会的两块基石") ["Social justice and good governance are the two pillars on which to build a harmonious society"]. *Lilun Dongtai* (理论动态) [*Theoretical Trends*], No. 1658 (January 10, 2005), pp. 1–12; *neibu* faxing.

———. "'Zhongguo moshi' bing mei you wanquan dingxing" ("'中国模式'并没有完全定型") ["'The China Model' actually has not been fixed yet in form."] *Shehui Guancha* (社会观察) [*Social Observation*], December 2010; retrieved on March 18, 2012, from Yu's website: www.cctb.net/zjxz/expertarticle/201103/t20110325_26832.htm; no pagination given.

Yu Xintian (俞新天). "Guoji wenhuaxue de goujian yicheng" ("国际文化学的构建议程") ["An agenda for constructing international culture studies"]. In Yu Xintian, ed., *Guoji*

Guanxi zhong de Wenhua (国际关系中的文化) [*Culture in International Relations*] (Shanghai: Shanghai Academy of Social Sciences Press, 2005), pp. 3–19.

———. "Zhongguo gonggong waijiao yu ruan shili jianshe" ("中国公共外交与软实力建设") ["China's public diplomacy and soft power construction"]. *Zhongguo Waijiao* (中国外交) [*China's Foreign Affairs*] 2010 (3), pp. 25–30.

———. "Zhongguo wenhua jiazhiguan de goujian yu chuanbo" ("中国文化价值观的构建与传播") ["The construction and dissemination of Chinese cultural values"]. *Guoji Wenti Yanjiu* (国际问题研究) [*International Studies*], 2011 (6), November 13, 2011, pp. 5–19.

Yu Yongding (余永定). "Zhongjie chukou daoxiang xing chuang hui zhengce" ("终结出口导向型创汇政策") ["Ending the policy of accumulating foreign exchange through exporting"]. *Gaige Neican* (改革内参) [*Internal Reference Materials on Reform*] No. 652 (April 23, 2010), pp. 21–23; *neibu* faxing.

Zai Fu (再富). "Jingti liyi jituan zuji budongchan shui" ("警惕利益集团阻击不动产税") ["Beware of interest groups blocking the real estate tax."] *Gaige Neican* (改革内参) [*Internal Reference Materials on Reform*] No. 653 (April 30, 2010), pp. 24–35; *neibu* faxing.

Zeng Ke (曾可). "Minzhu zhengzhi gaige di yu gongzhong yuqi: di er bufen" ("民主政治改革低于公众预期:第二部分") ["Political reform is not up to public expectations: part one."] In Renmin Luntan Zazhi, ed., *Shijie Da Qushi yu Weilai 10 Nian Zhongguo Mianlin de Tiaozhan* (世界大趋势于未来10年中国面临的挑战) [*World Megatrends and Challenges China Will Face in the Coming Decade*]. Beijing: Chang'an Chubanshe, [May] 2010), pp. 154–156.

Zhan Jiang (詹江). "Zhongguo ruan shili re de leng sikao" ("中国软实力热的冷思考") ["Some sober reflections on China's soft power fever"]. *Gaige Neican* (*Internal Reference Materials on Reform*), No. 651 (April 16, 2010), pp. 23–26; *neibu* faxing.

Zhang Fengqi (张风琪). "Xin shiqi wenhua fazhan zhanlue de yanbian" ("新时期文化发展战略的演变") ["The evolution of China's cultural development strategy in the new period"]. *Dangdai Zhongguo Shi Yanjiu* (当代中国史研究) [*Contemporary Chinese History Studies*] 16(3), May 2009, pp. 28–34.

Zhang Haisheng and Liu Xifeng (张海生, 刘希风). "Dangqian wo guo wenhua anquan mianlin de jiu da tiaozhan ji qi zhanlue sikao" ("当前我国文化安全面临的九大挑战及其战略思考") ["Nine great challenges our country's cultural security currently faces and reflections on their strategic implications."] In Ba Zhongtan (巴忠倓), ed., *Wenhua Jianshe yu Guojia Anquan* (文化建设与国家安全) [*Cultural Construction and National Security*] (Beijing: Shishi Chubanshe, 2007), pp. 63–73.

Zhang Monan (张茉楠). "Yingxiang weilai quanqiu jingji de shi da fengxian yu tiaozhan" ("影响未来全球经济的十大风险与挑战") ["Ten major risks and challenges that will influence the future global economy"]. *Jingji Yaocan* (经济要参) [*Essential Economic Reference Materials*] No. 1874 (October 22, 2009), pp. 11–16; *neibu* faxing.

———. "Zhongguo jingji fusu de waiyouneihuan" ("中国经济复苏的外忧内患") ["Internal and external threats to China's economic recovery"]. *Gaige Neican* (改革内参) [*Internal Reference Materials on Reform*] No. 625 (September 4, 2009), pp. 19–22; *neibu* faxing.

Zhang Monan. "China Has the Priciest Housing on the Planet and There's Nothing Beijing Can Do About It." *International Business Times*, July 3, 2013. Retrieved on March 1, 2014, from www.ibtimes.com/china-has-priciest-housing-planet-theres-nothing-beijing-can-do-about-it-1333635.

Zhang Wenmu (张文木). "Shijie diyuan zhengzhi tixi zhong de Zhongguo guojia anquan liyi" ("世界地缘政治体系中的中国国家安全利益") ["China's national security and interests within the world geopolitical system"]. *Xianggang Chuanzhen* (香港传真) [*Hong Kong Fax*] 2004-1 (January 6, 2004), pp. 1–58; *neibu* faxing.

Zhang Wenzong (张文宗). "Shixi dangqian Meiguo shehui huoli de kunjing ji zoushi" ("试析当前美国社会活力的困境及走势") ["Analyzing the difficulties facing social vitality in the contemporary U.S."]. *Xiandai Guoji Guanxi* (现代国际关系) [*Contemporary International Relations*] 2012 (2), pp. 8–14.

Zhang Yi (张翼). "Liushi nian jihua shengyu fengfengyuyu" ("六十年计划生育风风雨雨") ["Vicissitudes in family planning during the past sixty years"]. In Pan Wei [潘伟] and Ma Ya [玛雅], eds., *Renmin Gongheguo Liushi Nian yu Zhongguo Moshi* (人民共和国六十年与中国模式) [*Sixty Years of the People's Republic and the Chinese Model*] (Beijing: Sanlian Shudian, [February] 2010), pp. 72–82.

Zhao Chenchen and Wu Yumin (赵陈晨, 吴予敏). "Guanyu wangluo egao de ya wenhua yanjiu shuping" ("关与网络恶搞的亚文化研究述评") ["Assessing research on the subculture of trick-playing on the Internet"]. *Xiandai Chuanbo* (现代传播) [*Modern Communication*], No. 180 (July 2011), pp. 112–117.

Zhao Qizheng (赵启正). "Yu quanqiu duihua: dui gonggong waijiao zai renshi" ("与全球队会: 对公共外交在认识") ["Dialogue with the Global: Rethought of Public Diplomacy (official translation)"]. *Zhongguo Waijiao* (中国外交) [*China's Foreign Affairs*] 2011 (2), pp. 3–6. [The essay originally appeared in *Renmin Zhengxie Bao* (人民政协报), a publication of the Chinese People's Political Consultative Conference.]

Zhao, Suisheng. "The China Model: Can It Replace the Western Model of Modernization?" *Journal of Contemporary China* 19 (Issue 65), June 2010, pp. 419–436.

———. "Foreign Policy Implications of Chinese Nationalism Revisited: The Strident Turn." *Journal of Contemporary China* 22(82), 2013, pp. 535–553.

———. "Understanding China's assertive foreign policy behavior during the global financial meltdown." *The European Financial Review*, December 2011–January 2012, pp. 40–41.

Zhao, Yuezhi. *Communication in China: Political Economy, Power, and Conflict.* Lanham, MD: Rowman & Littlefield, 2008, pp. 245–338.

Zheng Bingwen (郑秉文). "Quebao ziyuan anquan, tuozhan La Mei bukehuoque" ("确保资源安全, 拓展拉美不可或缺") ["To guarantee resource security, expanding efforts in Latin America is indispensable"]. *Gaige Neican* (改革内参) [*Internal Reference Materials on Reform*] 651 (April 16, 2010), pp. 10–12; *neibu* faxing.

———. "Wo guo zai La Mei fazhan liyi de xuanze" ("我国在拉美发展利益的选择") ["Our country's strategic choices for developing our interests in Latin America"]. *Lingdao Canyue* (领导参阅) [*Leadership Reference*] 517 (February 5, 2010), pp. 39–44; *neibu* faxing.

Zheng Gongcheng (郑功成). "Shehui fenpei gaige xu jinru jiasu qi" ("社会分配改革需进入加速期") ["Reform of social distribution must enter the high-speed phase"]. In Renmin Luntan Zazhi, ed., *Shijie Da Qushi yu Weilai 10 Nian Zhongguo Mianlin de Tiaozhan* (世界大趋势于未来10年中国面临的挑战) [*World Megatrends and Challenges China Will Face in the Coming Decade*] (Beijing: Chang'an Chubanshe, [May] 2010), pp. 63–70.

Zheng Yongnian (郑永年). "Jinfang Zhongguo siwei Meiguohua" ("谨防中国思维美国化") ["Urgently prevent the Americanization of Chinese thought patterns"]. *Gaige Neican* (改革内参) [*Internal Reference Materials on Reform*] 558 (October 20, 2007), pp. 40–41; *neibu* faxing.

"Zhonggong zhongyang guanyu quanmian shenhua gaige ruogan zhongda wenti de jueding" ("中共中央关于全面深化改革若干重大问题的决定") ["Decision of the Central

Committee of the Chinese Communist Party Regarding Certain Important Questions Related to Comprehensively Deepening Reform"]. Xinhua News Agency, November 15, 2013. Retrieved on November 17, 2013, from http://news.xinhuanet.com/politics/2013-11/15/c_118164235.htm.

Zhongguo Faxuehui Xinxi Faxue Yanjiuhui and Zhongguo Shekeyuan Faxuesuo Lianhe Ketizu (中国法学会信息法学研究会, 中国社科院法学所联合课题组) [Joint Study Group of the China Legal Studies Society Information Legal Studies Research Association and the Chinese Academy of Social Sciences Legal Studies Institute]. "Wo guo xinxi anquan guanli tizhi jixu lishun" ("我国信息安全管理体制亟需理顺") ["Our nation's information security management system urgently needs rationalization"]. *Lingdao Canyue* (领导参阅) [*Leadership Reference*] 358, September 5, 2005, pp. 3–5; *neibu* faxing.

Zhongguo Shekeyuan Jingjixuebu Jingji Xingshi Genzong Fenxi Keti Zu. (中国社科院经济学部经济形势跟踪分析课题组) [CASS Department of Economics Economic Tracking Analysis Study Group]. "Dui Dangqian jingji xingshi de fenxi yu yuce" ("对当时经济形势的分析与预测") ["Current economic conditions: analysis and outlook"]. *Lingdao Canyue* (领导参阅) [*Leadership Reference*] No. 526 (May 5, 2010), pp. 3–11; *neibu* faxing.

Zhongguo Shekeyuan Wenhua Yanjiu Zhongxin Ketizu (中国社科院文化研究中心课题组) [Study Group at the Chinese Academy of Social Sciences' Culture Research Center]. "Xinjiang gonggong wenhua fuwu tixi cunzai de wenti, yuanyin, he jiejue banfa" ("新疆公共文化服务体系存在的问题, 原因, 和解决办法") ["Problems, reasons for the problems, and solutions in Xinjiang's public culture service system"]. *Lingdao Canyue* (领导参阅) [*Leadership Reference*], No. 588 (January 25, 2012), pp. 11–16; *neibu* faxing.

Zhongguo Shekeyuan Xinxihua Yanjiu Zhongxin (中国社科院信息化研究中心) [Chinese Academy of Social Sciences Informationalization Research Center]. "Zhiding shi er wu xinxihua guihua, jiakuai wo guo xinxihua jincheng" ("制定十二五信息化规划, 加快我国信息化进程") ["Formulate the informationalization measures in the Twelfth Five-Year Plan, accelerate the pace of our country's informationalization"]. *Lingdao Canyue* (领导参阅) [*Leadership Reference*] 510 (November 25, 2009), pp. 17–20; *neibu* faxing.

Zhongguo Sixiang Zhengzhi Gongzuo Yanjiuhui and Zhongxuanbu Sixiang Zhengzhi Gongzuo Yanjiusuo (中国思想政治工作研究会 and 中宣部思想政治工作研究所), [China Political Thought Work Research Committee and Chinese Communist Party Central Propaganda Department Political Thought Work Research Institute], eds. *Weida de Minzu Jingshen—Zhonghua Minzu de Jingshen X-Liang* (伟大的民族精神 – 中华民族的精神X梁) [*A Great National Spirit—The Chinese Nation's Spiritual Pillar*]. Beijing: 党建读物出版社, 2006.

Zhongguo Weilai Zouxiang Editorial Group (中国未来走向编写组), ed. *Zhongguo Weilai Zouxiang: Juji Gaoceng Juece yu Guojia Zhanlue Buju* (中国未来走向: 聚集高级决策与国家战略布局) [*China's Future Direction: Uniting High-Level Policy-Making and National Strategic Arrangements*]. Beijing: Renmin Chubanshe, [May] 2009.

Zhou Ruijin (周瑞金). "Jingti 'teshu liyi jituan' weidabudiao" ("警惕 '特殊利益集团' 尾大不掉") ["Beware of 'special interest groups' becoming too powerful to control"]. *Gaige Neican* (改革内参) [*Internal Reference Materials on Reform*], No. 633 (November 10, 2009), pp. 34–35; *neibu* faxing.

Zhou Tianyong (周天勇). *Zhongguo xiang Hechu Qu: Zou Bie Ren Zouduile de Dao, Bu Zou Bie Ren Zoucuole de Lu* (中国向何处去: 走别人走对了的道, 不走别人走错了的路) [*What Road Should China Take? It Should Take Roads That Others Have Chosen Correctly but Not Take Roads That Others Have Chosen Mistakenly*]. Beijing: Renmin Ribao Chubanshe, 2010.

Zhu Huaxin, Dan Xuegang, and Hu Jiangchun (祝华新, 单学刚, 胡江春). "Weibo zhengzhi tiaozhan shehui guanli" ("微博政治挑战社会管理") ["Microblog politics challenges social management"]. *Gaige Neican* (改革内参) [*Internal Reference Materials on Reform*], No. 686 (January 7, 2011), pp. 15–17; *neibu* faxing.

Zhu Liqun (朱立群). "Zhongguo yu guoji tixi: shuangxiang shehuihua de shijian luoji" ("中国与国际体系: 双向社会化的实践逻辑") ["China and the international system: the practical logic of bidirectional socialization"]. *Zhongguo Waijiao* (中国外交) [*China's Foreign Affairs*] 2012 (4), pp. 20–30. [The essay originally appeared in Waijiao Pinglun (外交评论), a publication of the 外交学院 (China Foreign Affairs University).]

Zhu Majie (朱马杰). "Guoji guanxi liliang jiegou zhong de ruan guoli" ("国际关系力量结构中的软国力") ["National soft power within the power structure of international relations"]. In Yu Xintian, ed., *Guoji Guanxi zhong de Wenhua* (国际关系中的文化) [*Culture in International Relations*] (Shanghai: Shanghai Academy of Social Sciences Press, 2005), pp. 69–84.

Zhu Min (朱敏). "Dui wo guo jingji fusu jichu shang bu wengu de fenxi" ("对我国经济复苏上不稳固的分析") ["Why the basis of our country's economic recovery is still not firm"]. *Jingji Yaocan* (经济要参) [*Essential Economic Reference Materials*] No. 1884 (1 December 2009), pp. 36–38; *neibu* faxing.

Zhu Xufeng. "The Influence of Think Tanks in the Chinese Policy Process." *Asian Survey* 49(2), March/April 2009, pp. 333–357.

Index